g r o w

The Art of Koyamori

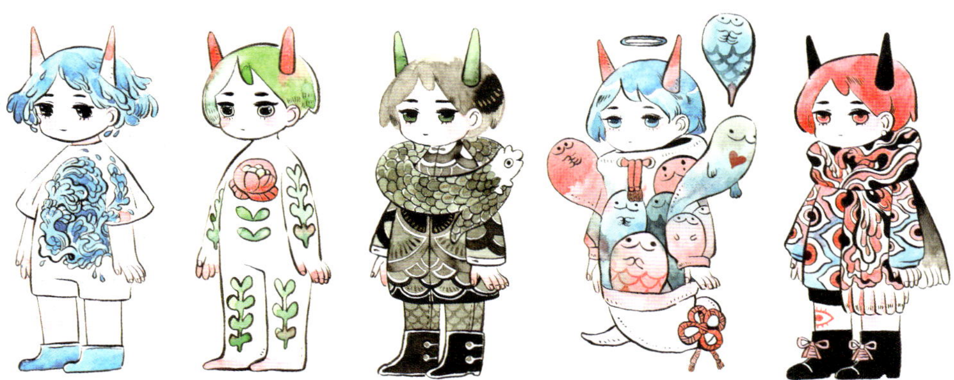

grow

The Art of Koyamori

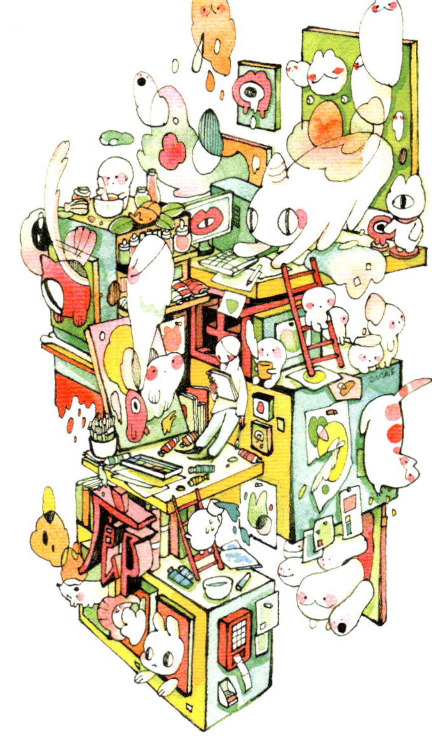

Author: Koyamori

Editorial Design: YUTO HAMA DESIGN

Editor: Masashi Miyauchi, Megumi Michihira

Publisher: Hiromoto Miyoshi

PIE International Inc.
2-32-4 Minami-Otsuka, Toshima-ku, Tokyo 170-0005 JAPAN
comic@pie.co.jp

ISBN978-4-7562-5121-3 (Outside Japan)
Printed in Japan

When I was a child, I lived near mountains.
The journey to school was a one hour up hill hike,
with trees and rice fields on all sides.

The song of the birds and cicadas would fill the air,
and sometimes the fog would be so thick you could not see a thing.
I remember sunny afternoons,
biking to nearby waterfalls, and catching frogs in streams.

Even now, those moments shine bright in my mind.
Many things have changed since then,
but the memories of those mountains are as vivid as ever.

|||||

私が小さなころに住んでいたのは、木々や田んぼに囲まれた山の近くで
学校へ通うだけでも一時間の小旅行になるようなところでした

そこは、鳥たちの歌うさえずりや蝉のなき声に包まれることもあれば
ときには何も見えなくなるほどの濃い霧が立ち込めることもあるような場所
晴れた昼の午後に近くの滝まで自転車で出かけ
流れの中に入ってカエルを捕まえたことをよく覚えています

私の心の中でいまもキラキラと輝き続けている──そうしてすごした大切な時間
すっかり変わってしまったことも多いけれど
その山々がくれた思い出だけは、私の中で永遠に鮮やかなままなのです

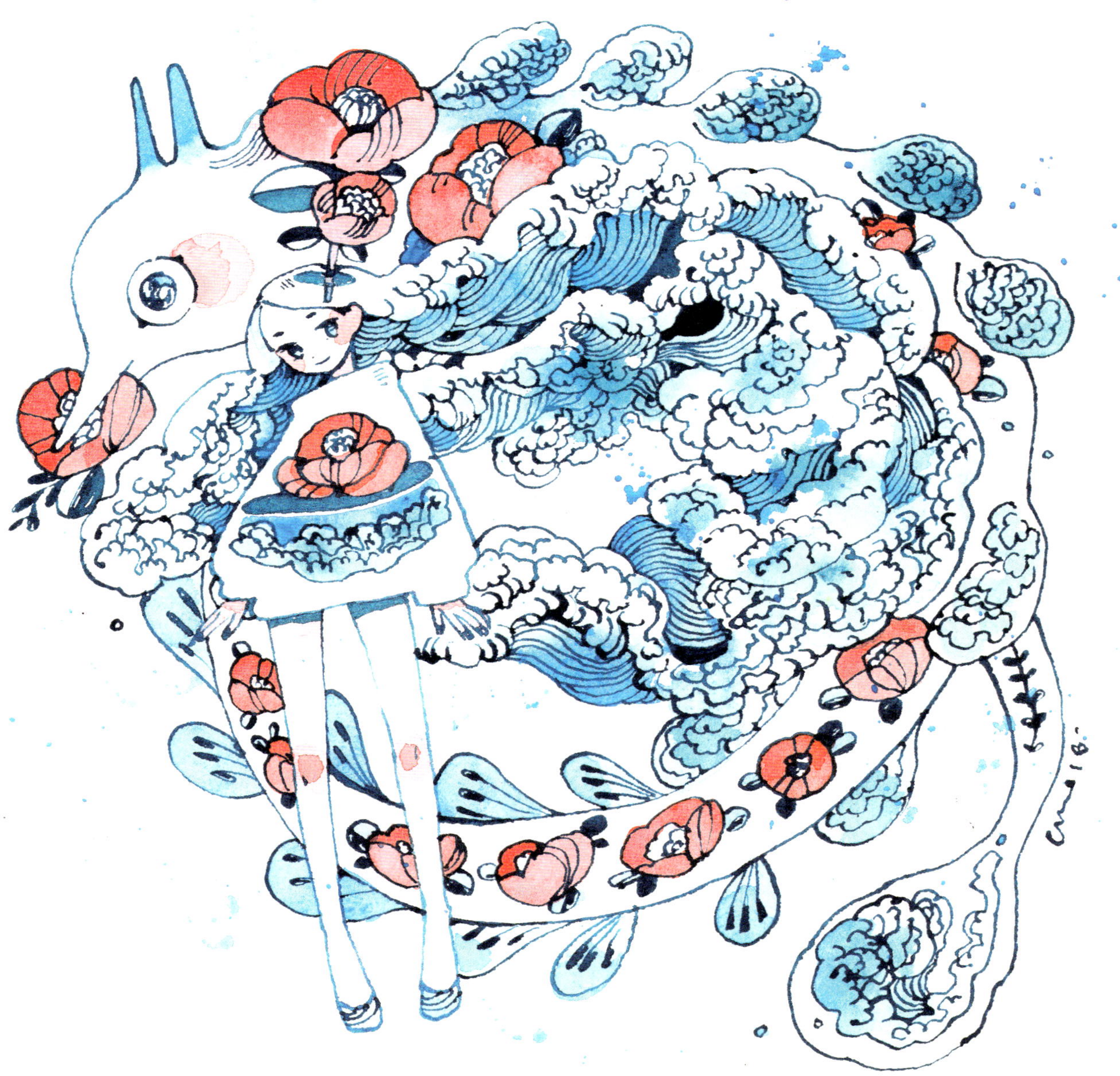

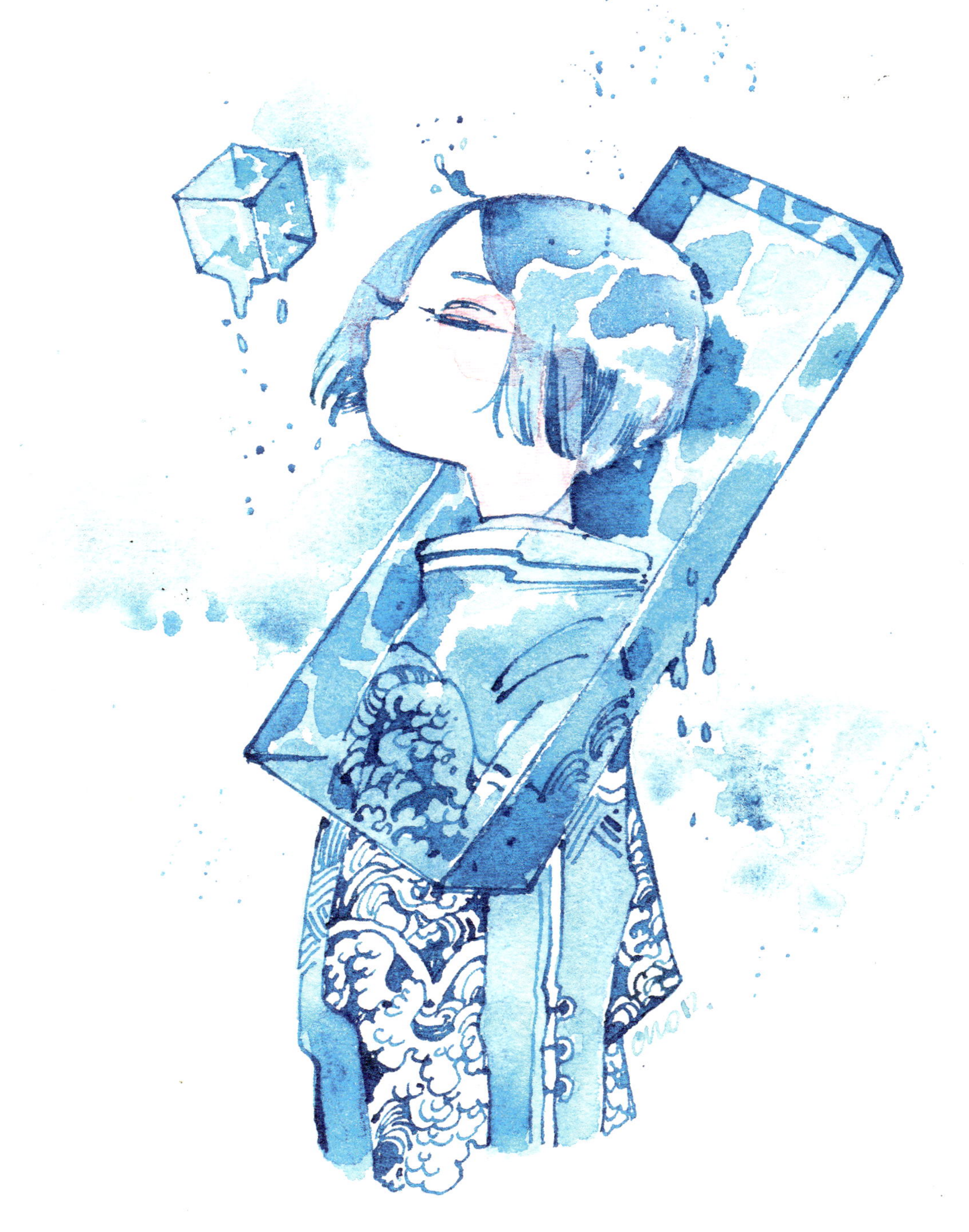

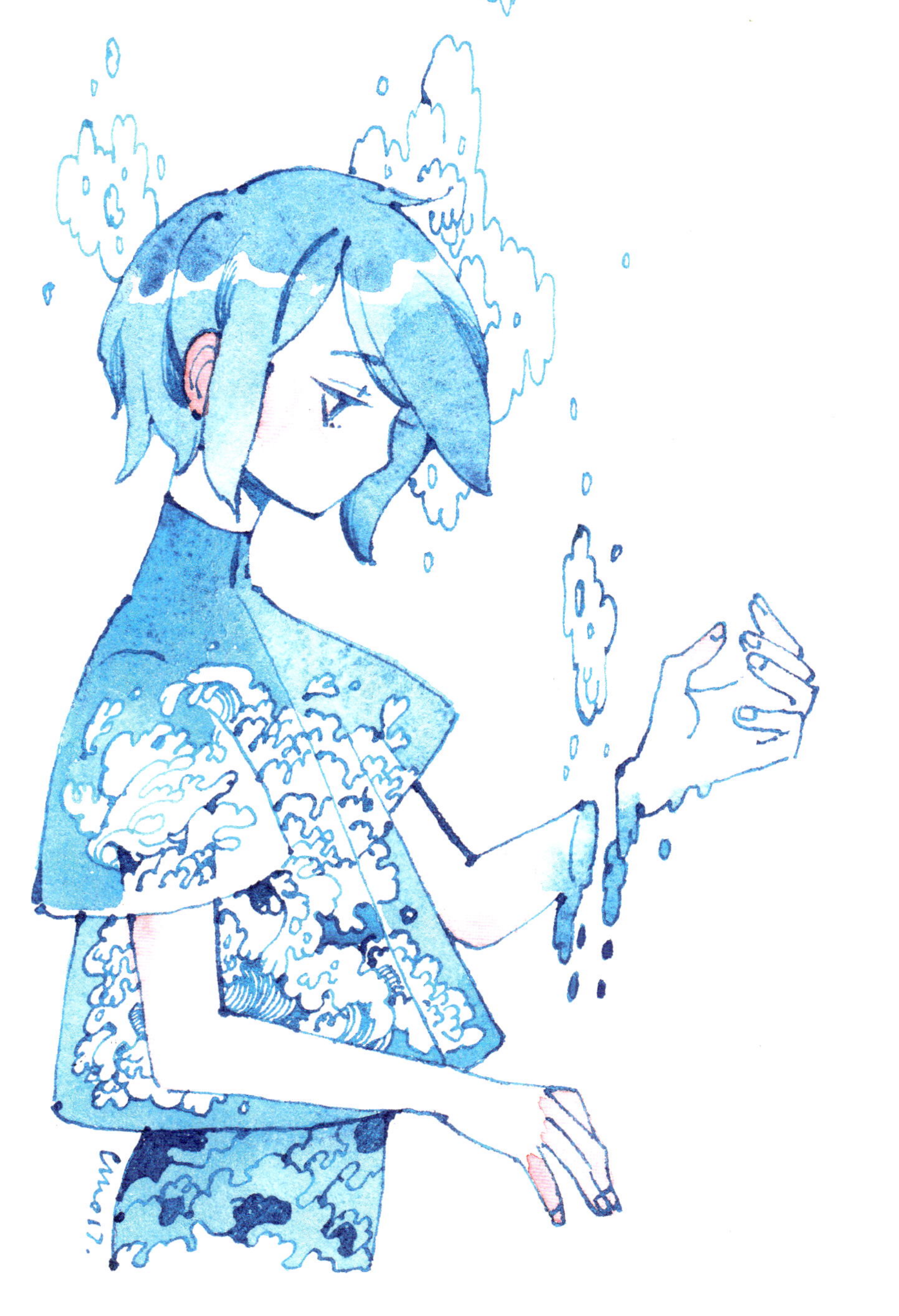

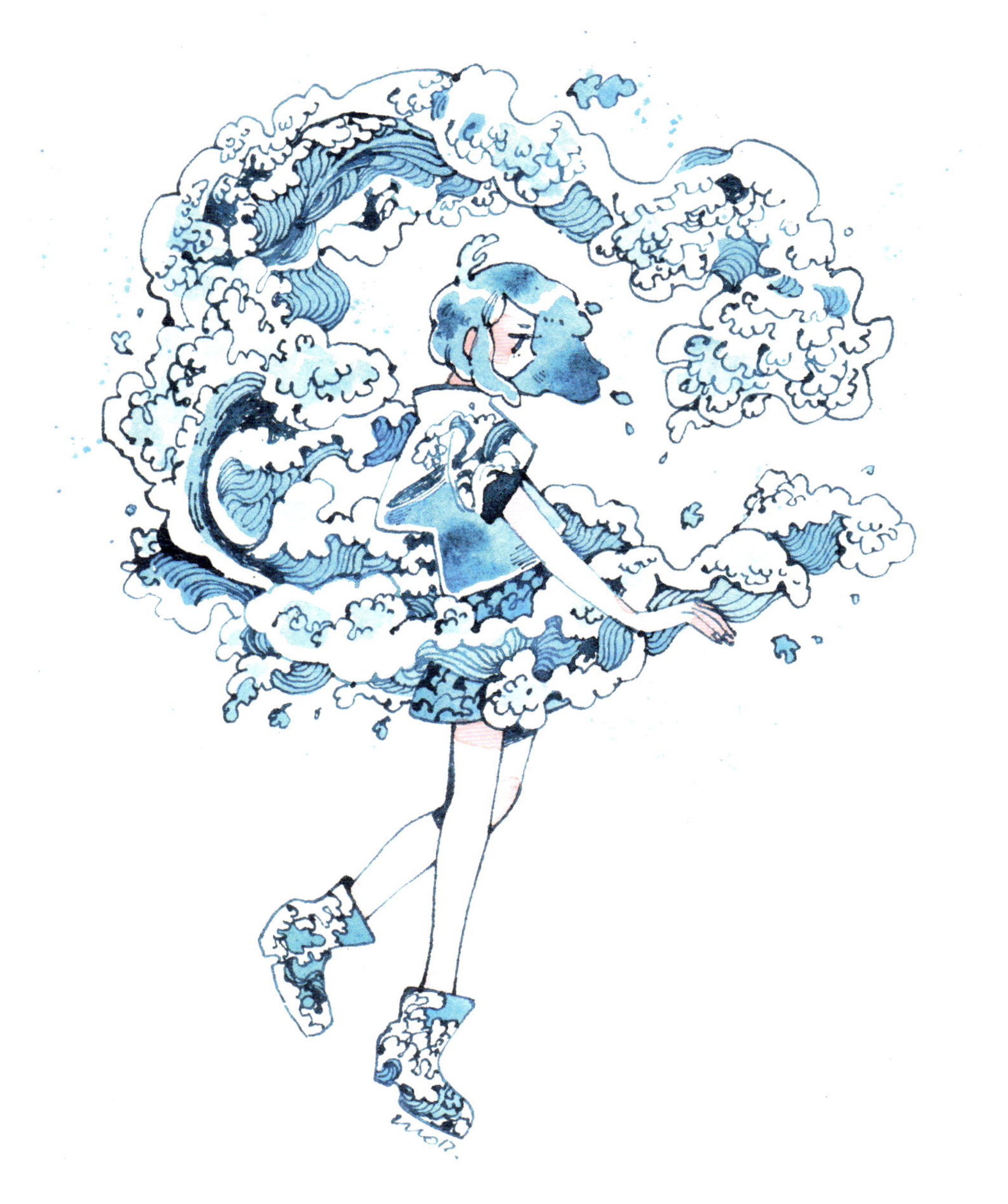

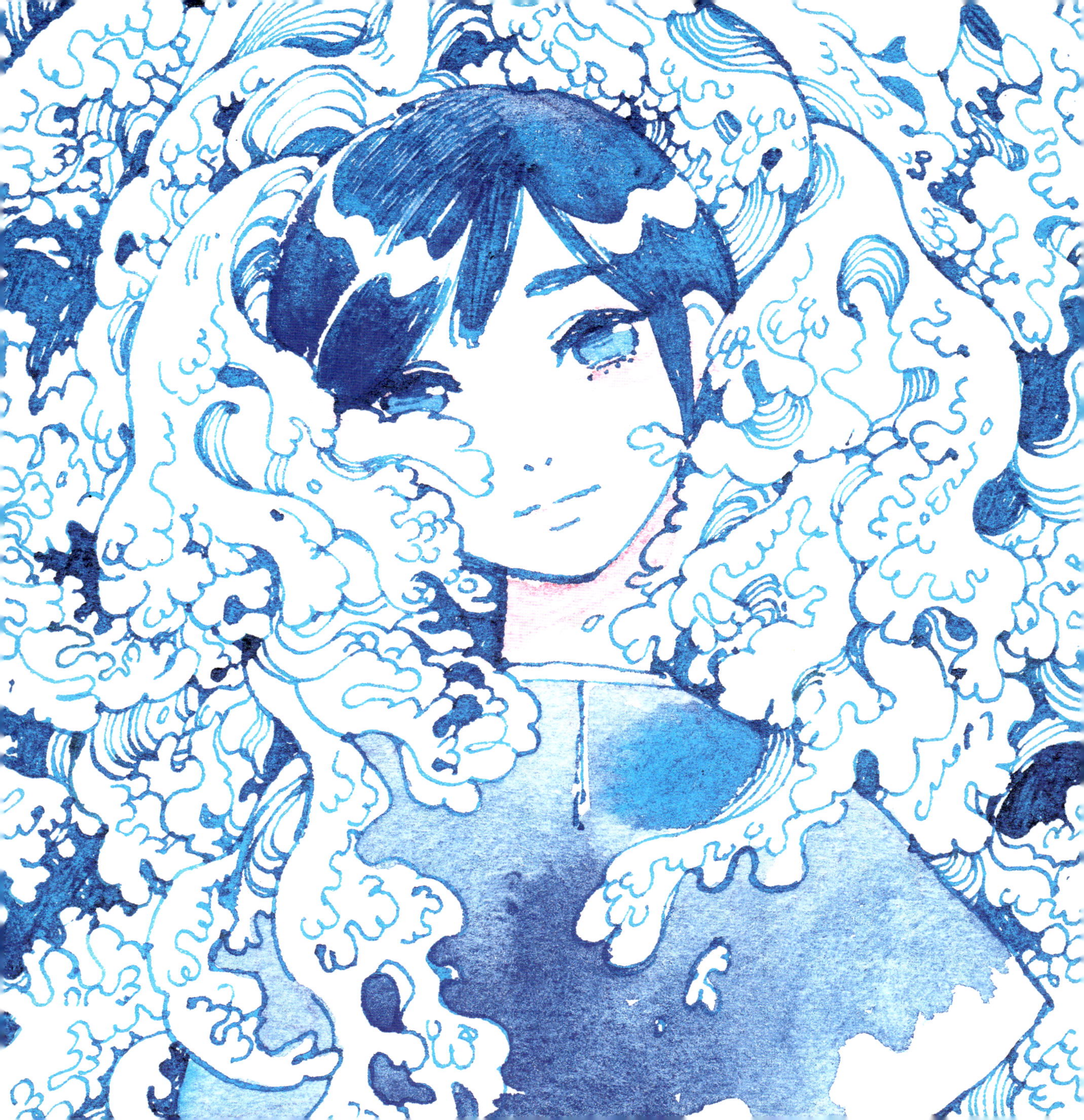

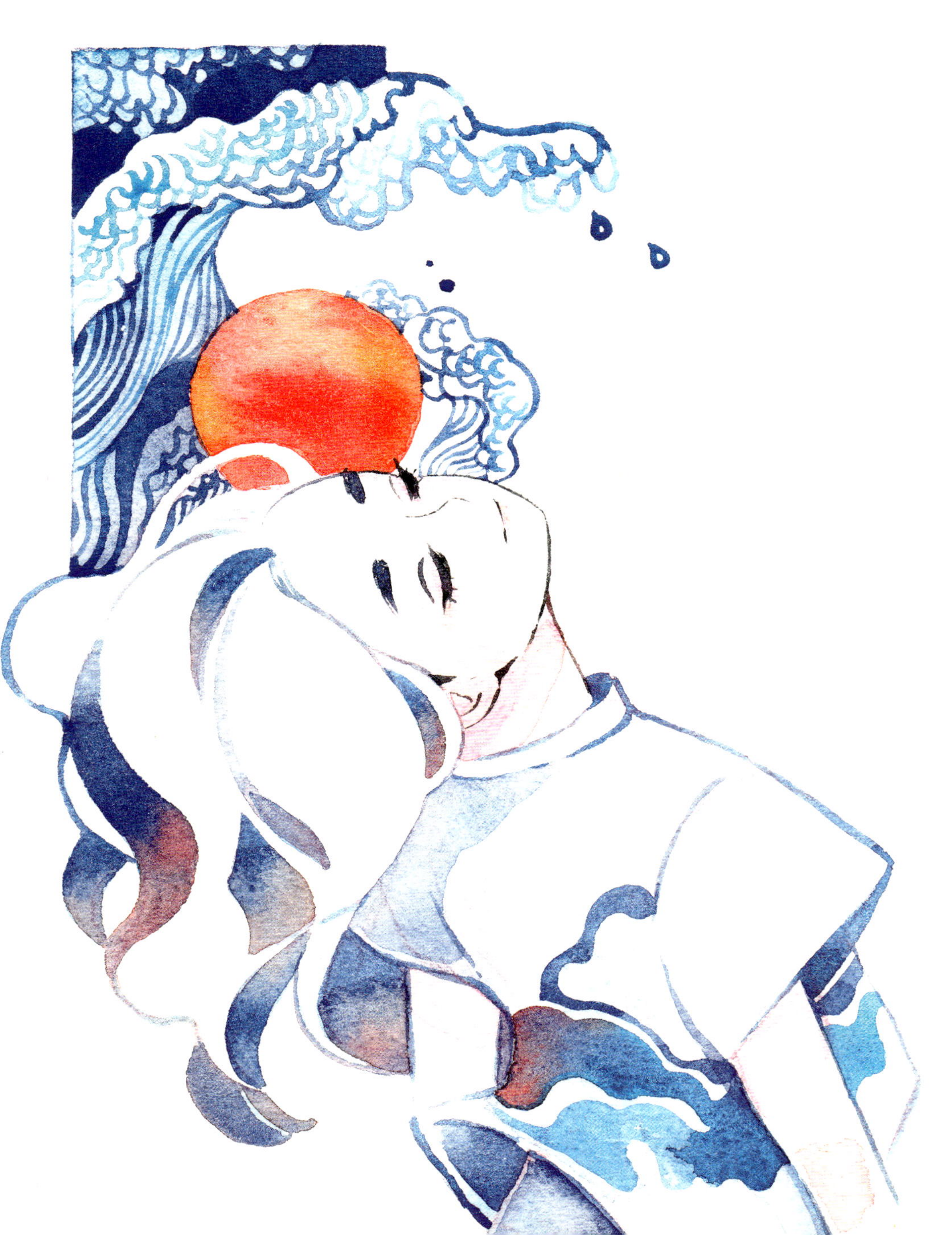

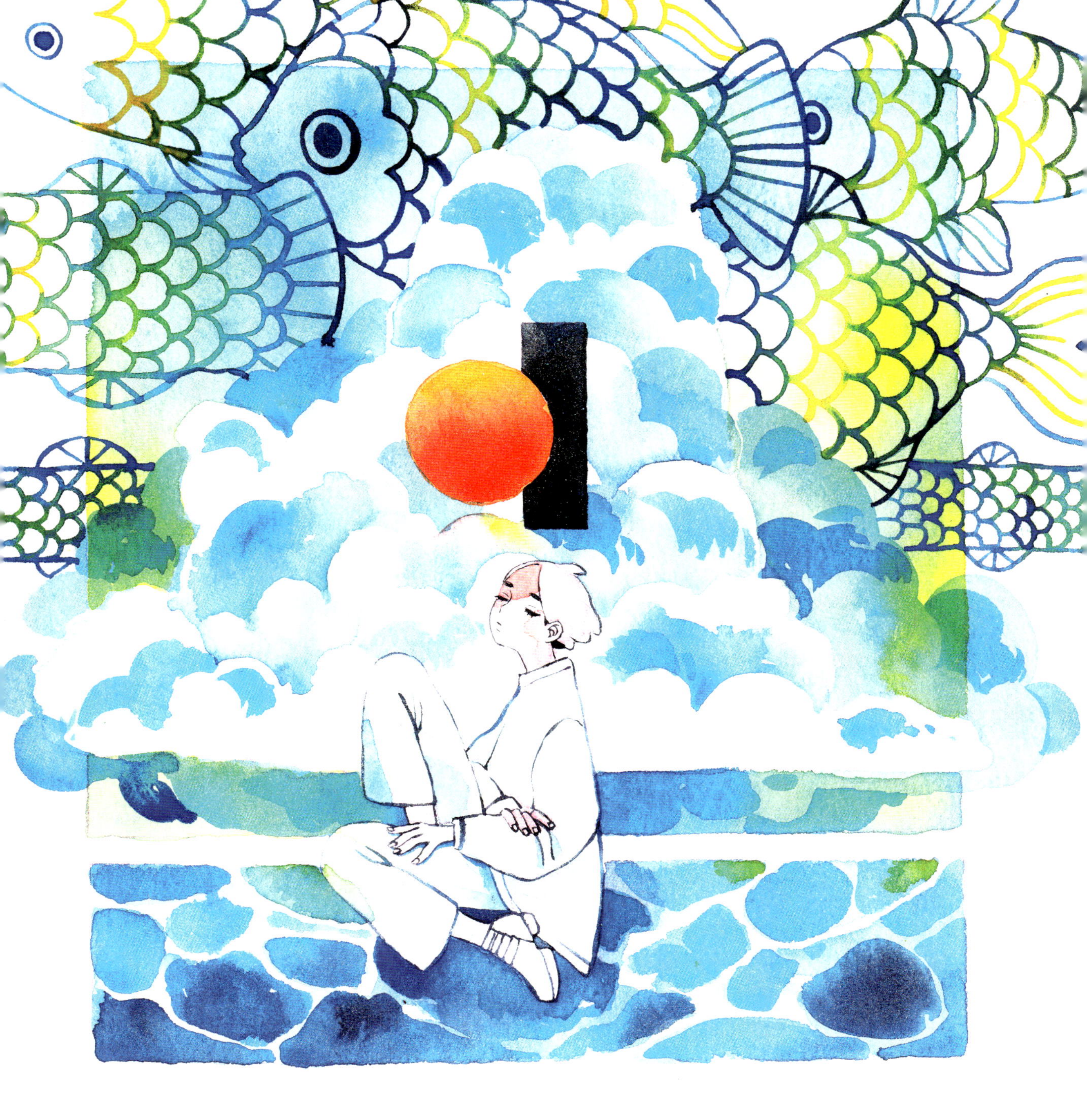

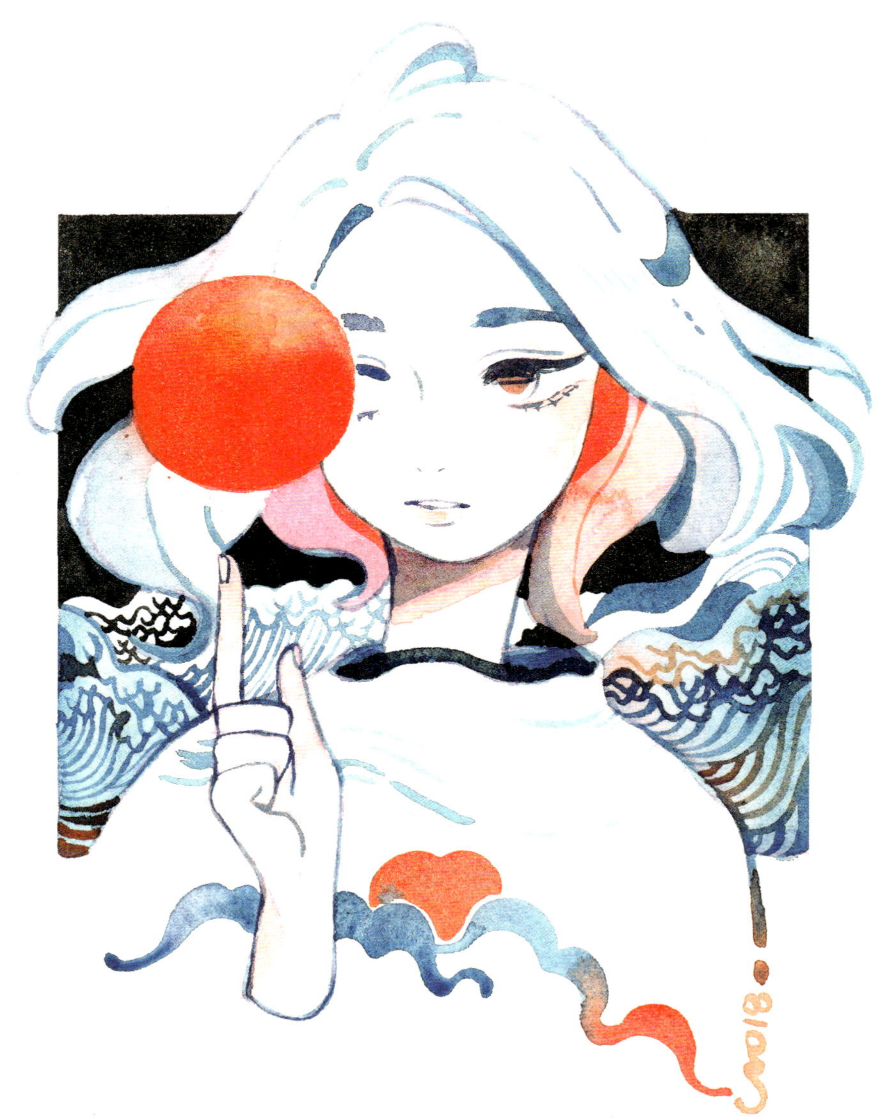

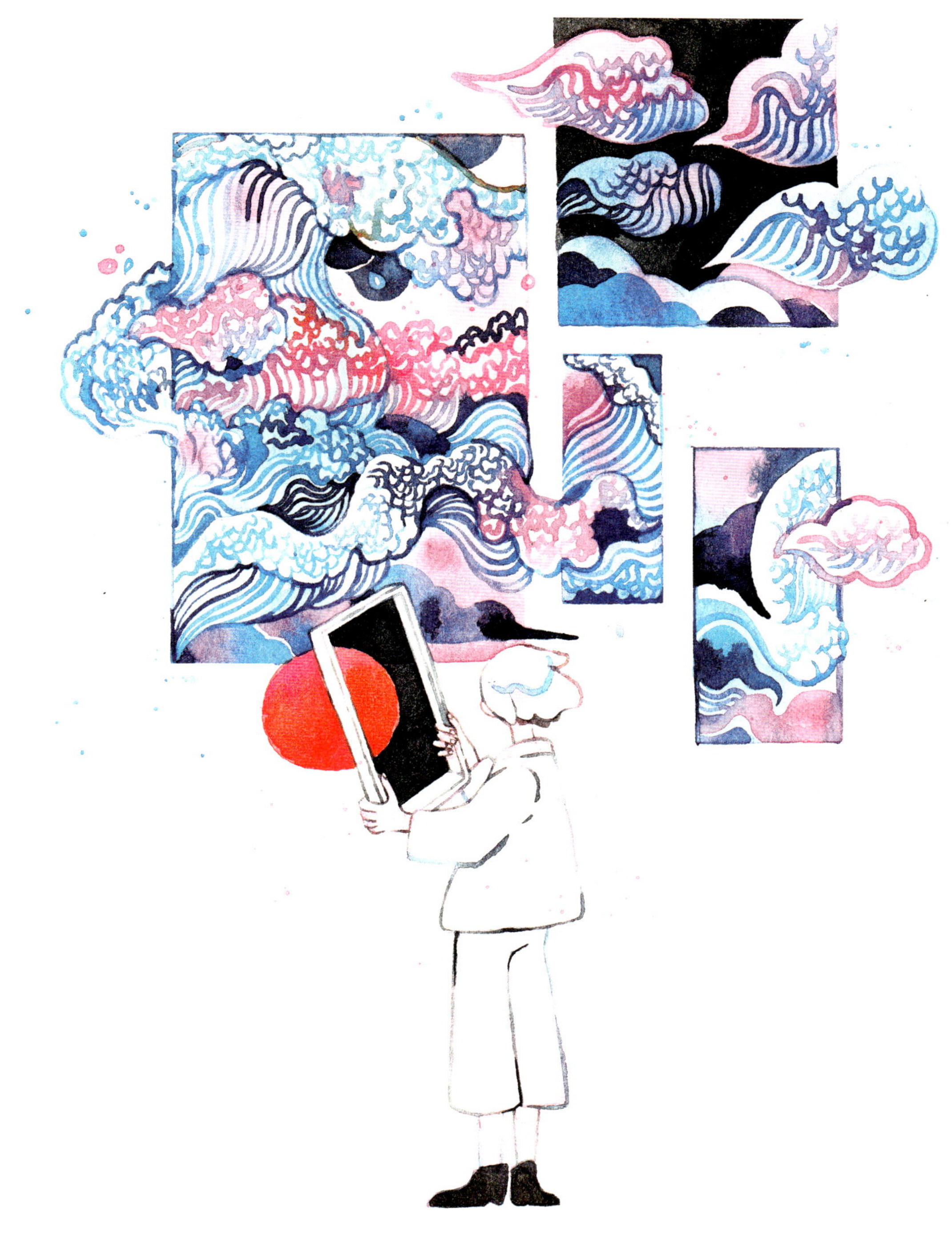

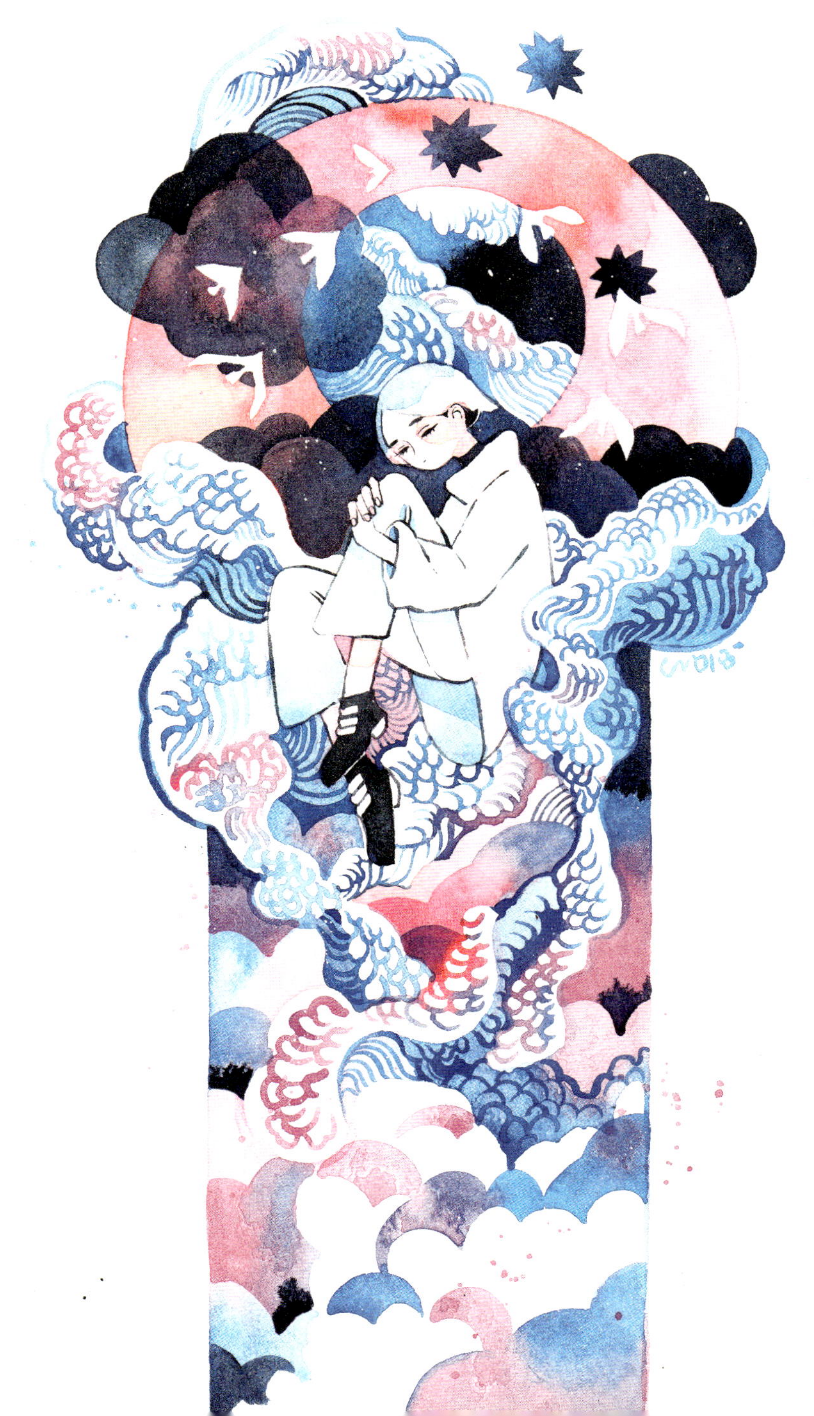

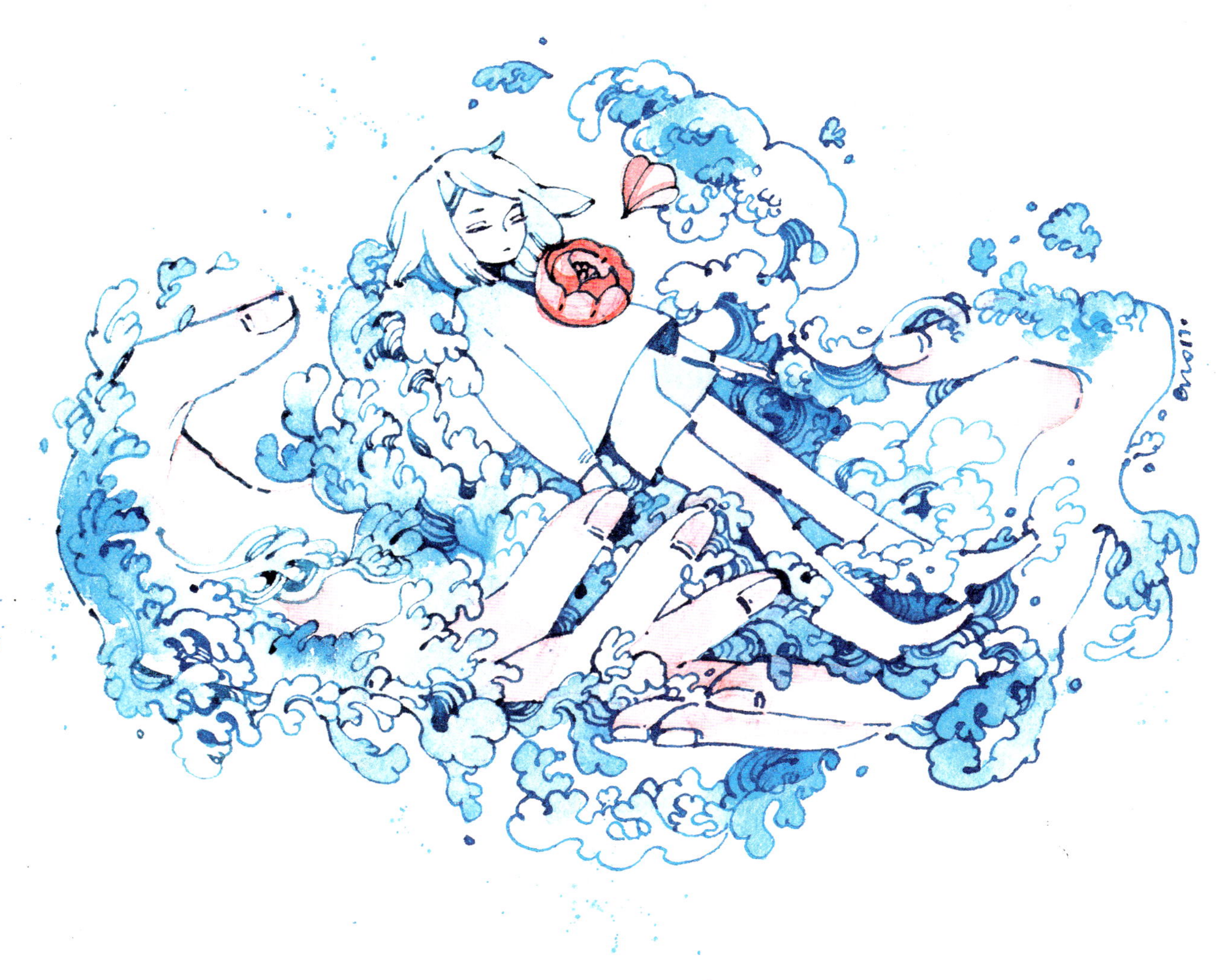

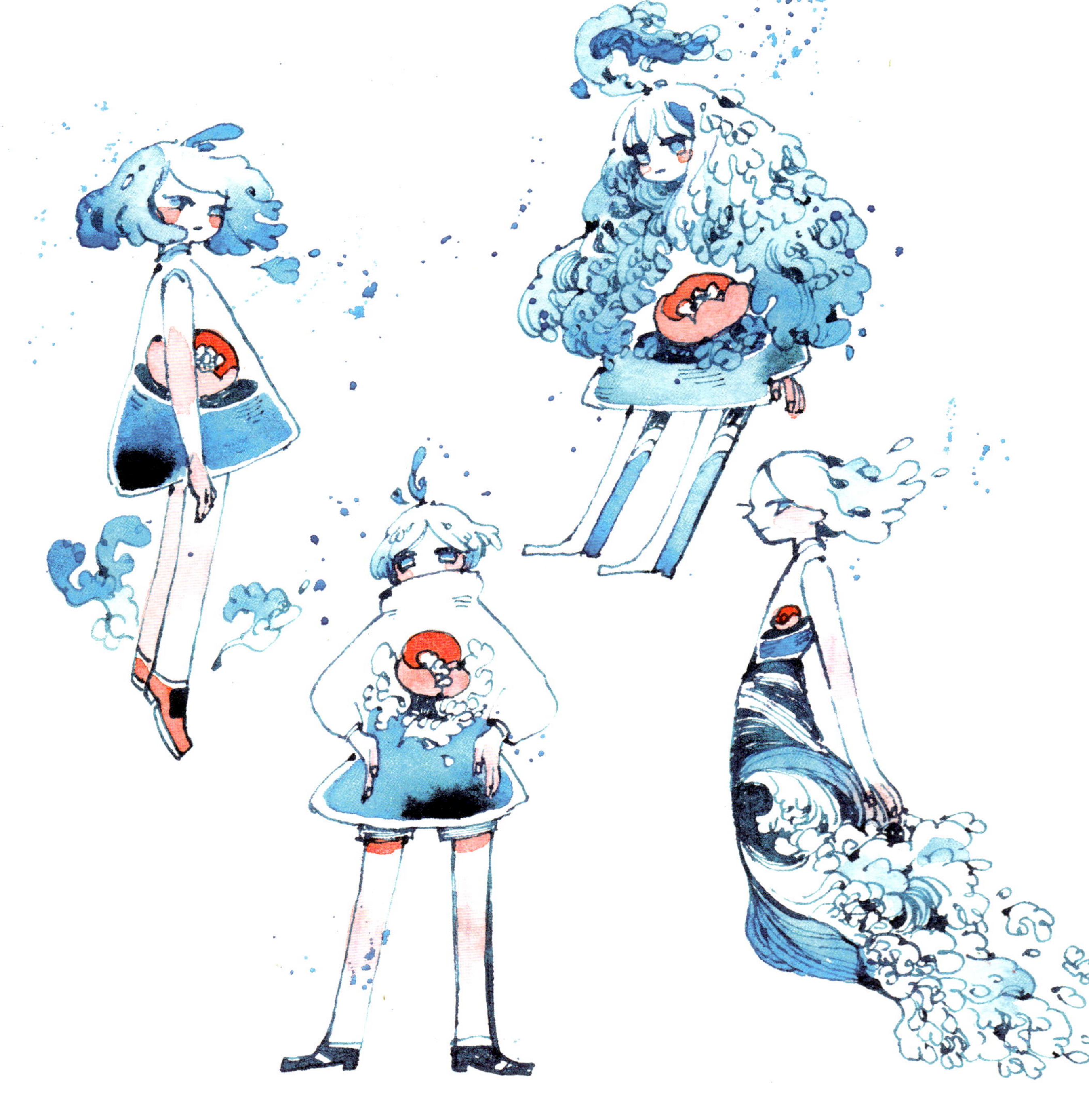

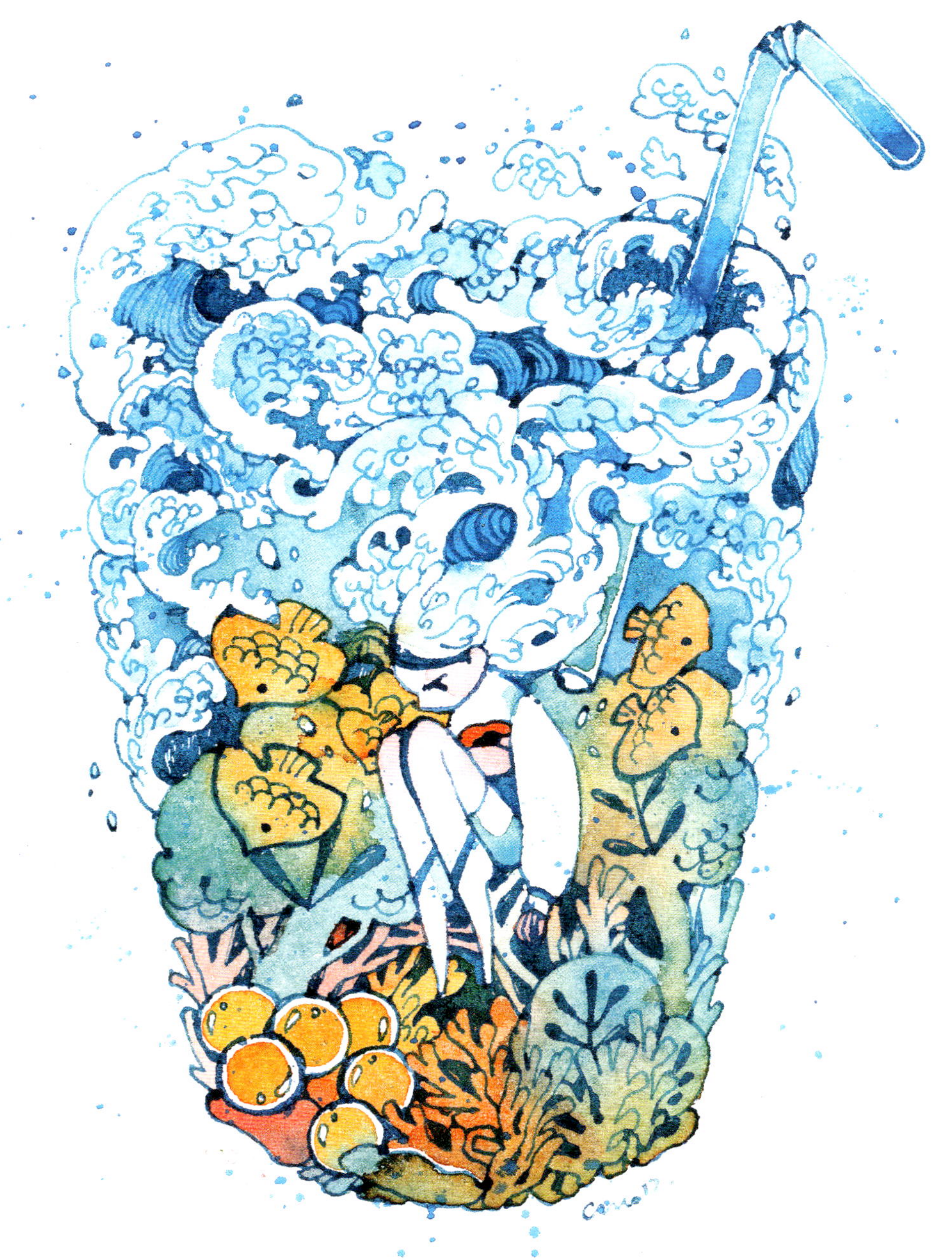

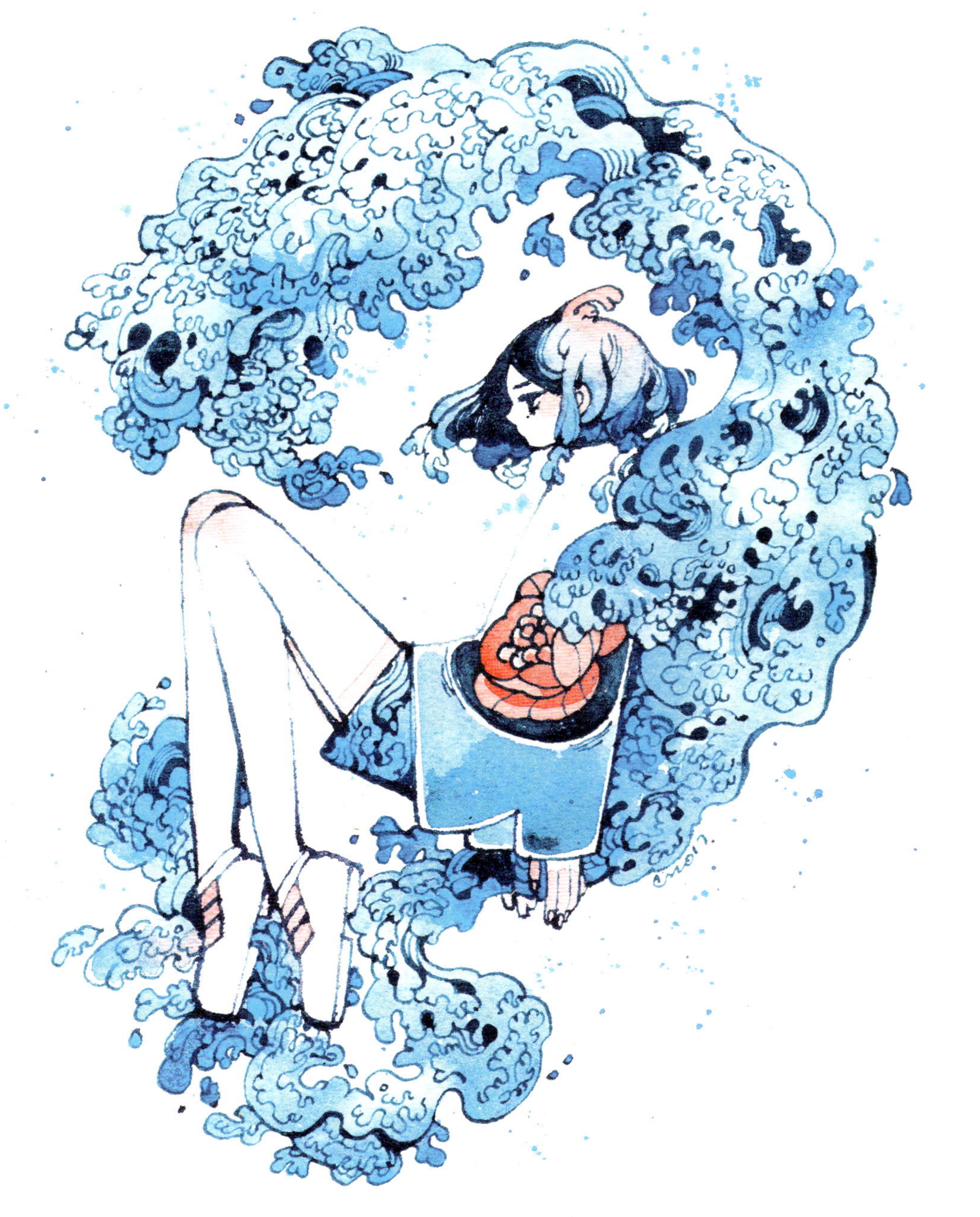

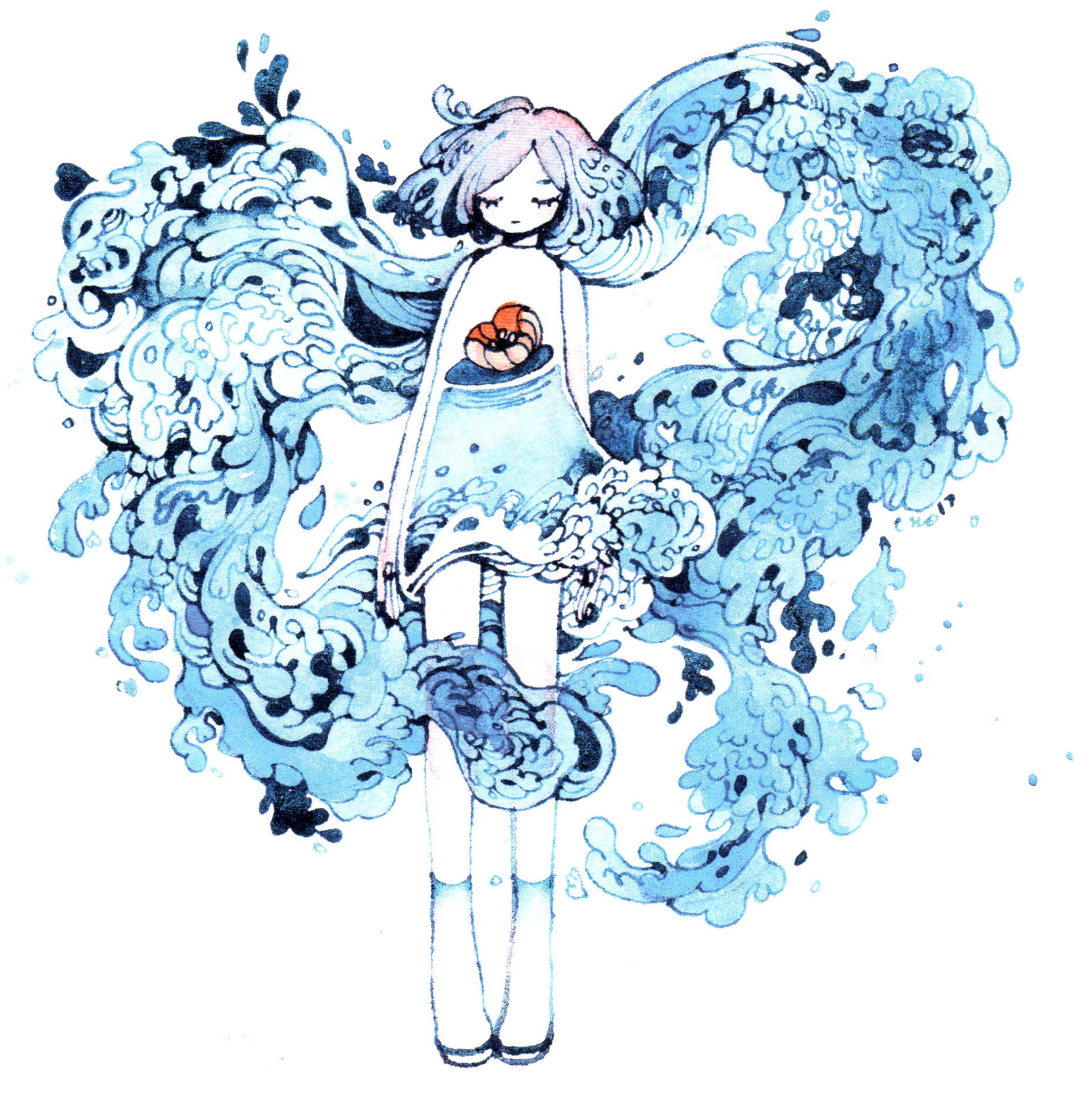

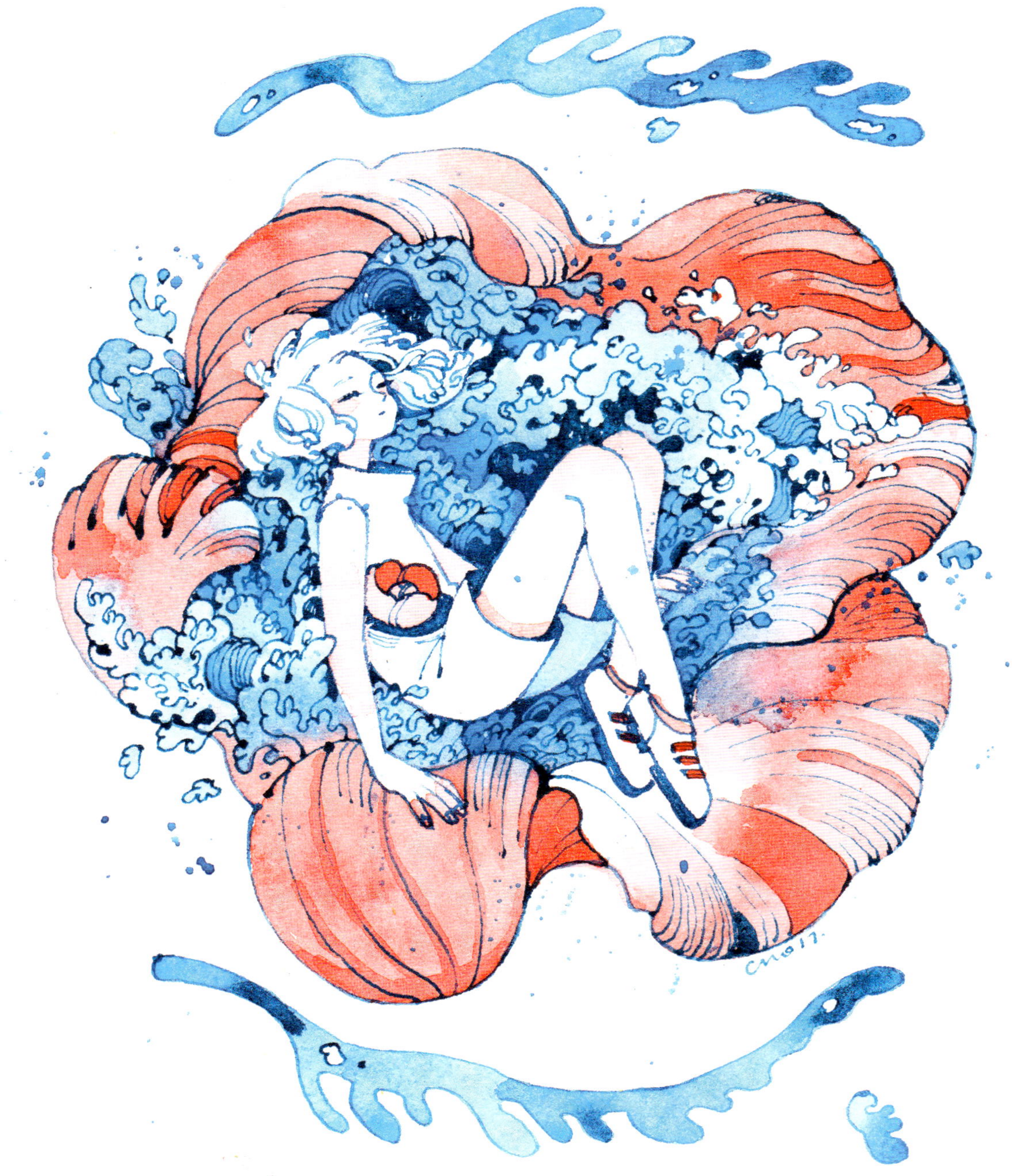

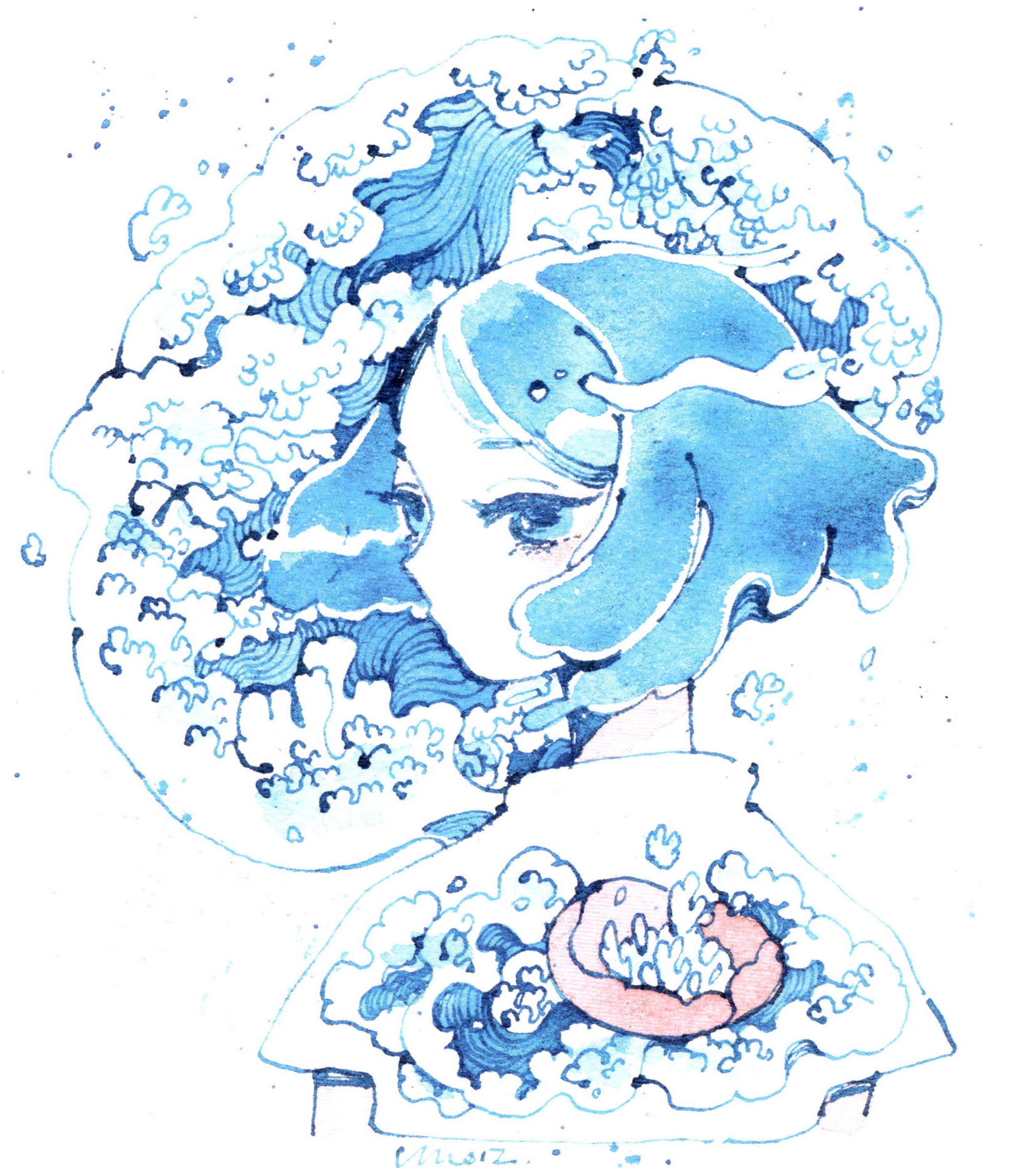

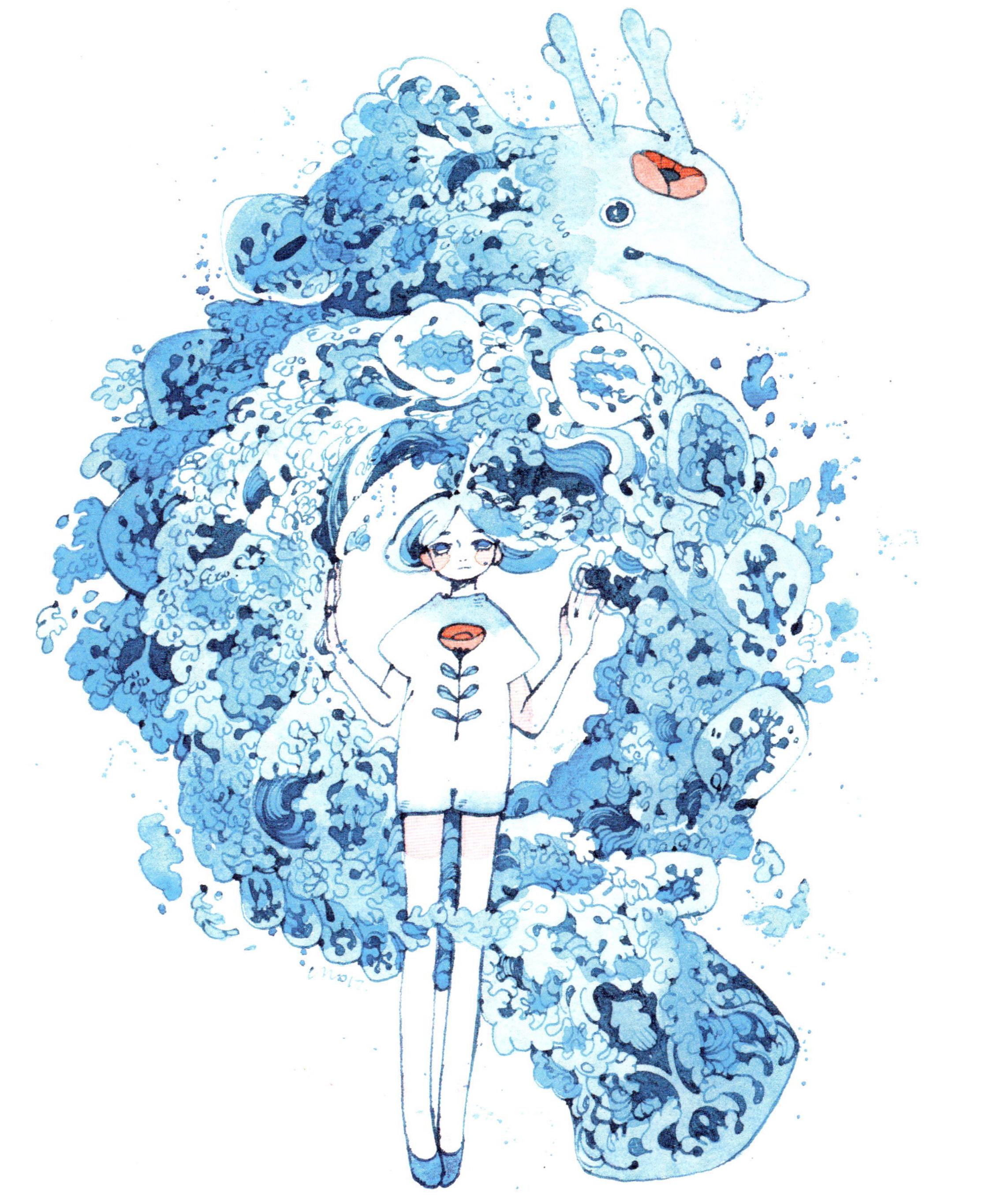

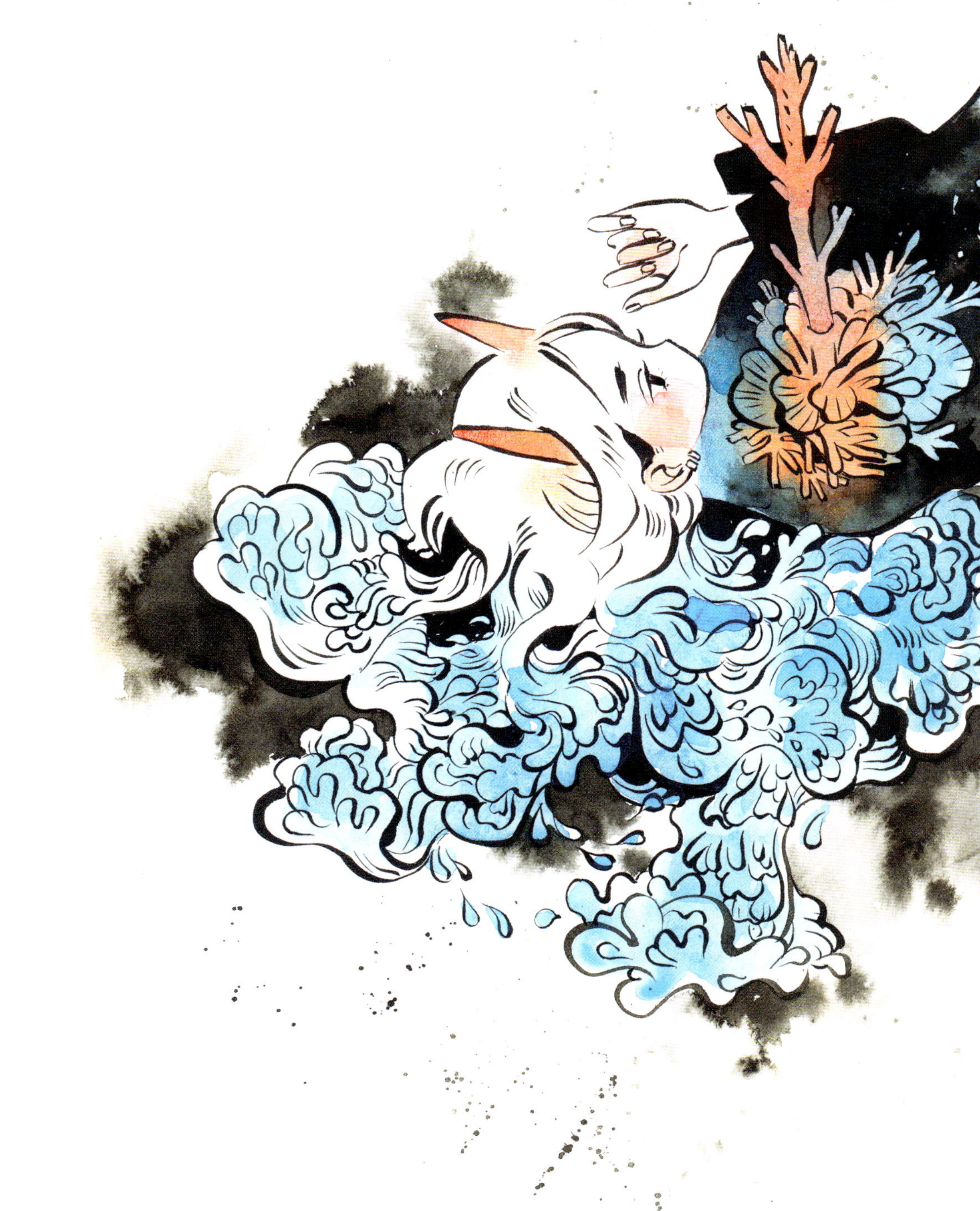

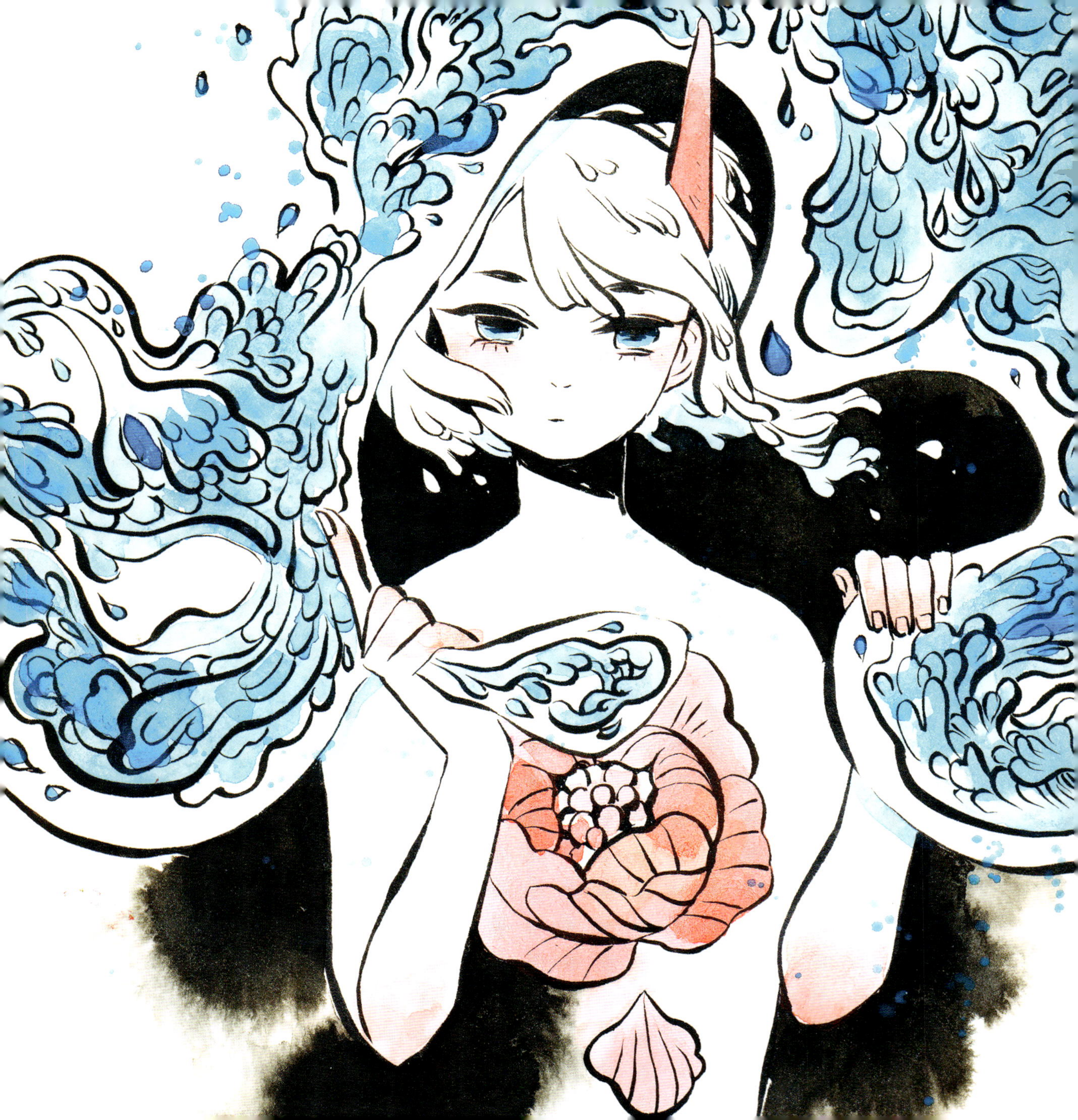

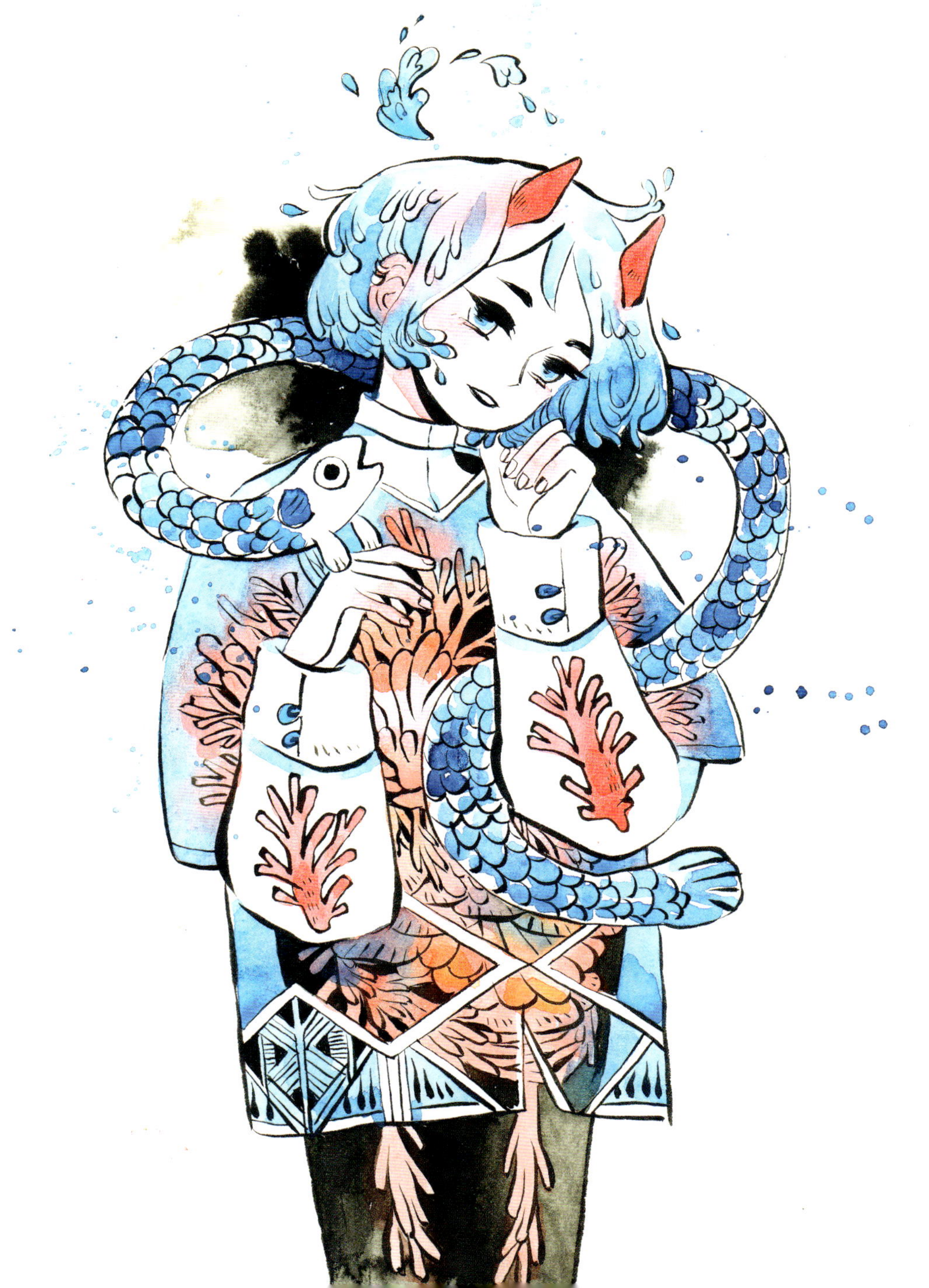

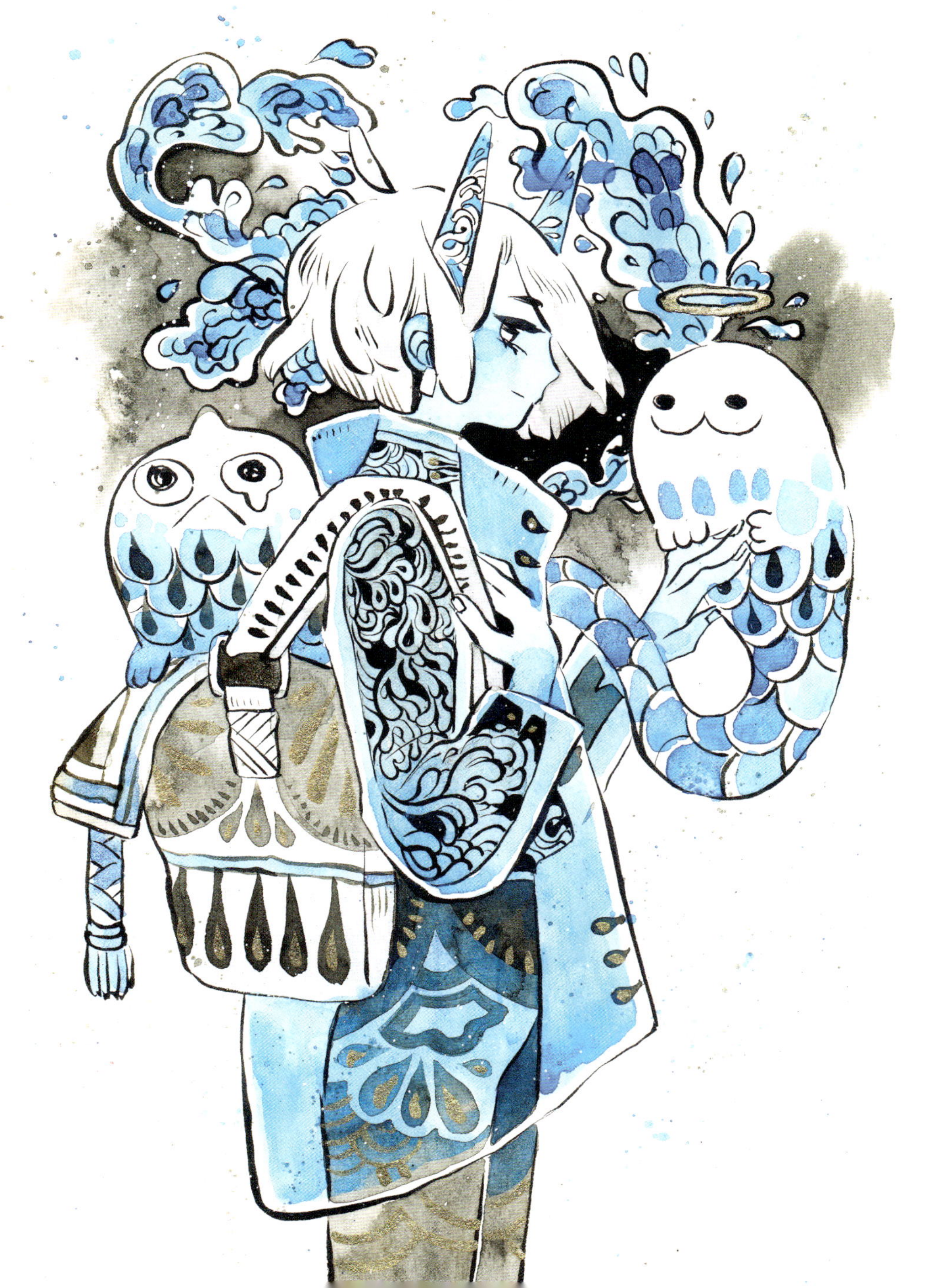

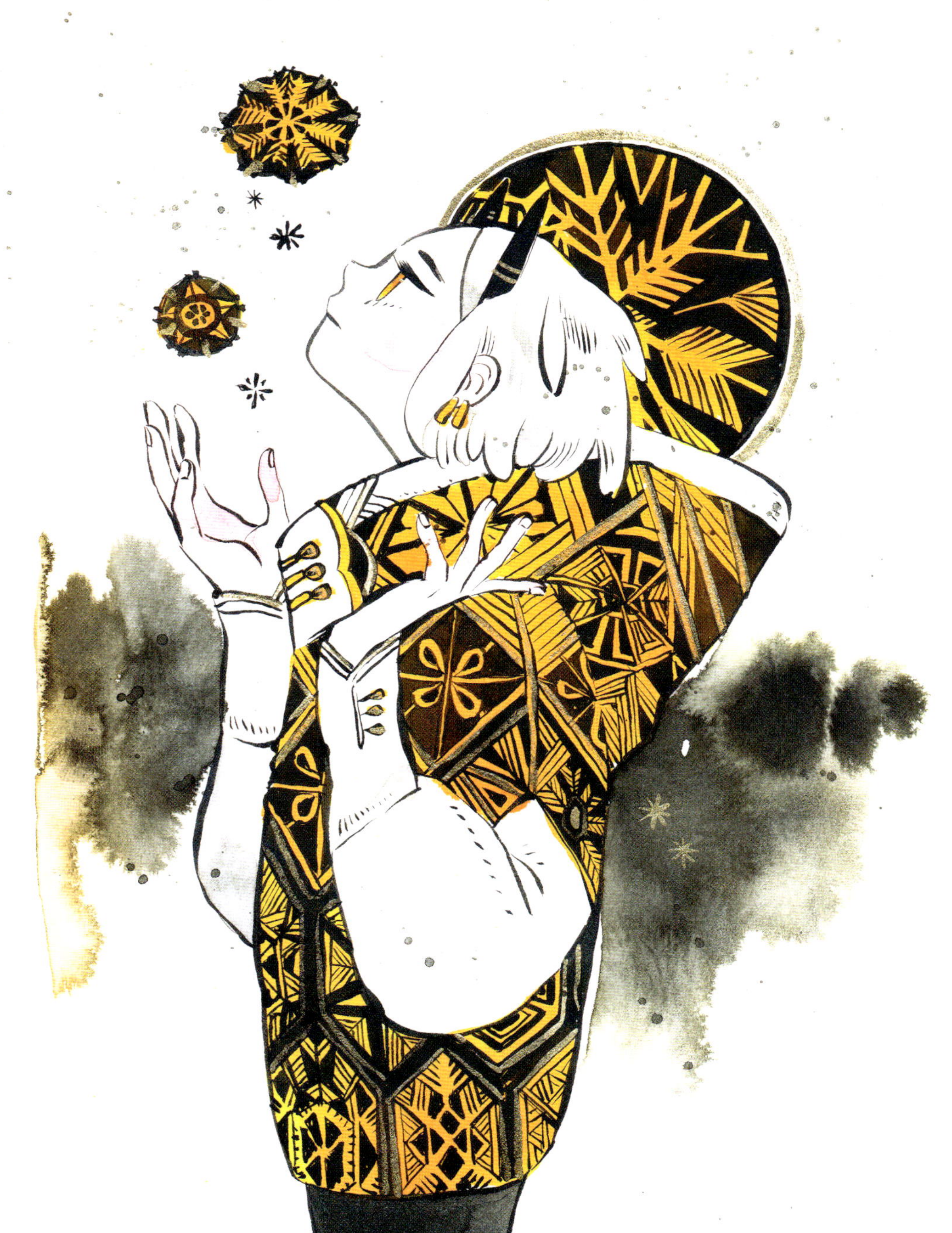

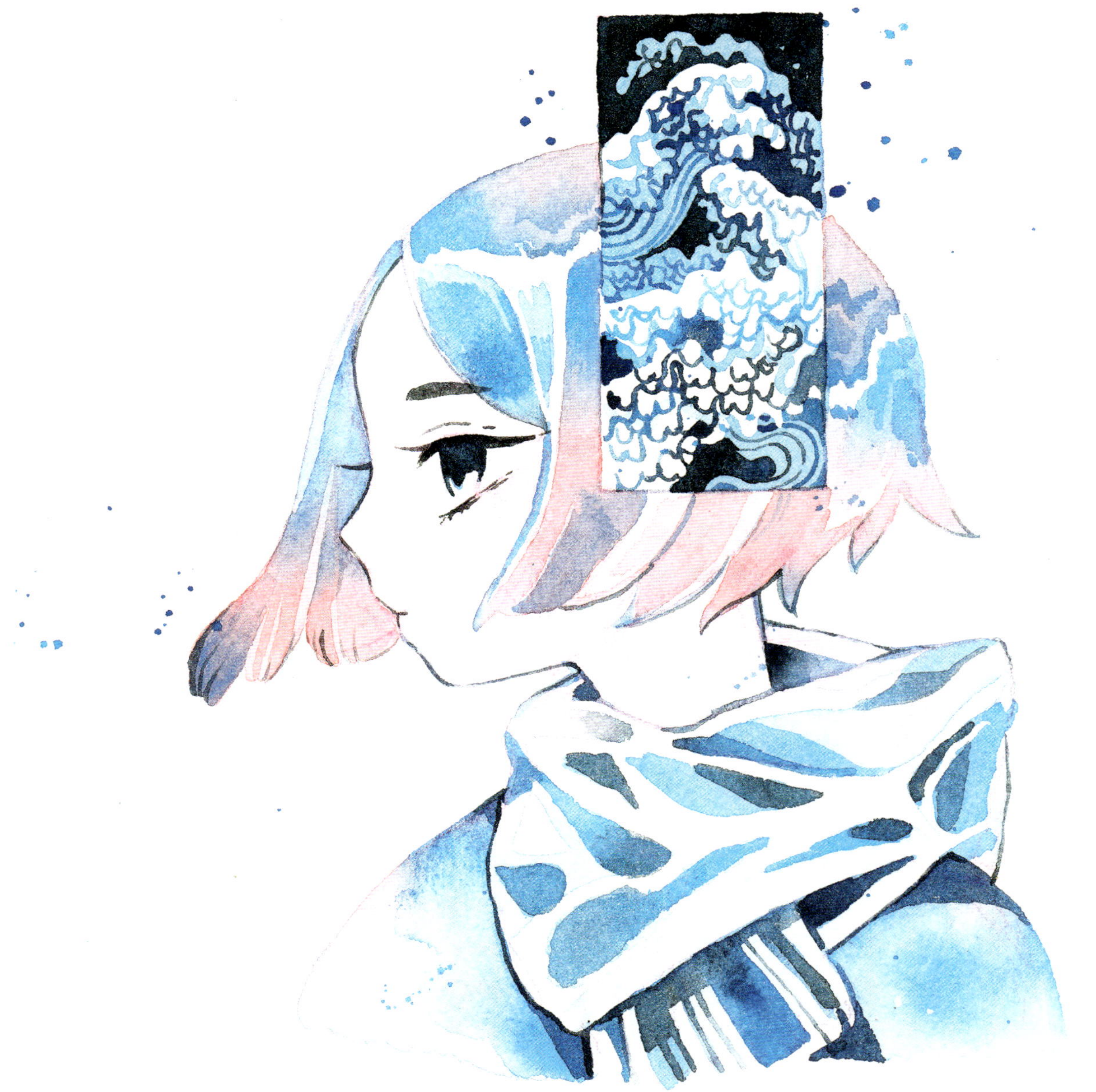

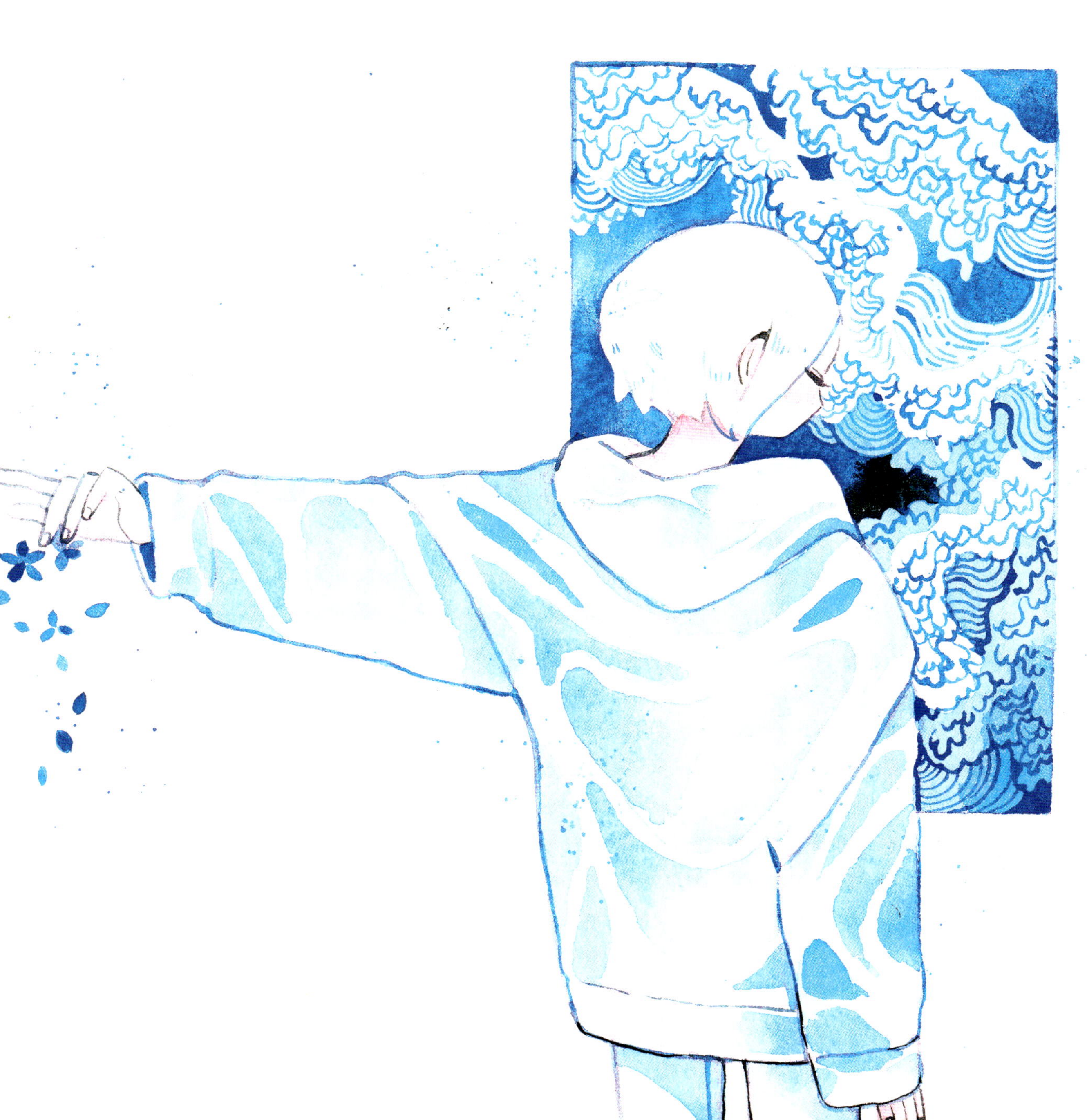

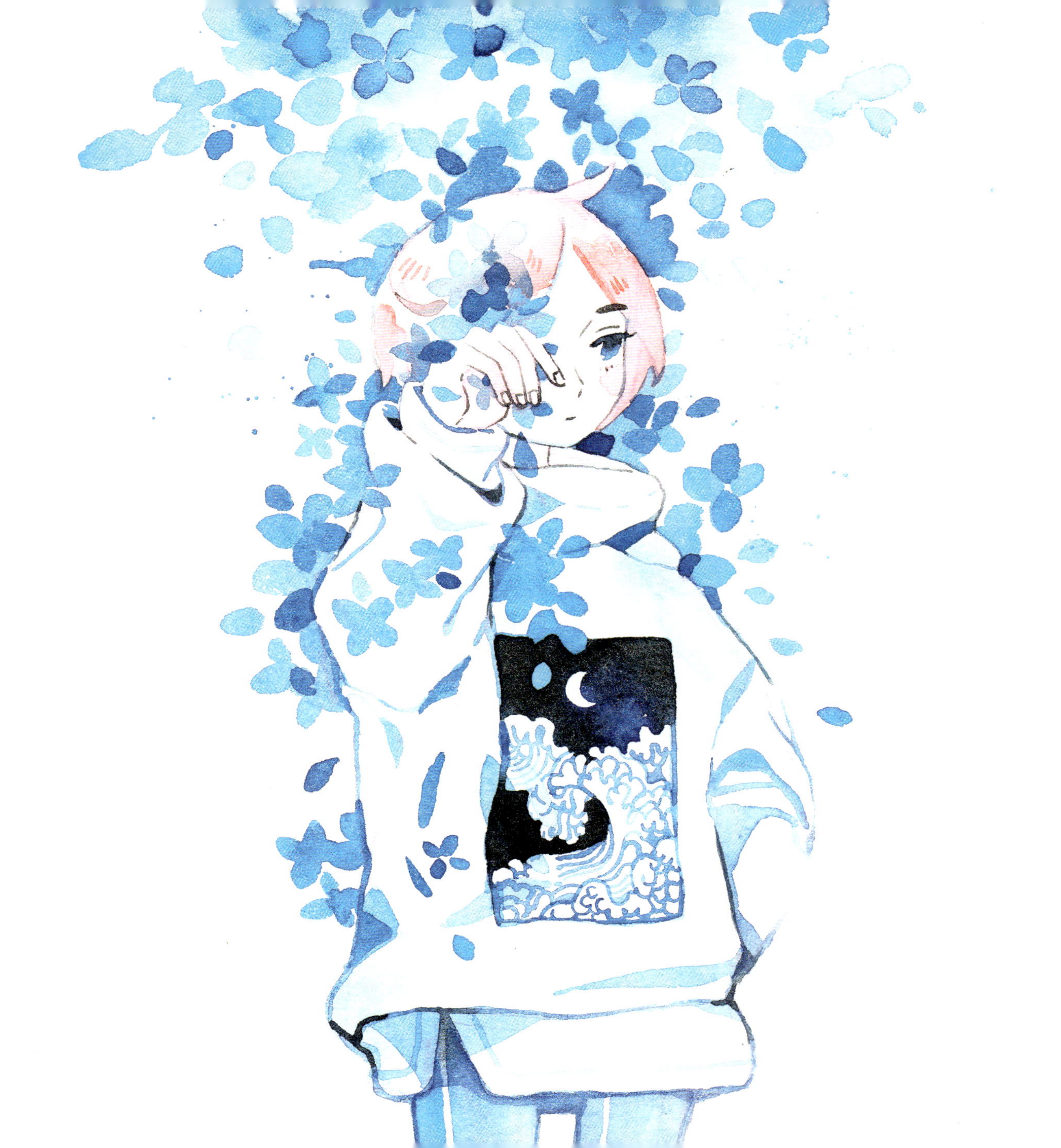

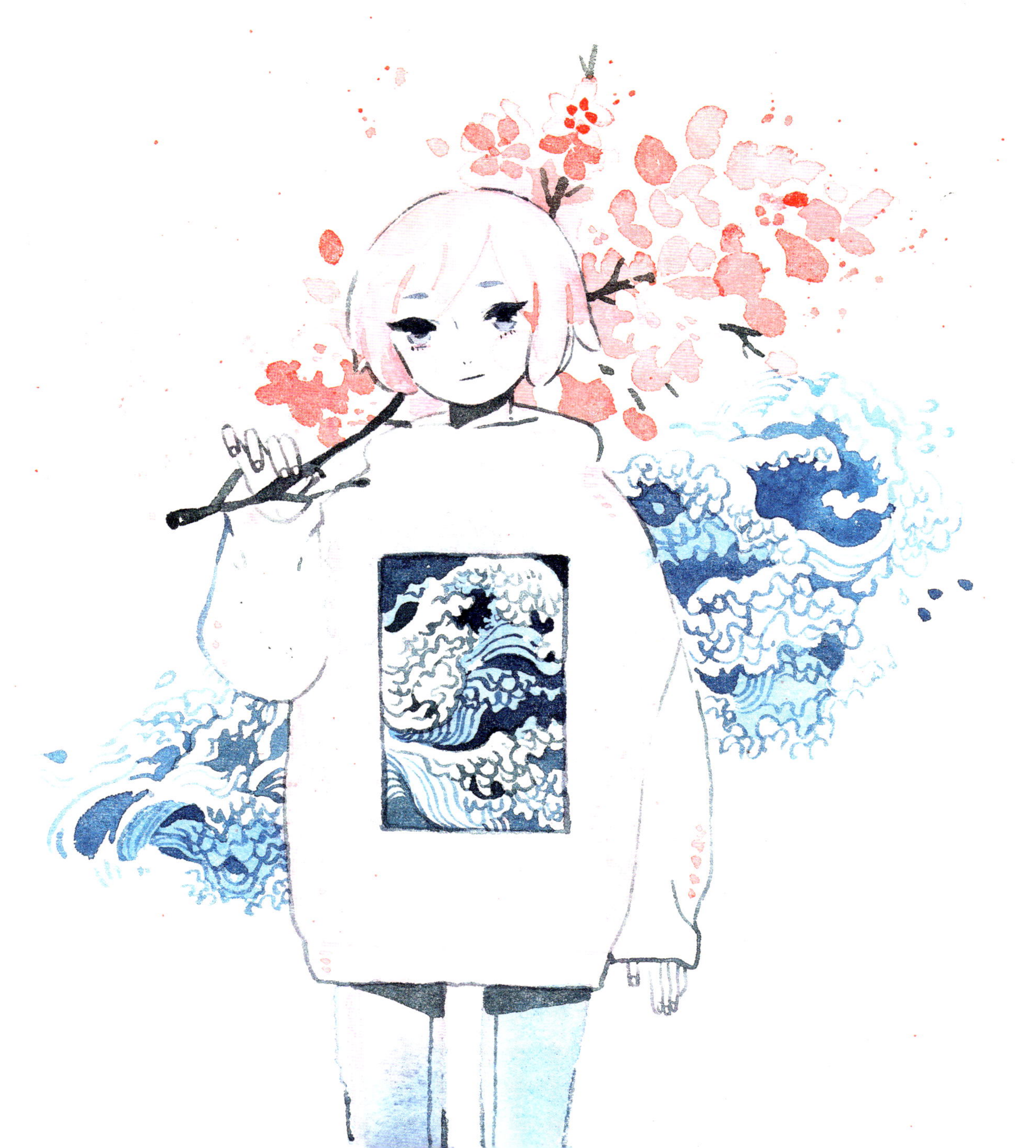

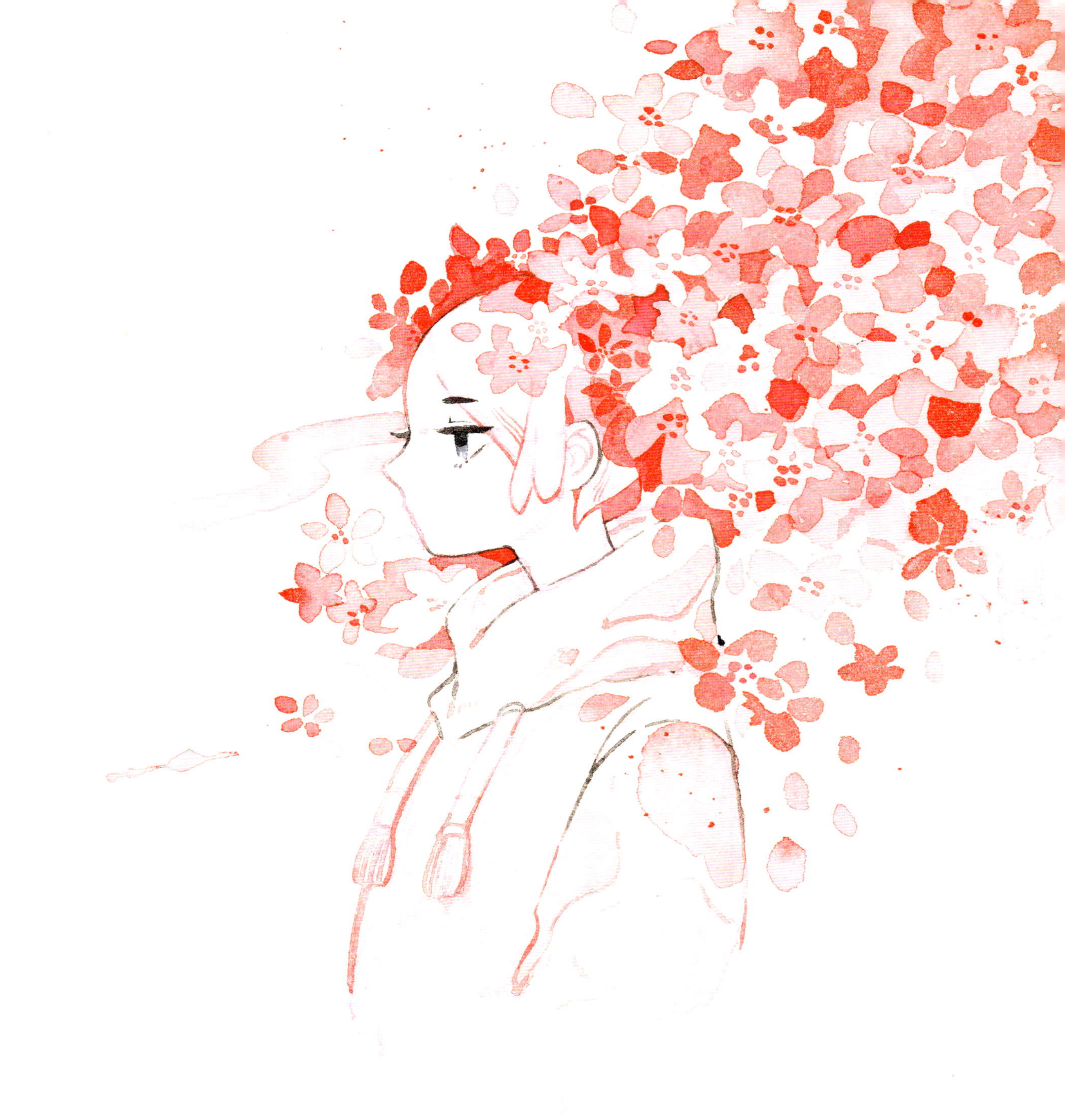

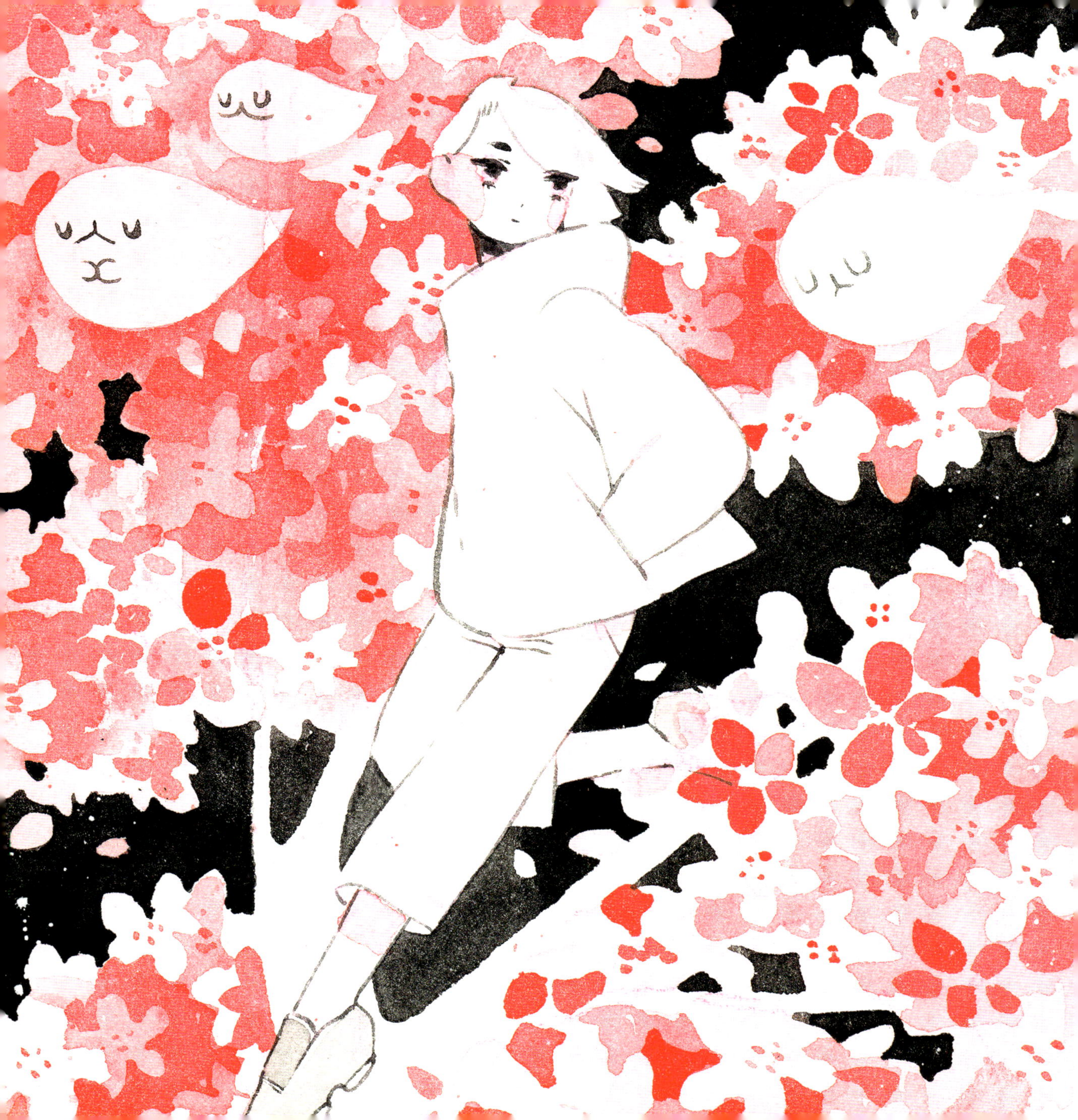

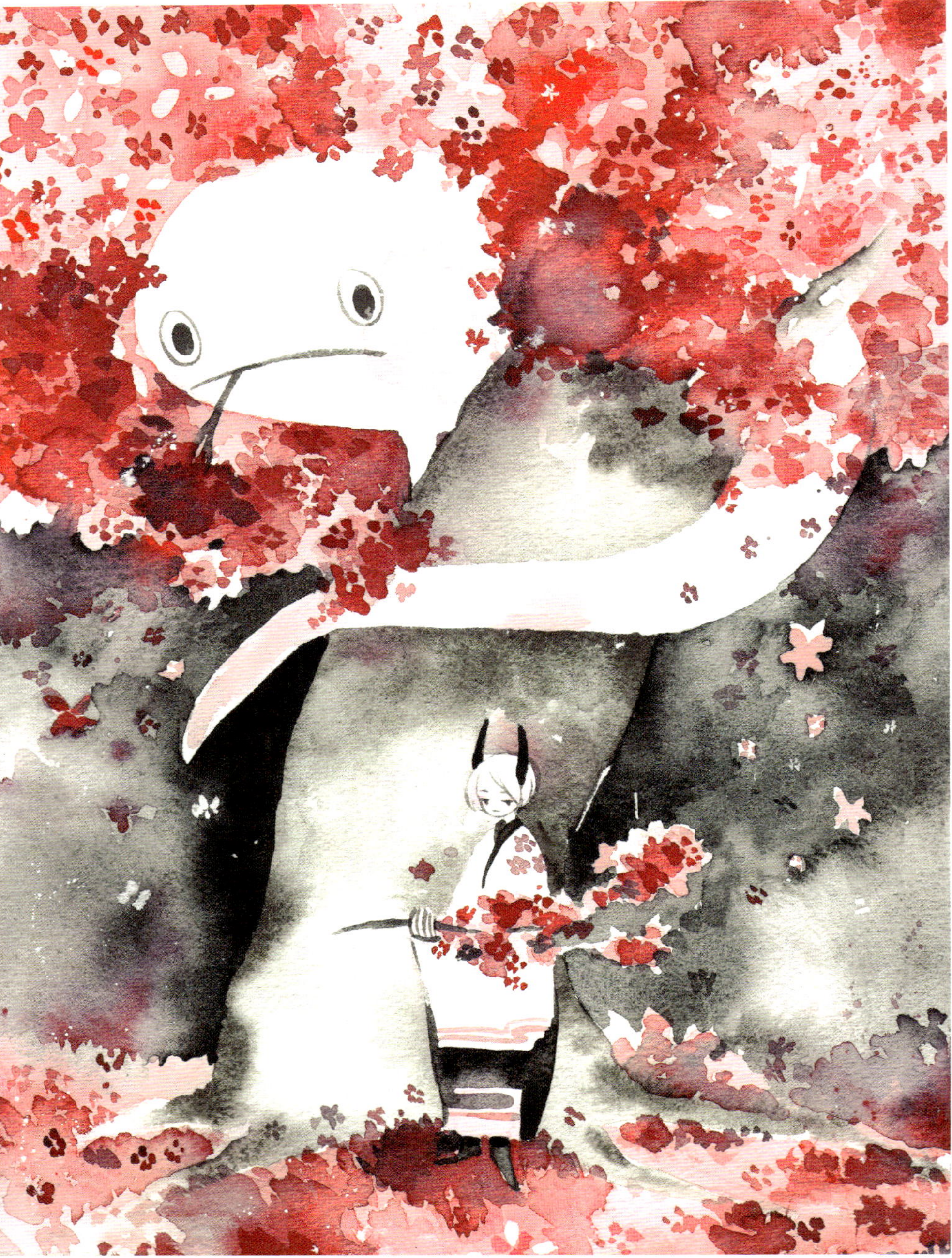

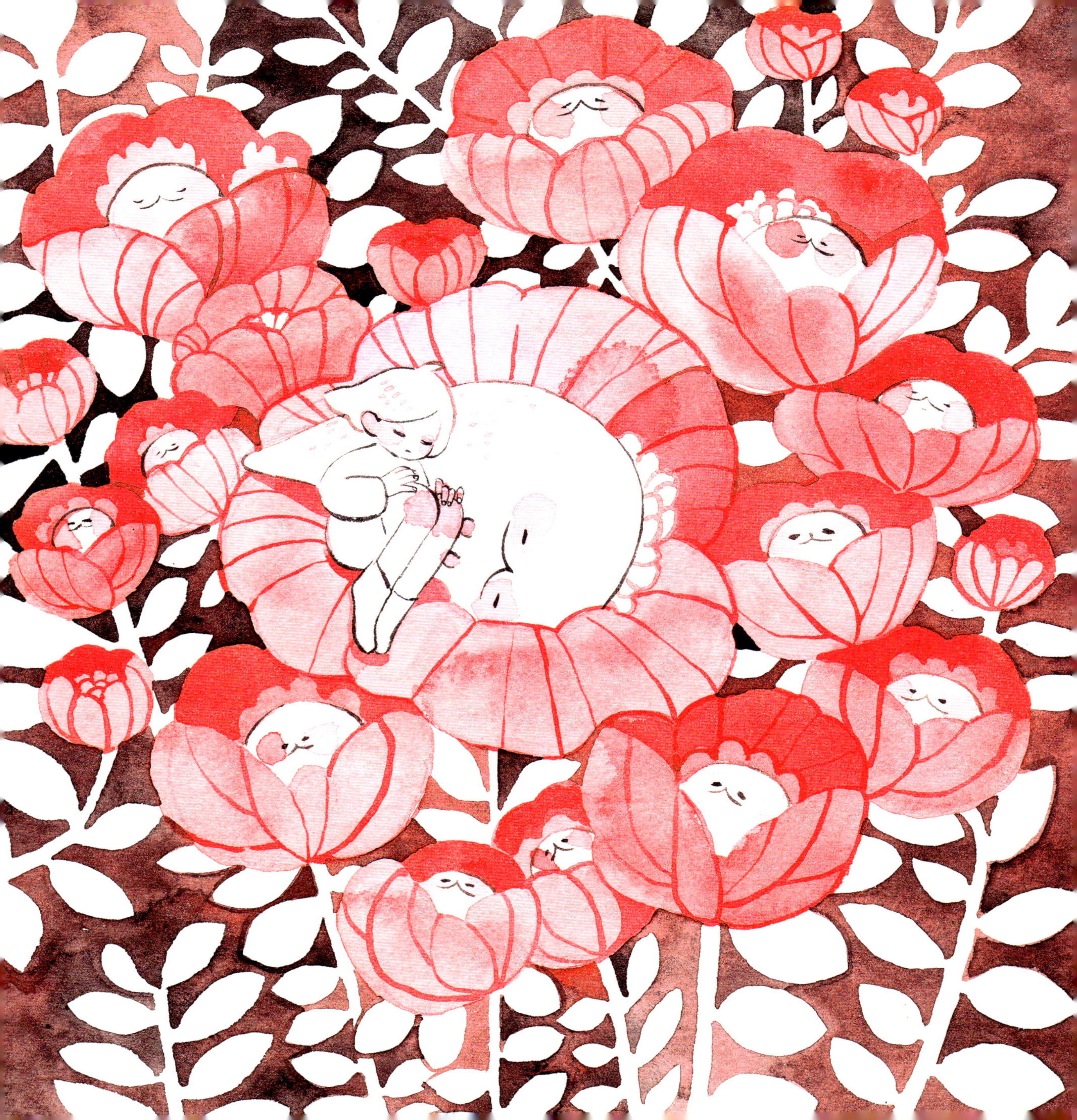

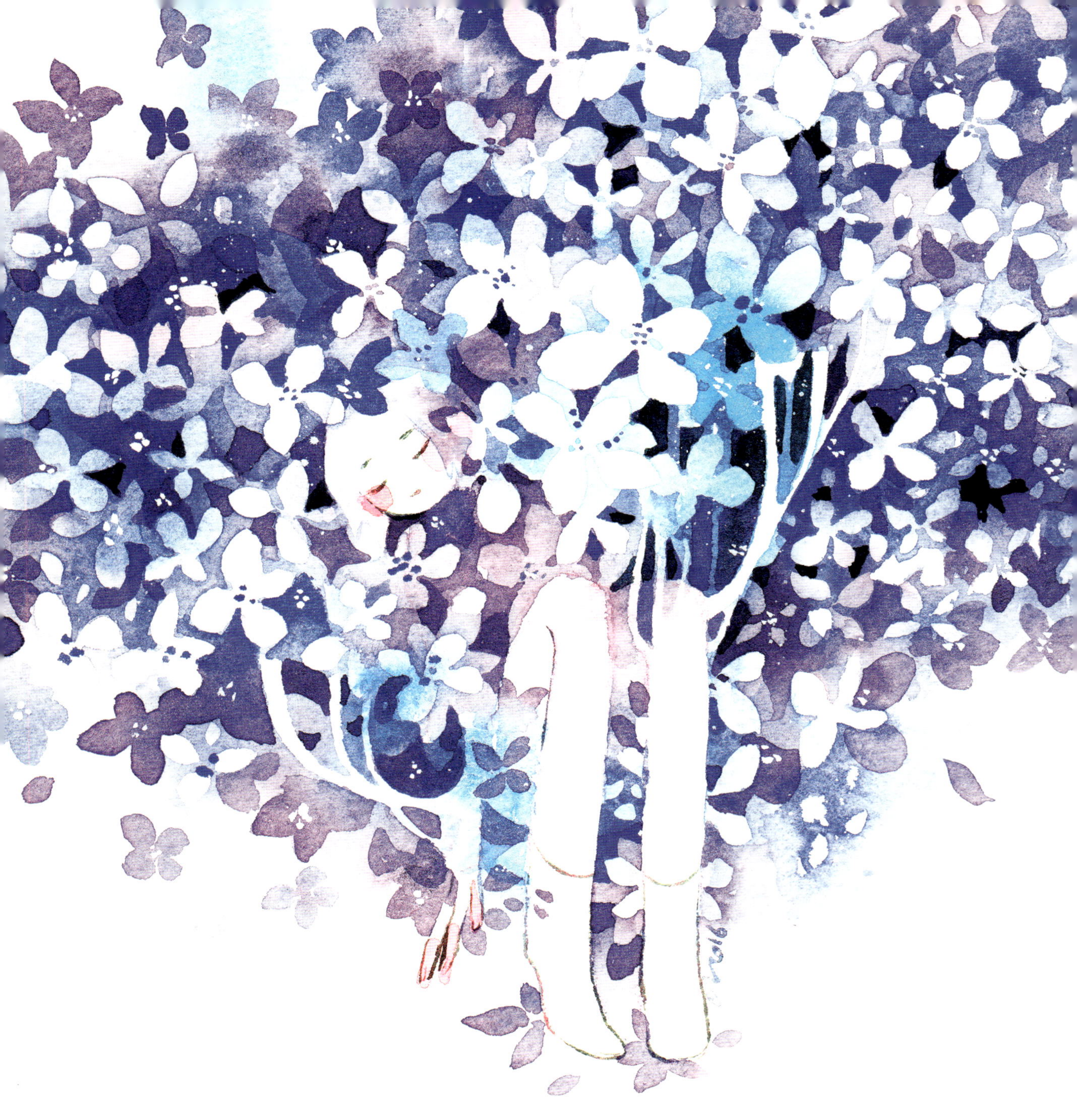

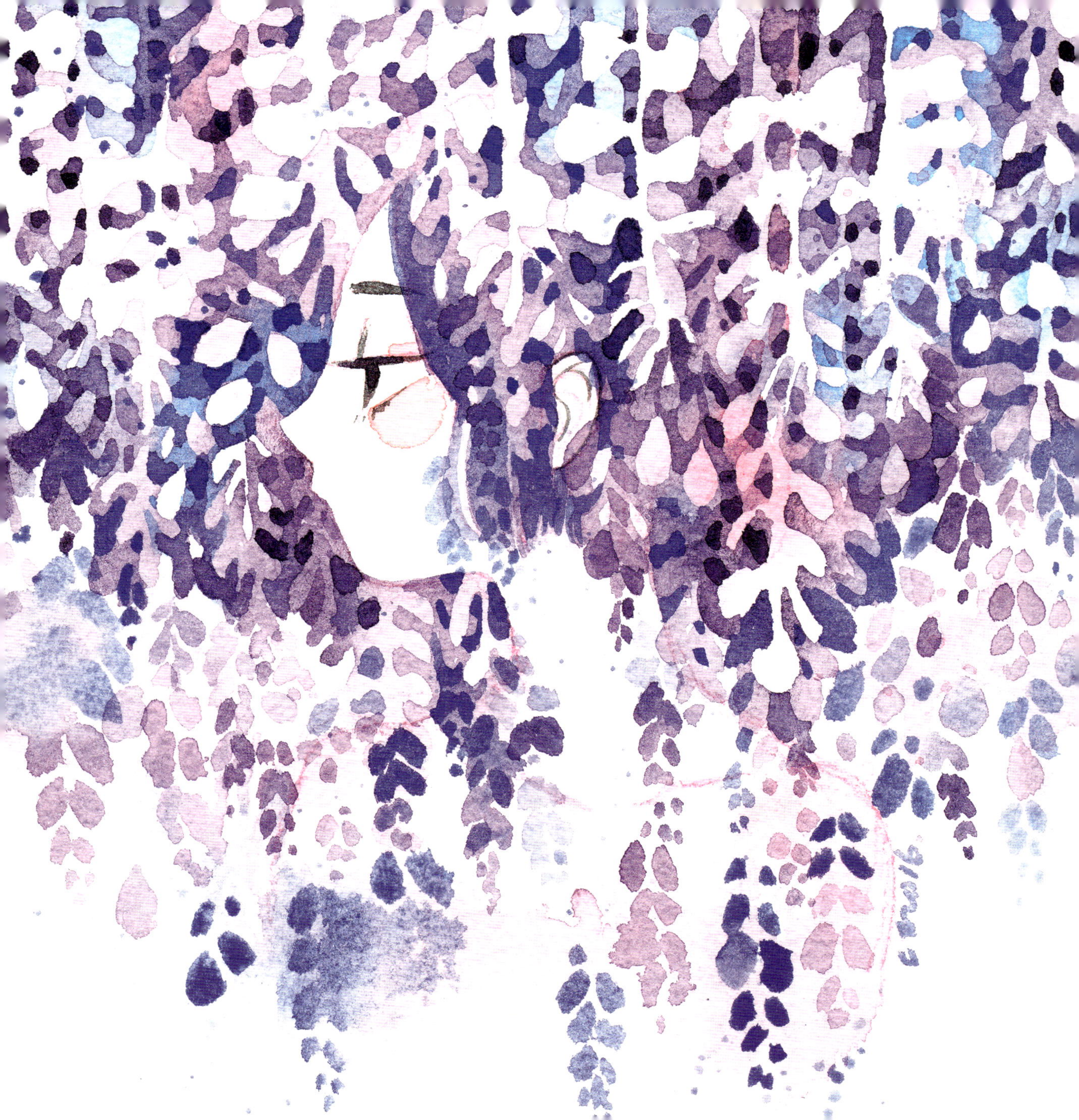

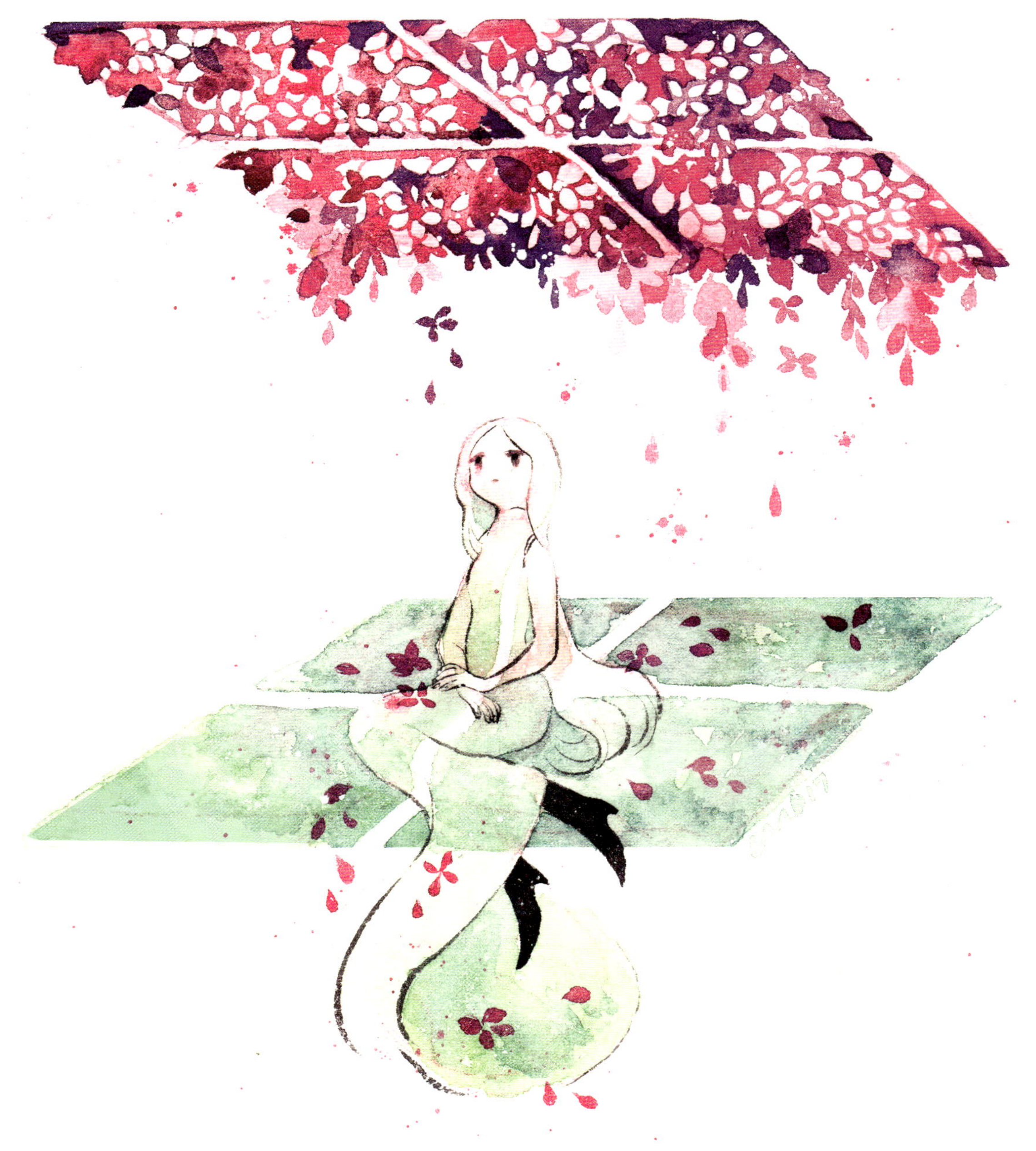

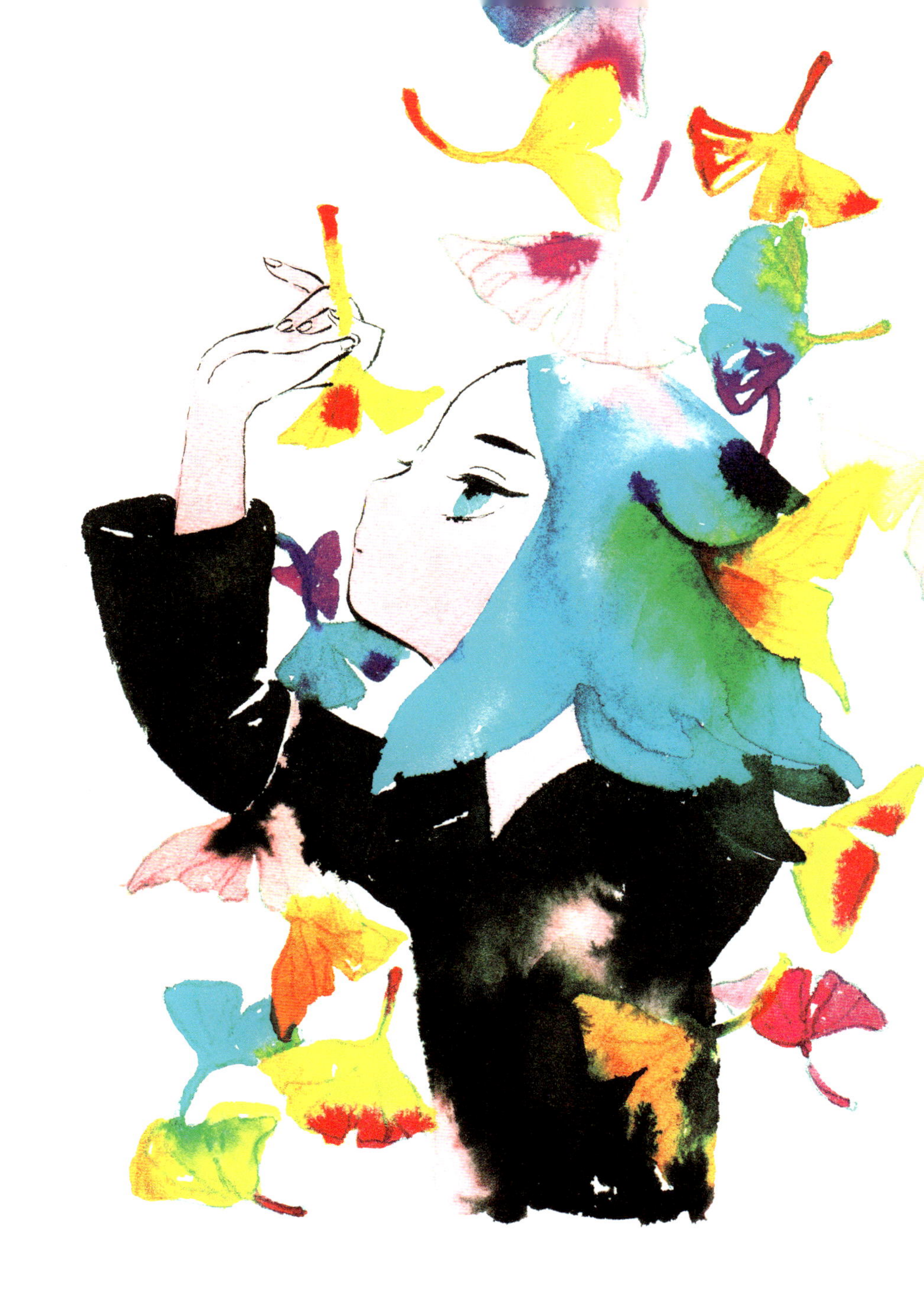

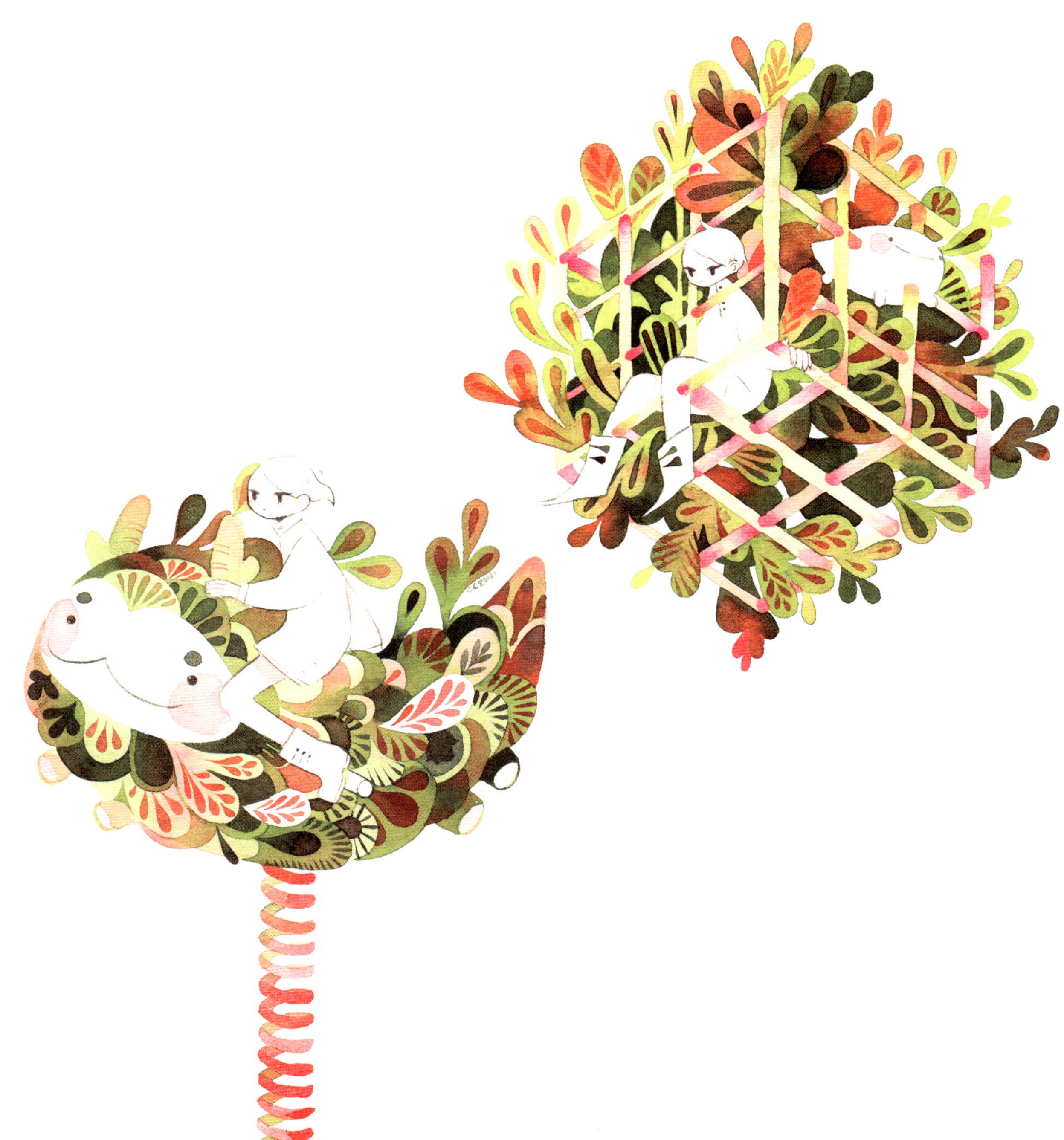

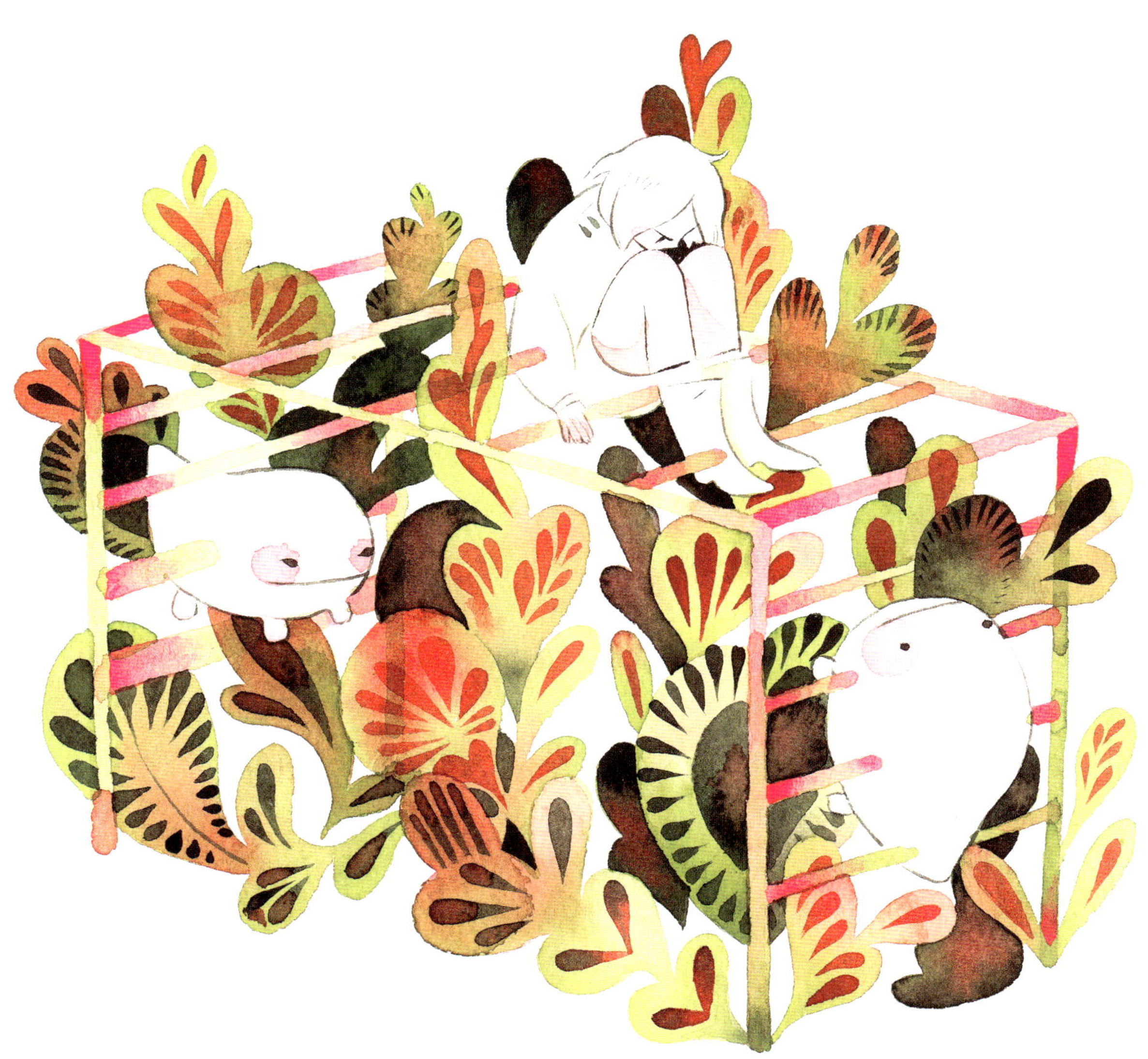

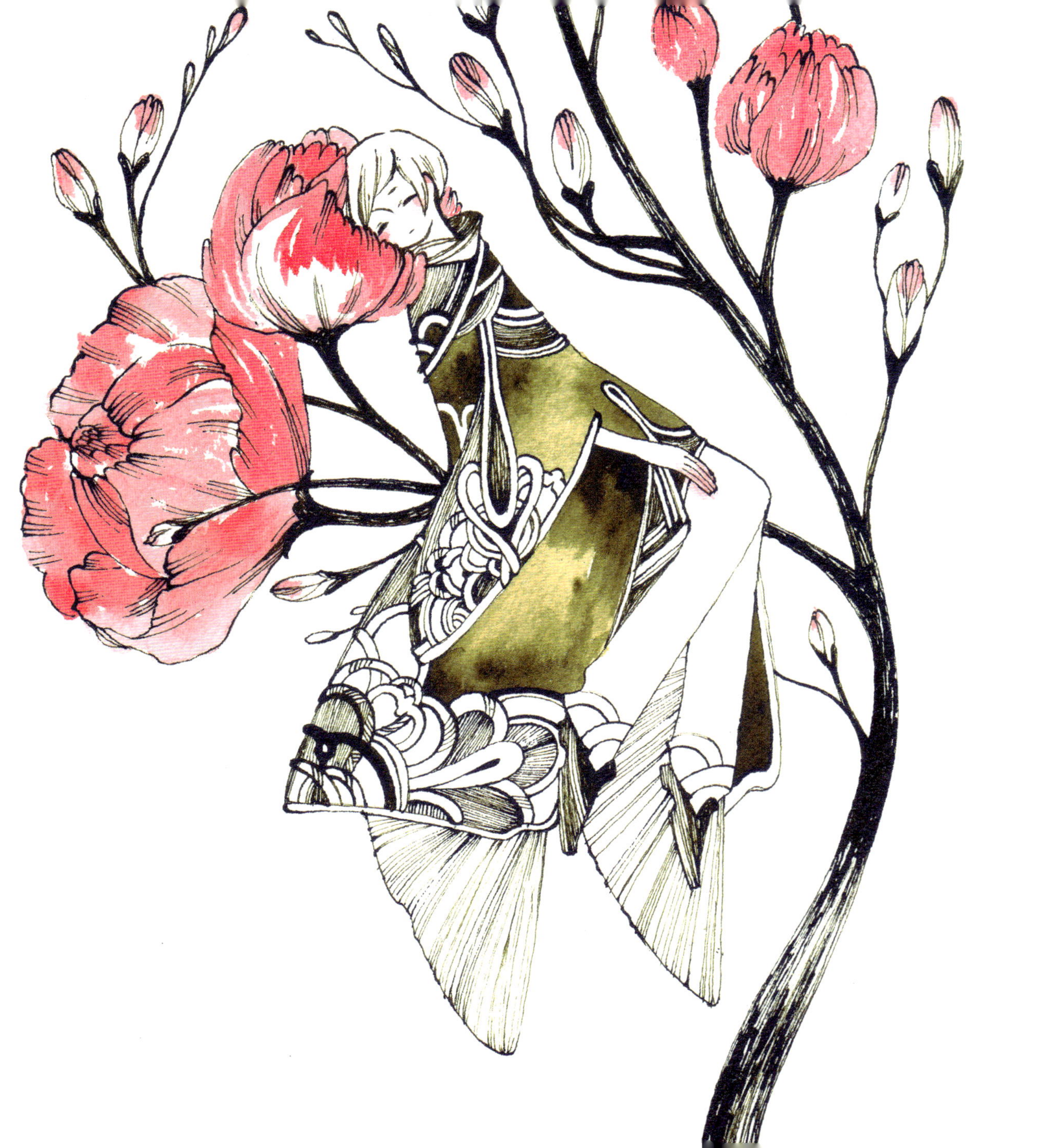

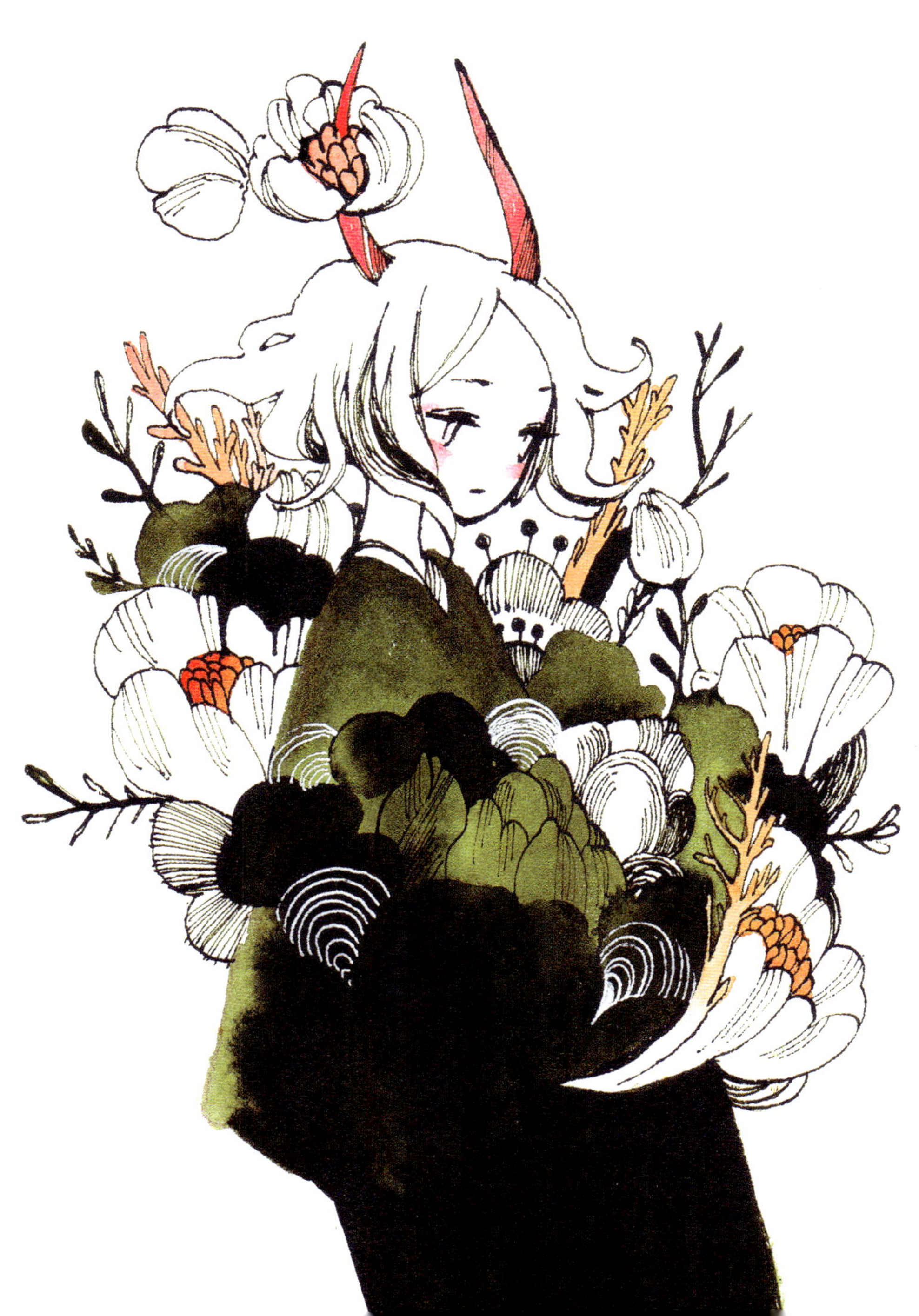

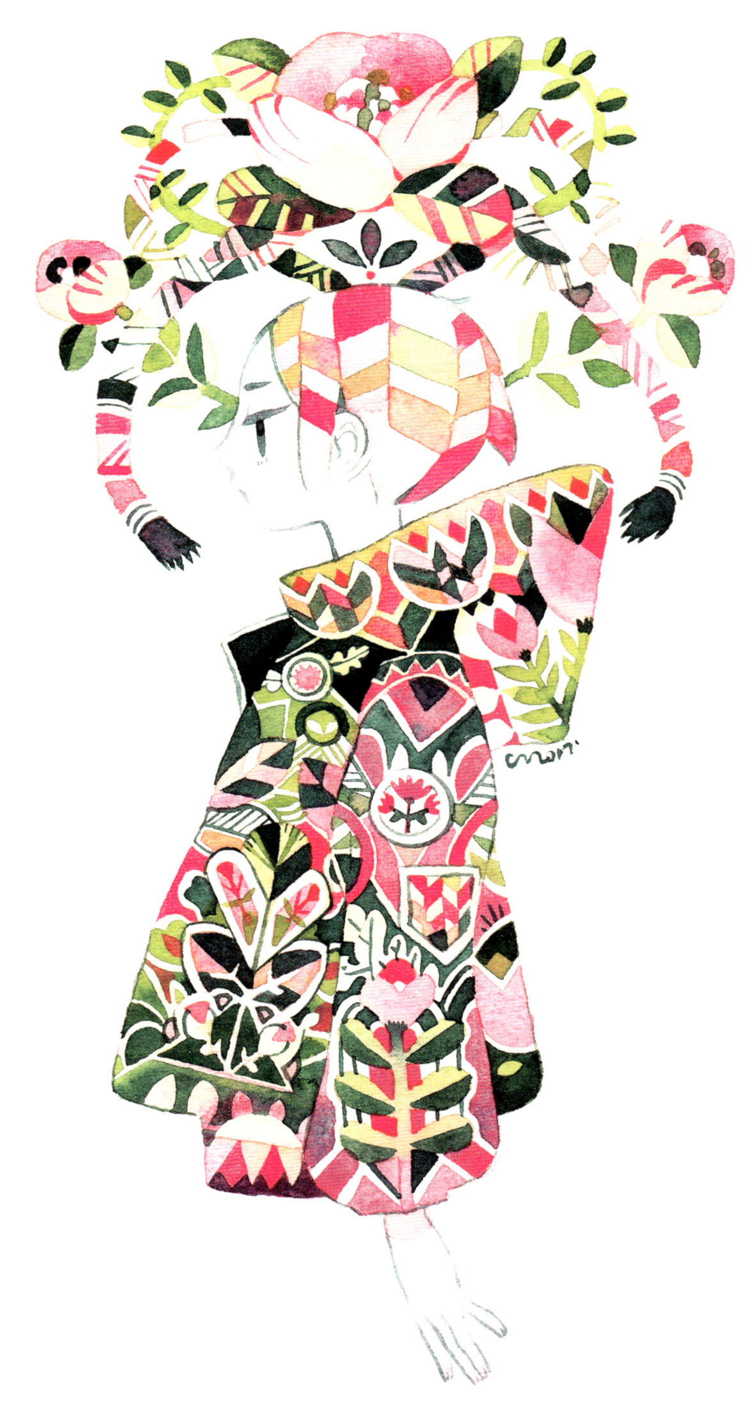

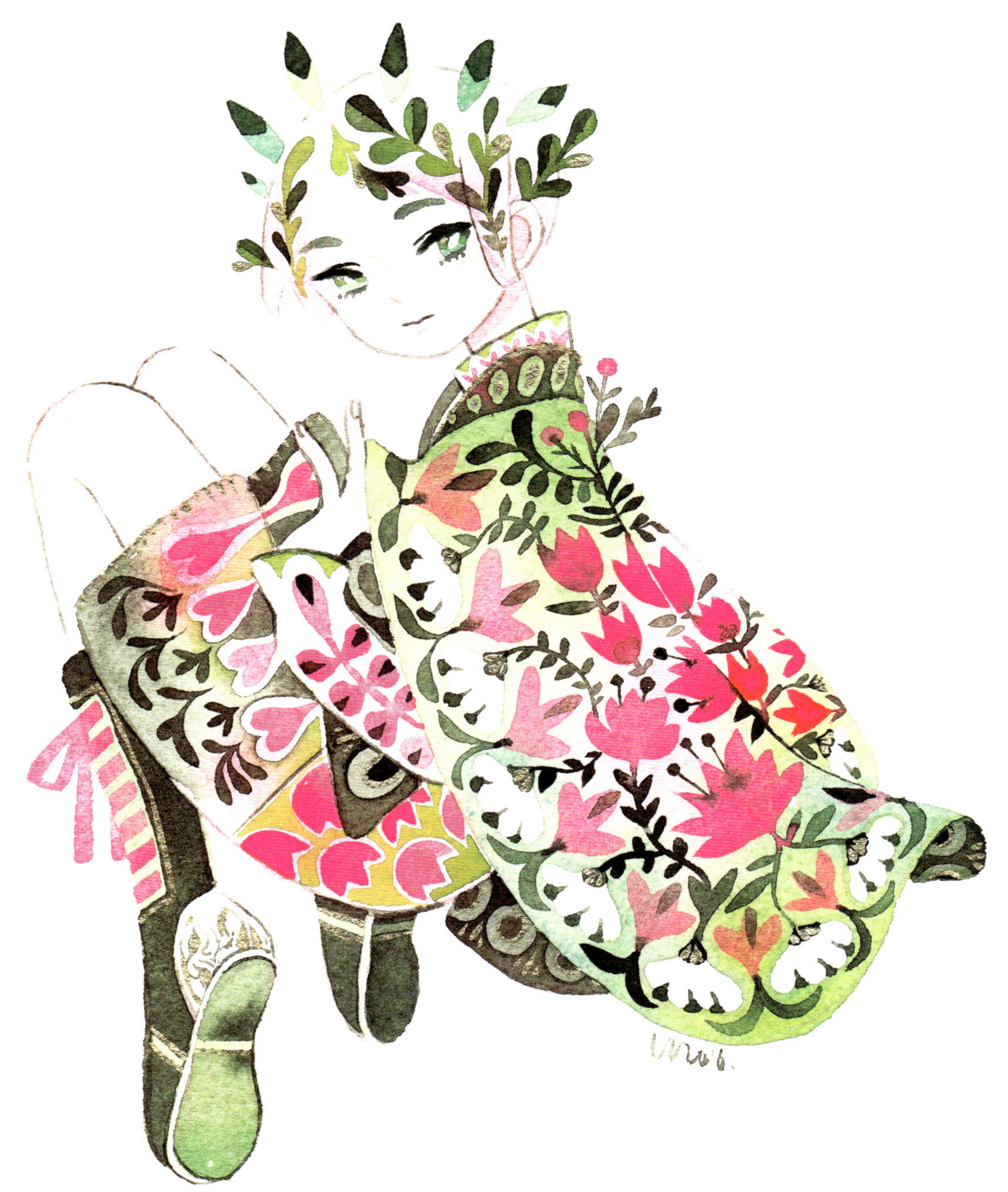

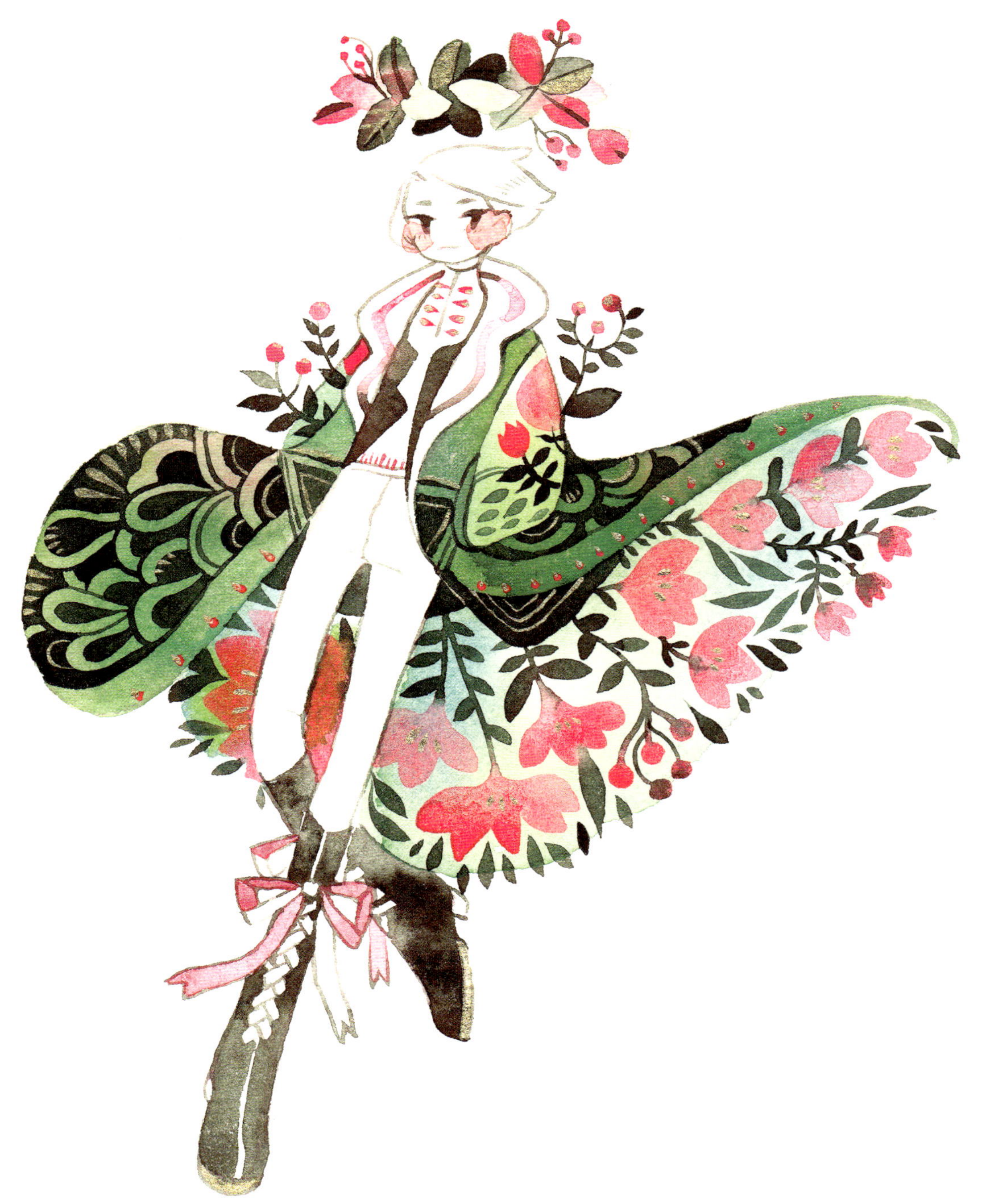

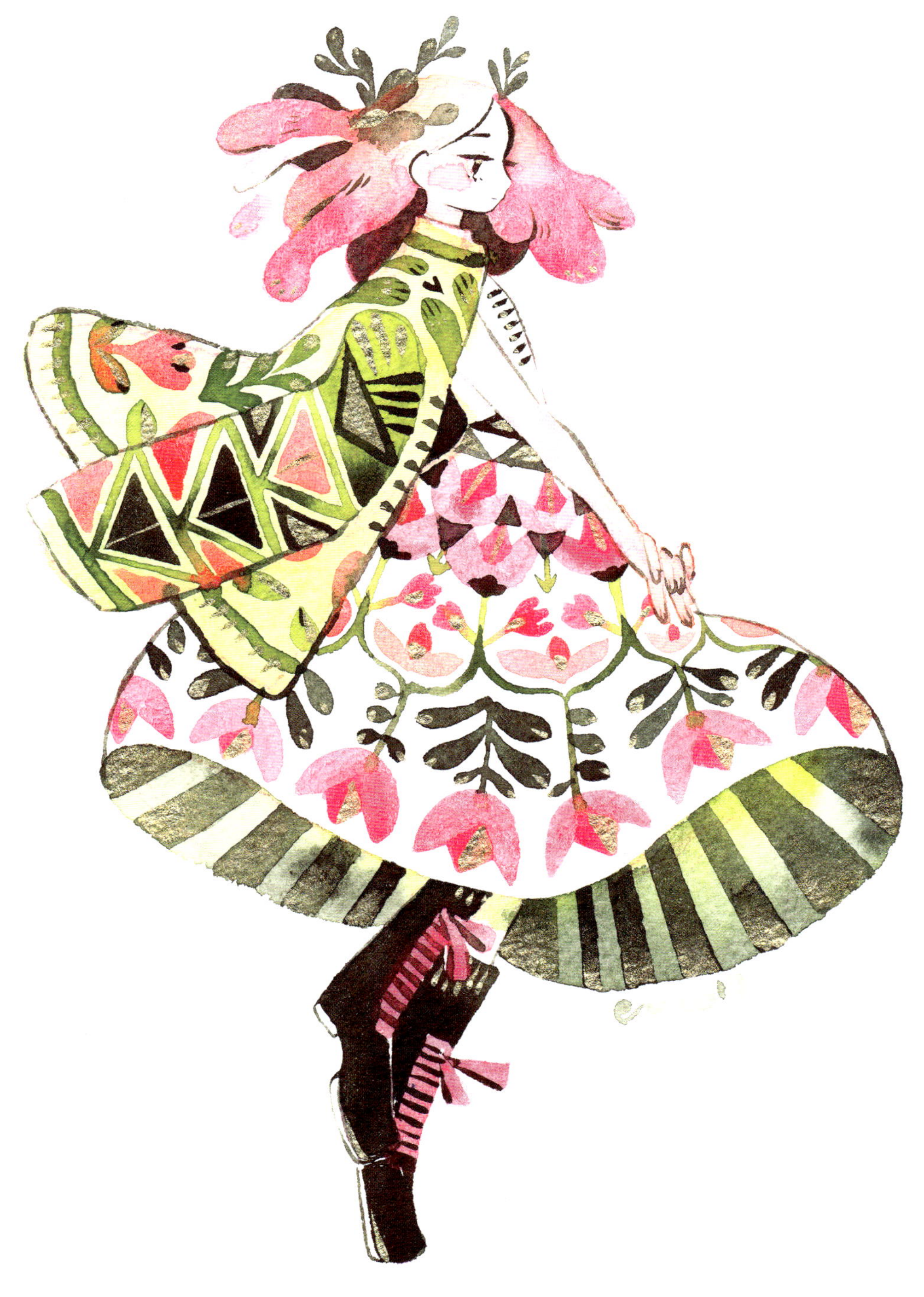

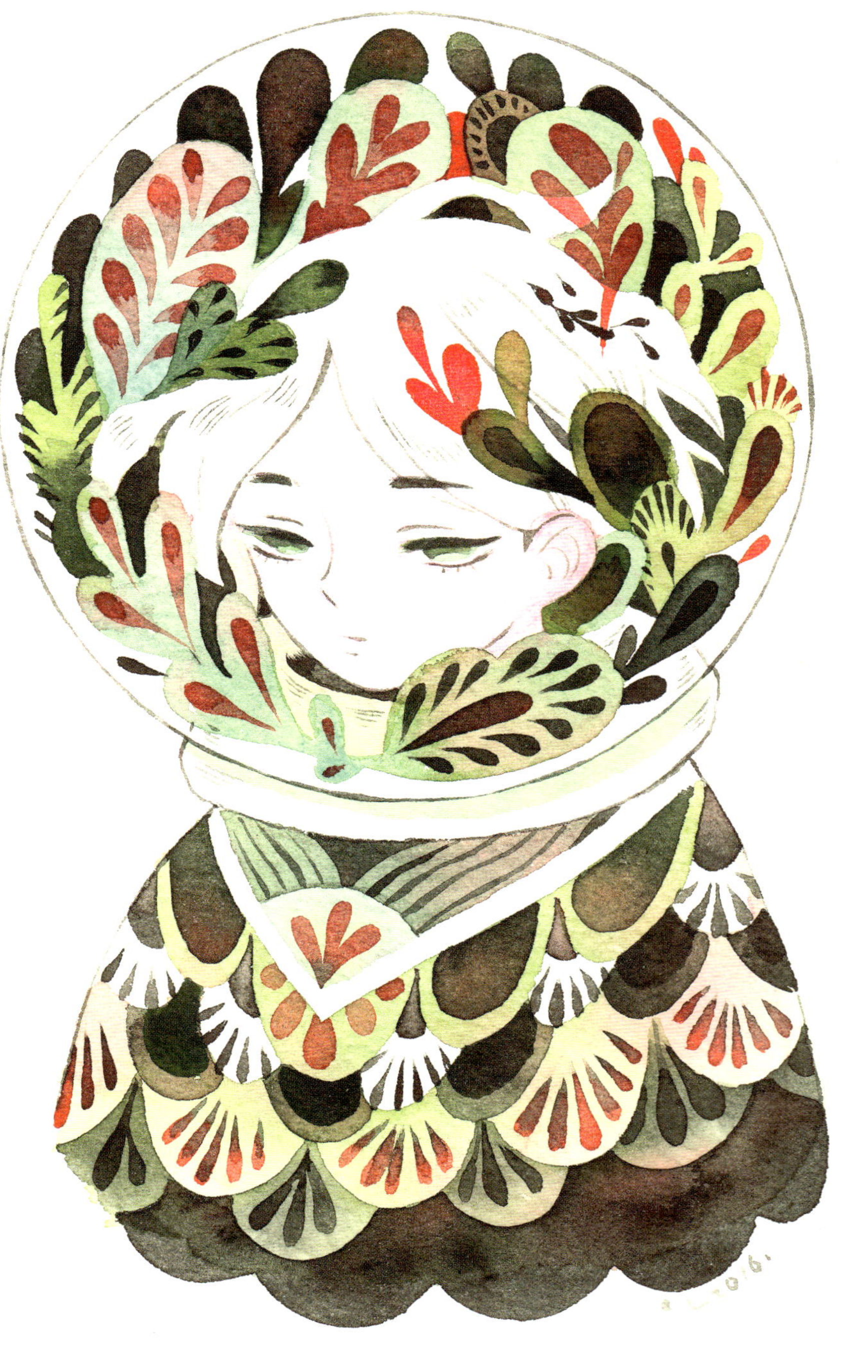

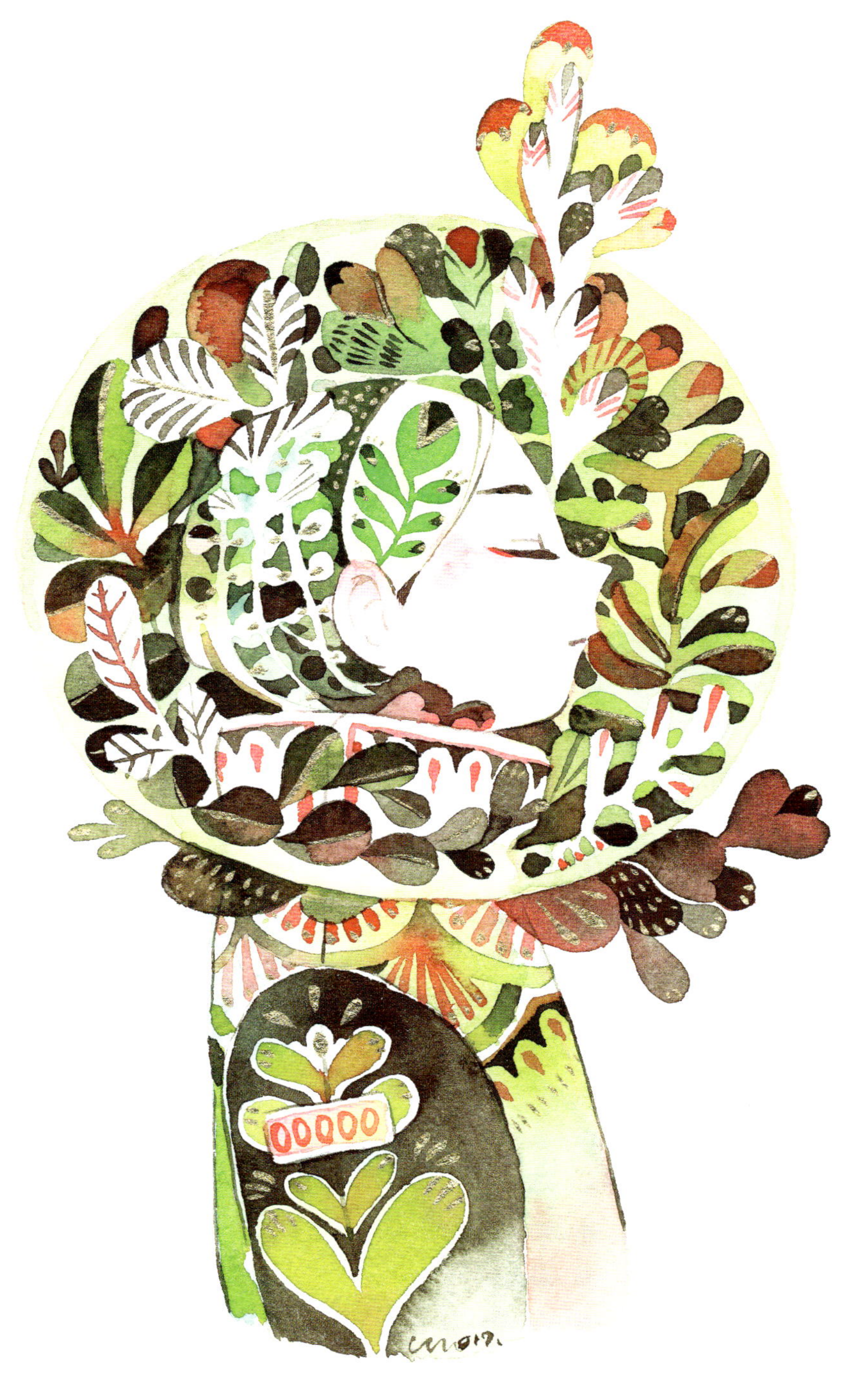

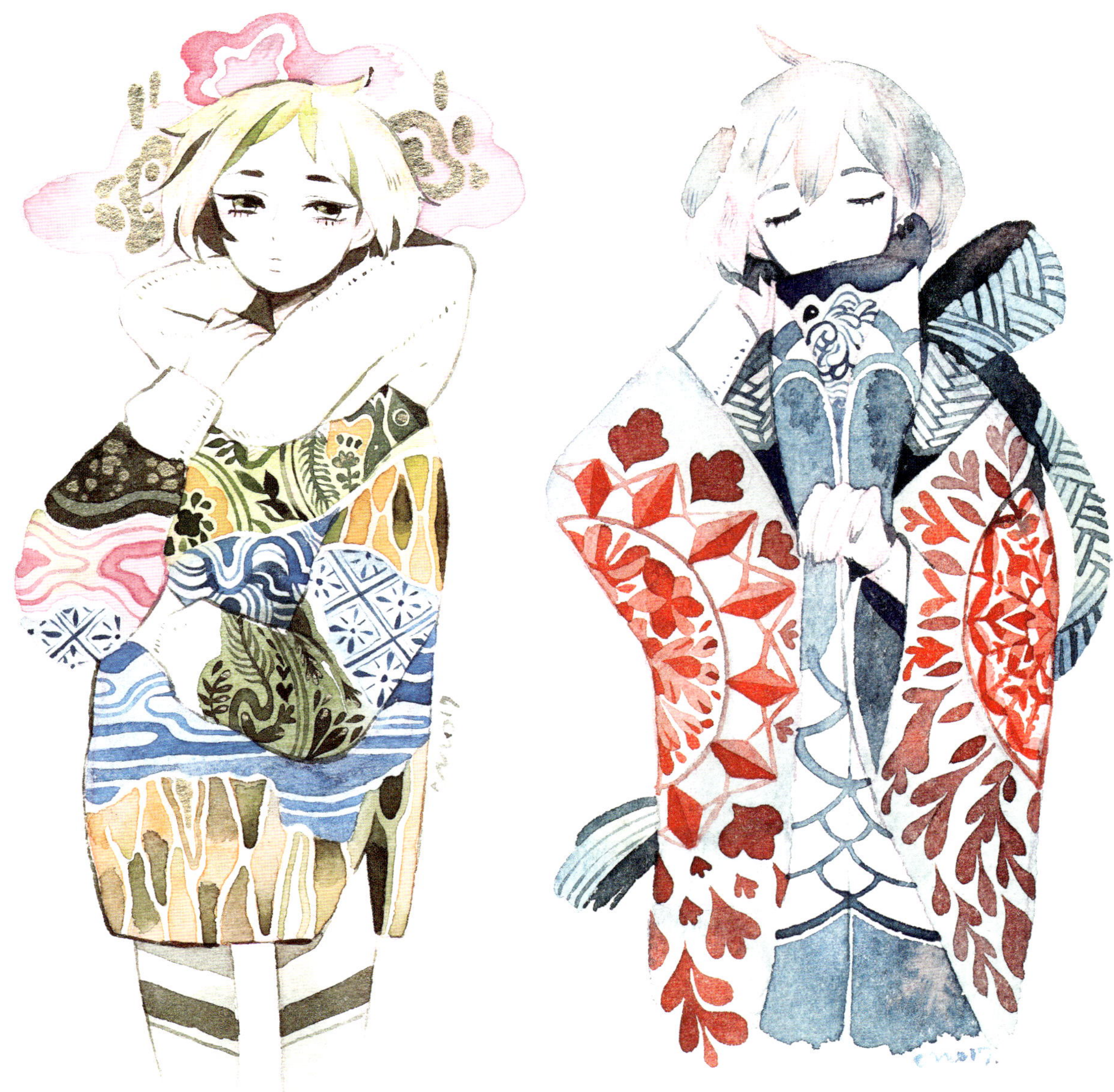

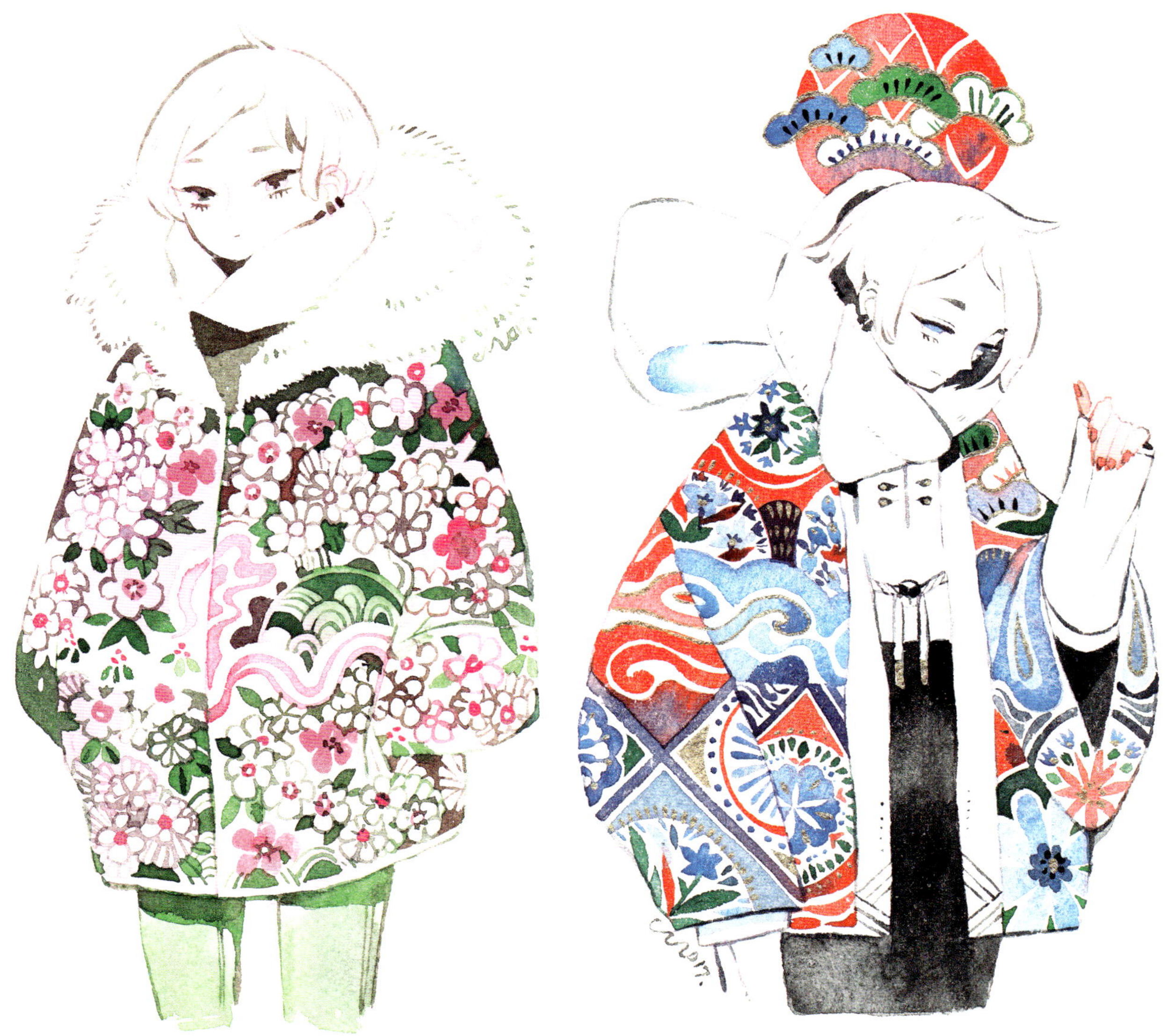

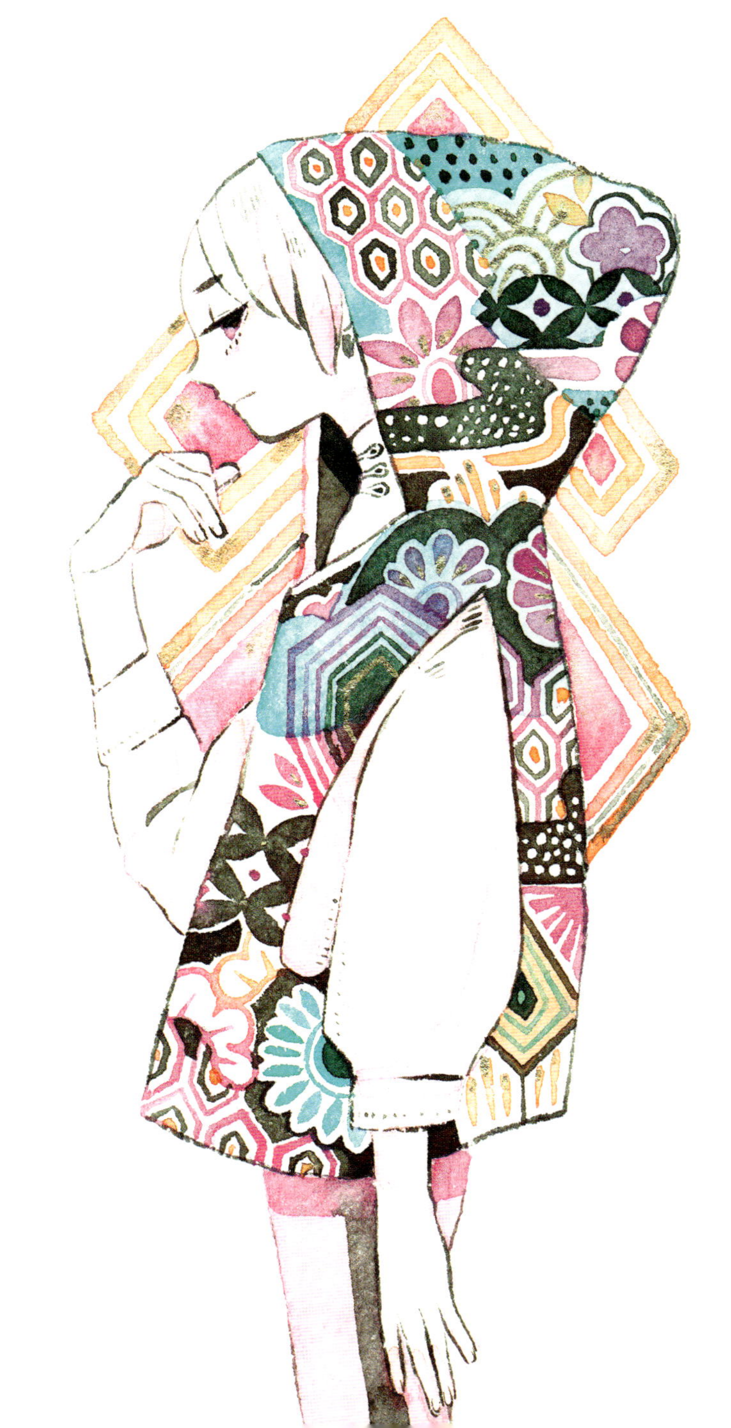

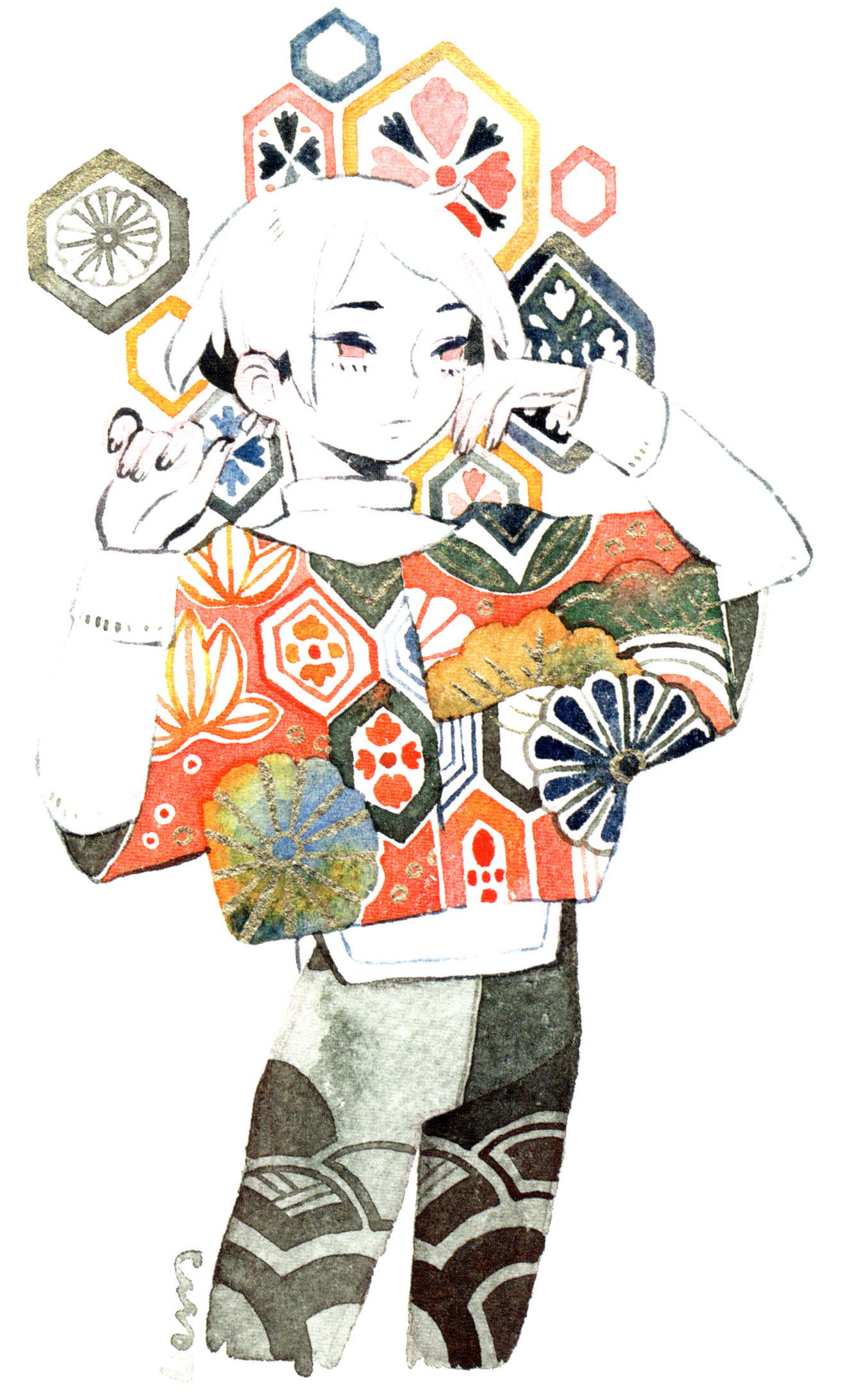

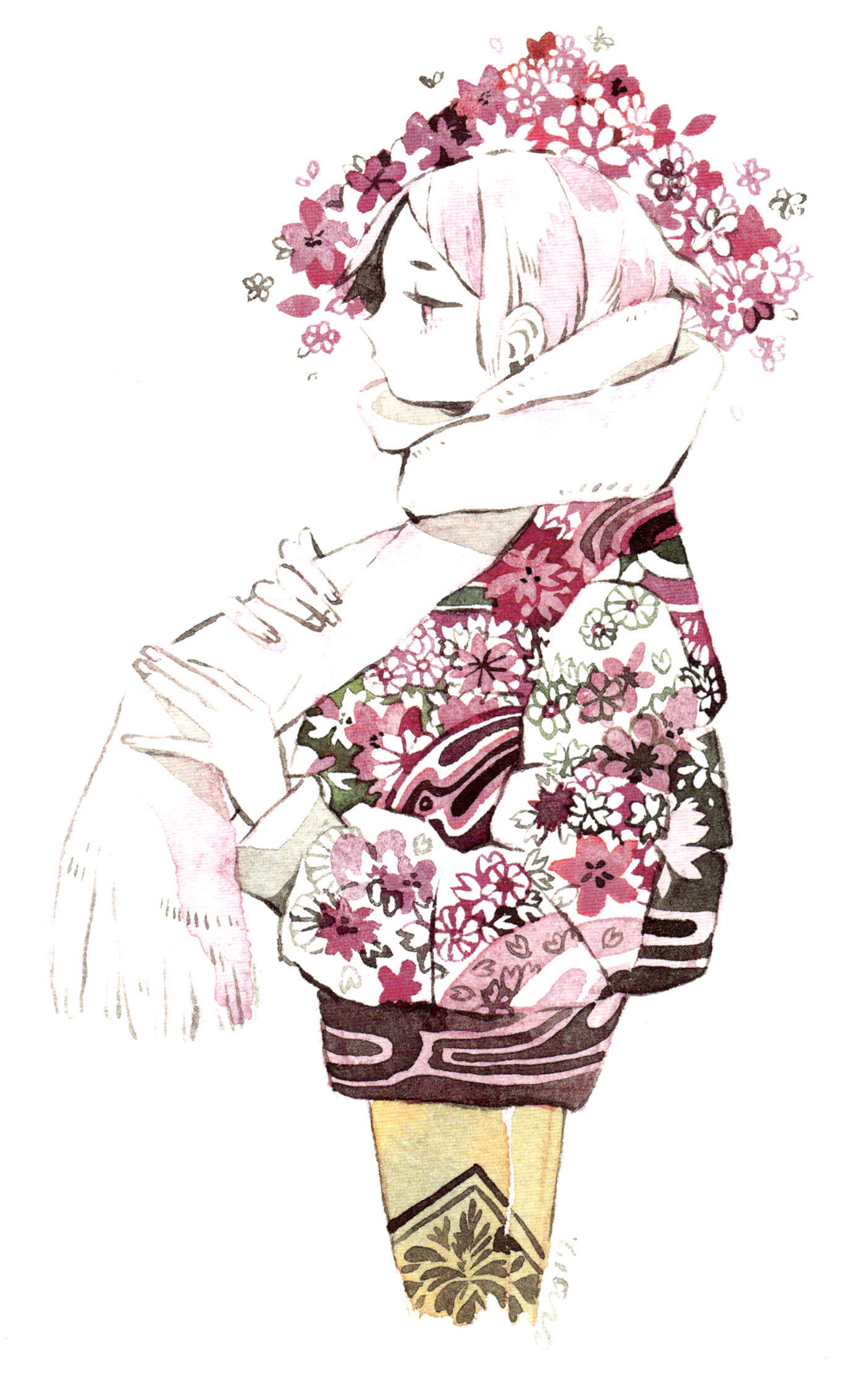

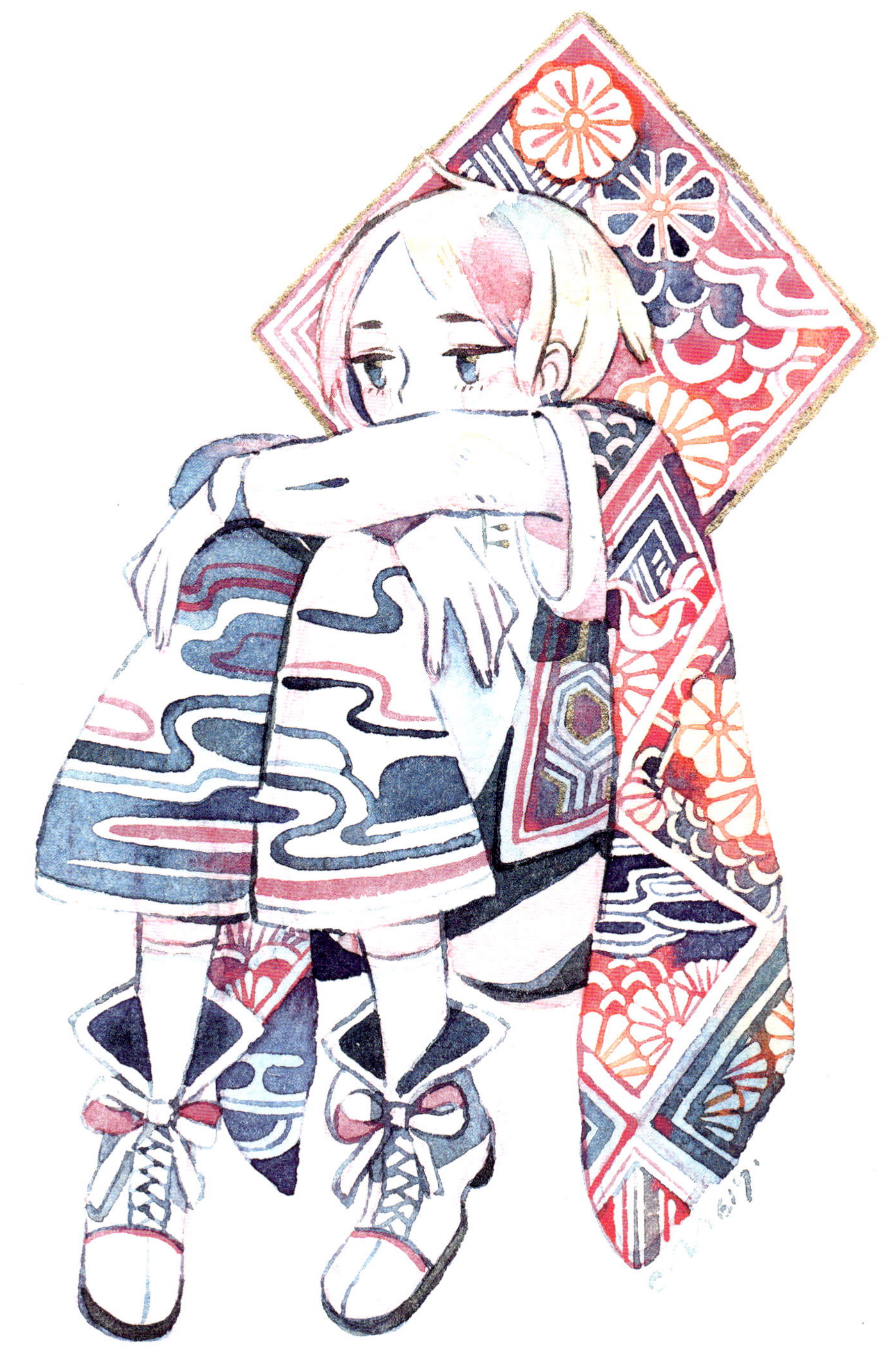

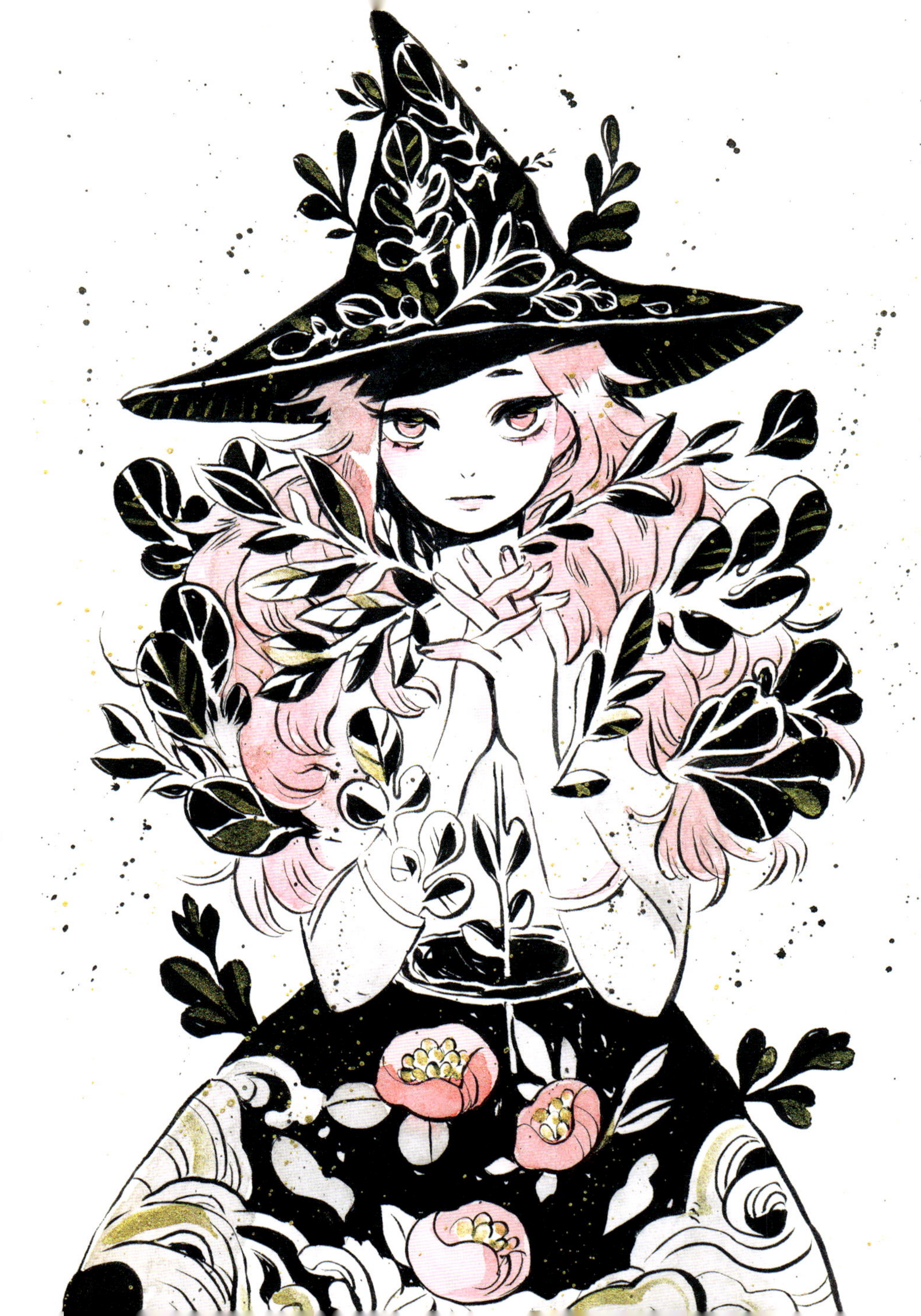

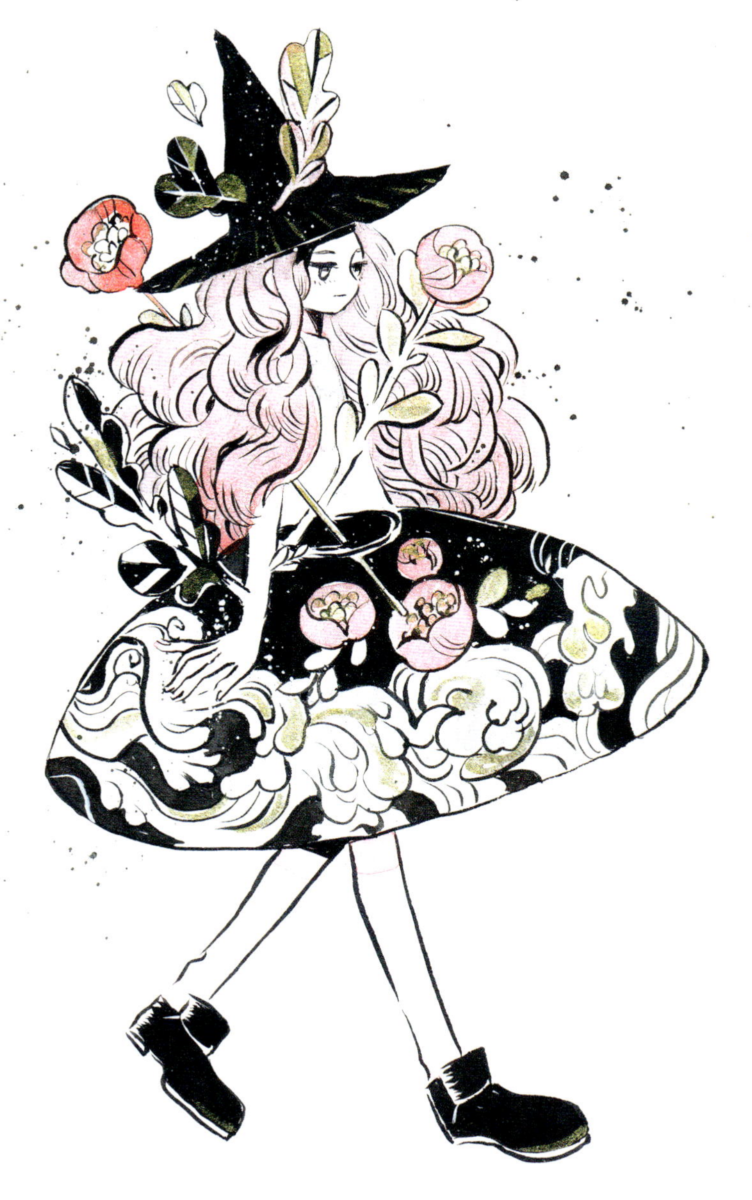

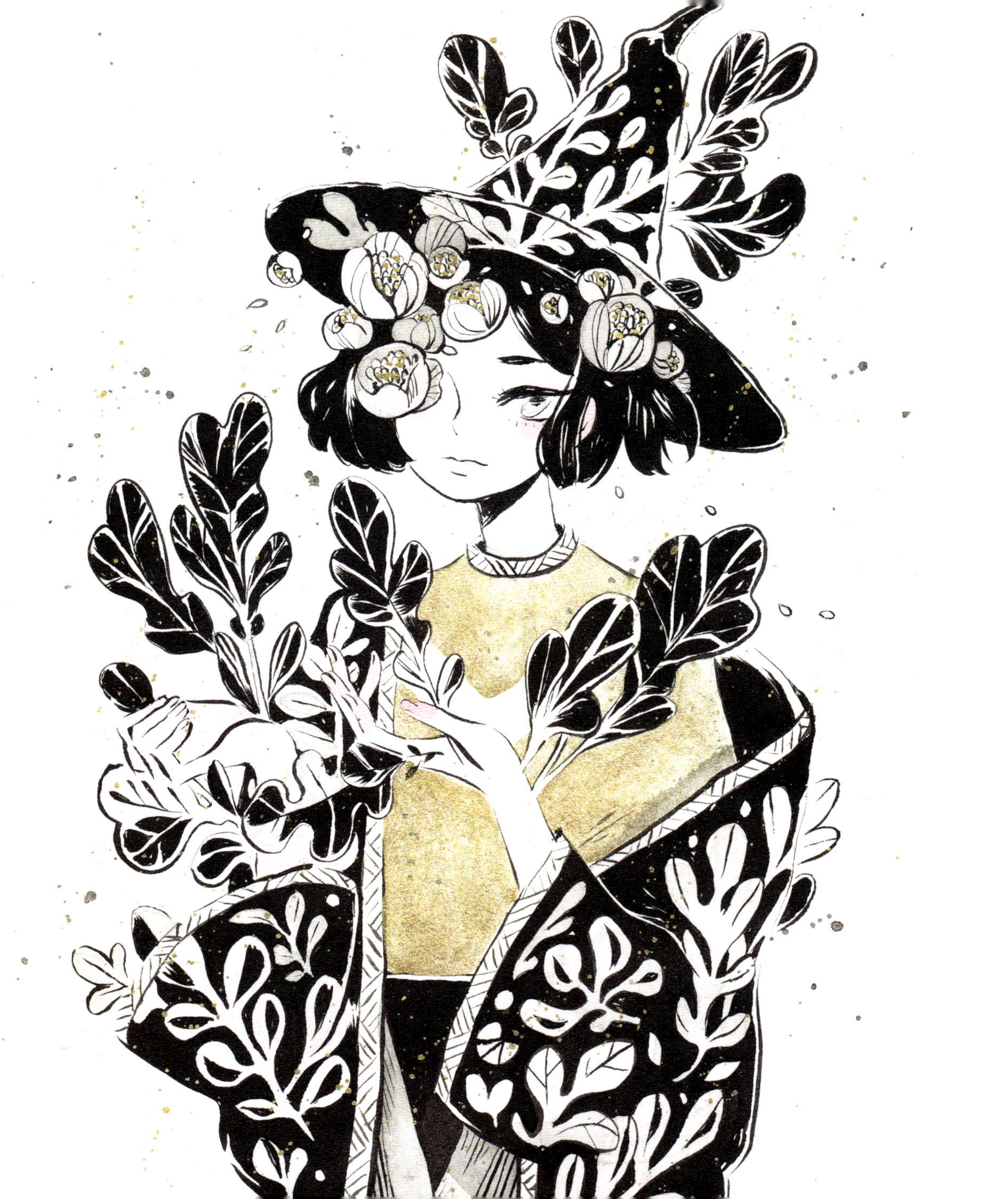

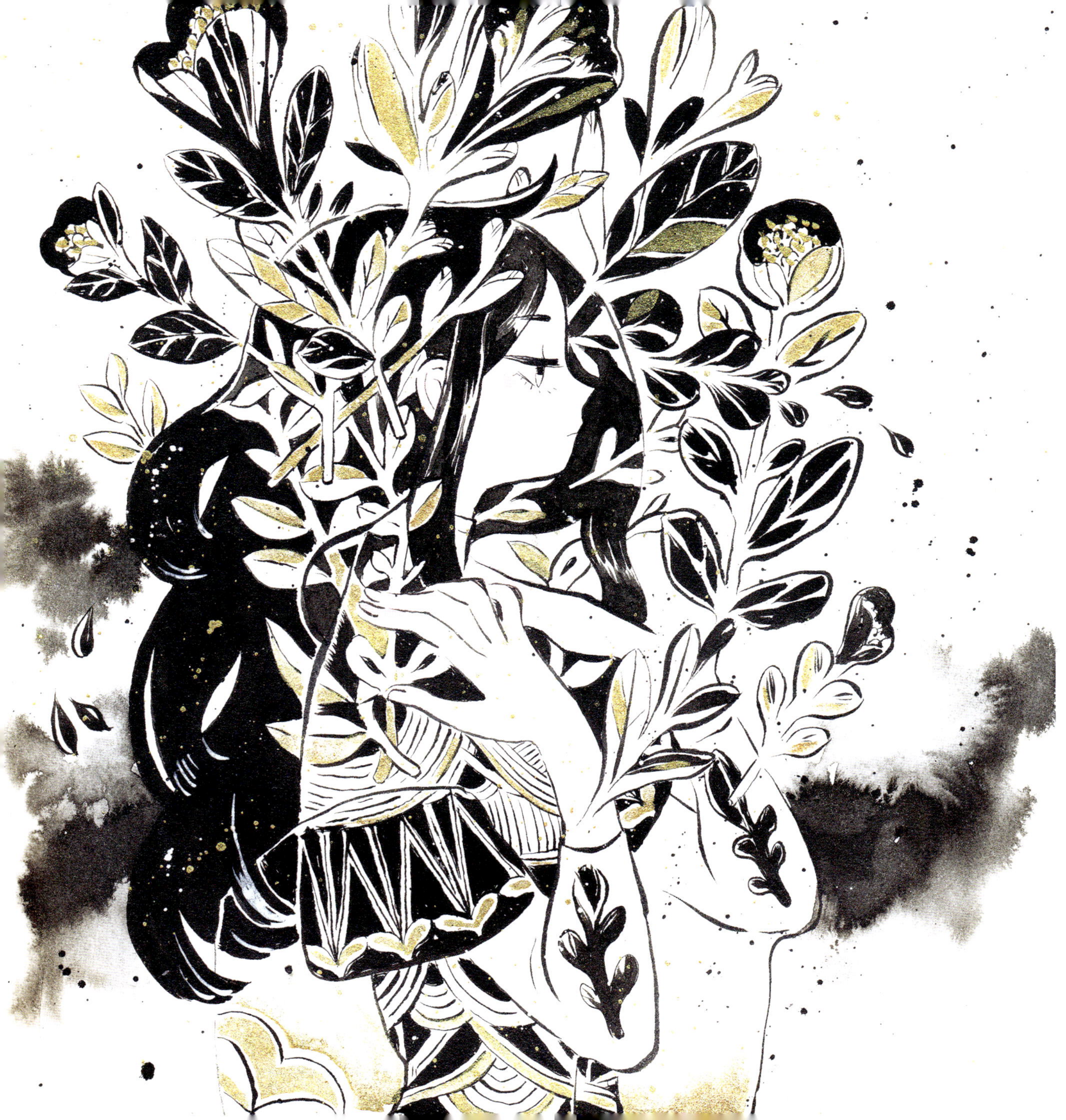

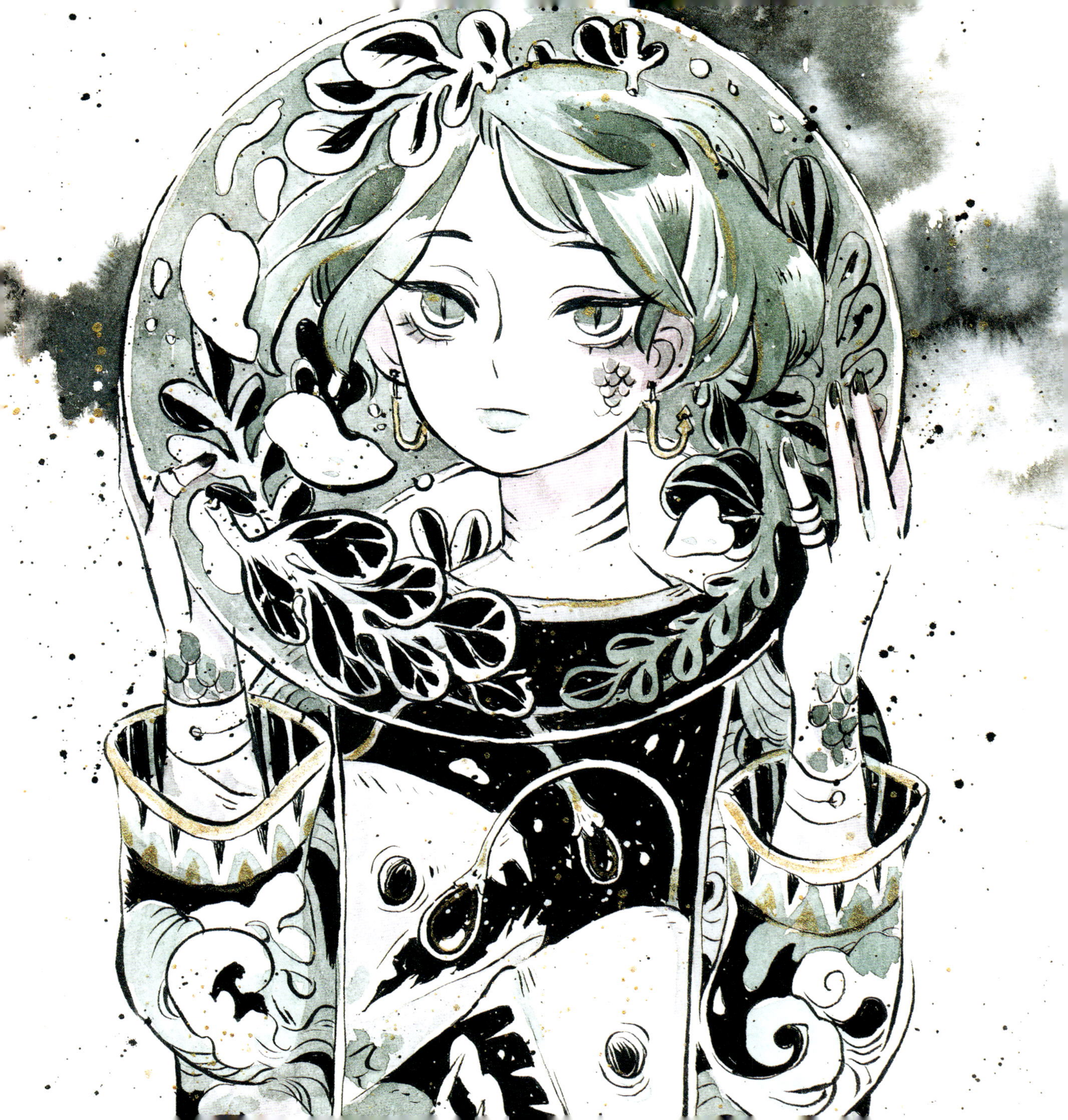

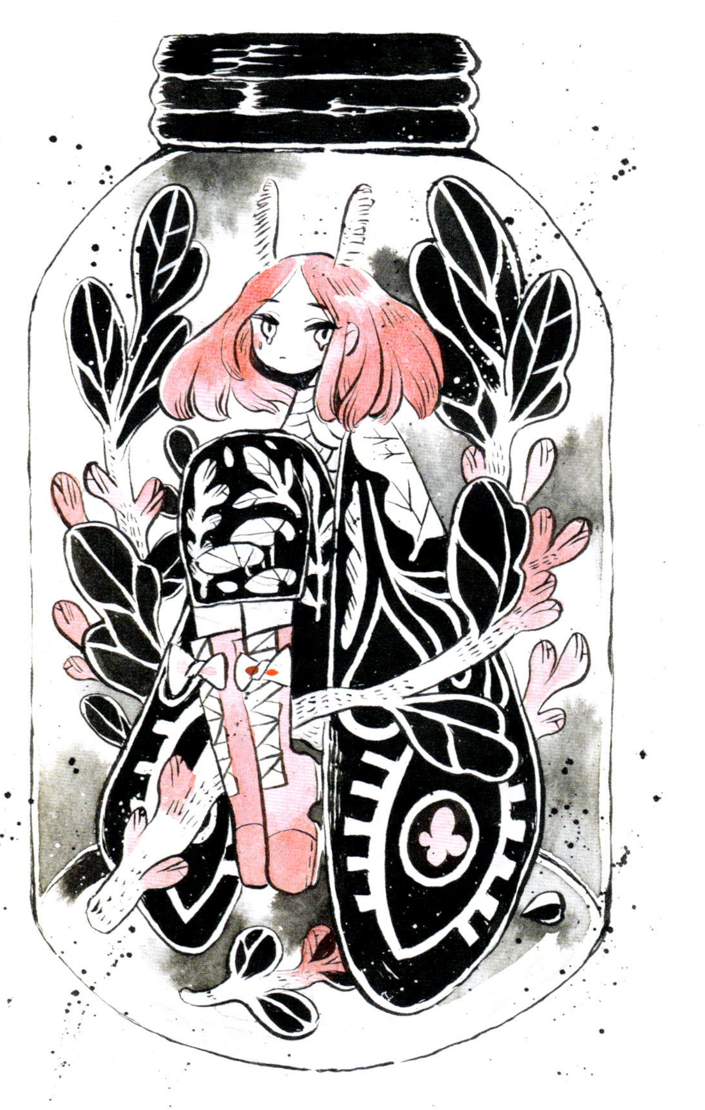

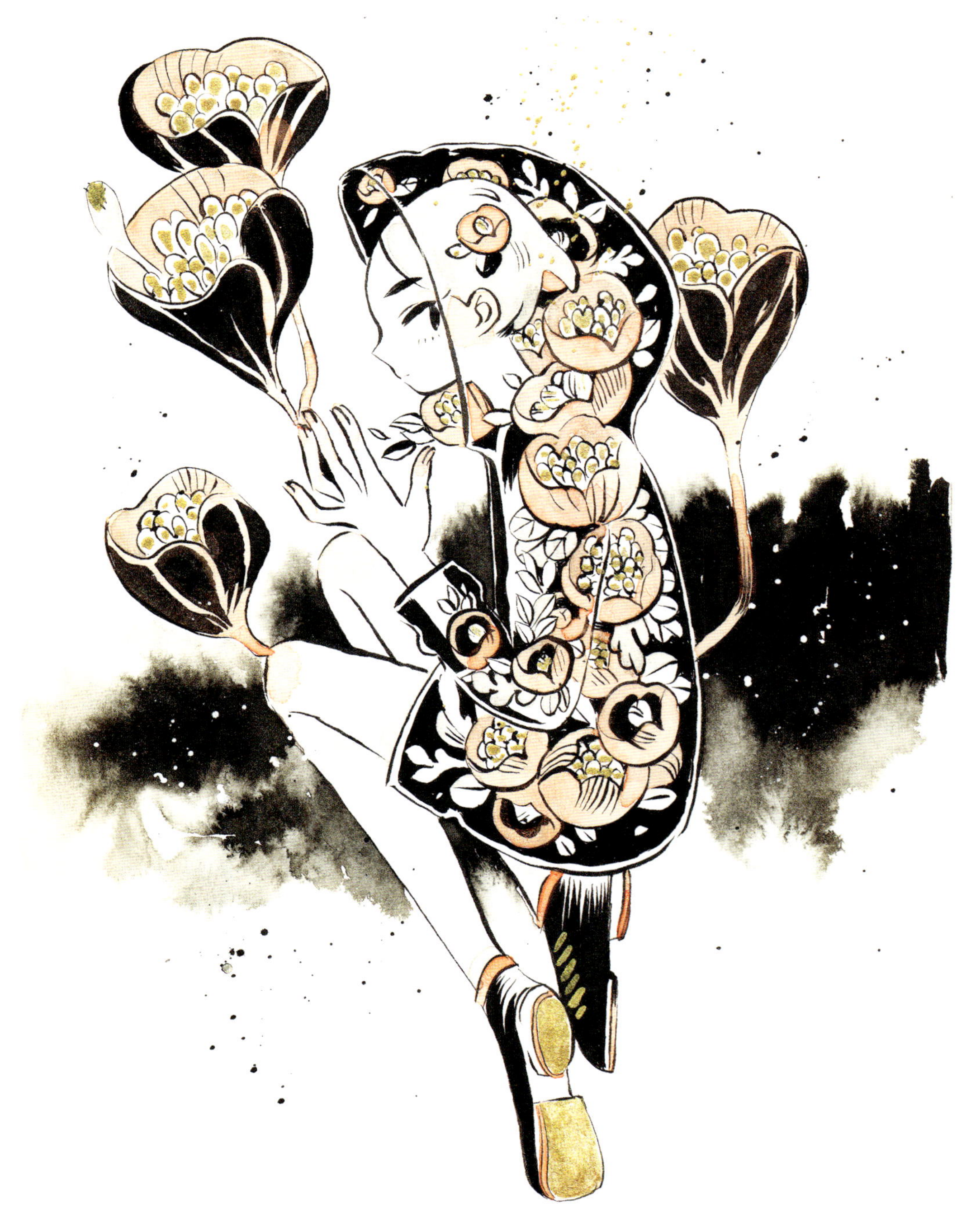

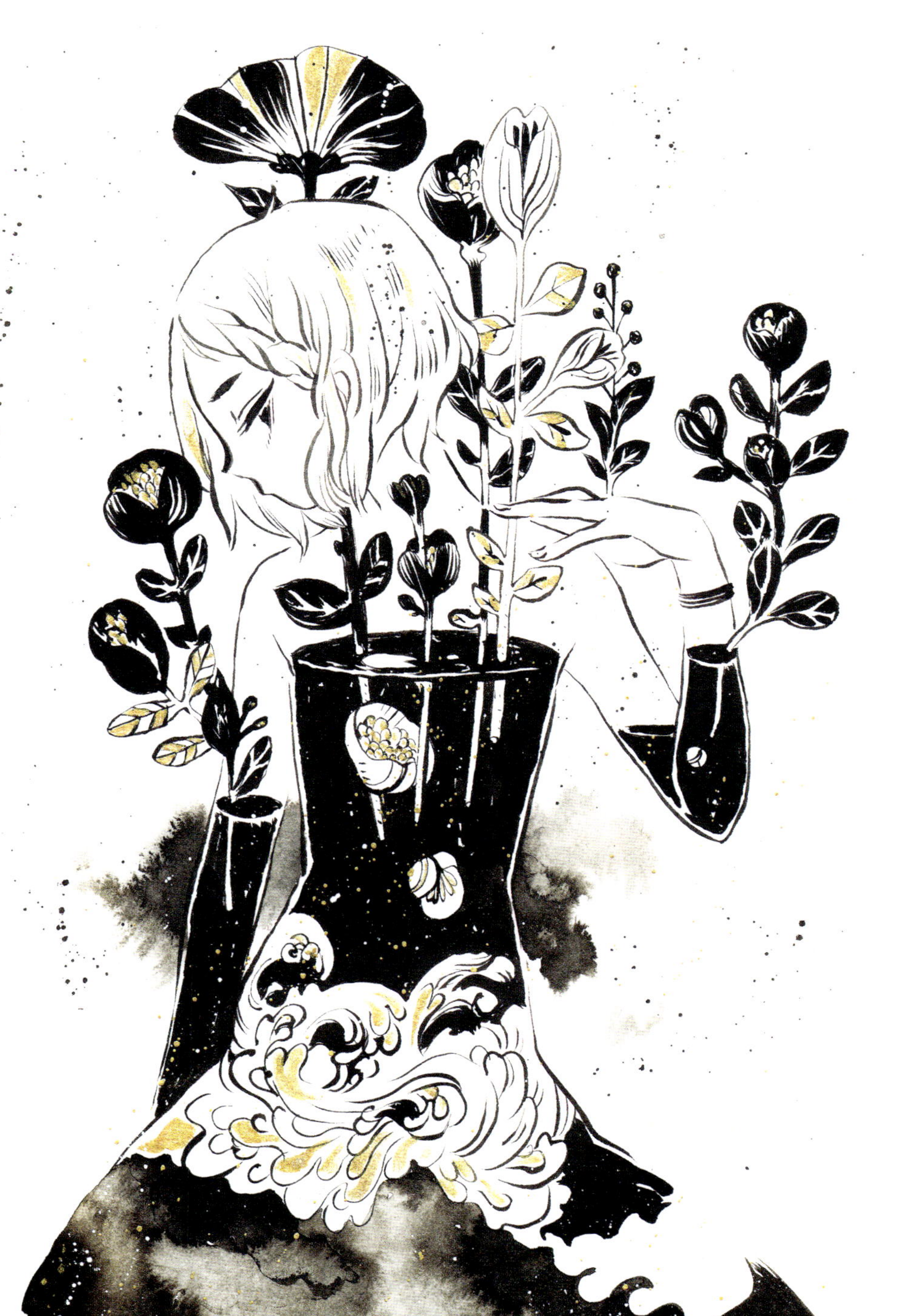

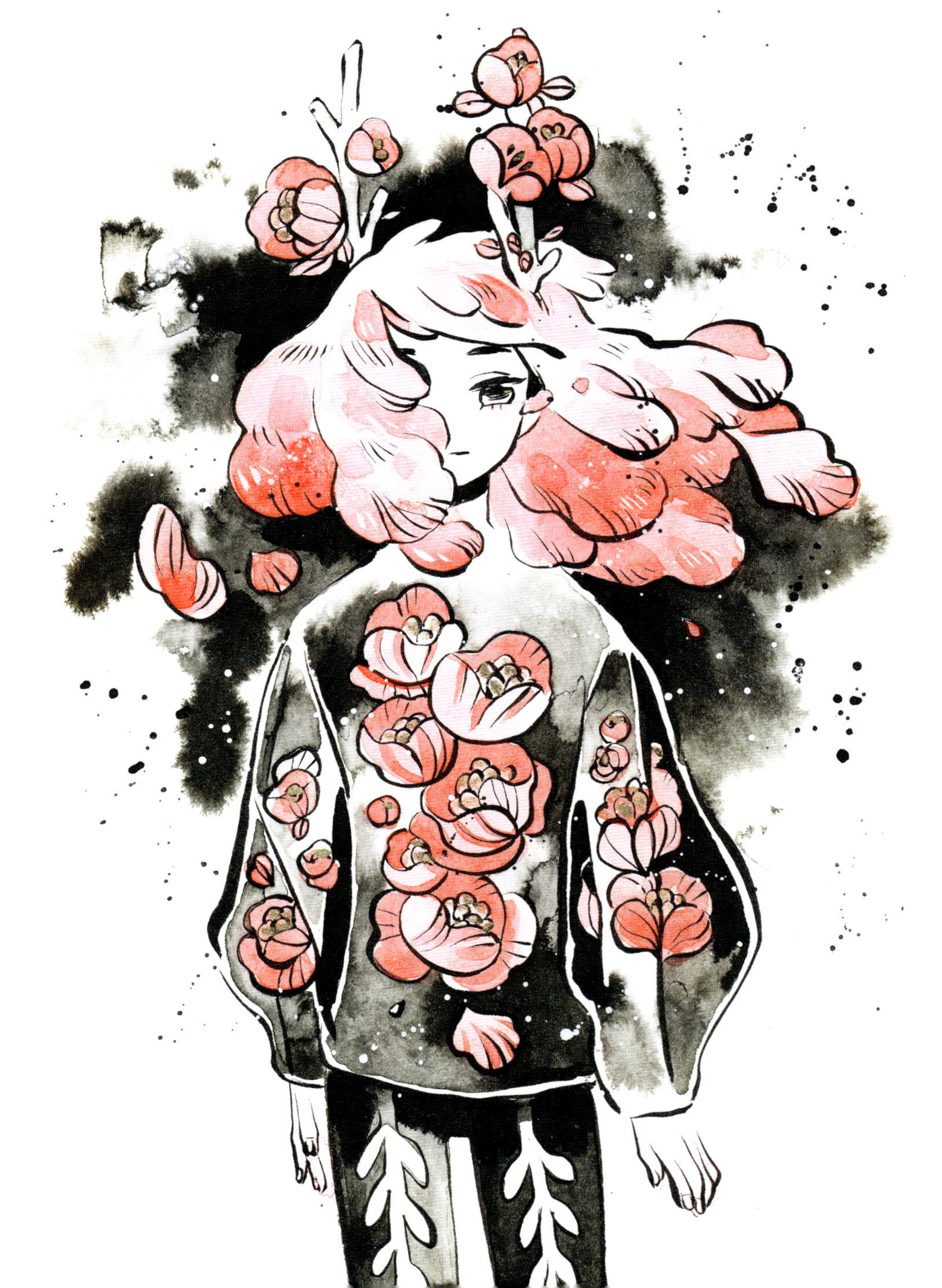

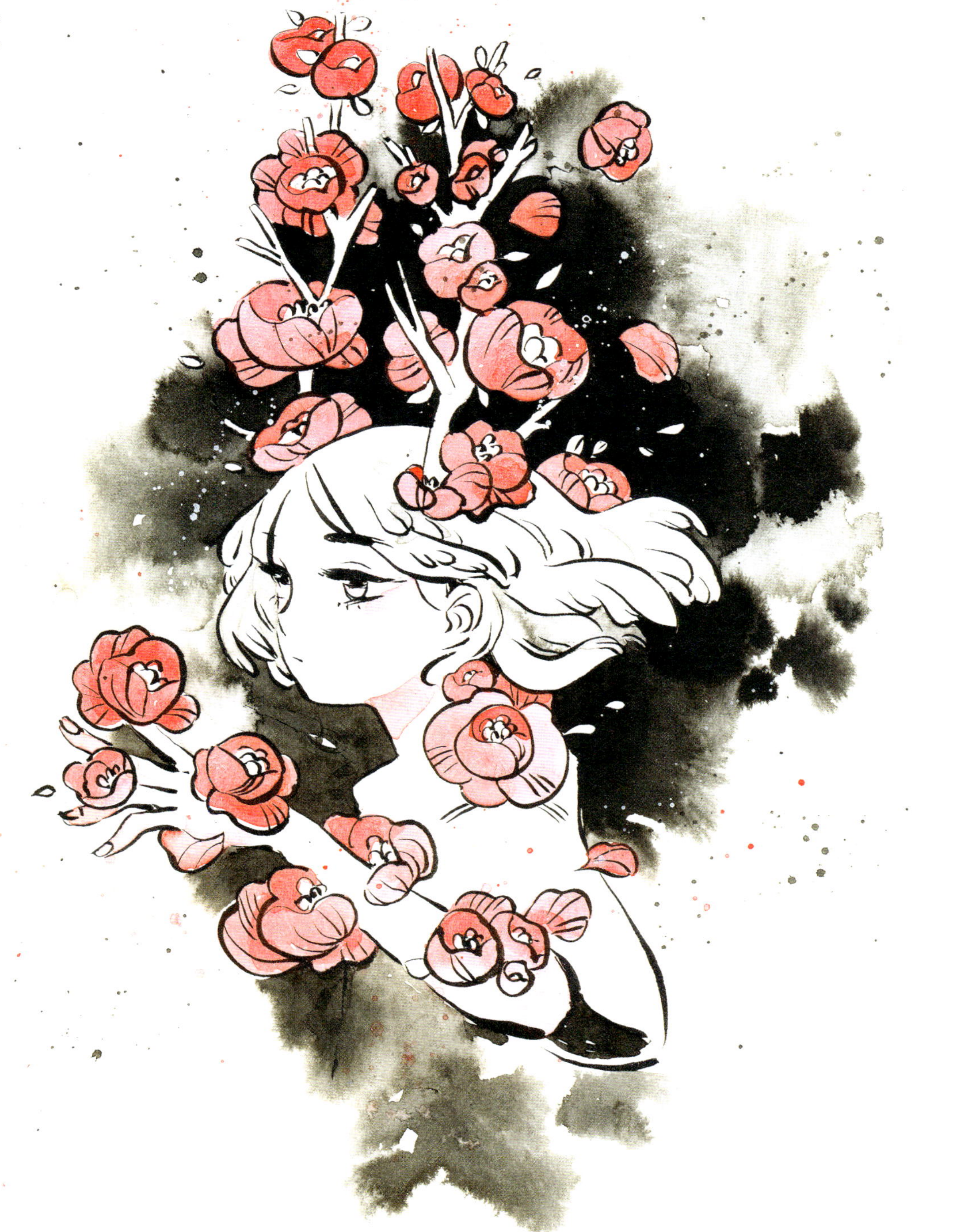

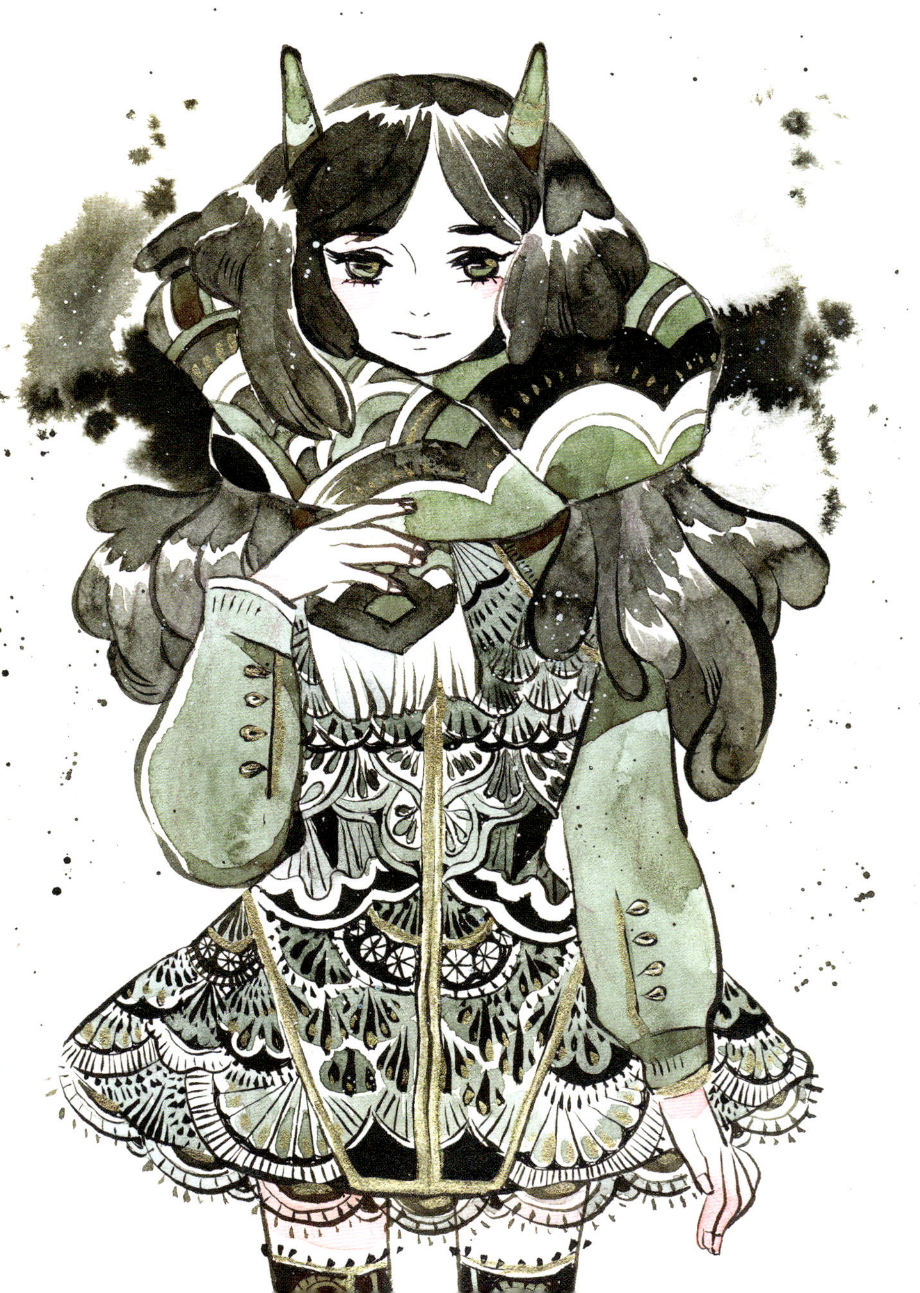

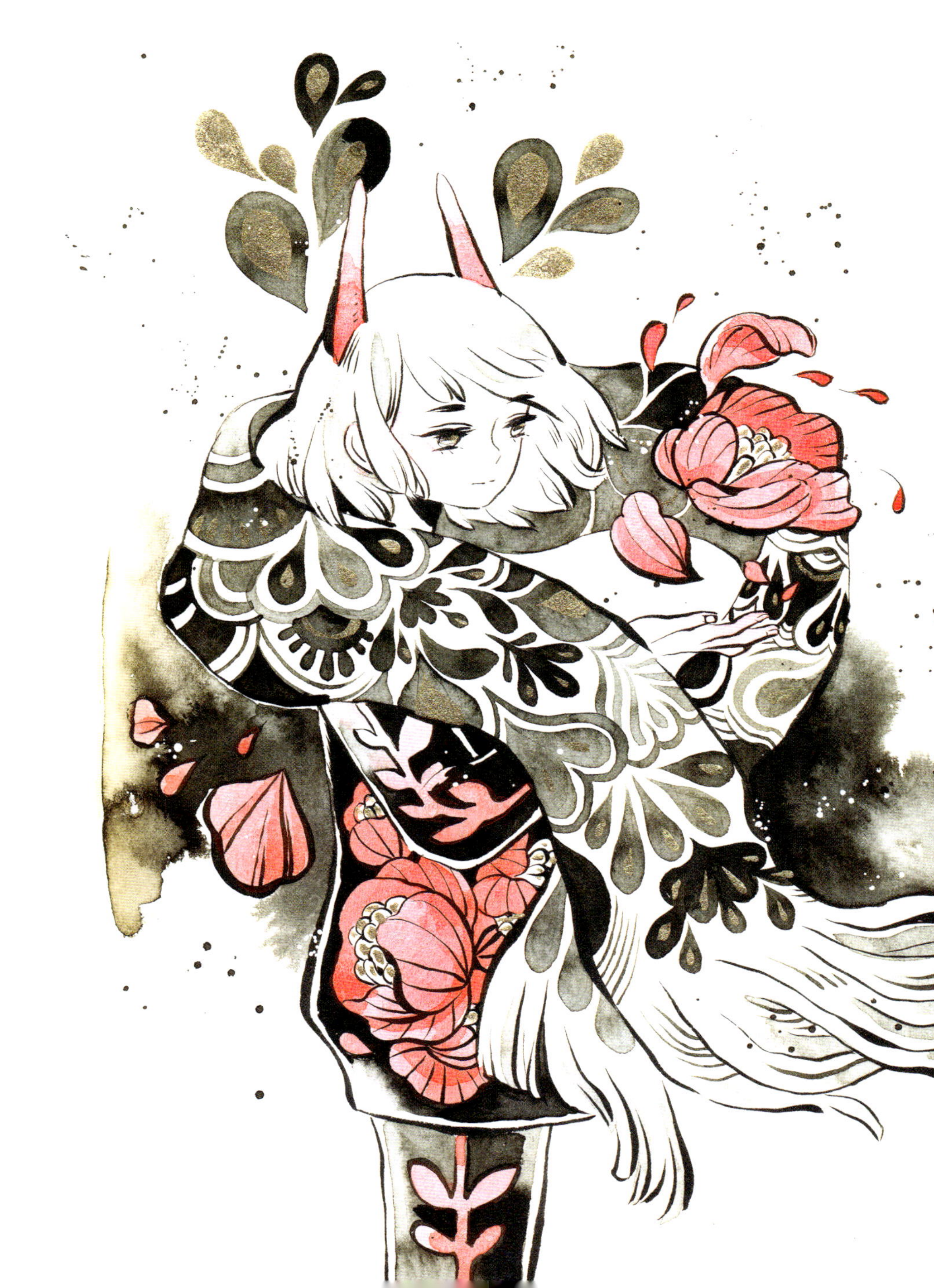

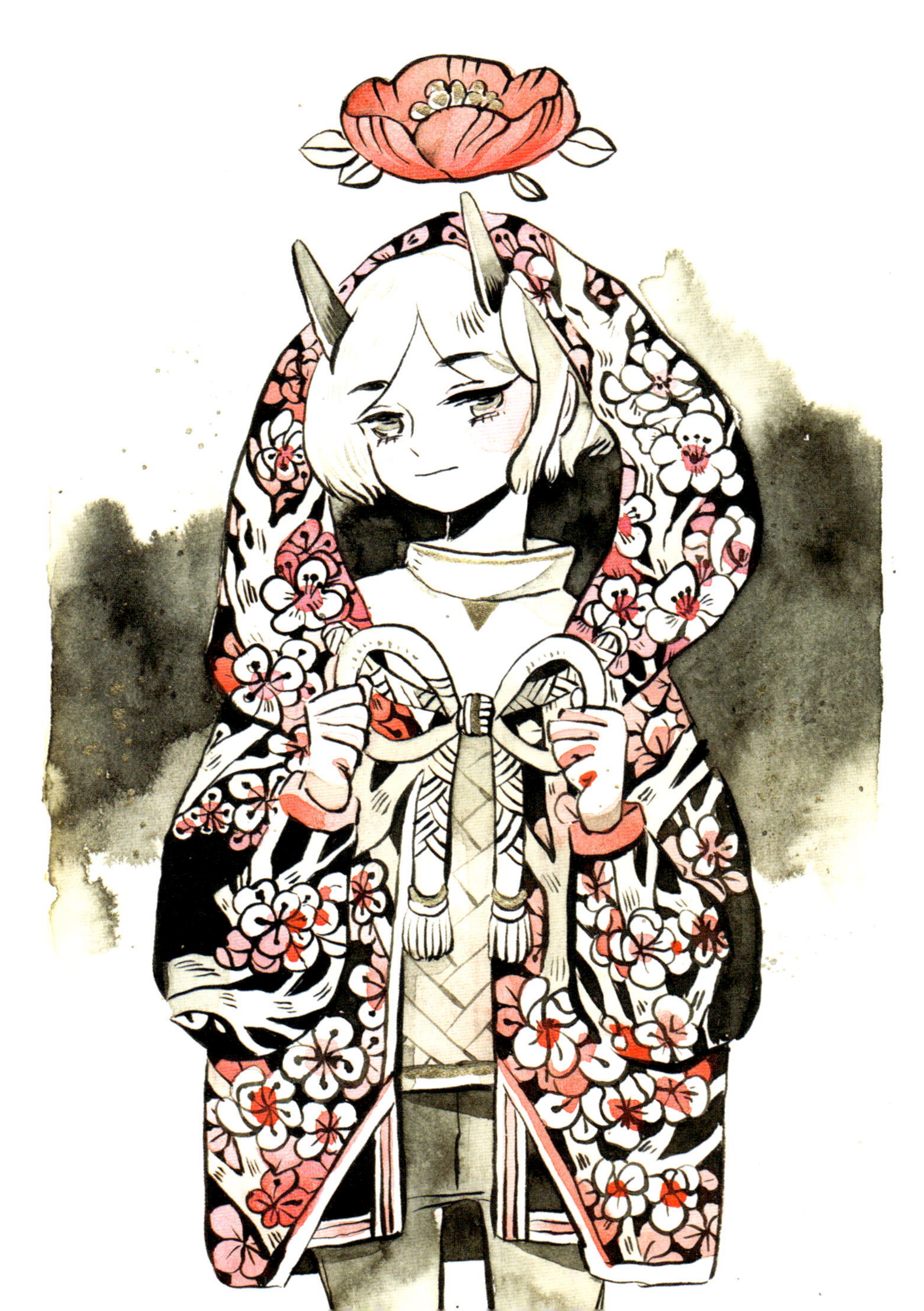

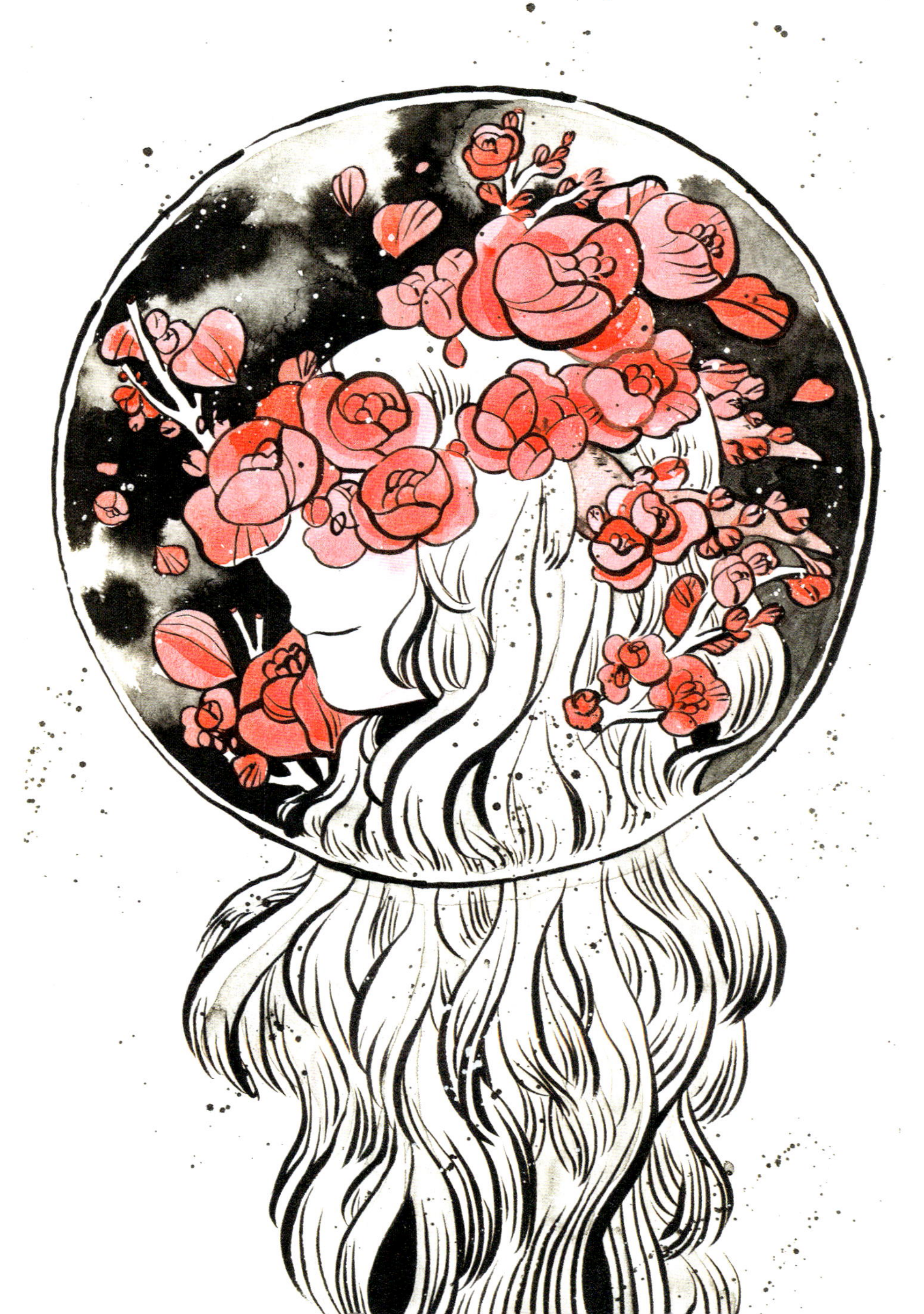

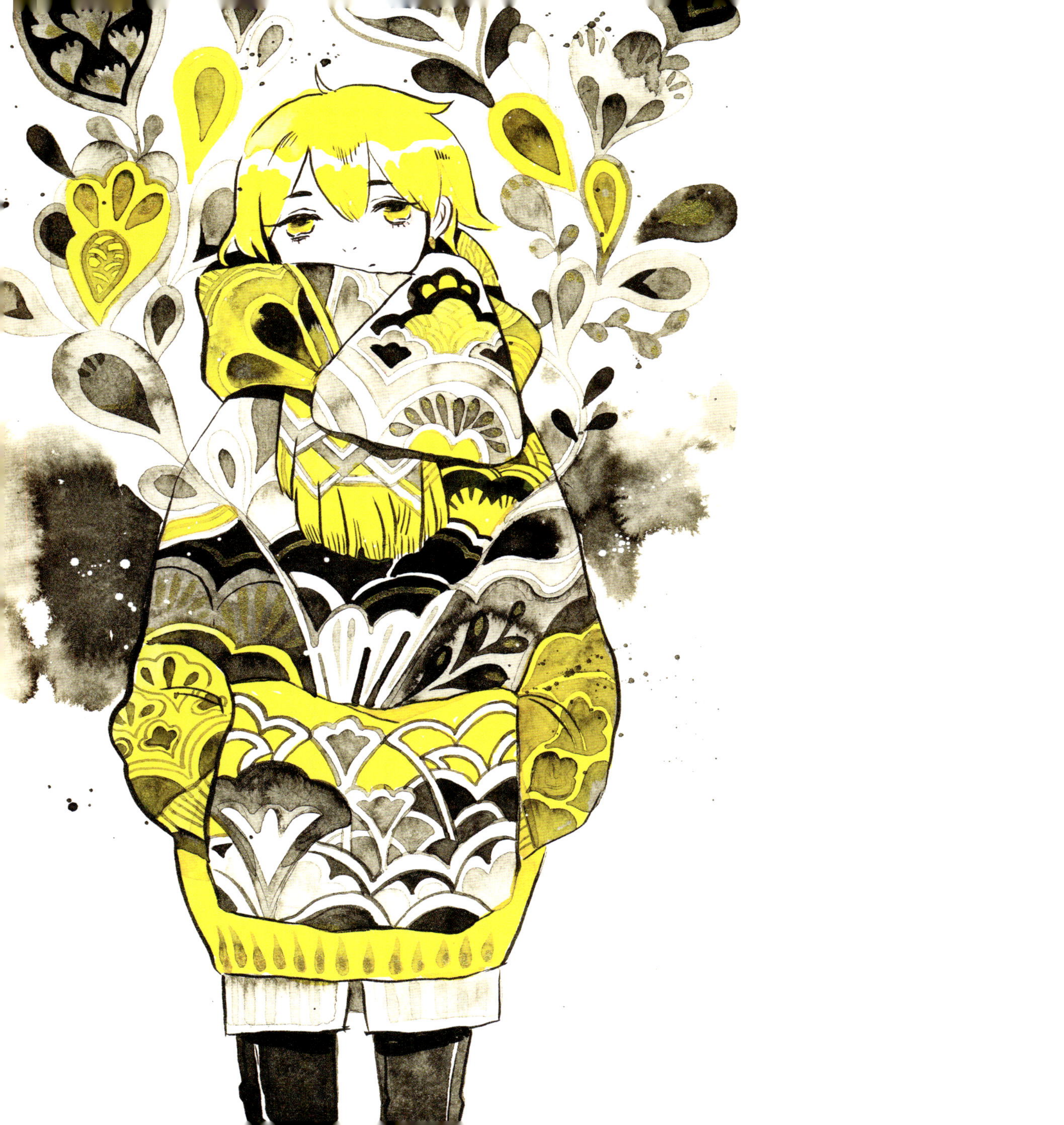

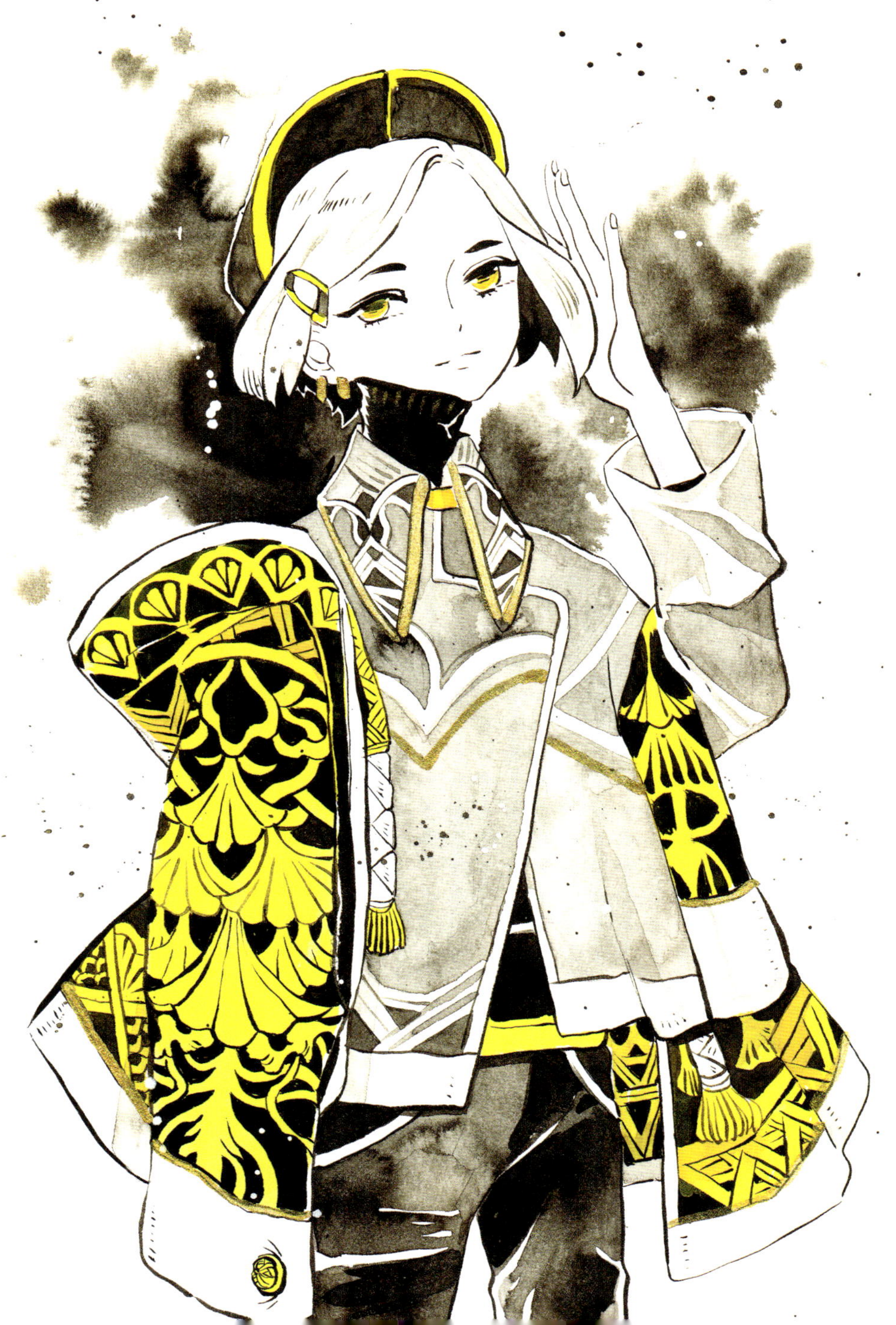

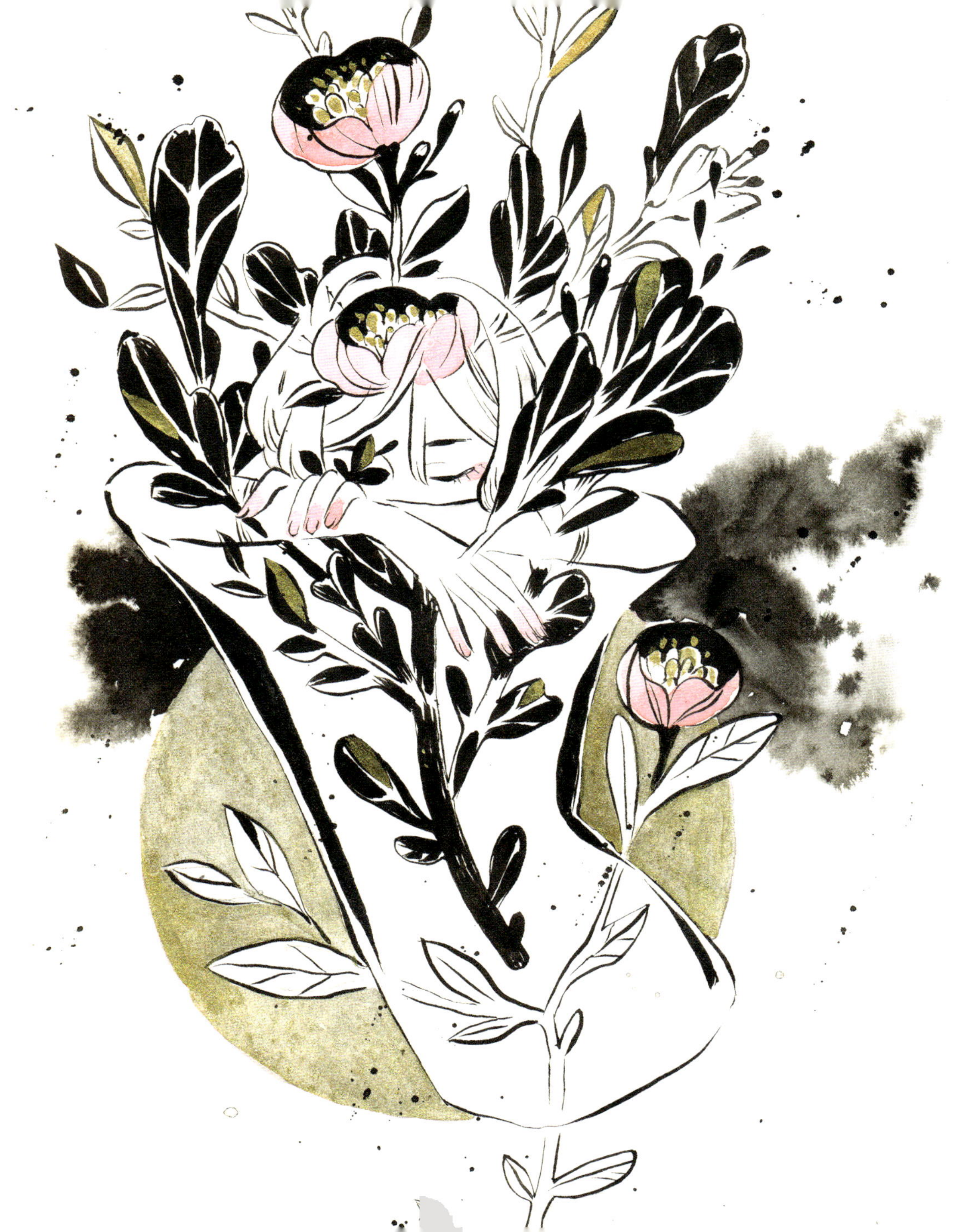

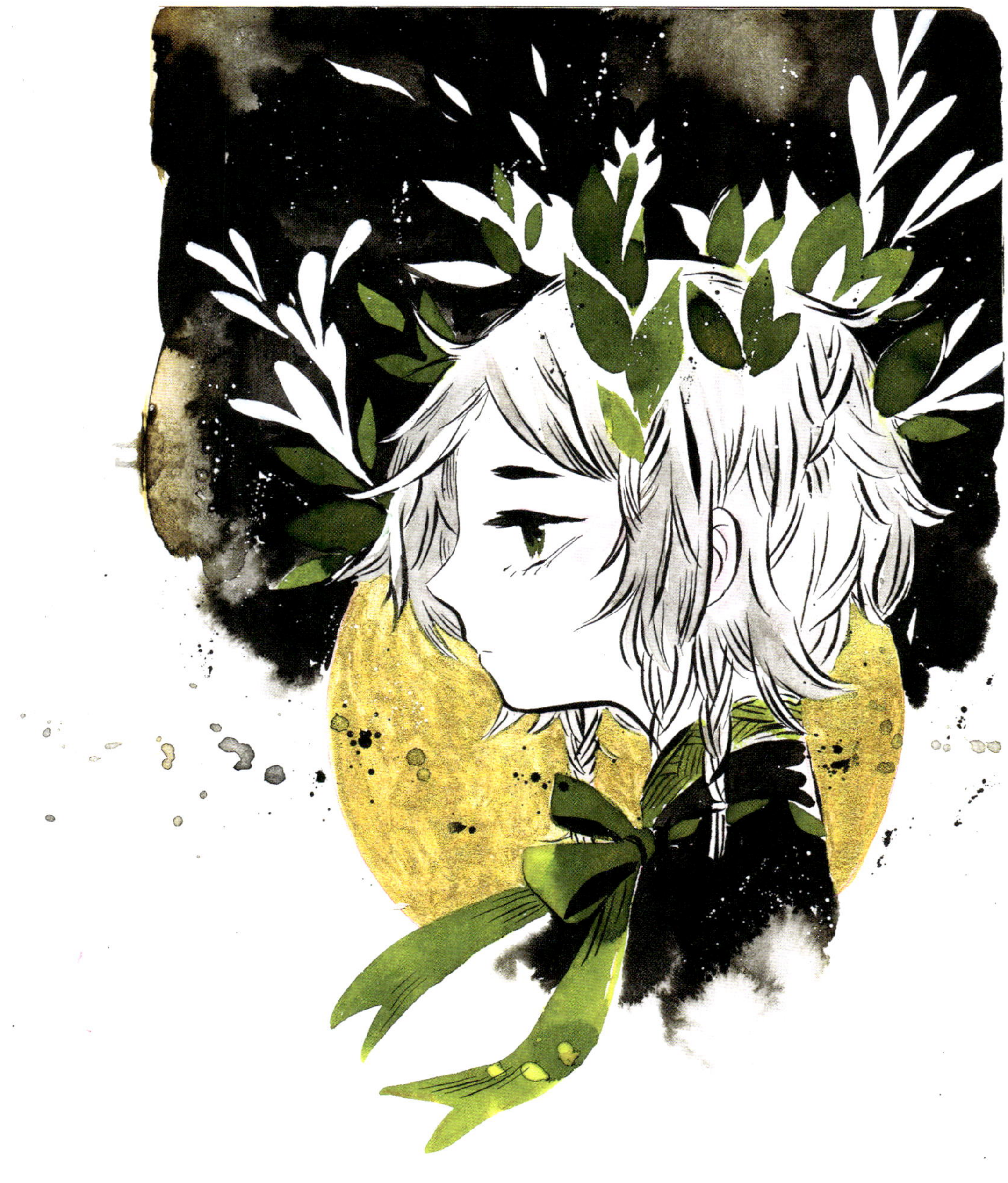

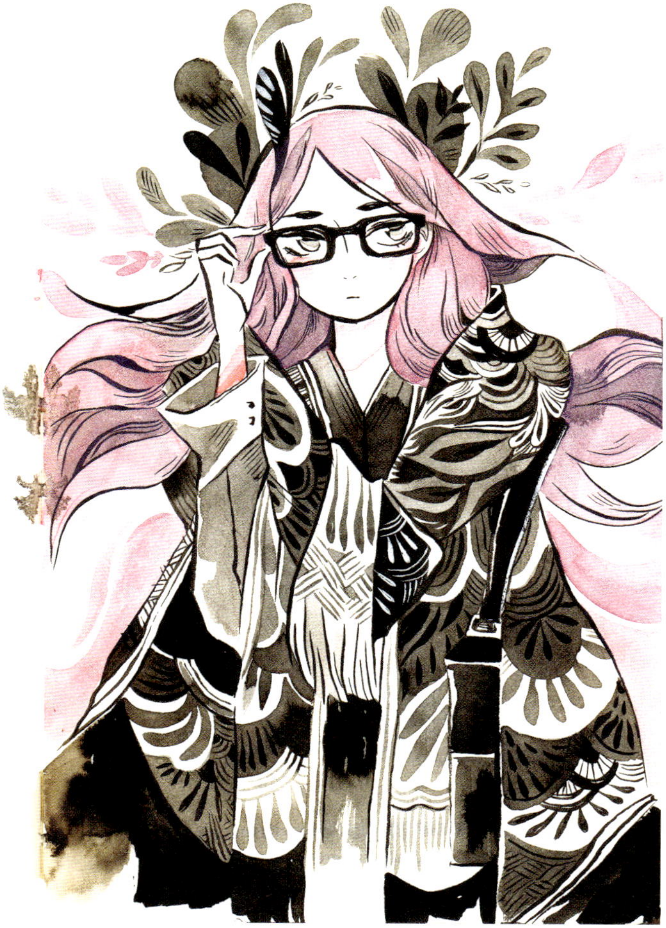

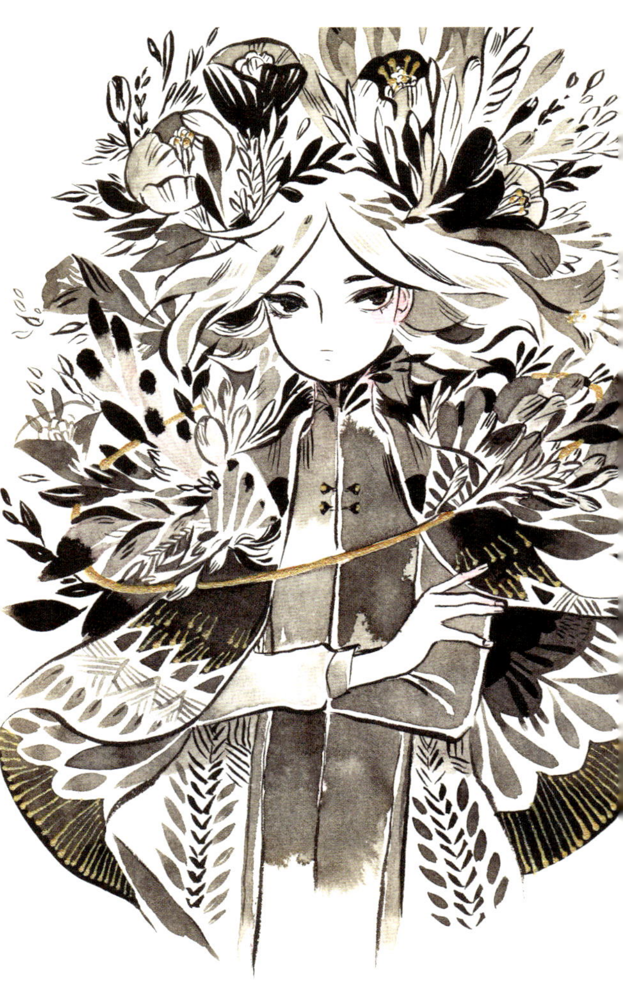

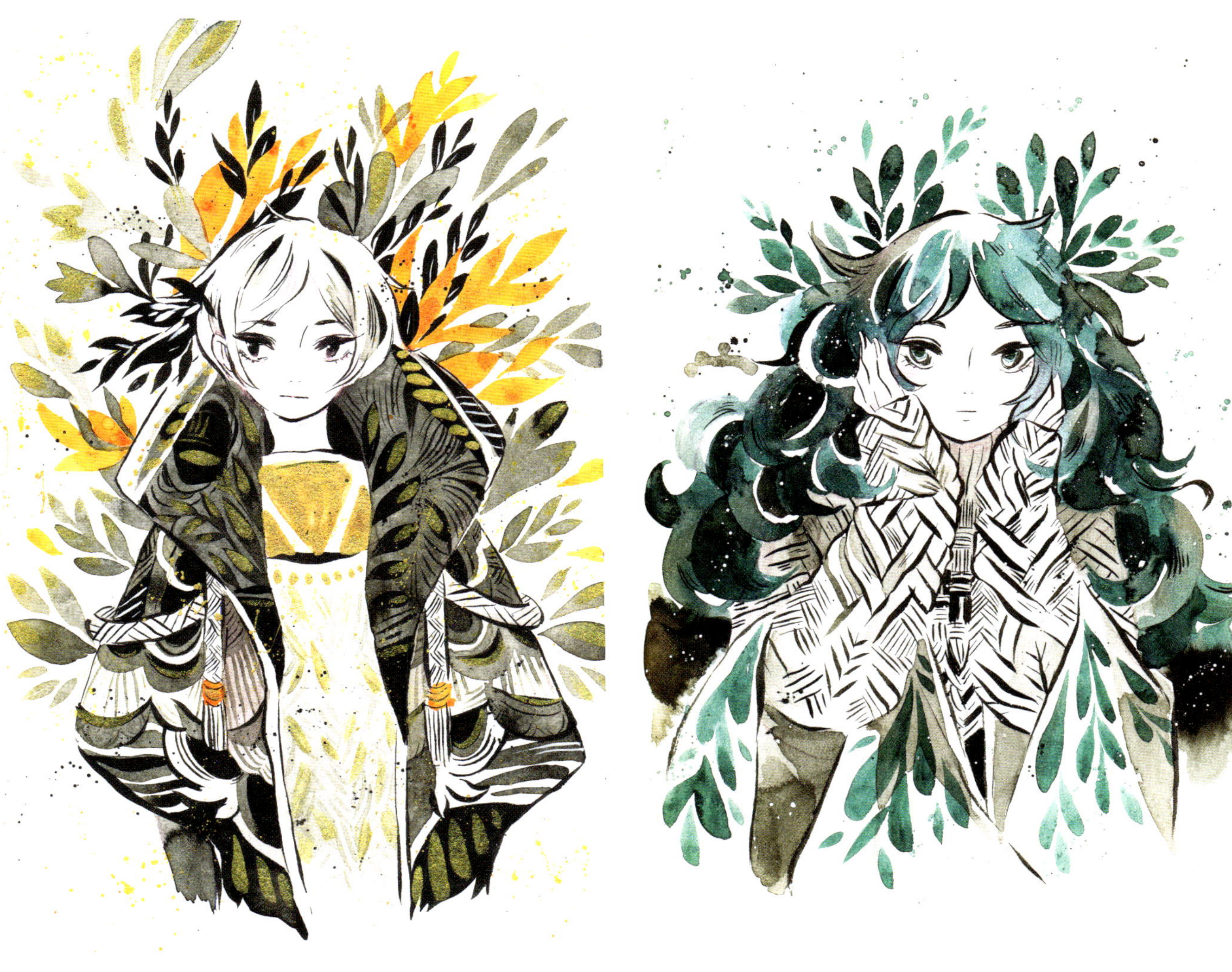

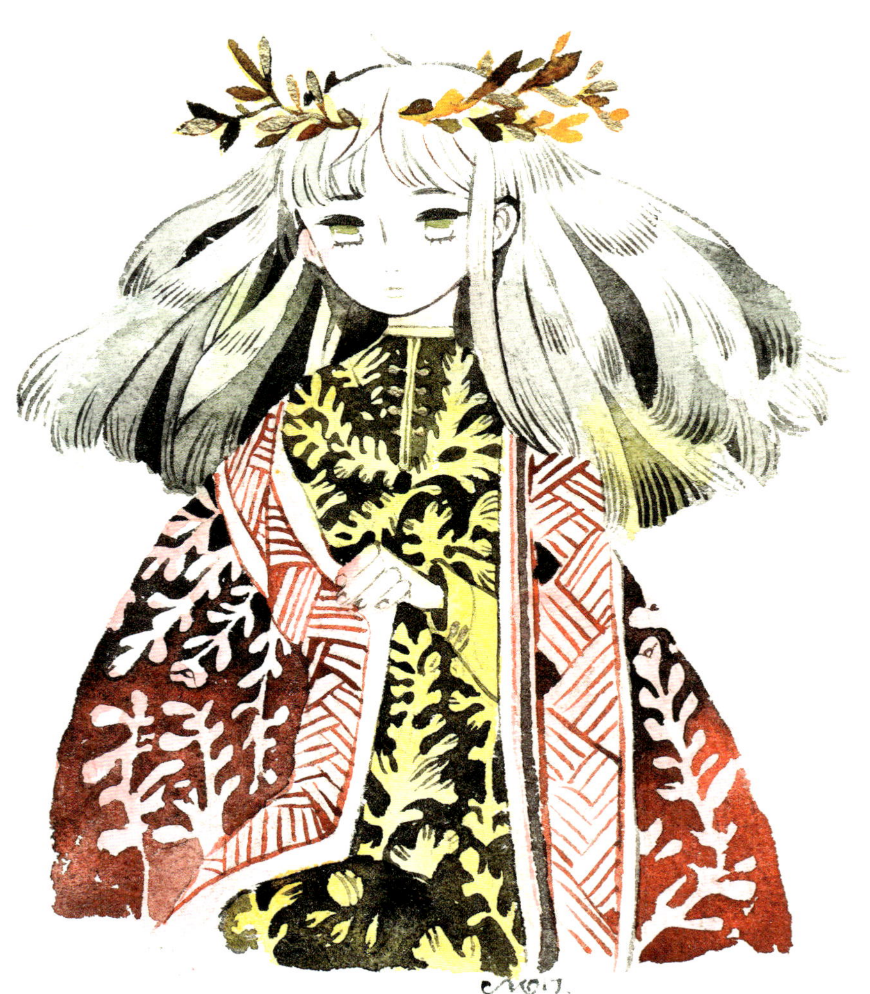

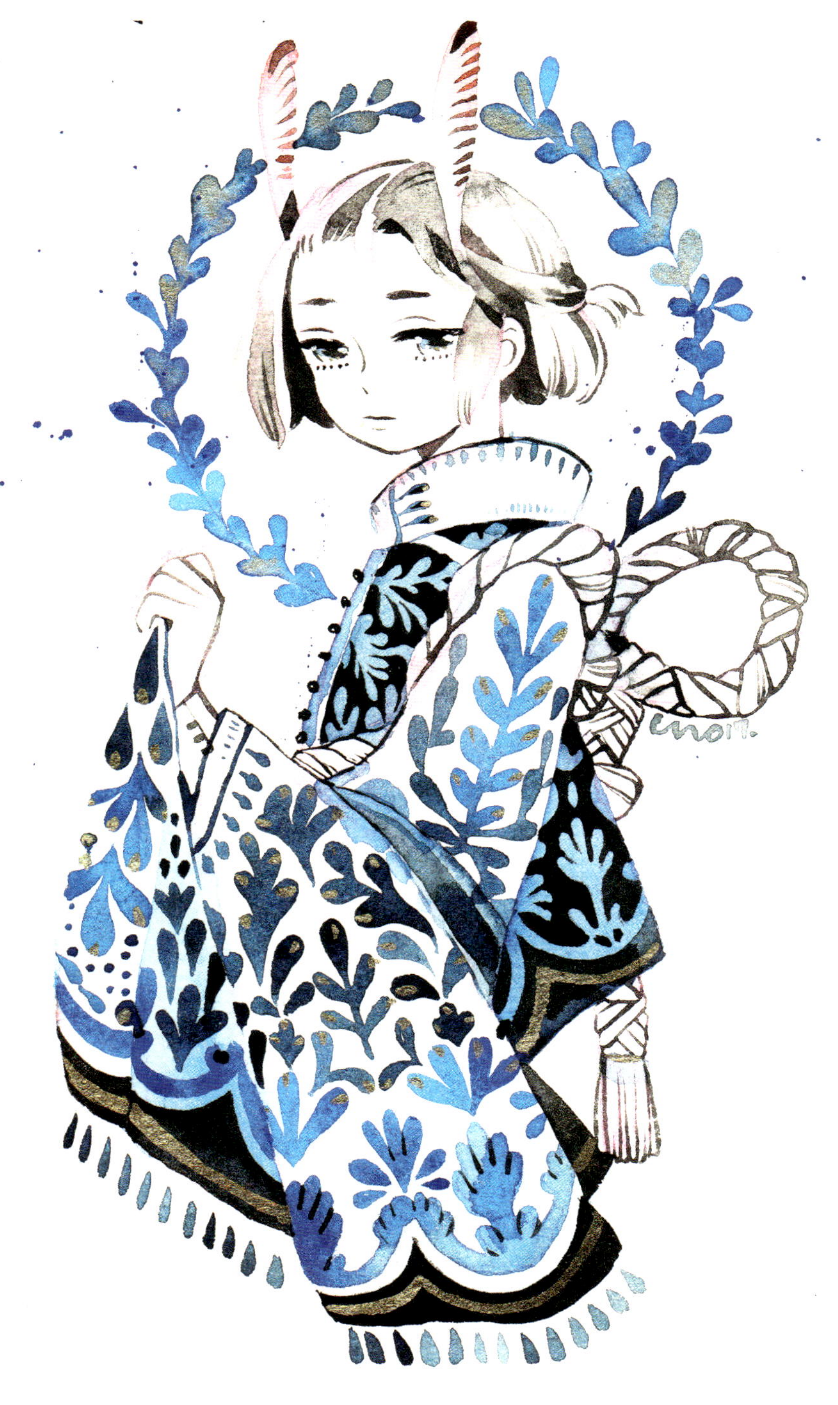

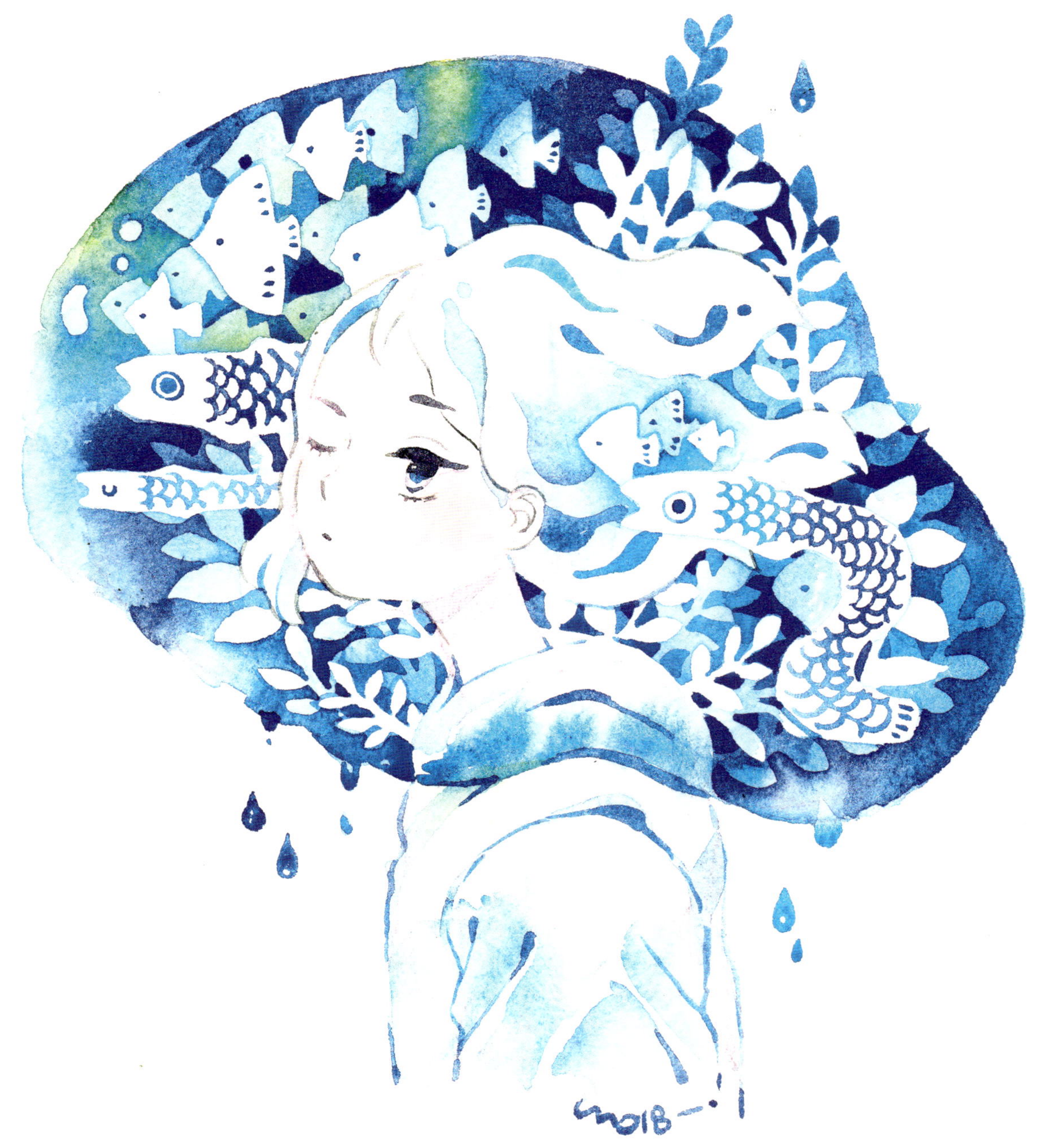

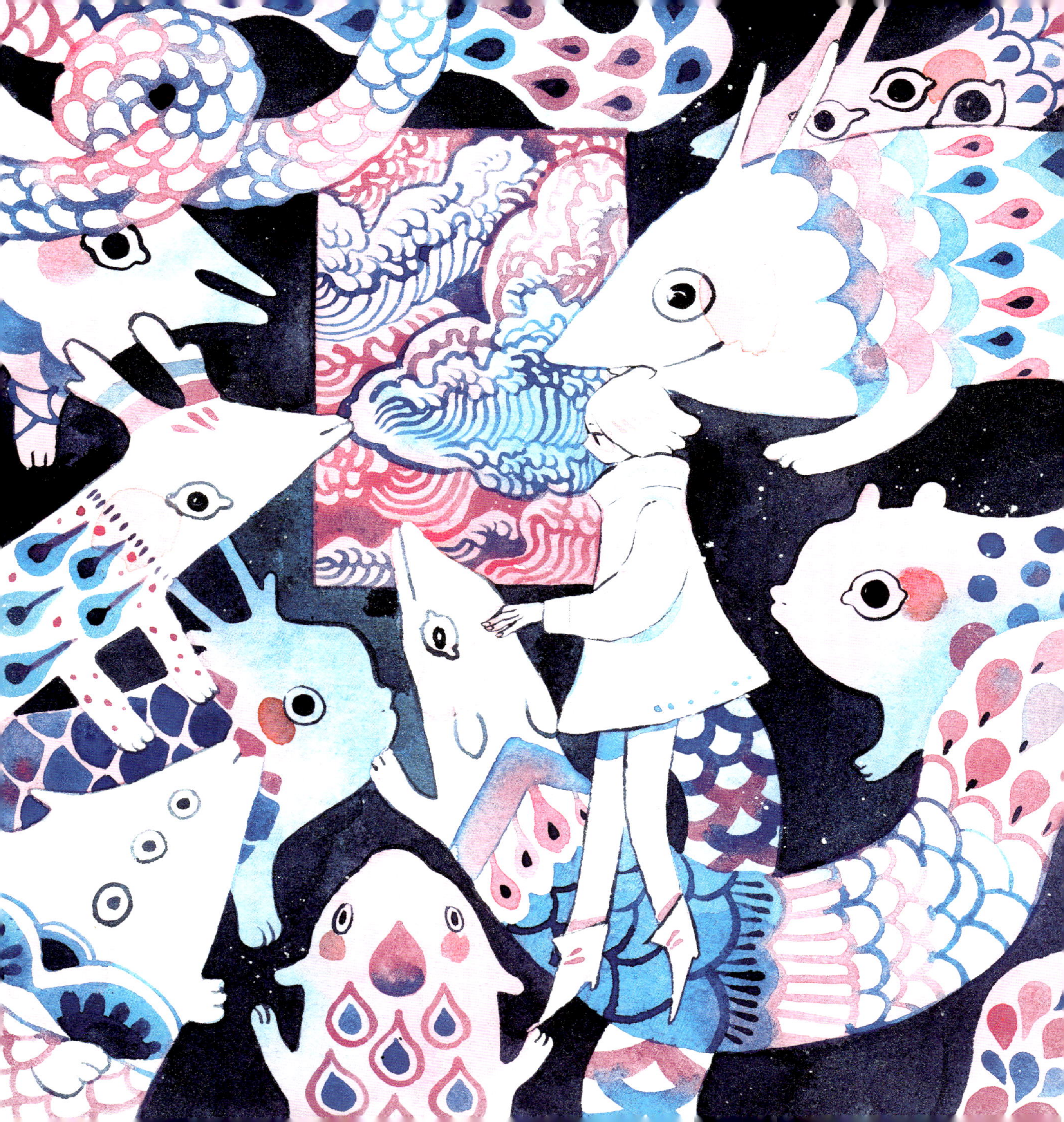

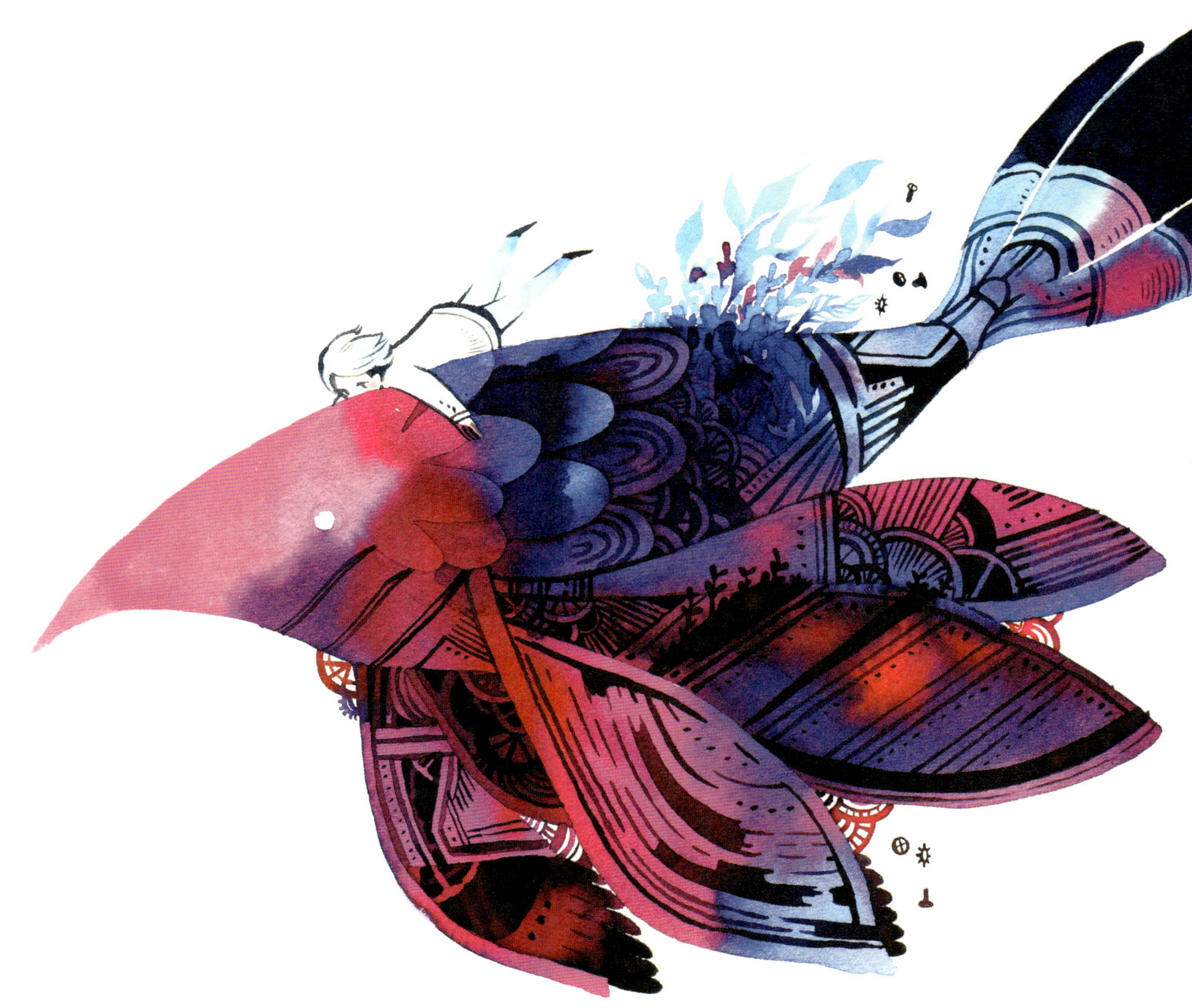

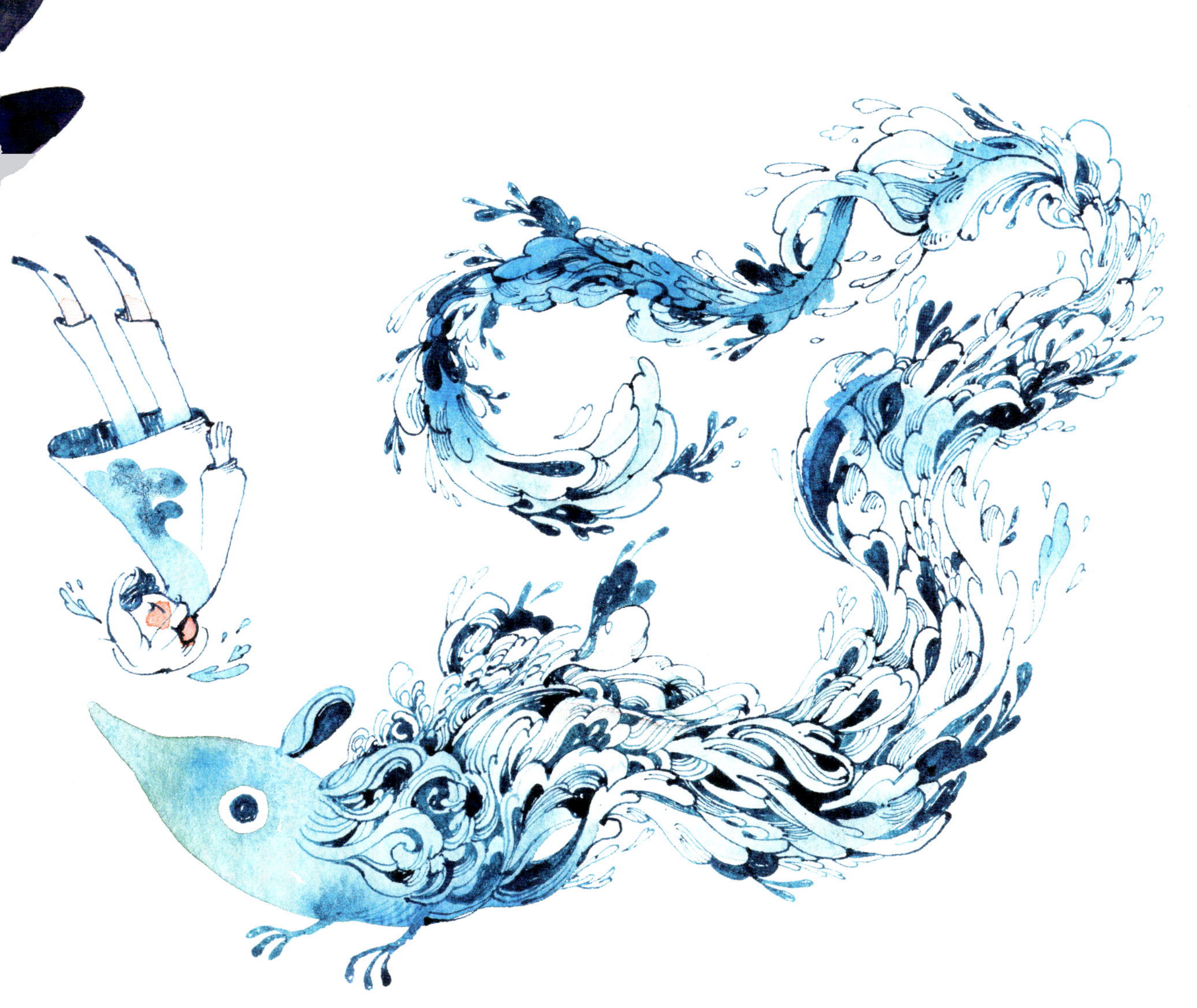

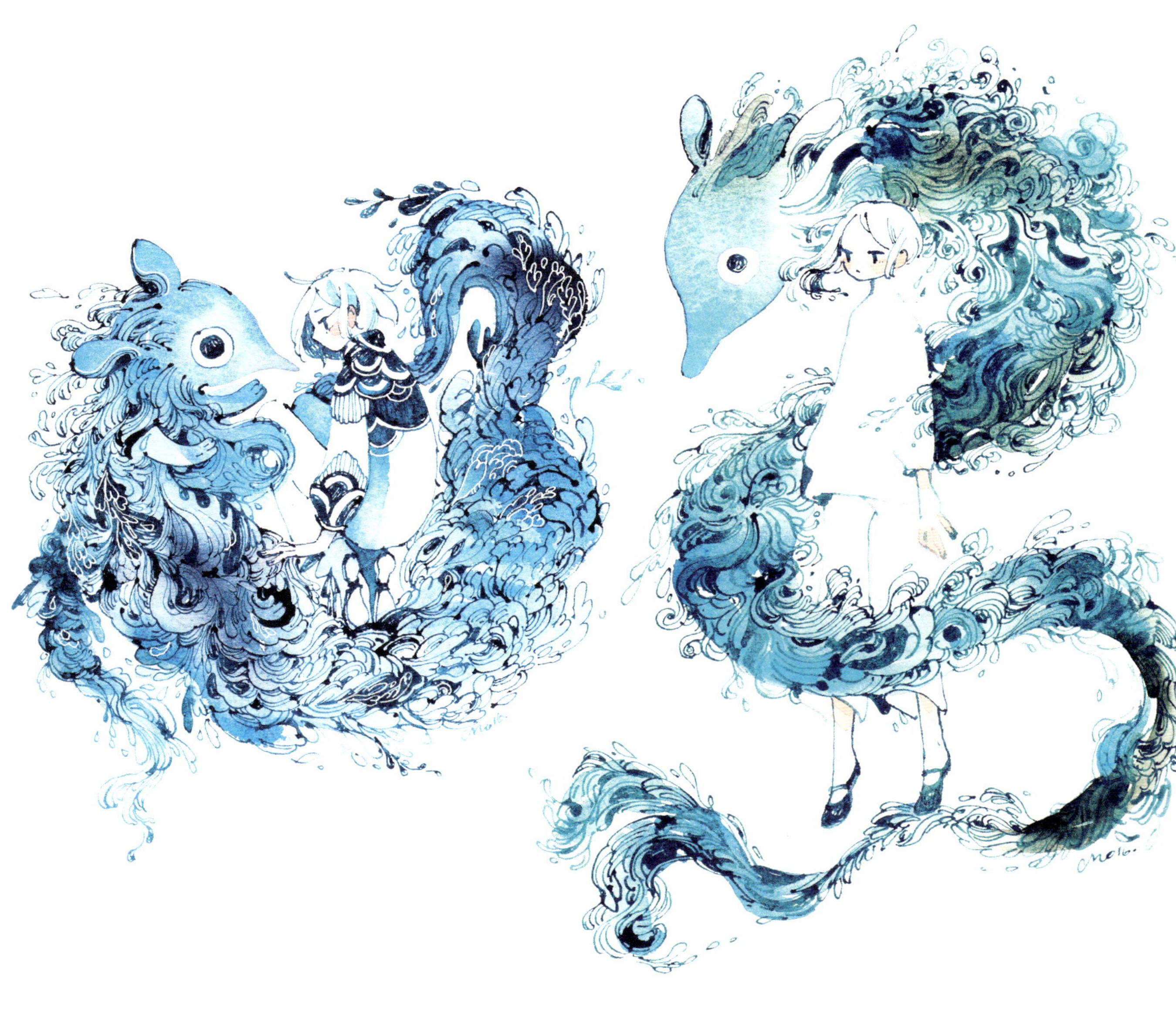

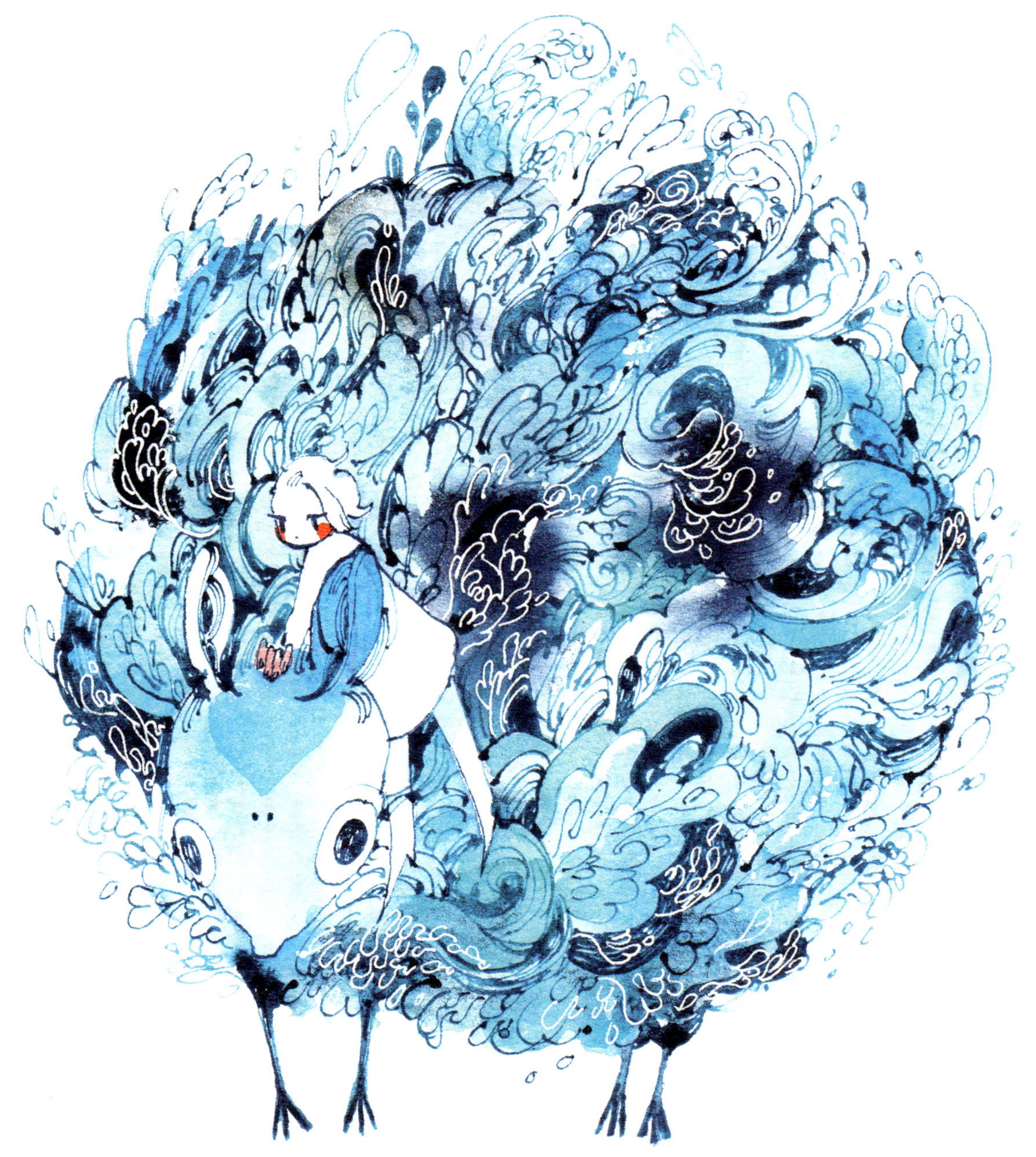

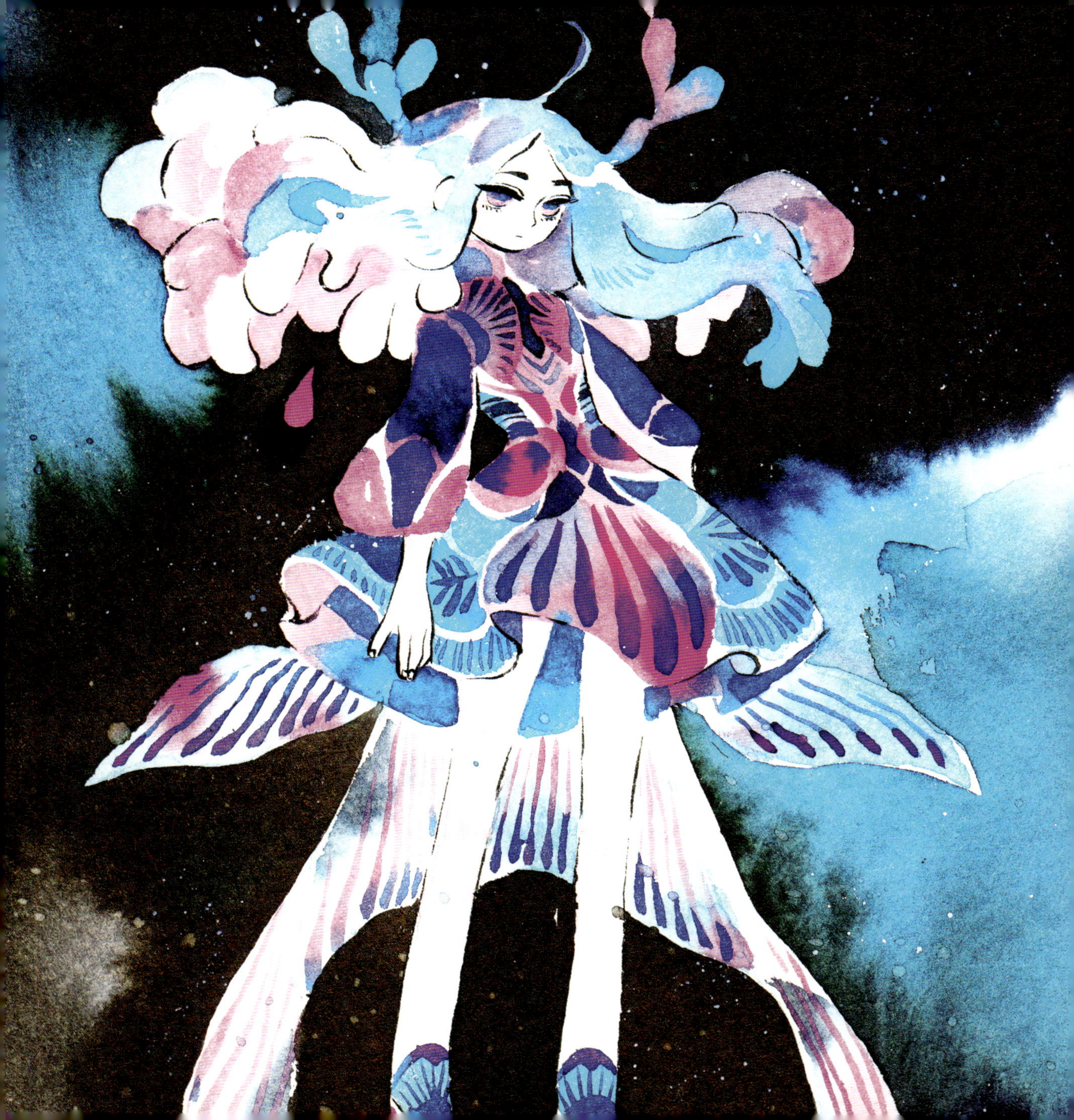

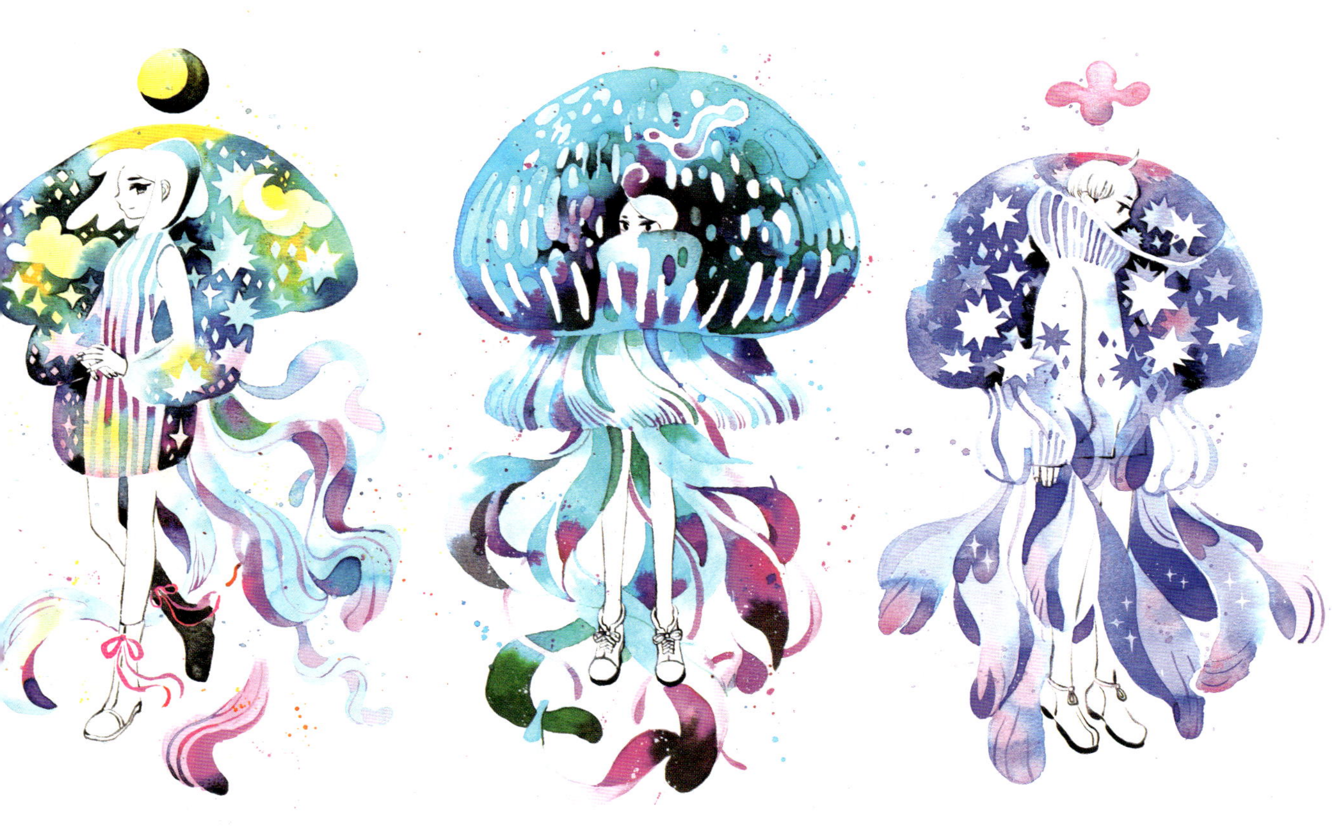

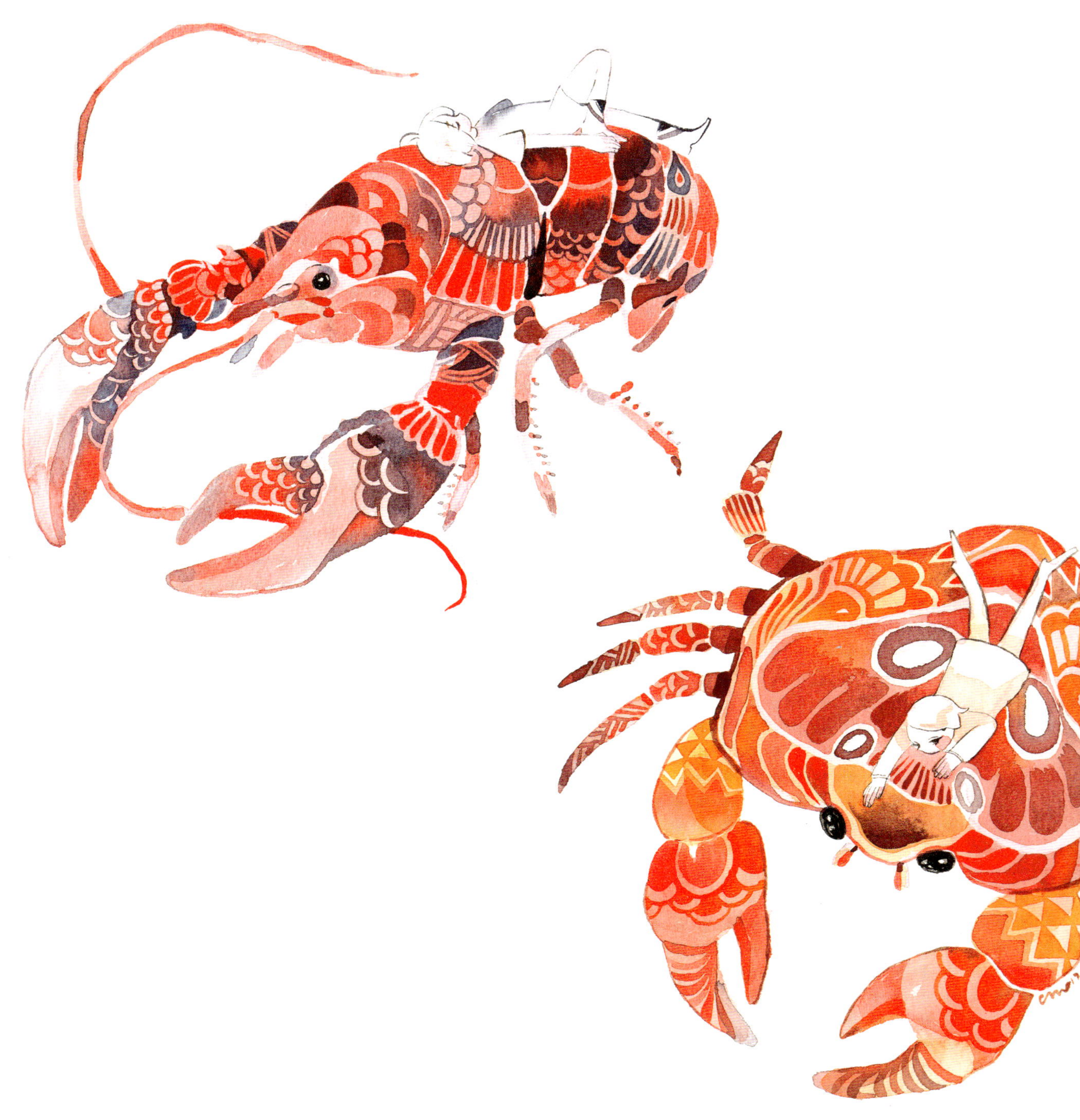

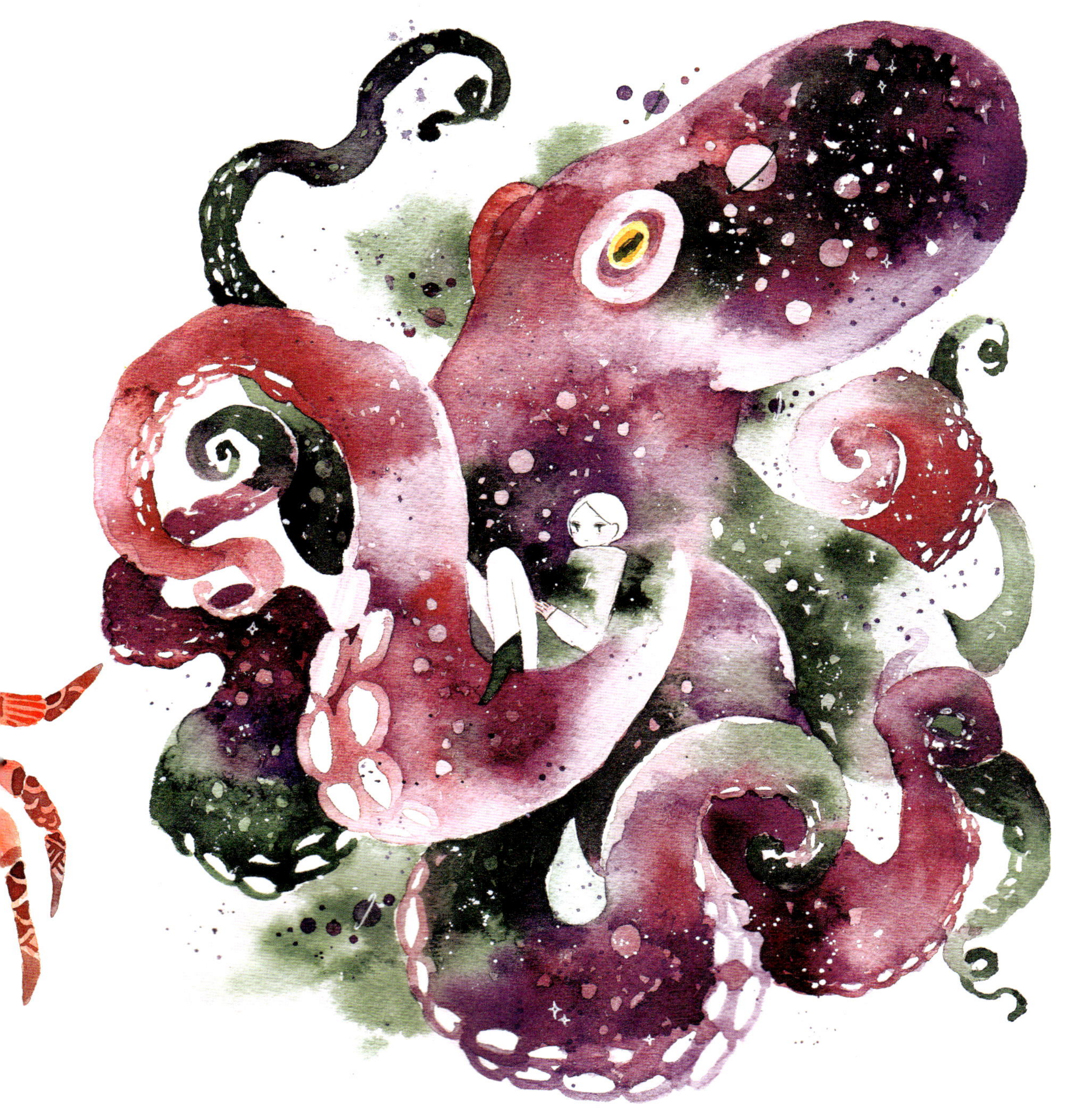

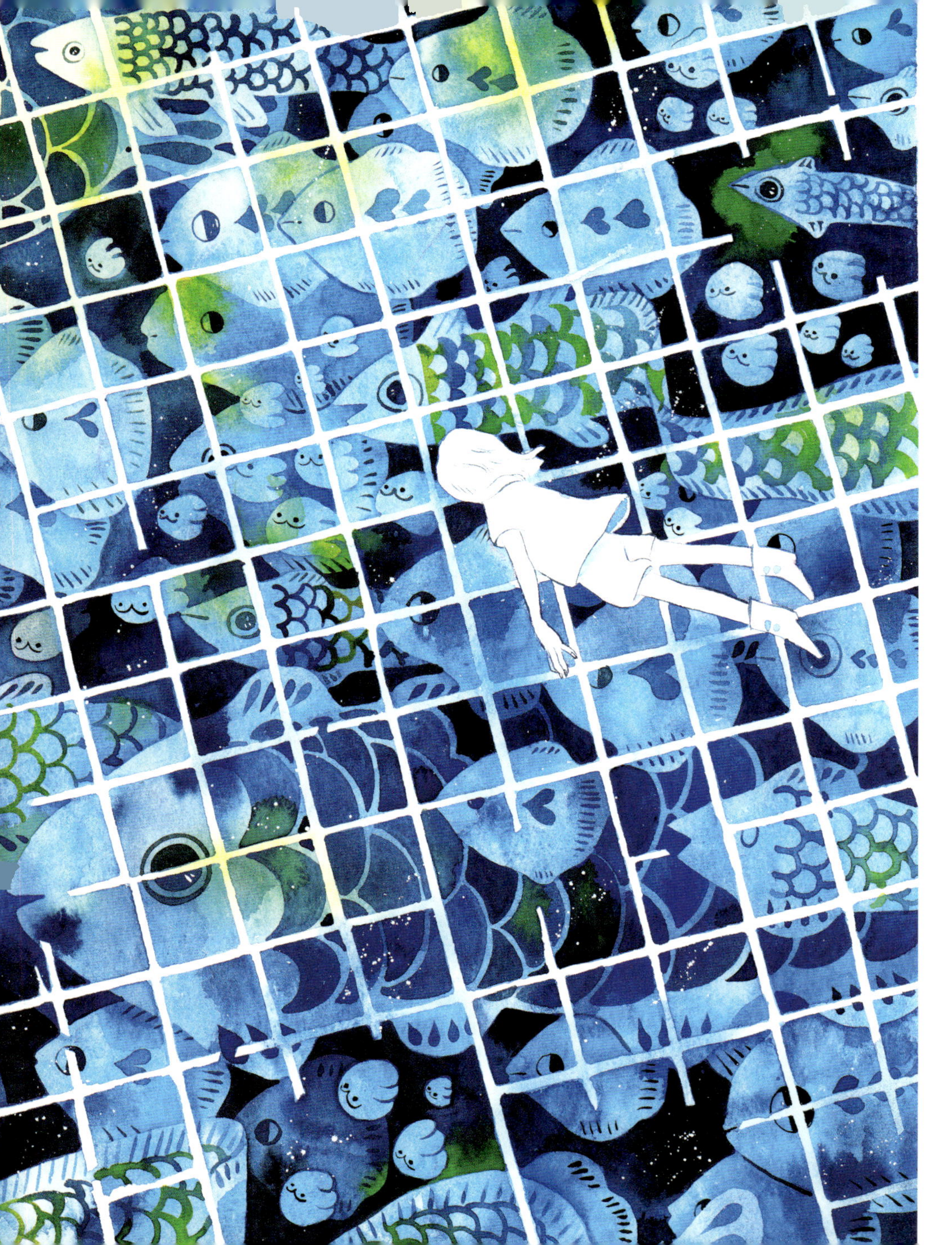

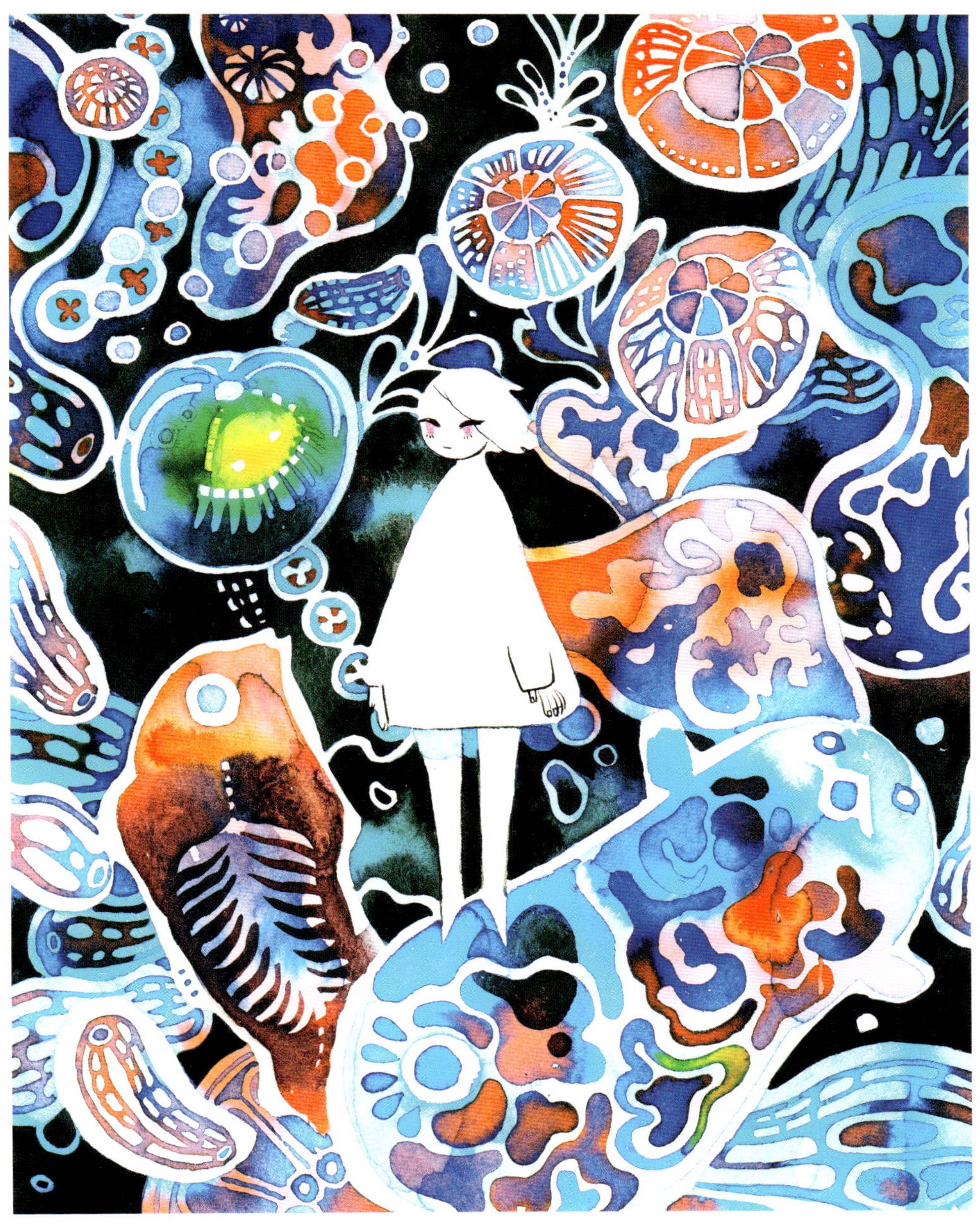

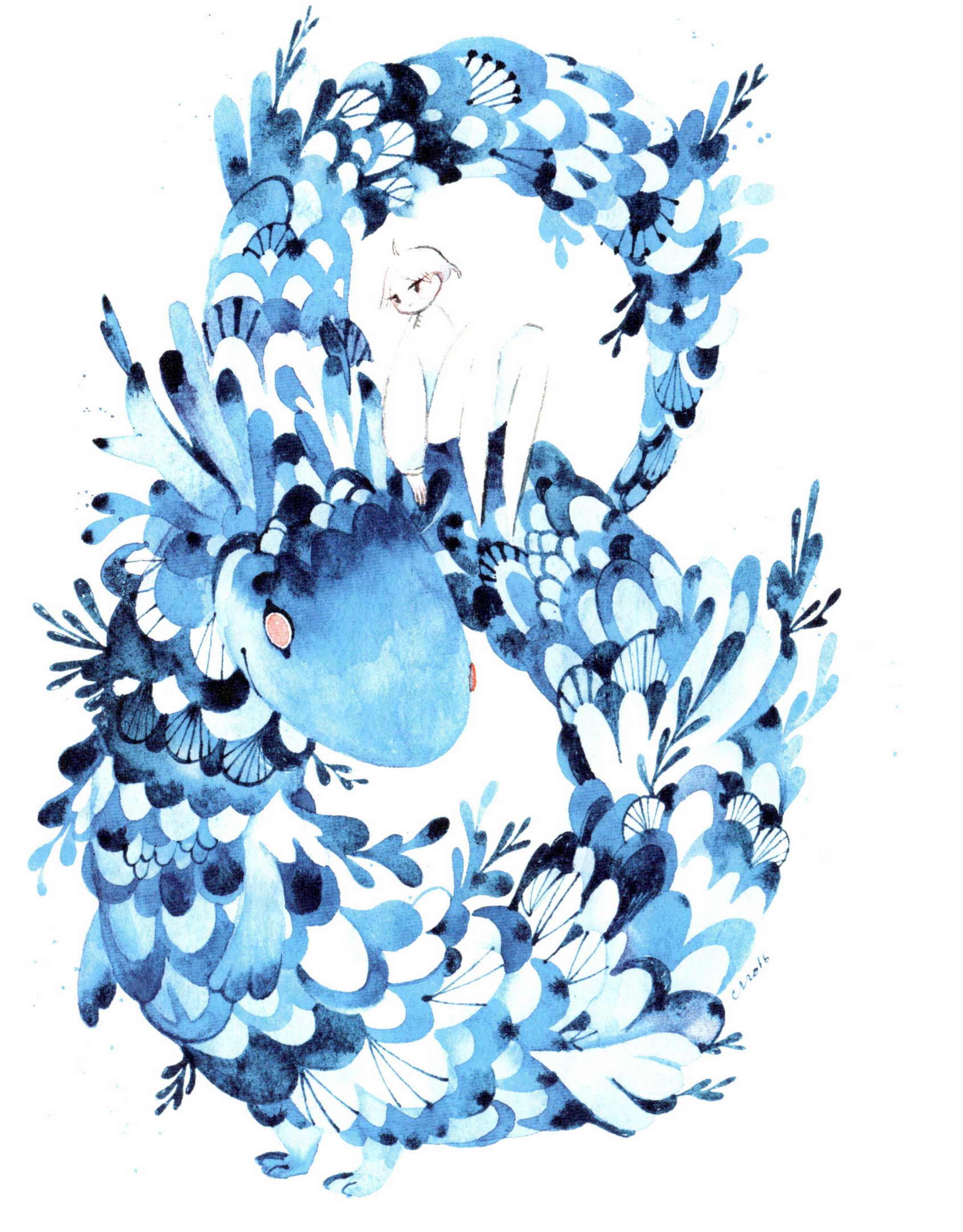

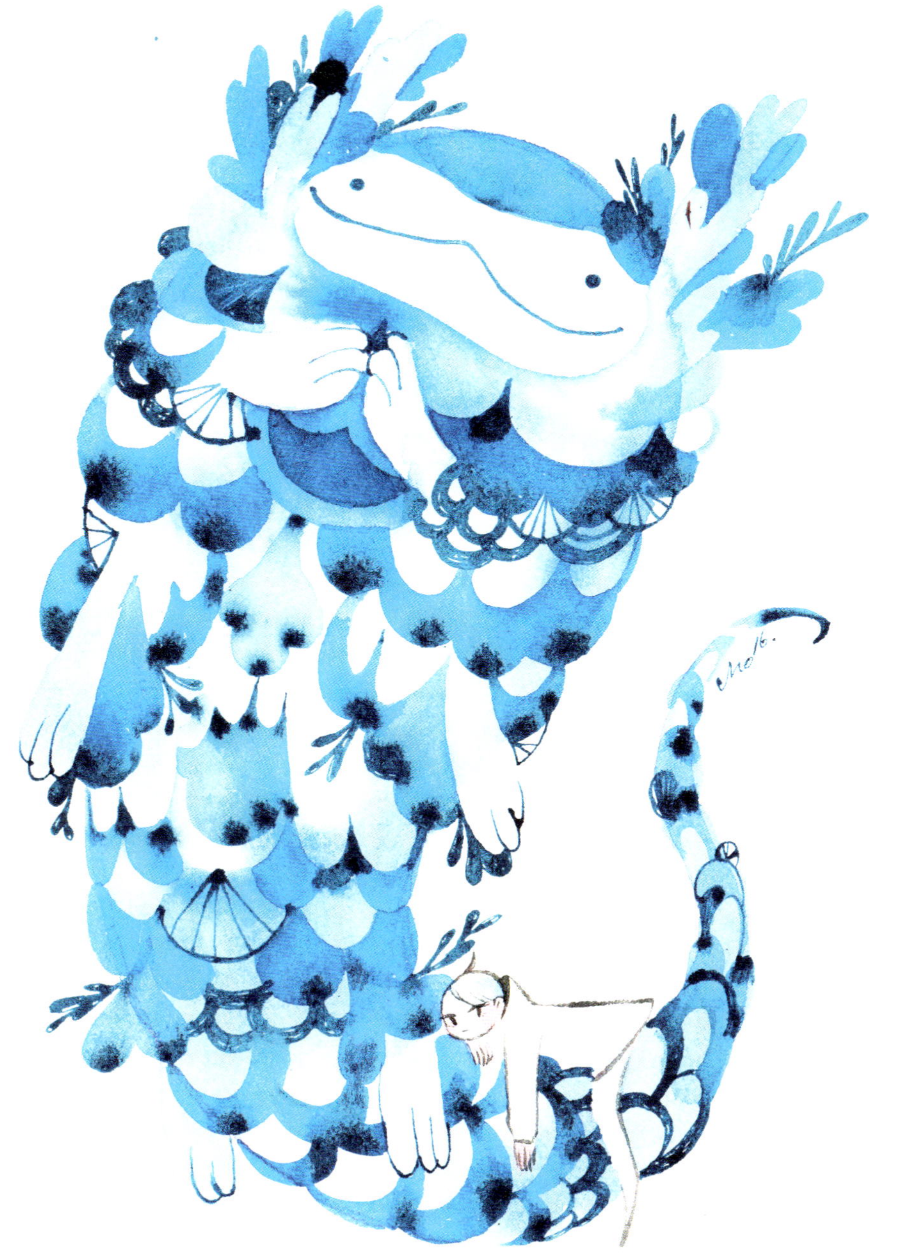

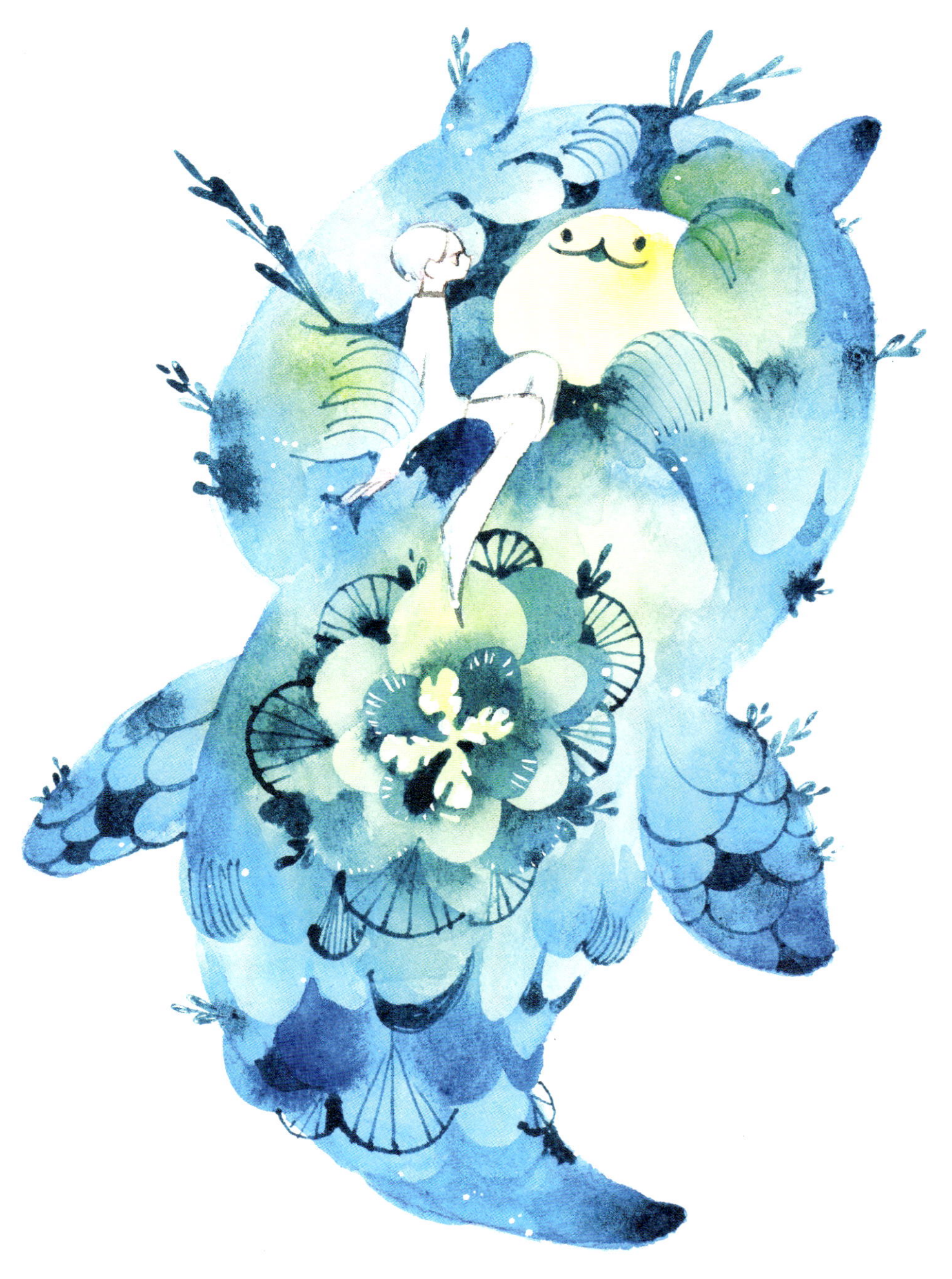

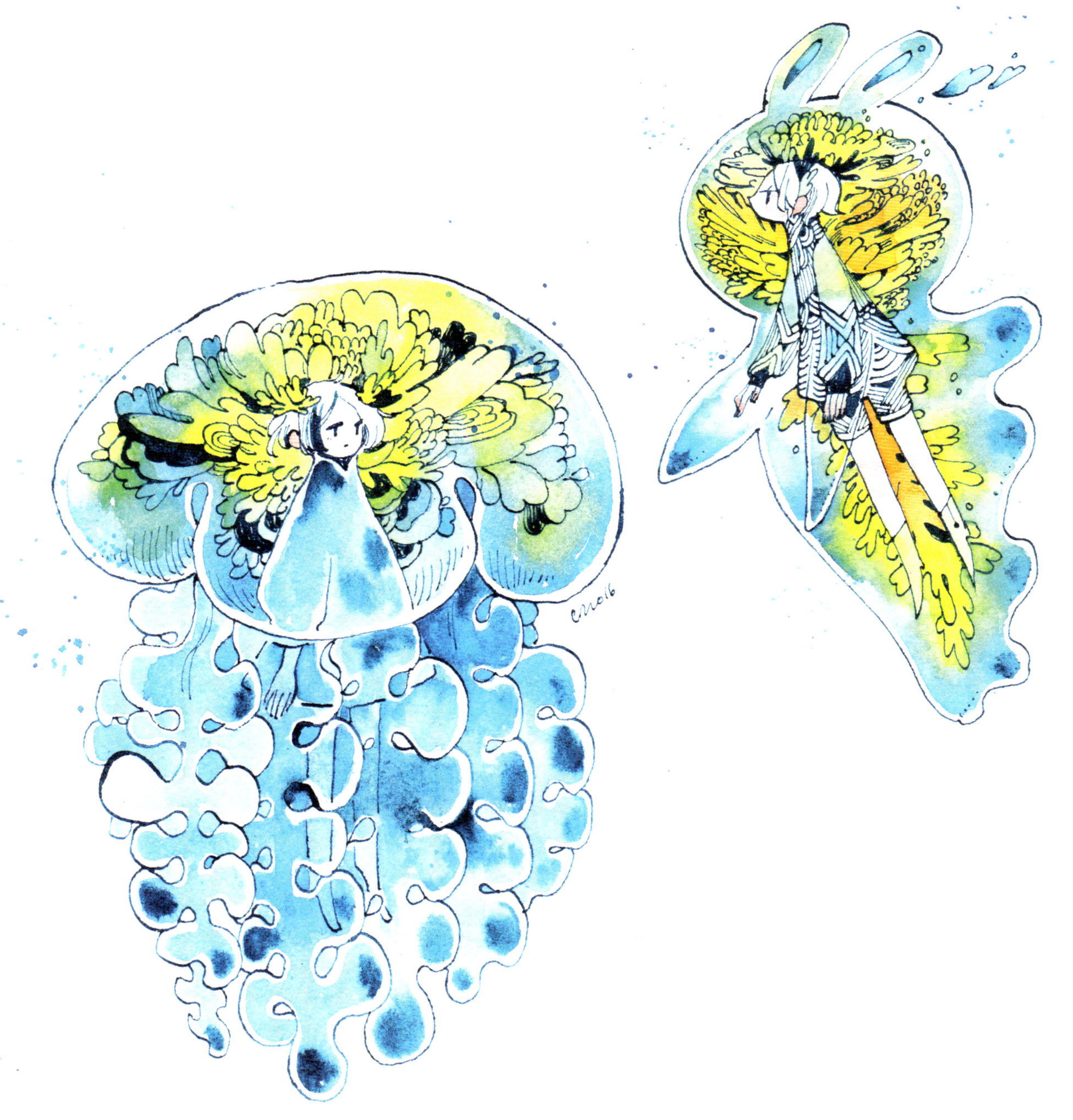

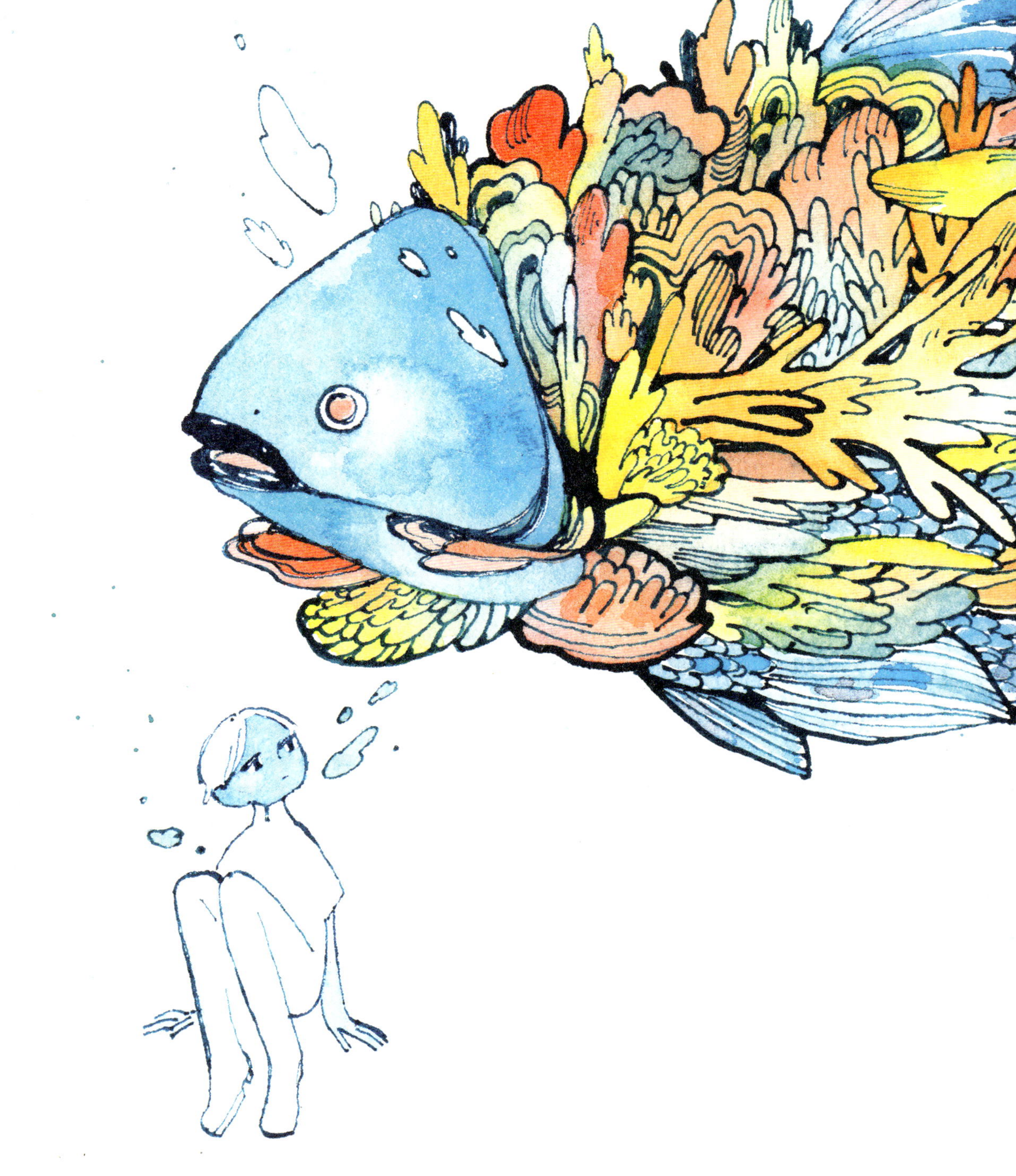

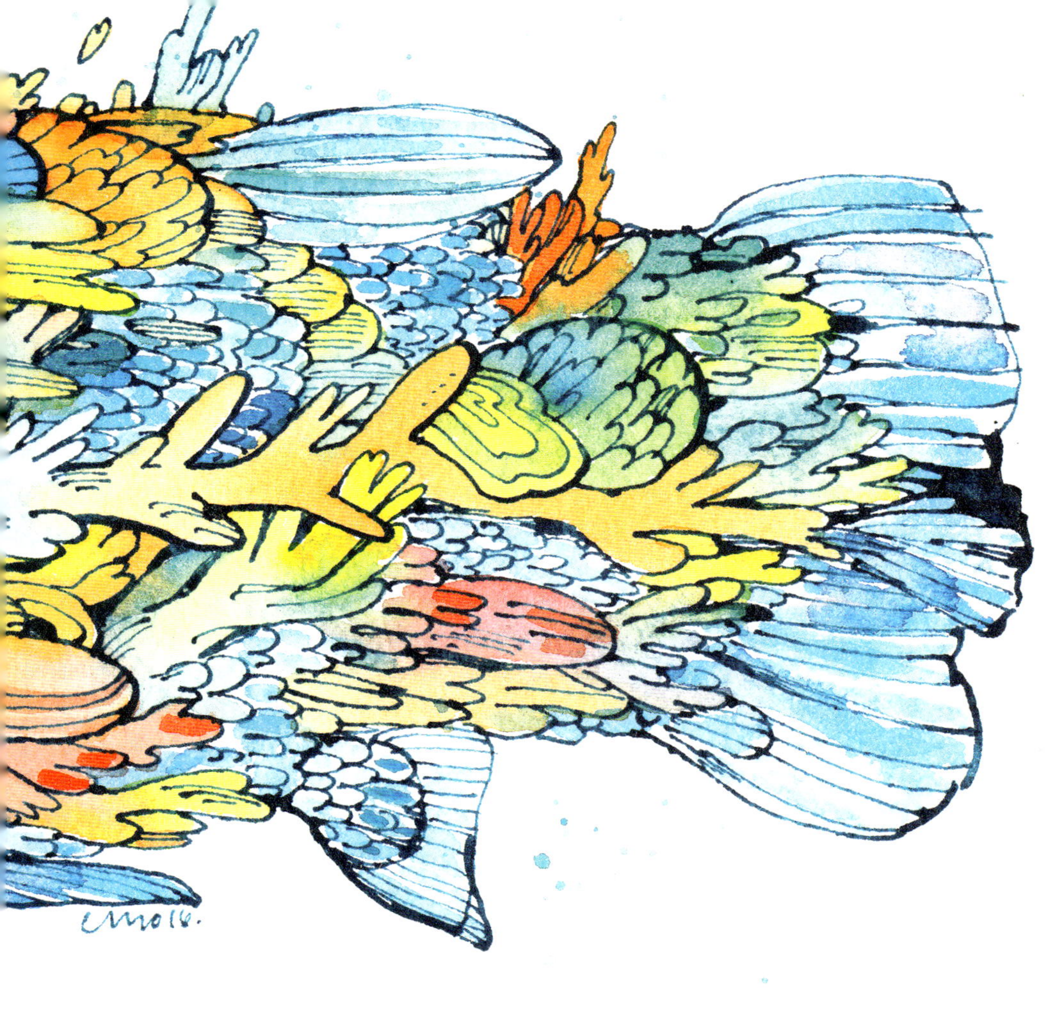

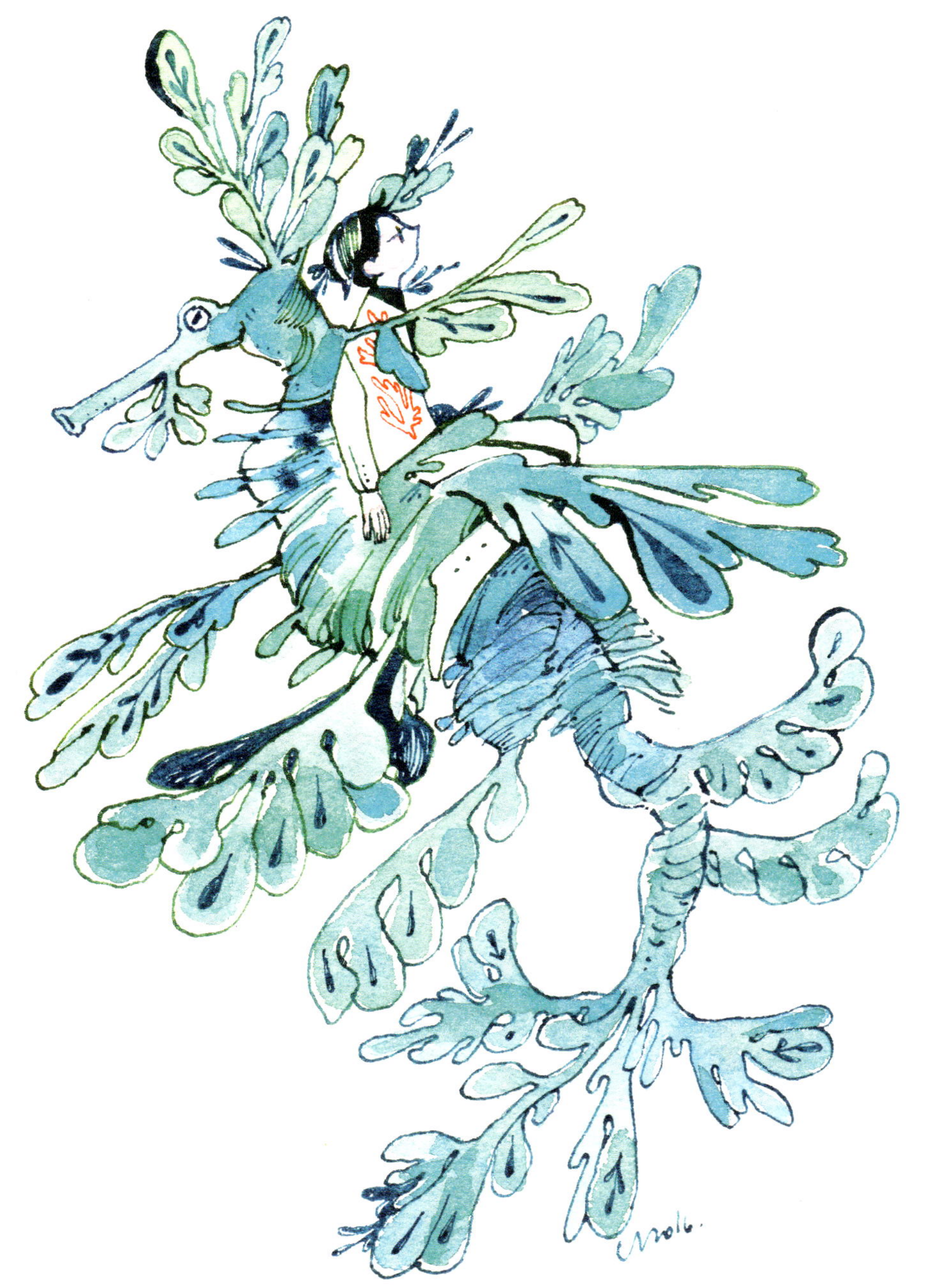

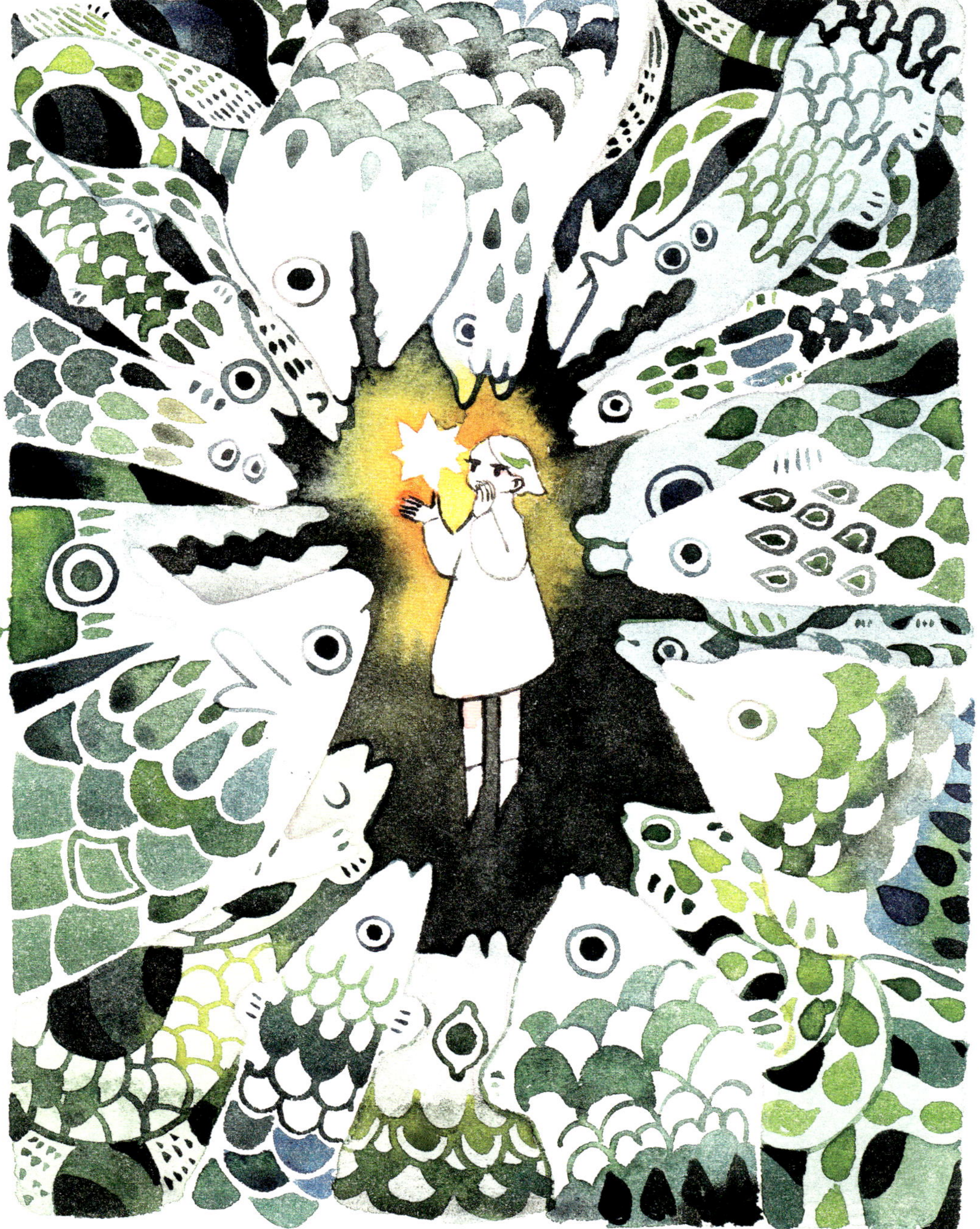

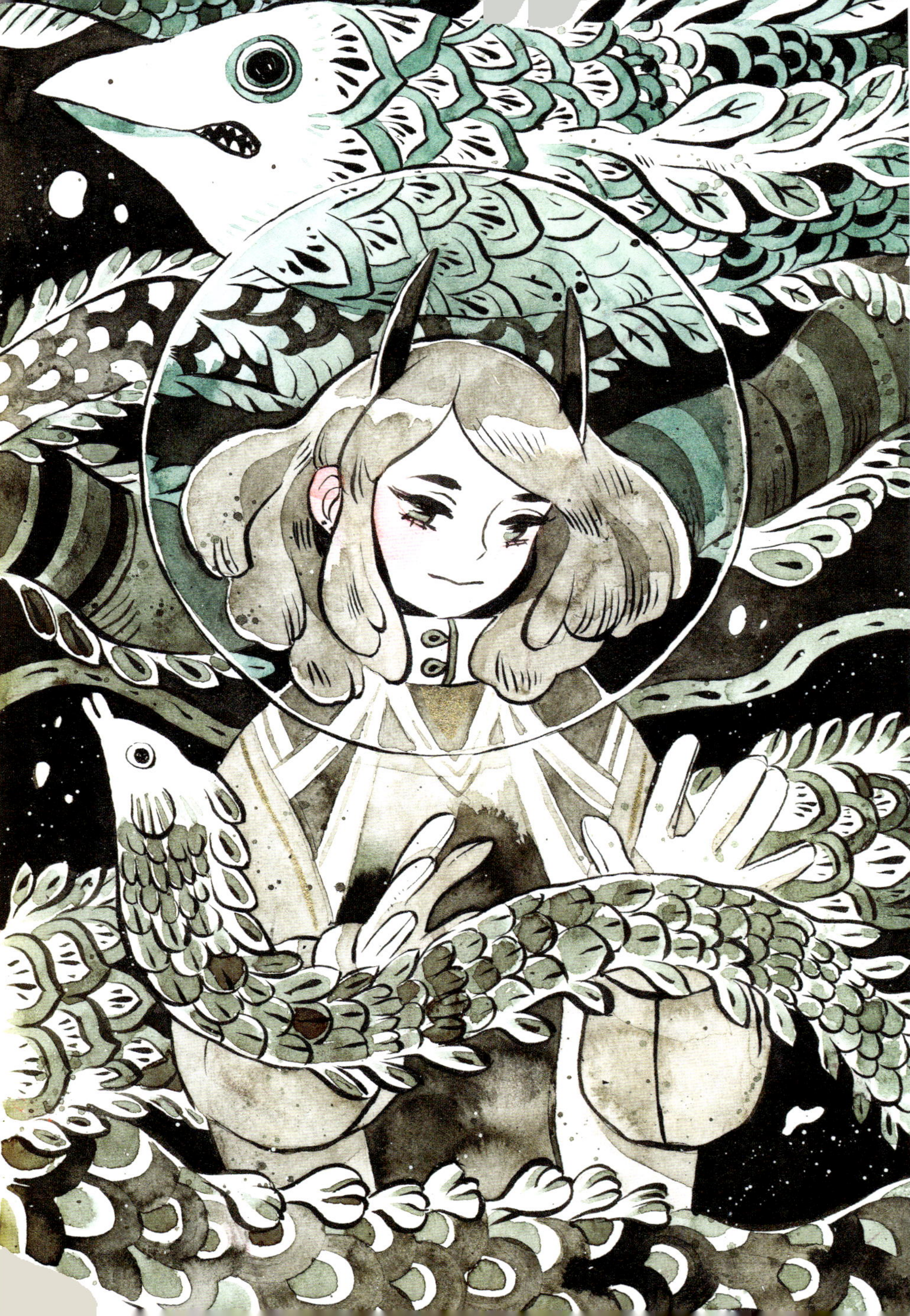

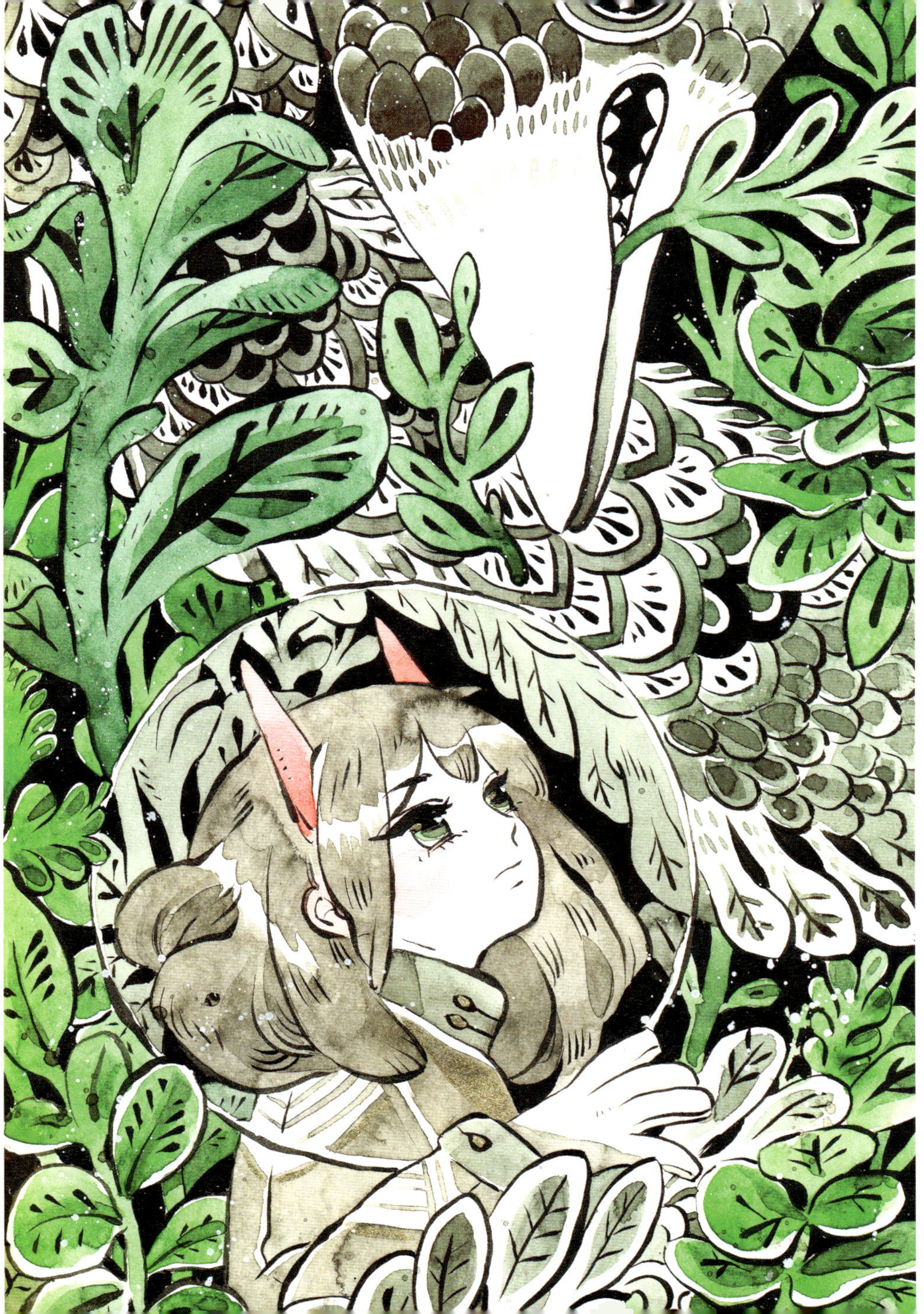

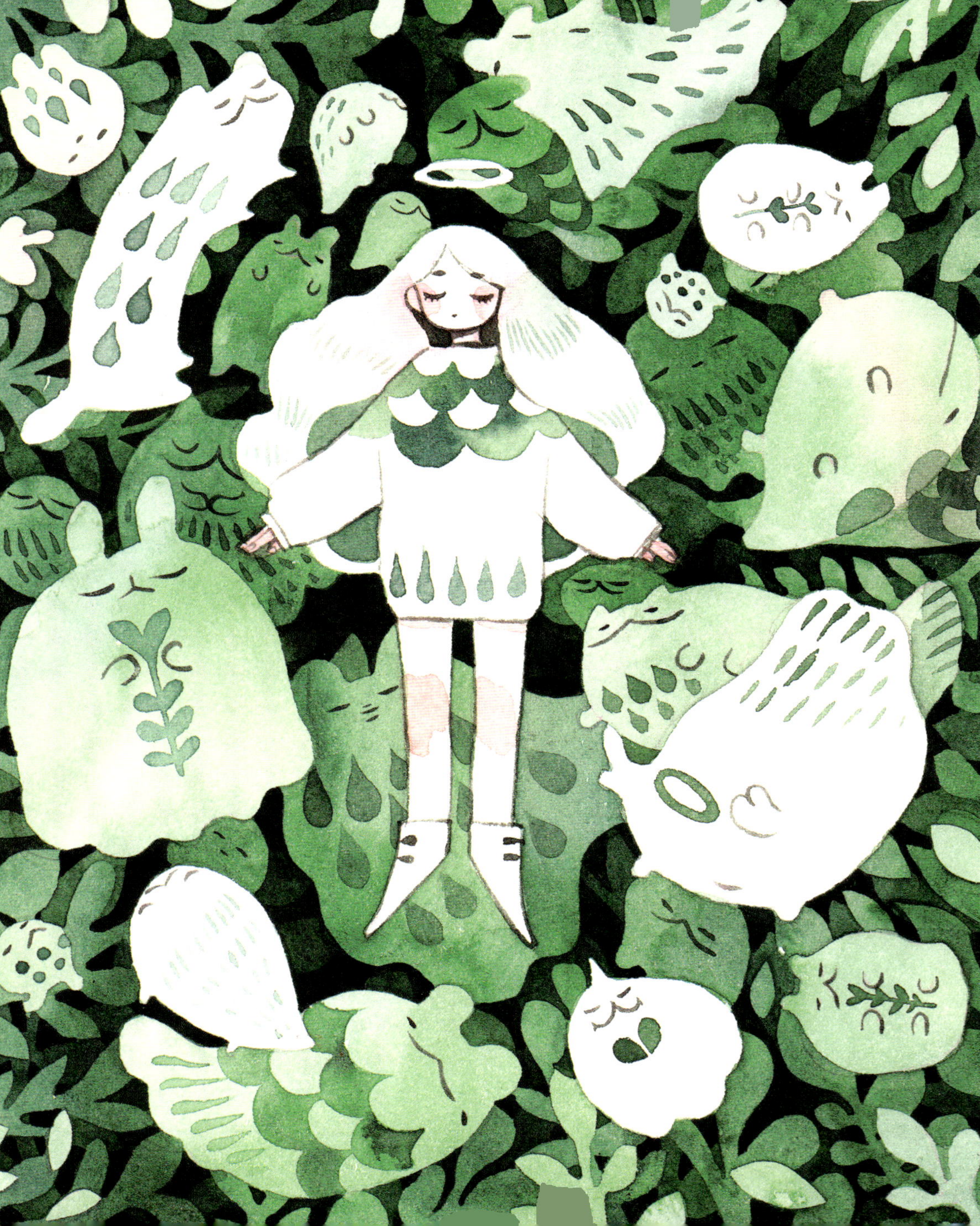

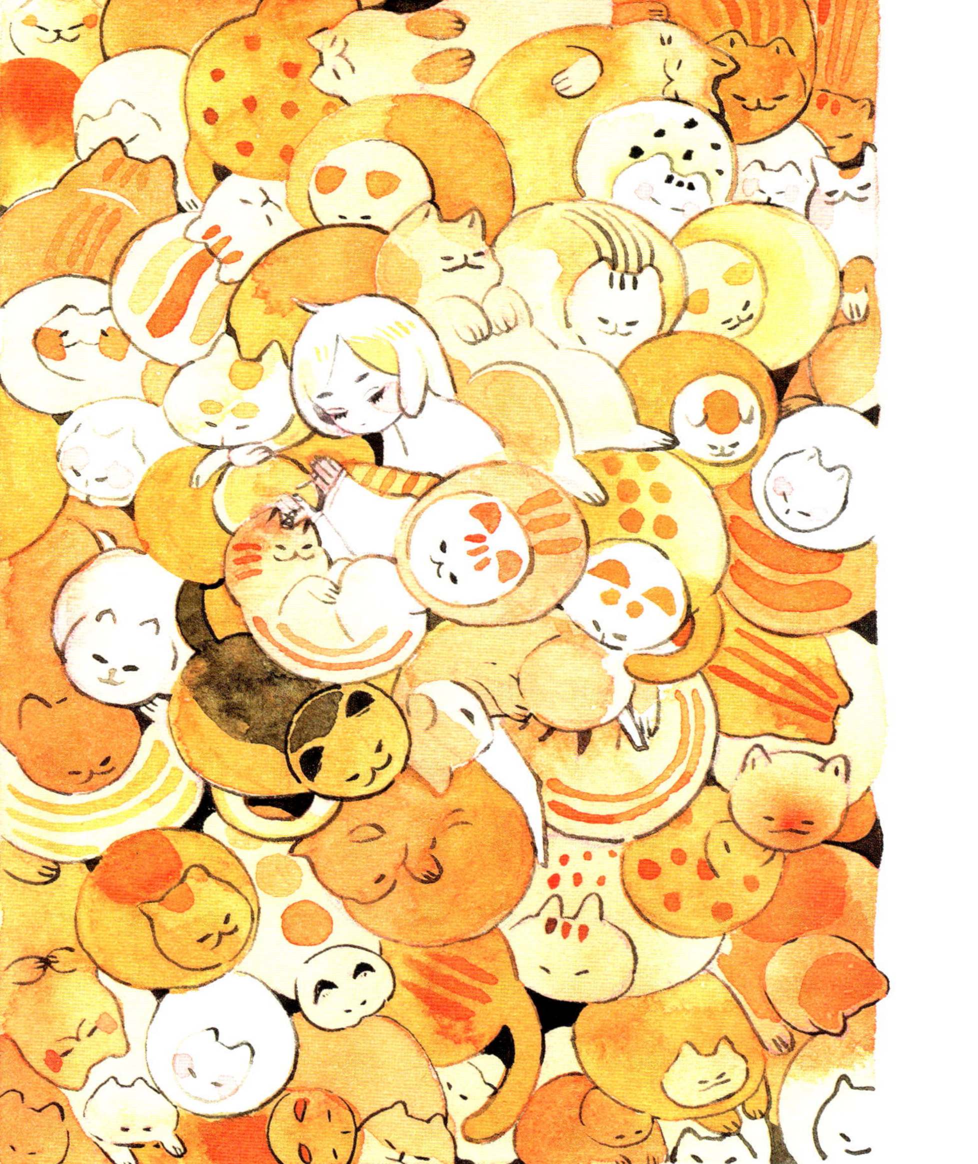

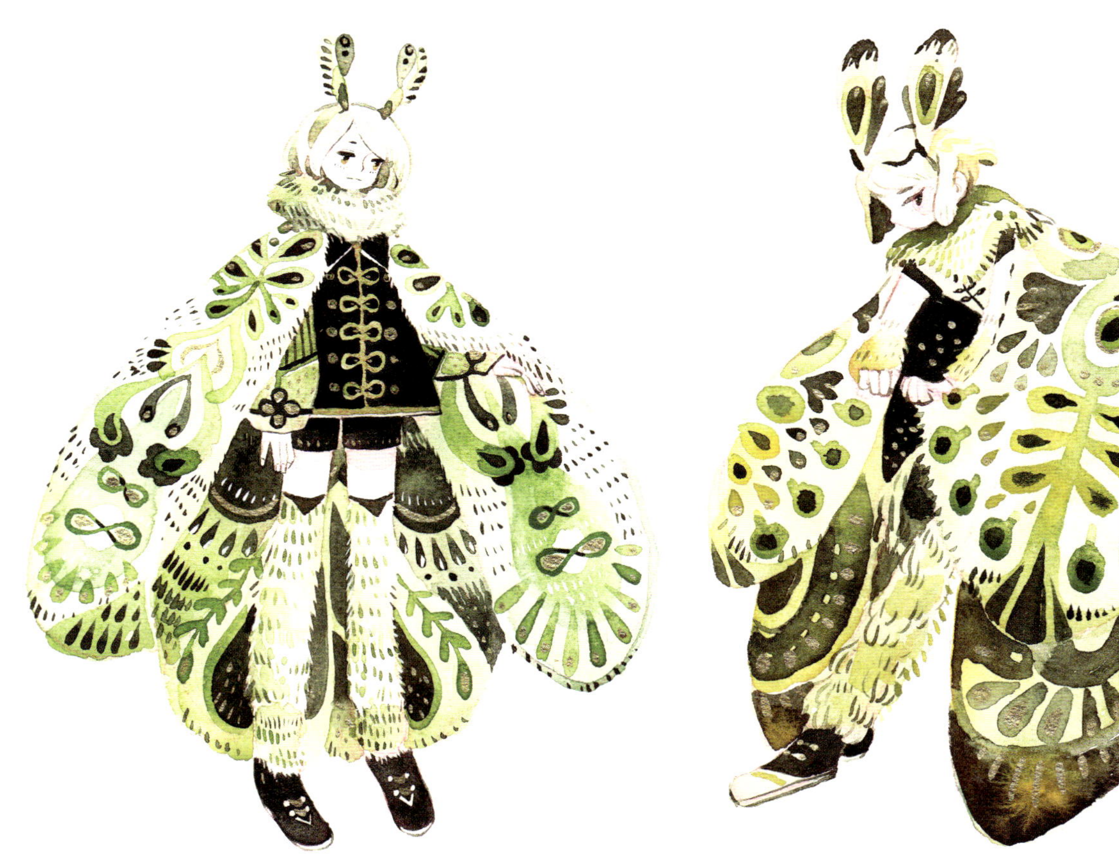

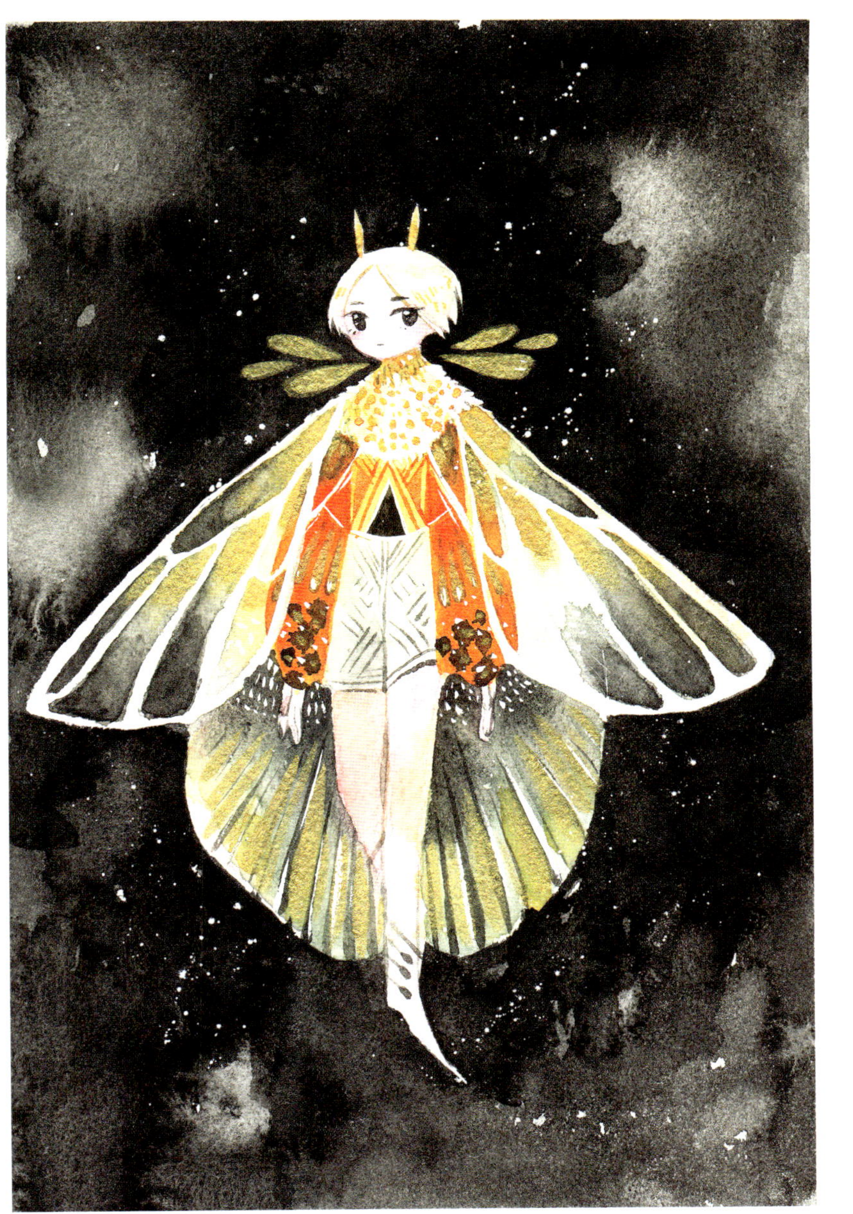

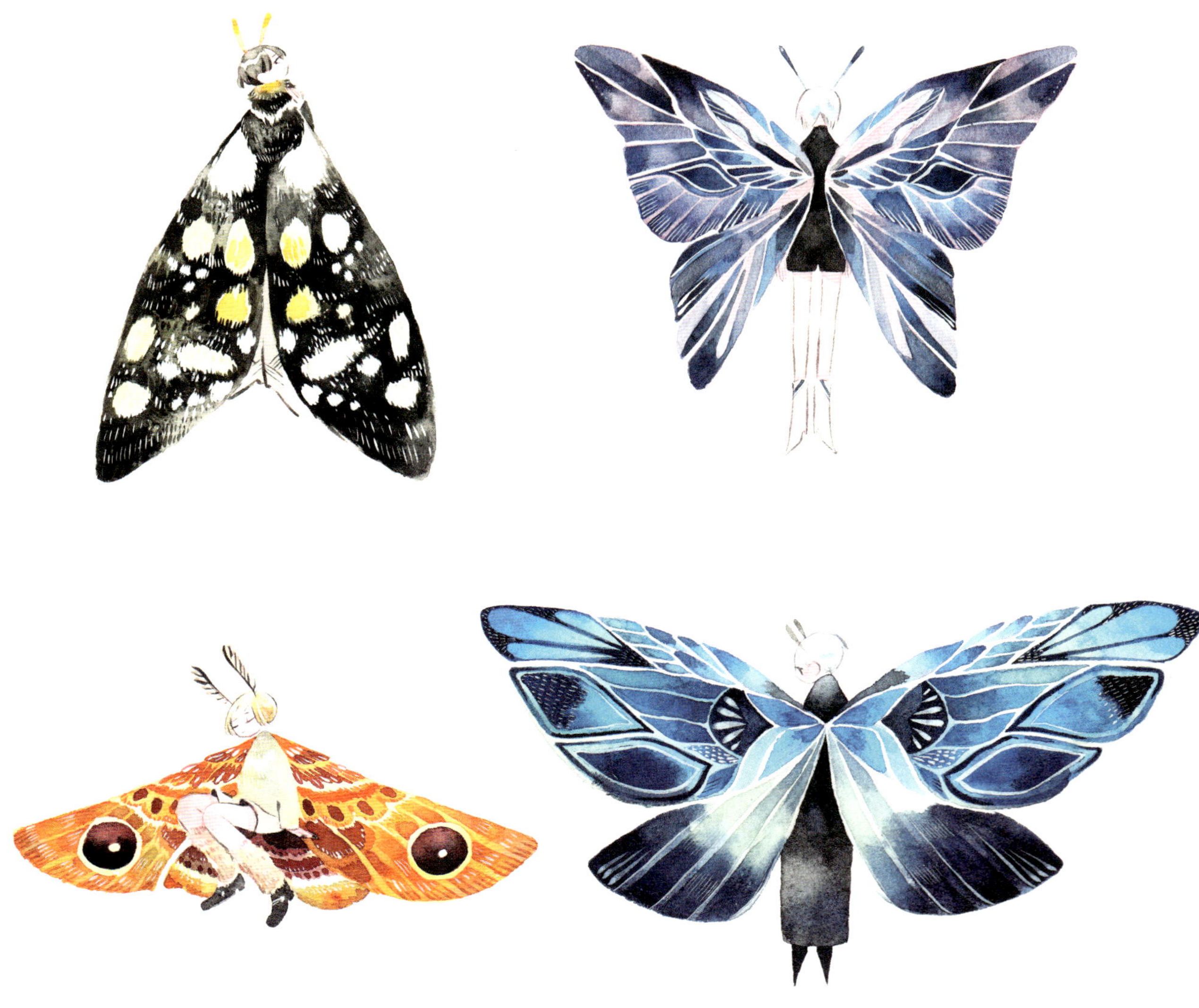

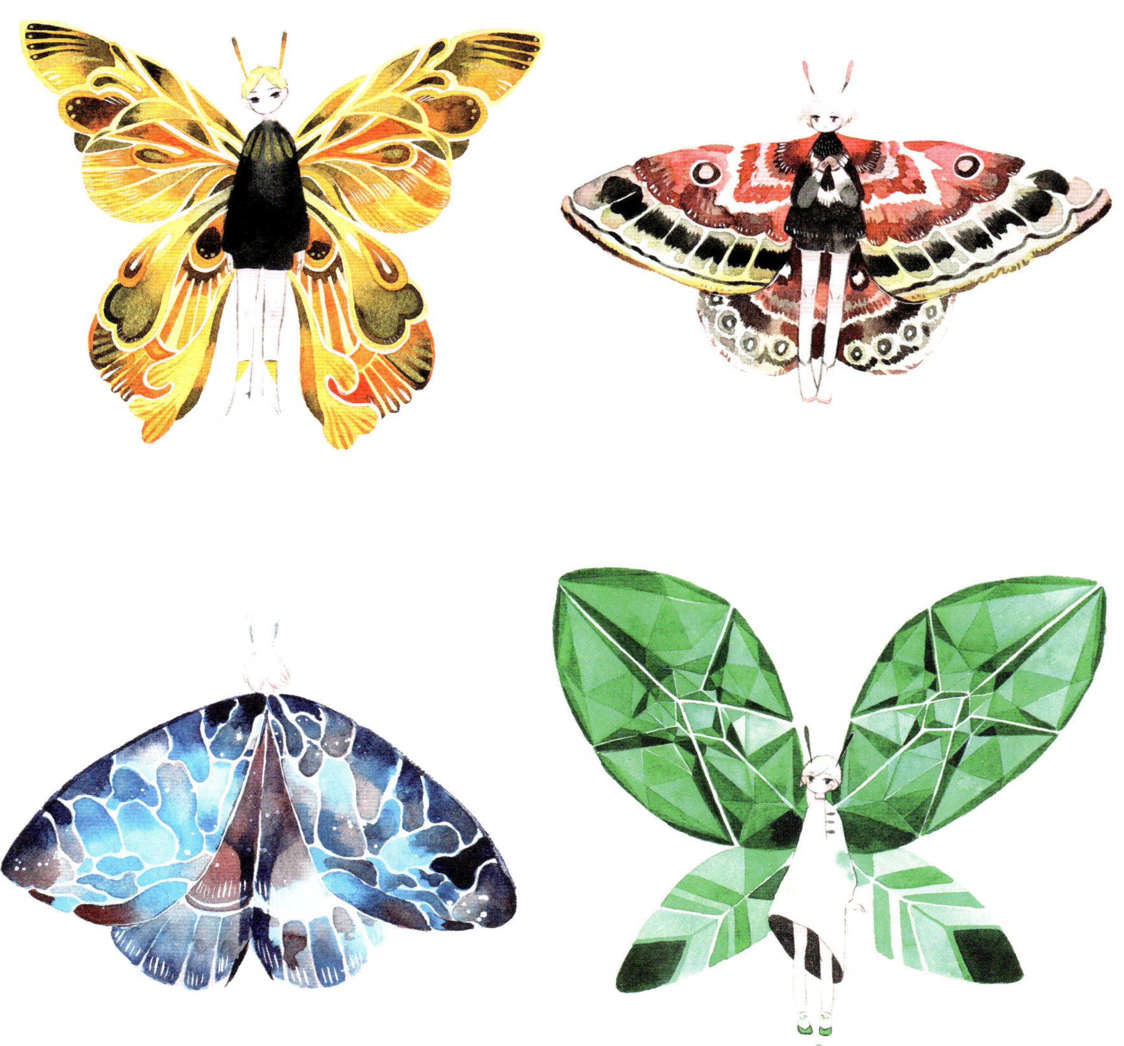

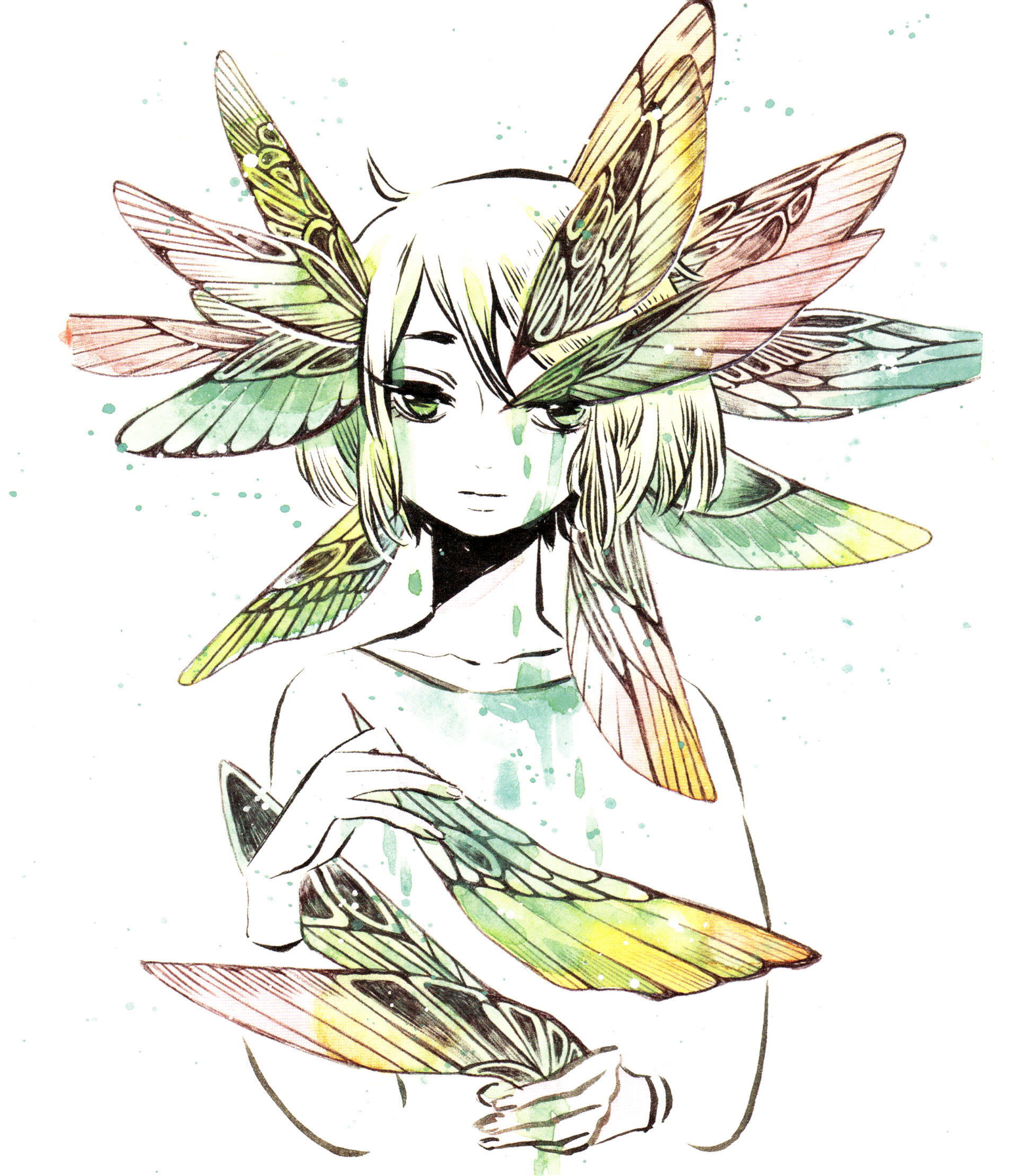

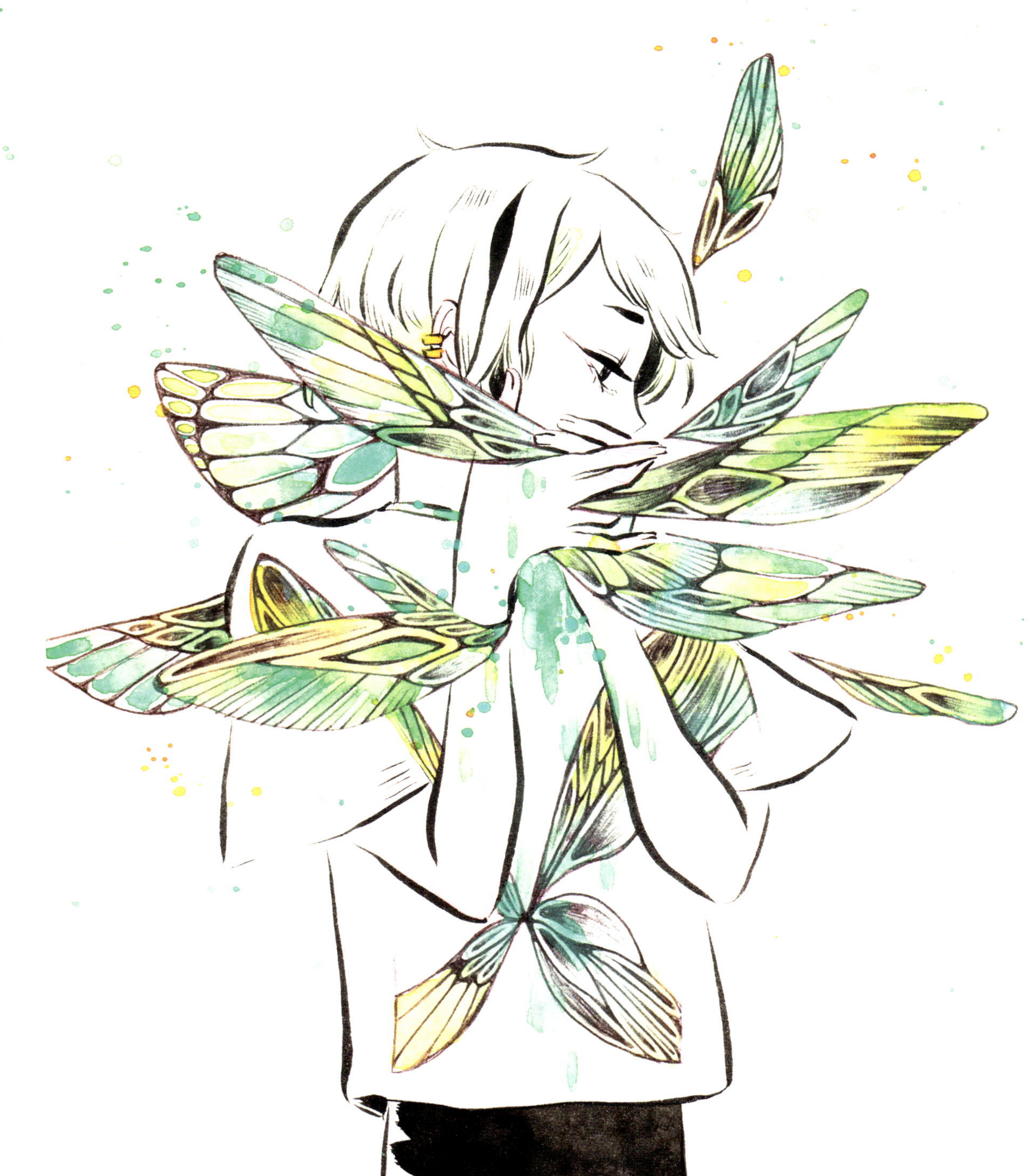

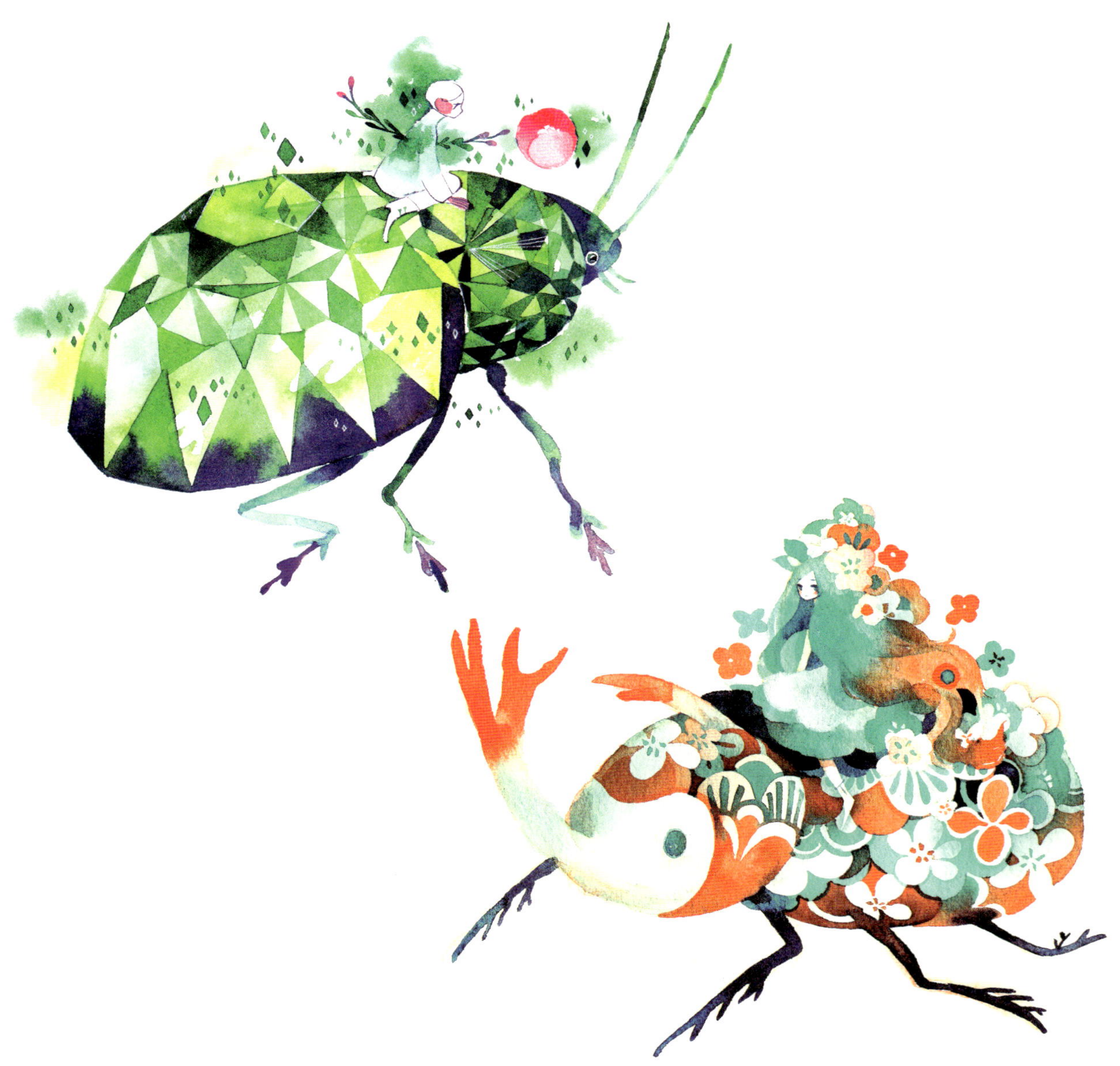

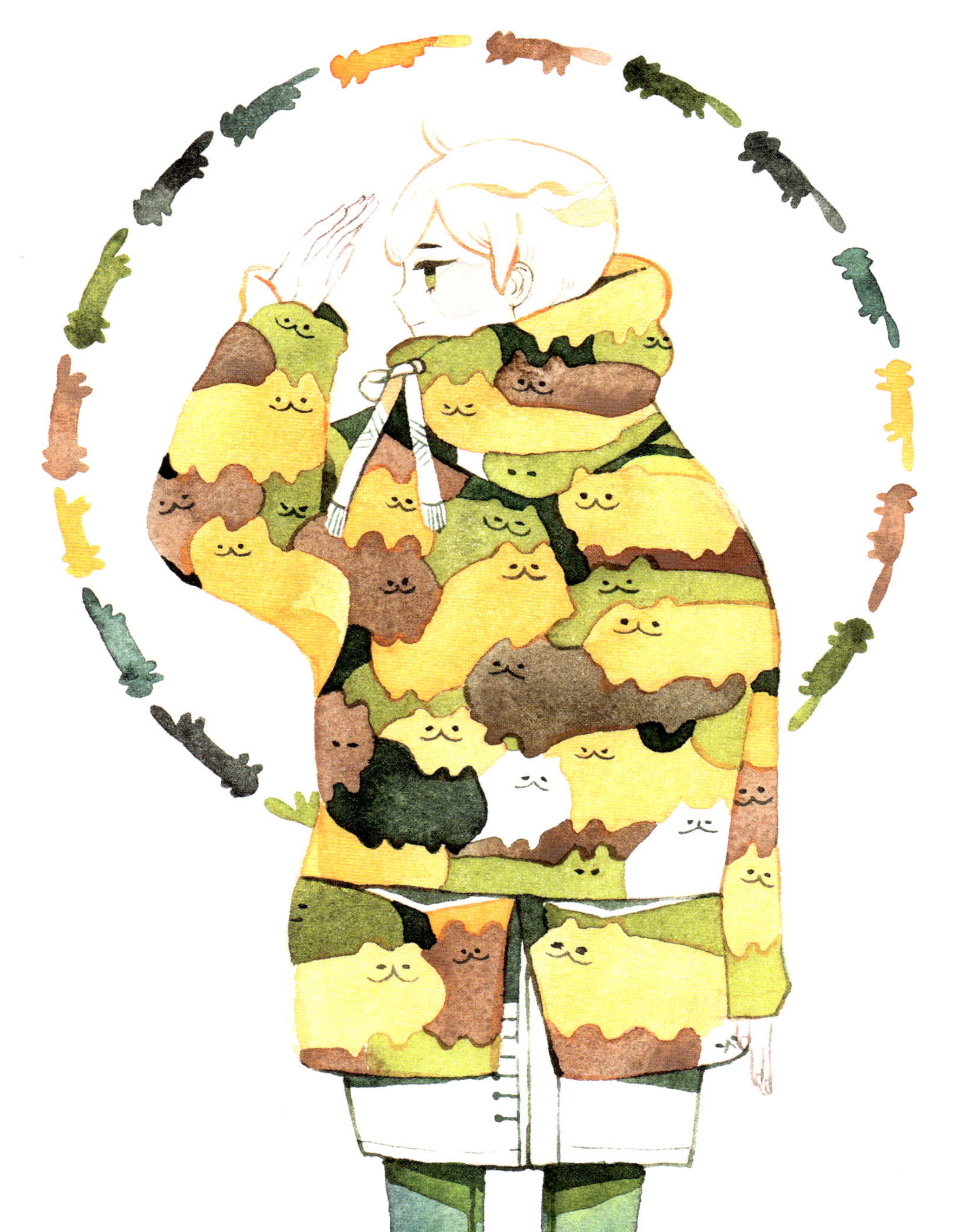

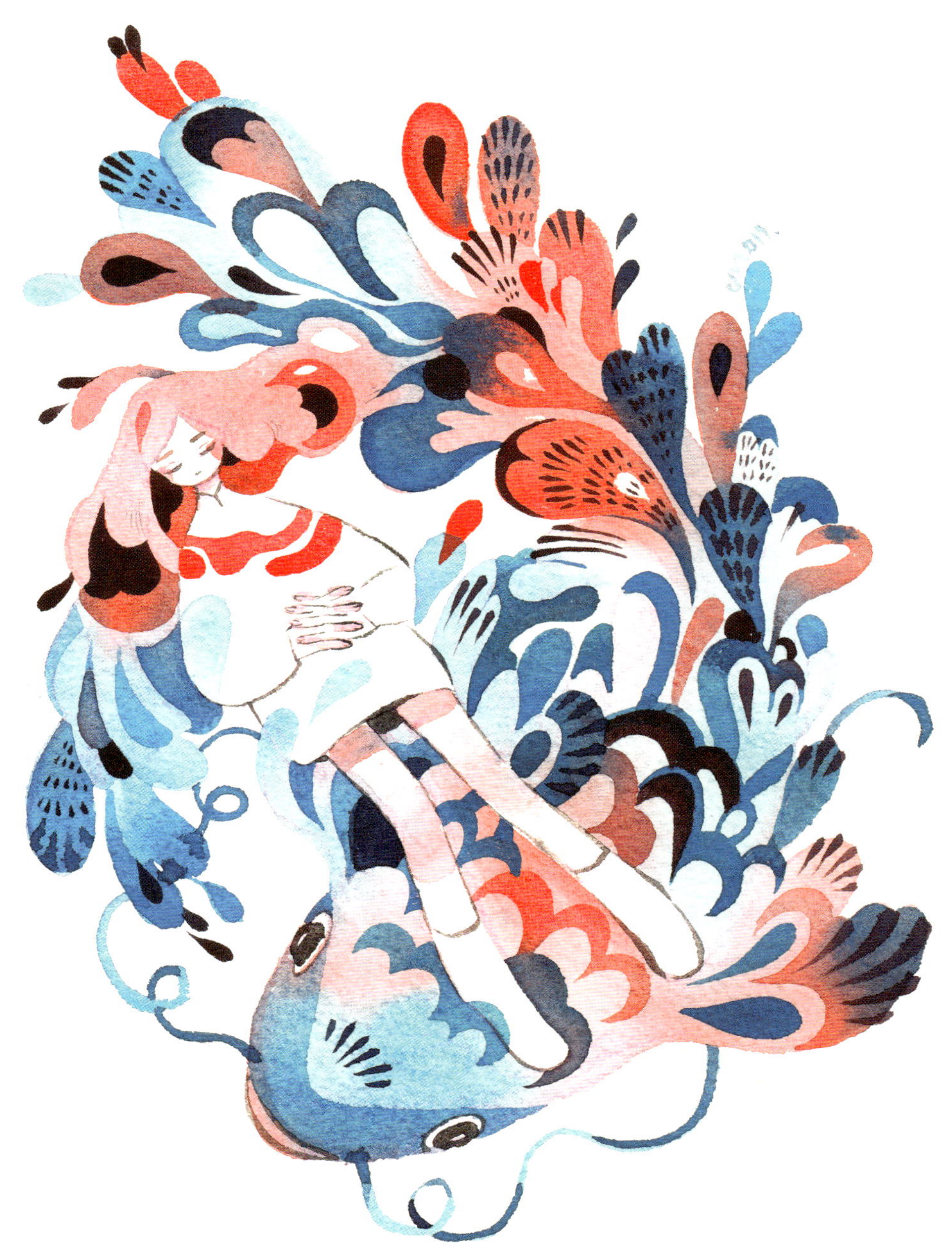

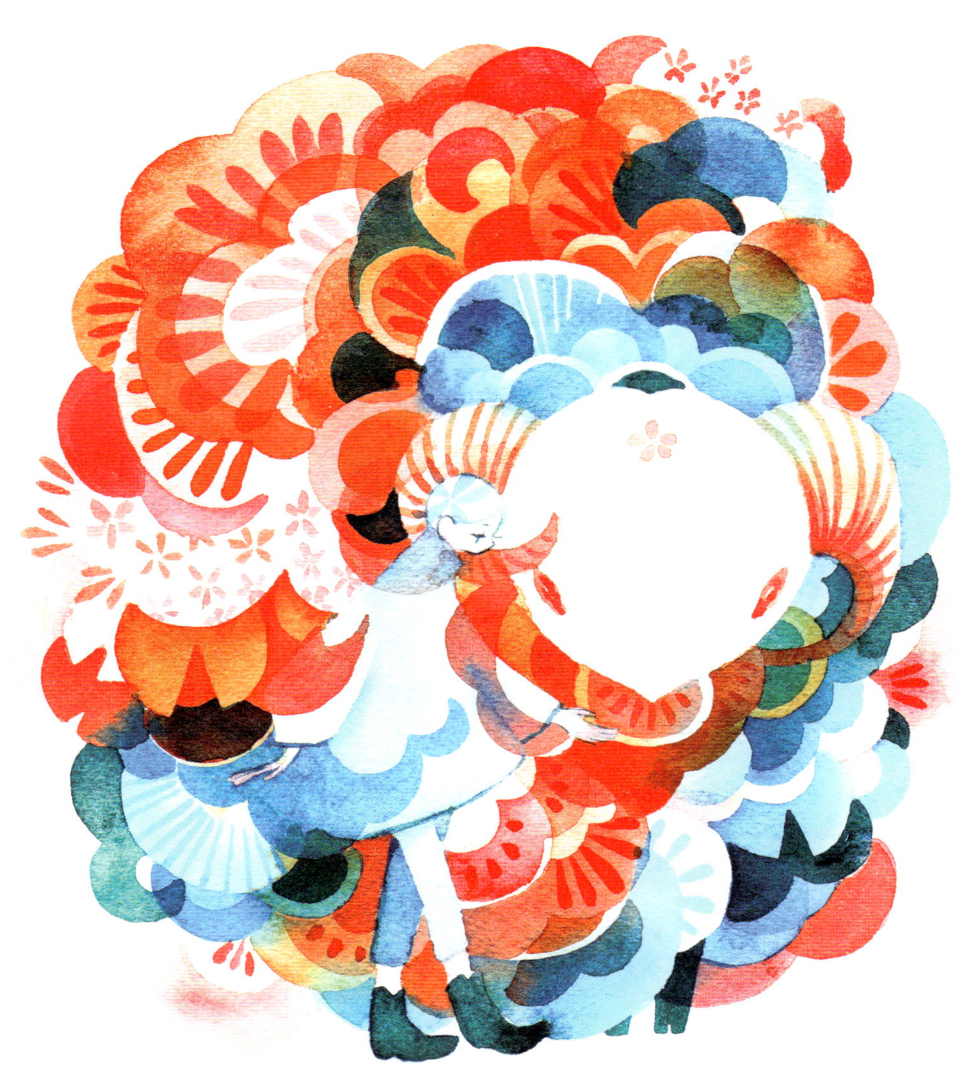

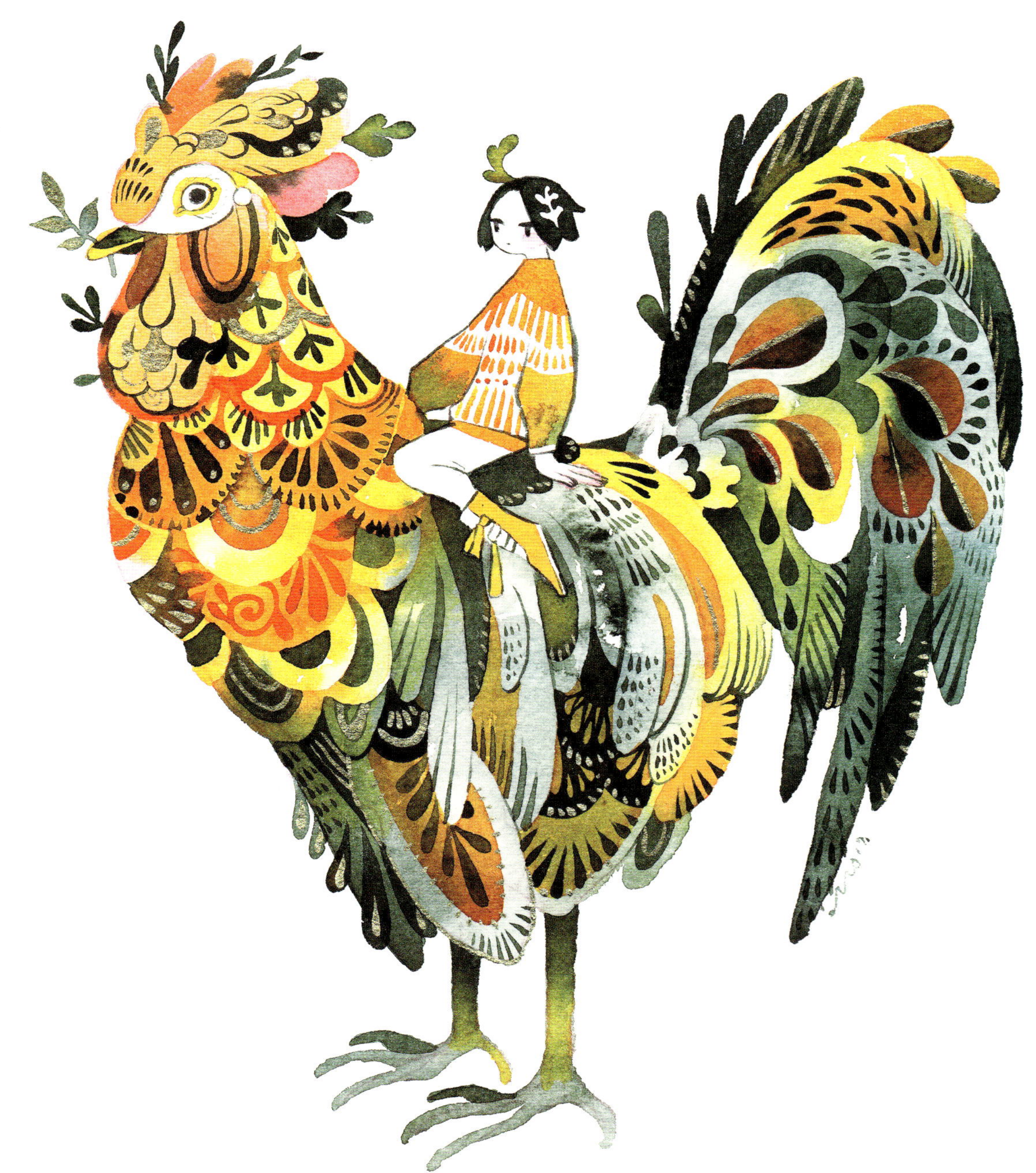

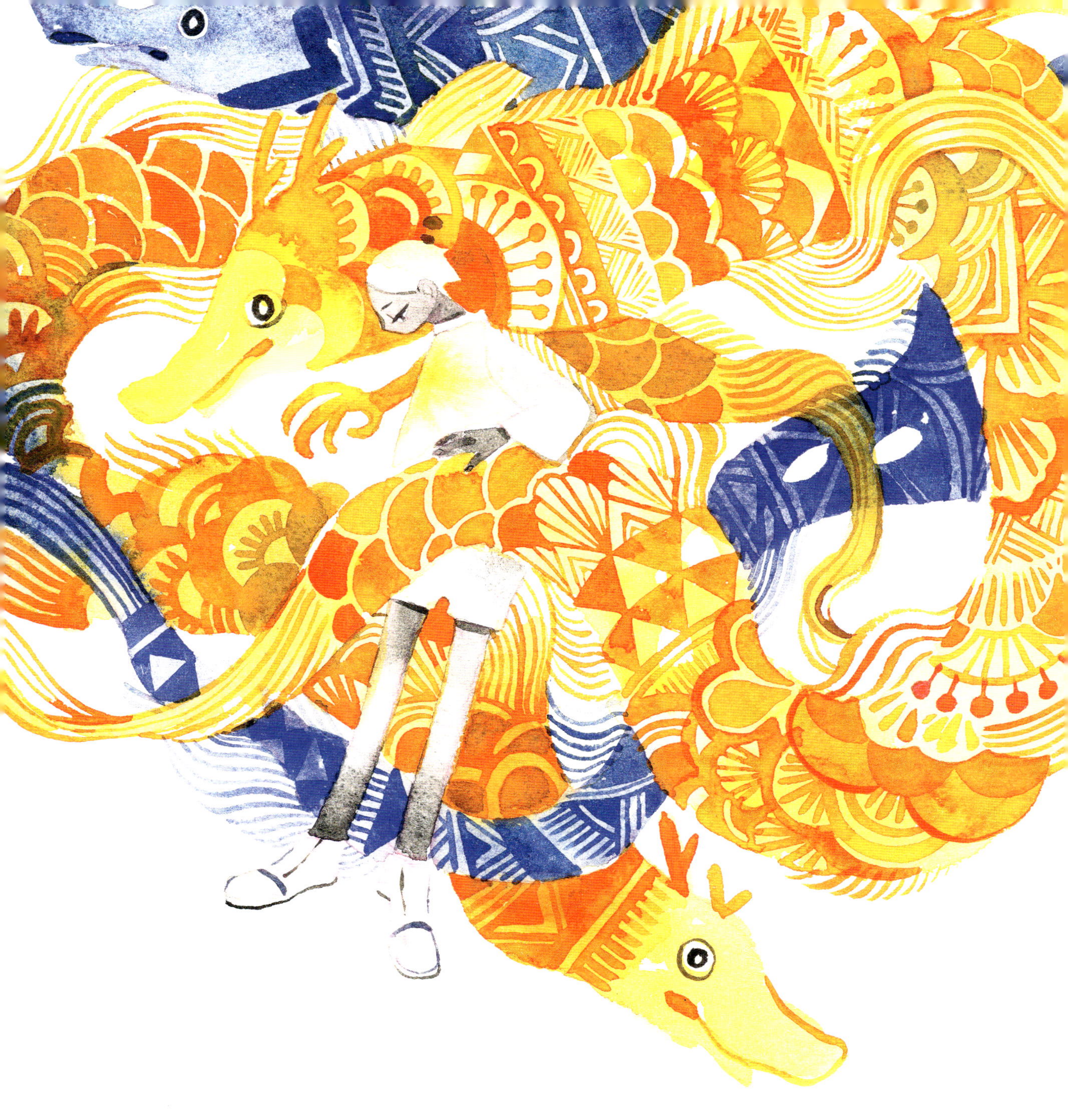

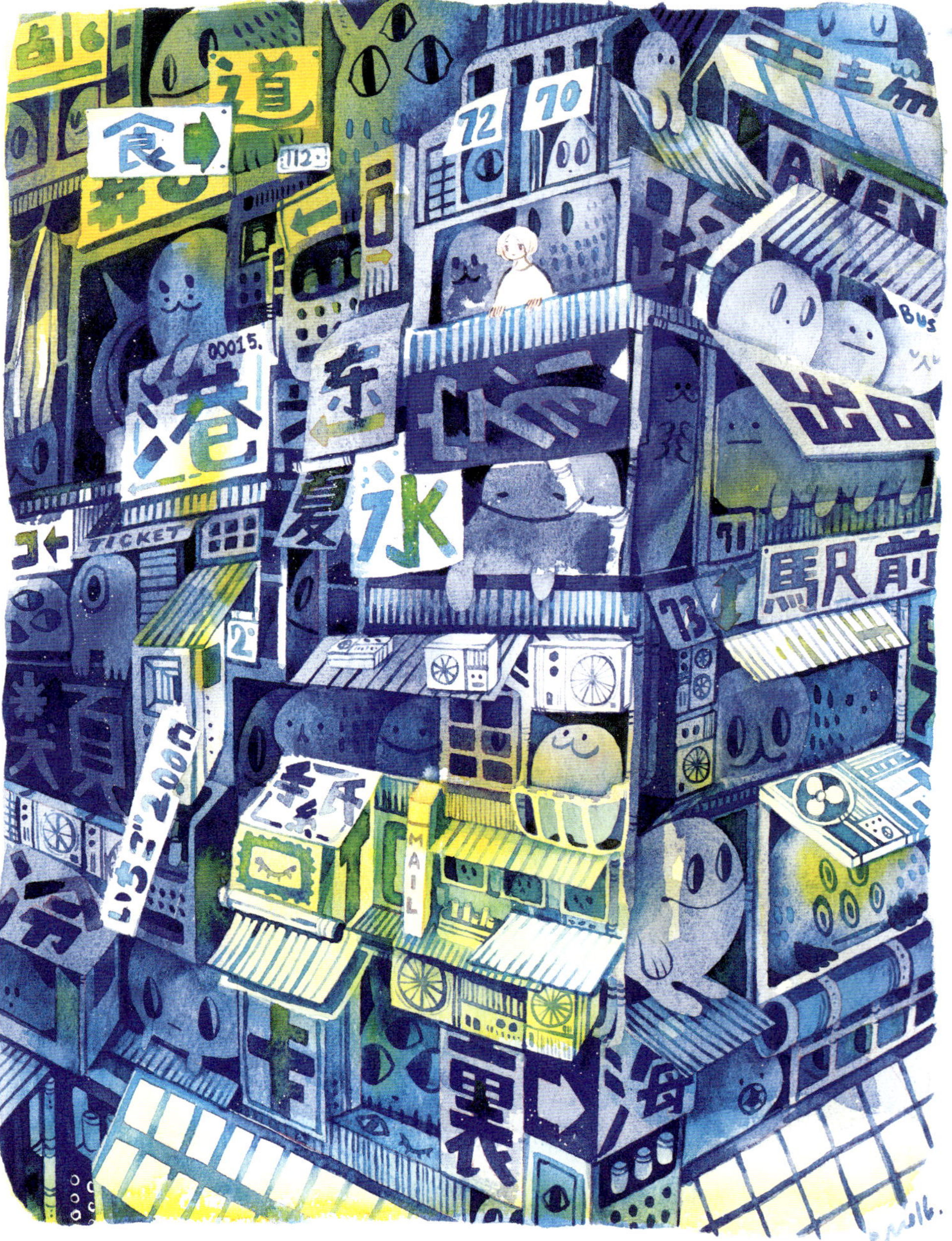

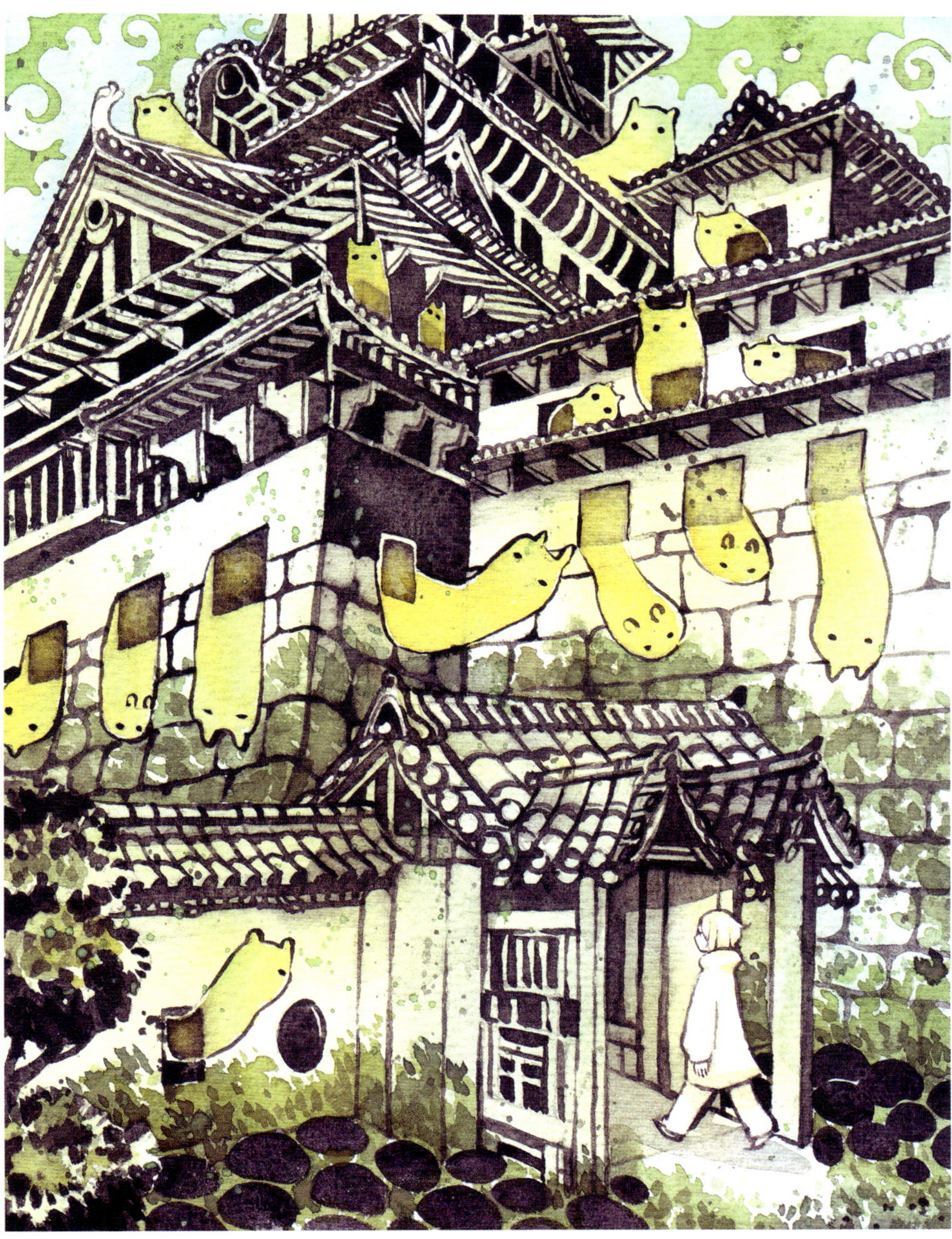

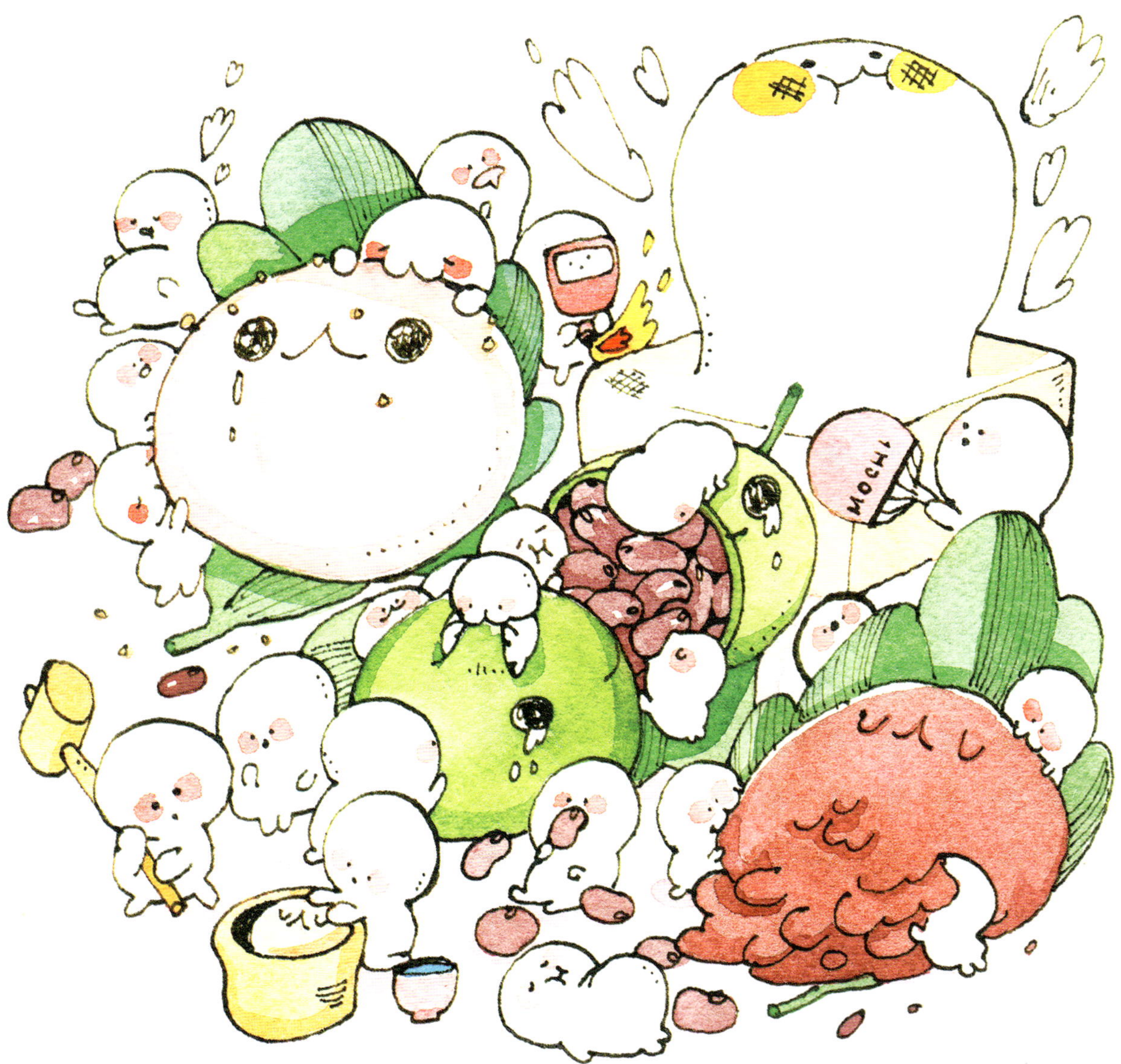

柚
塩
MOCHI

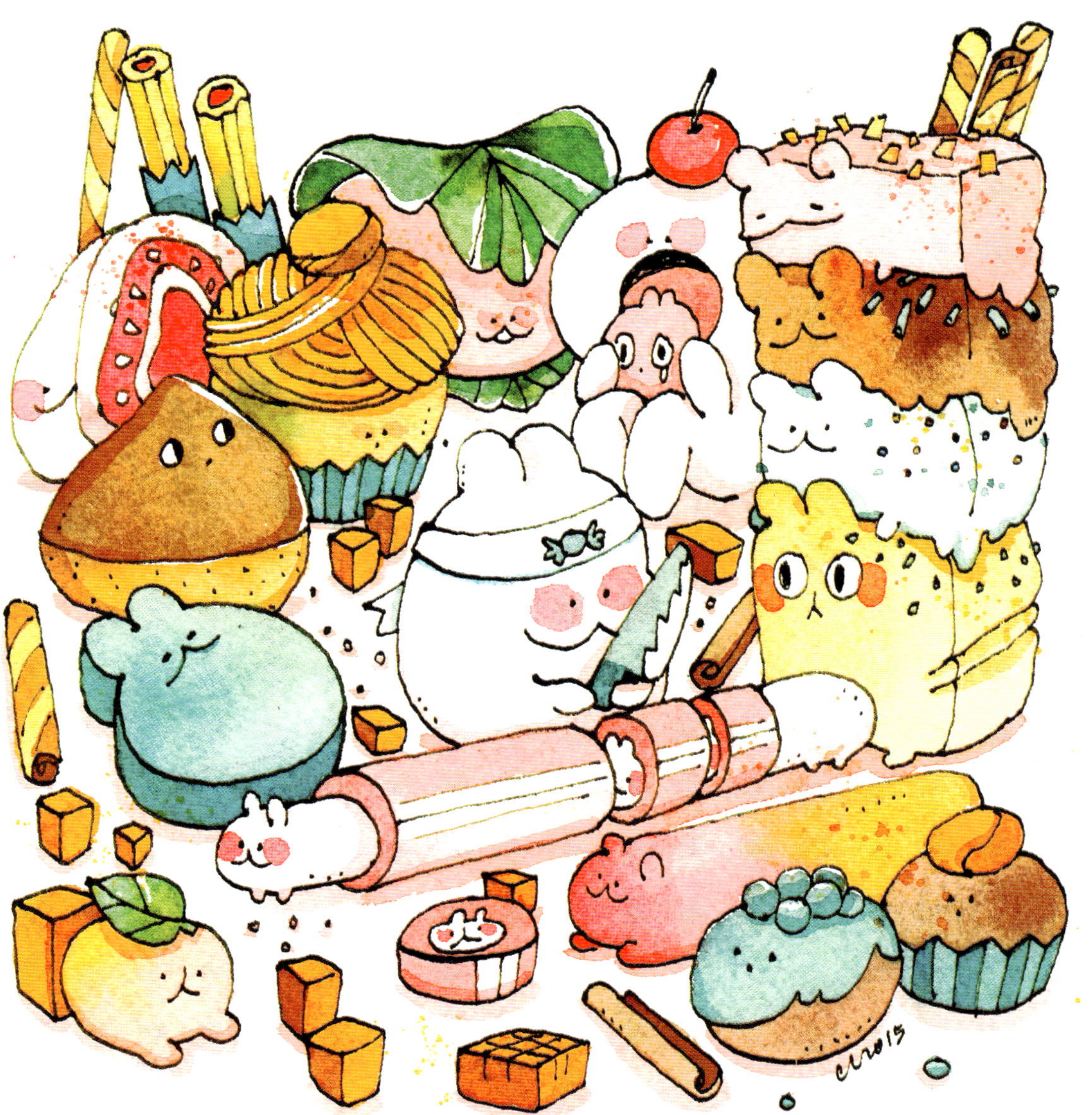

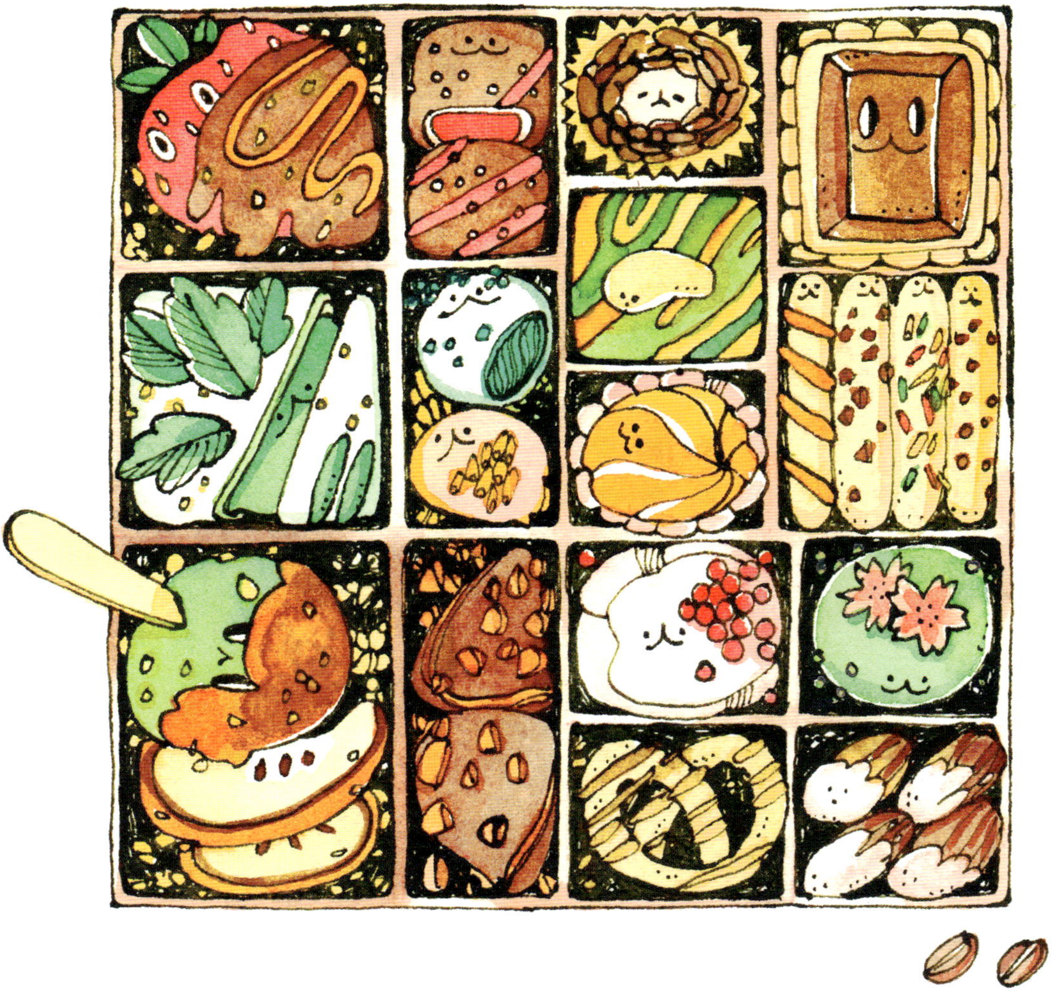

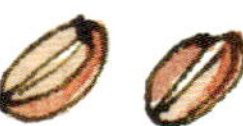

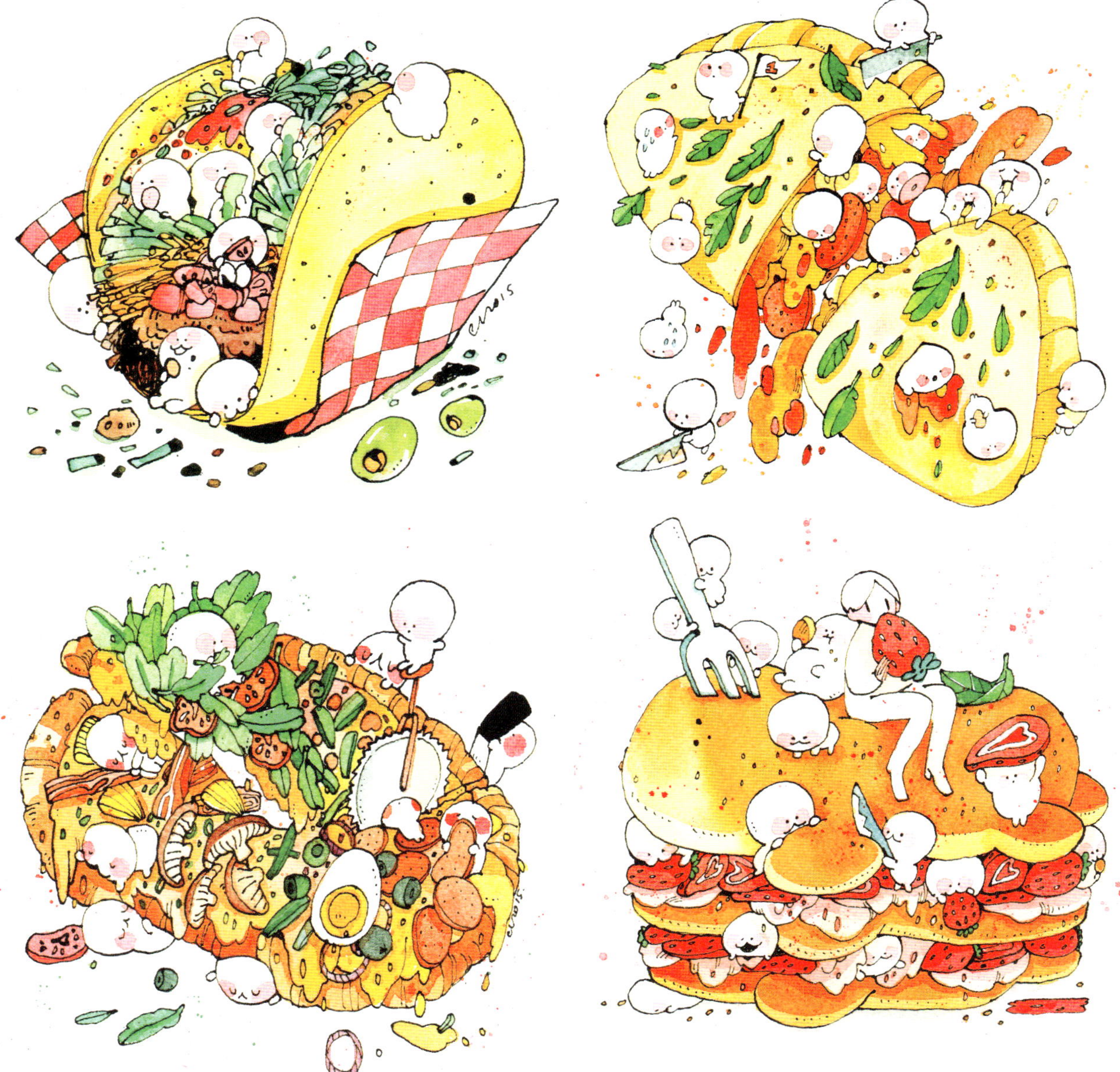

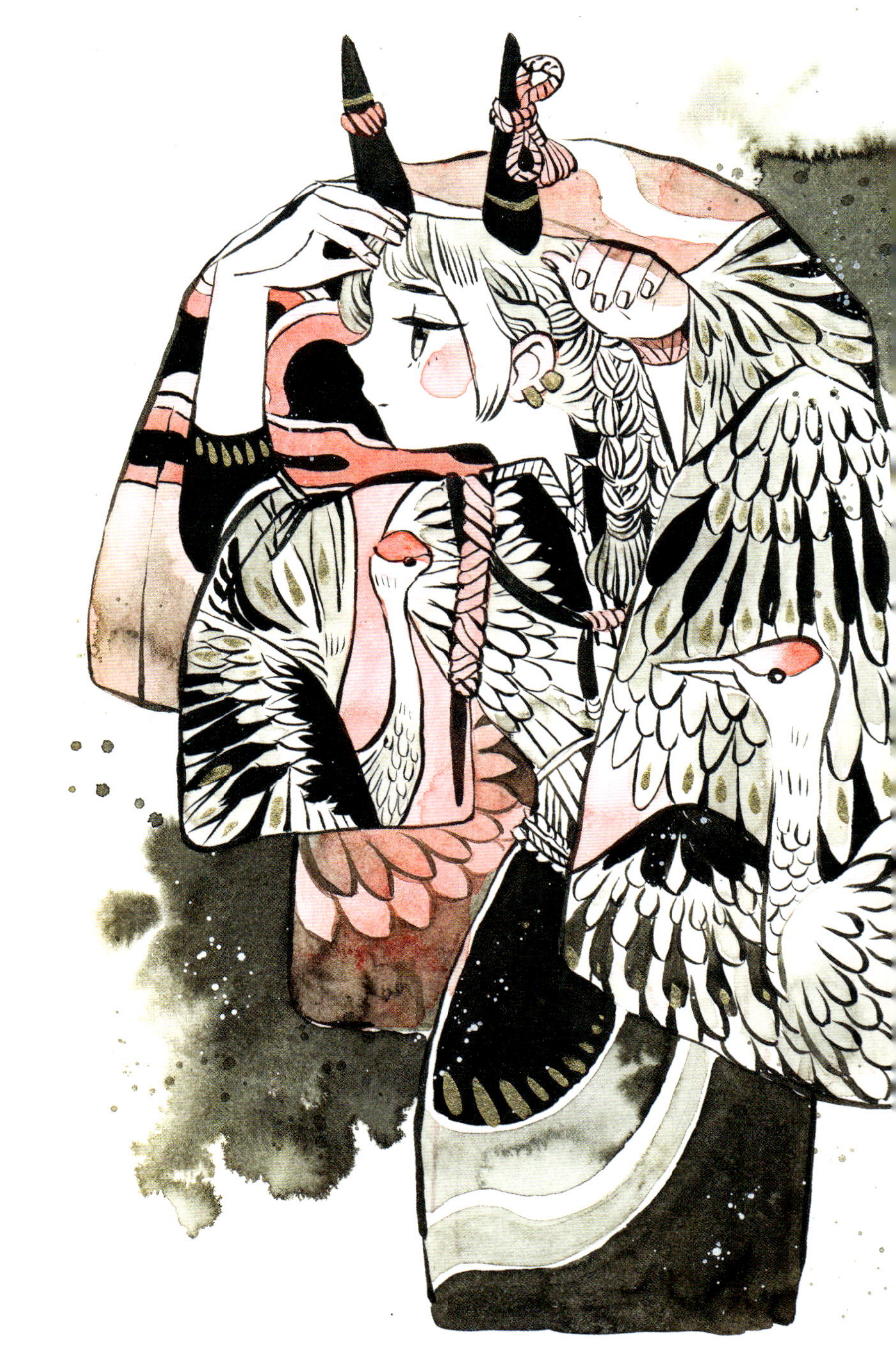

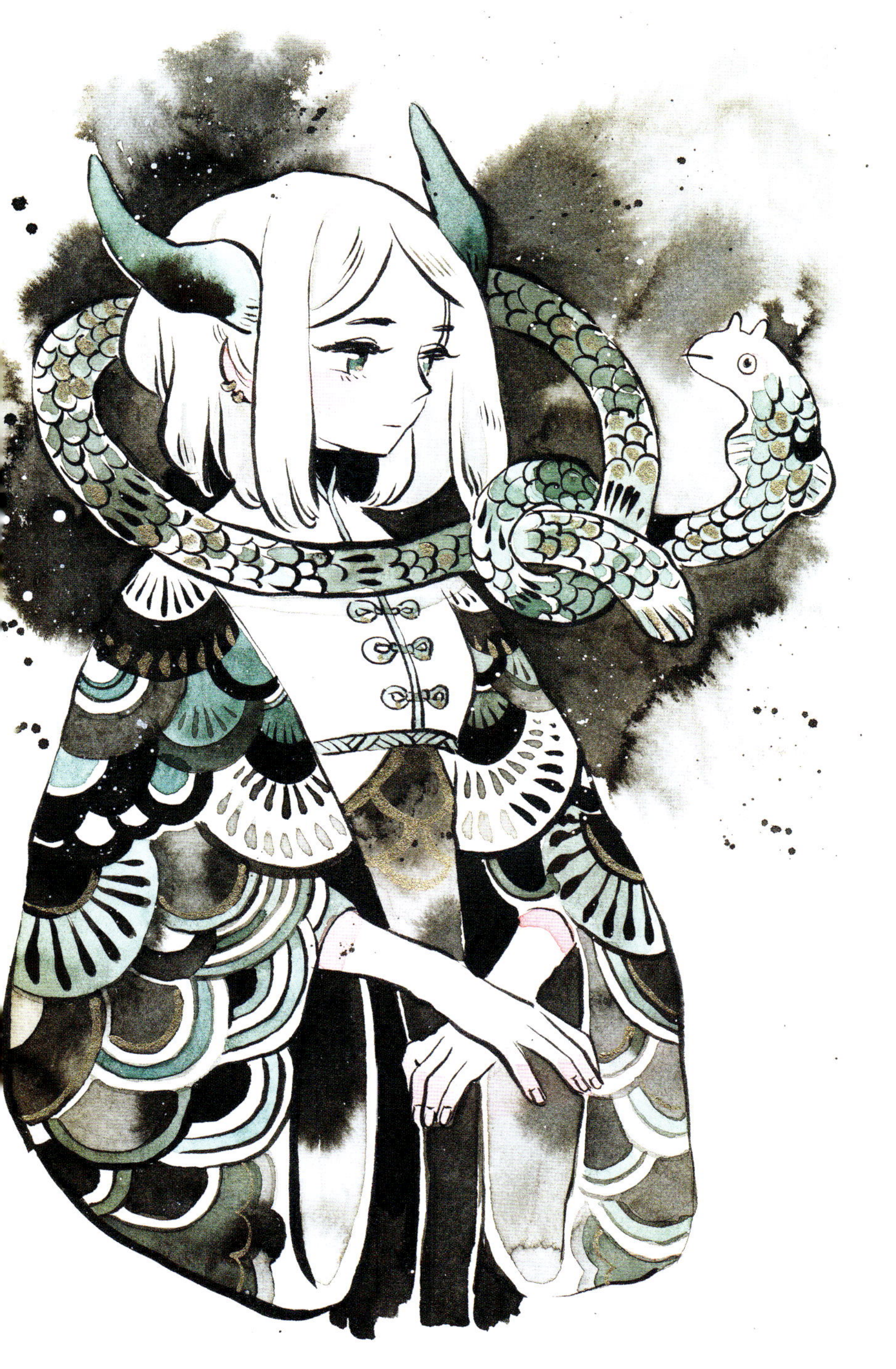

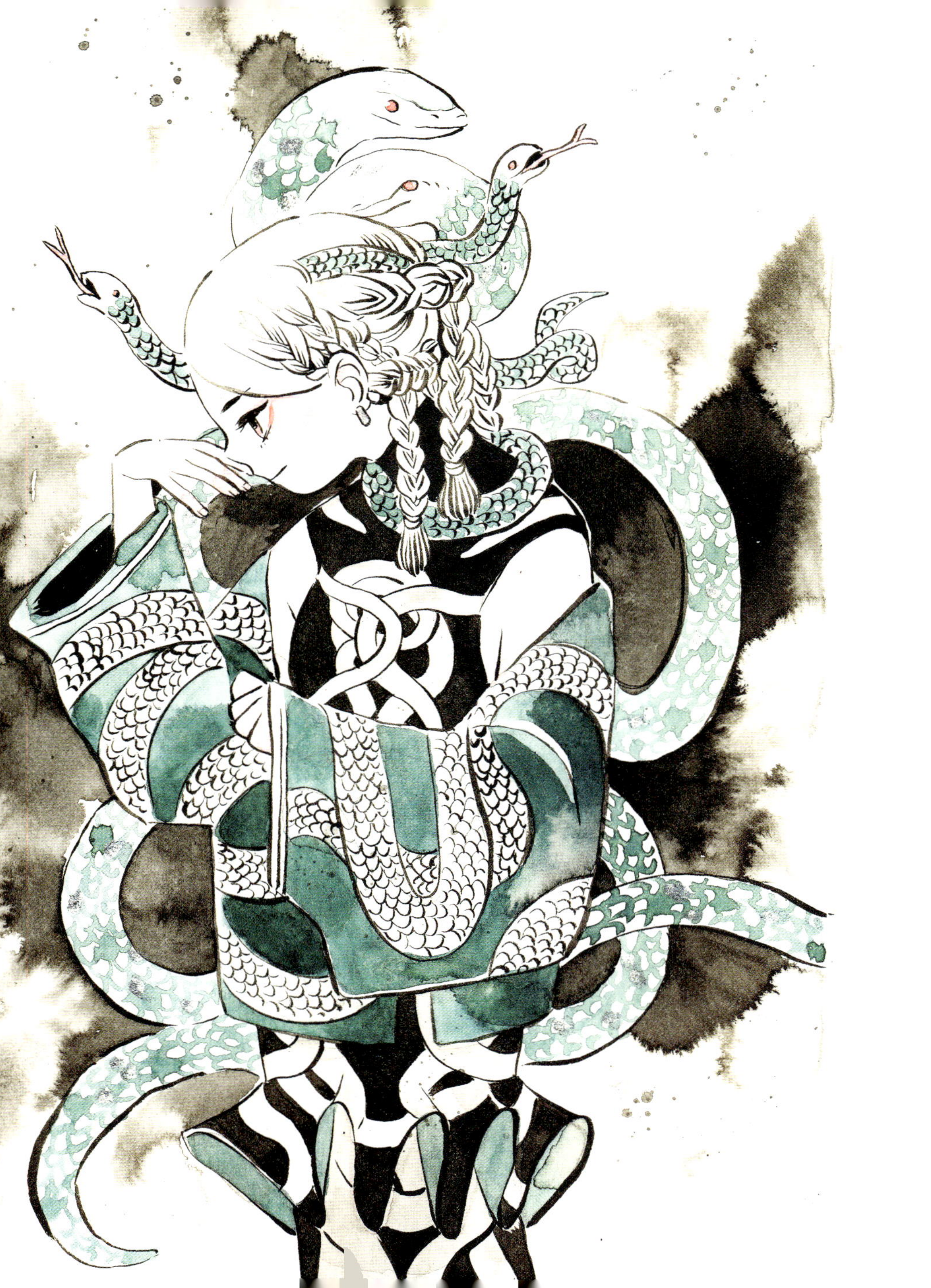

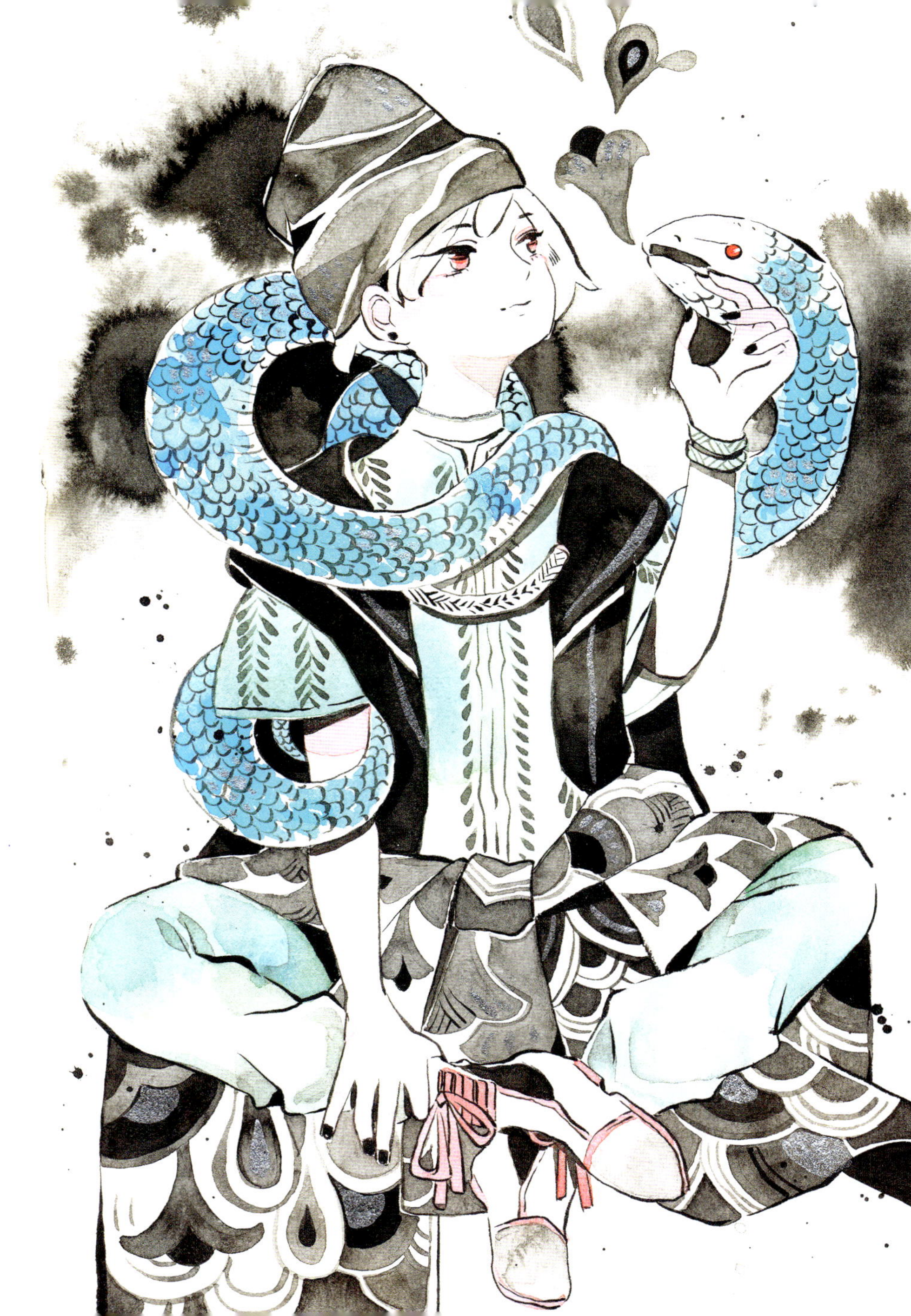

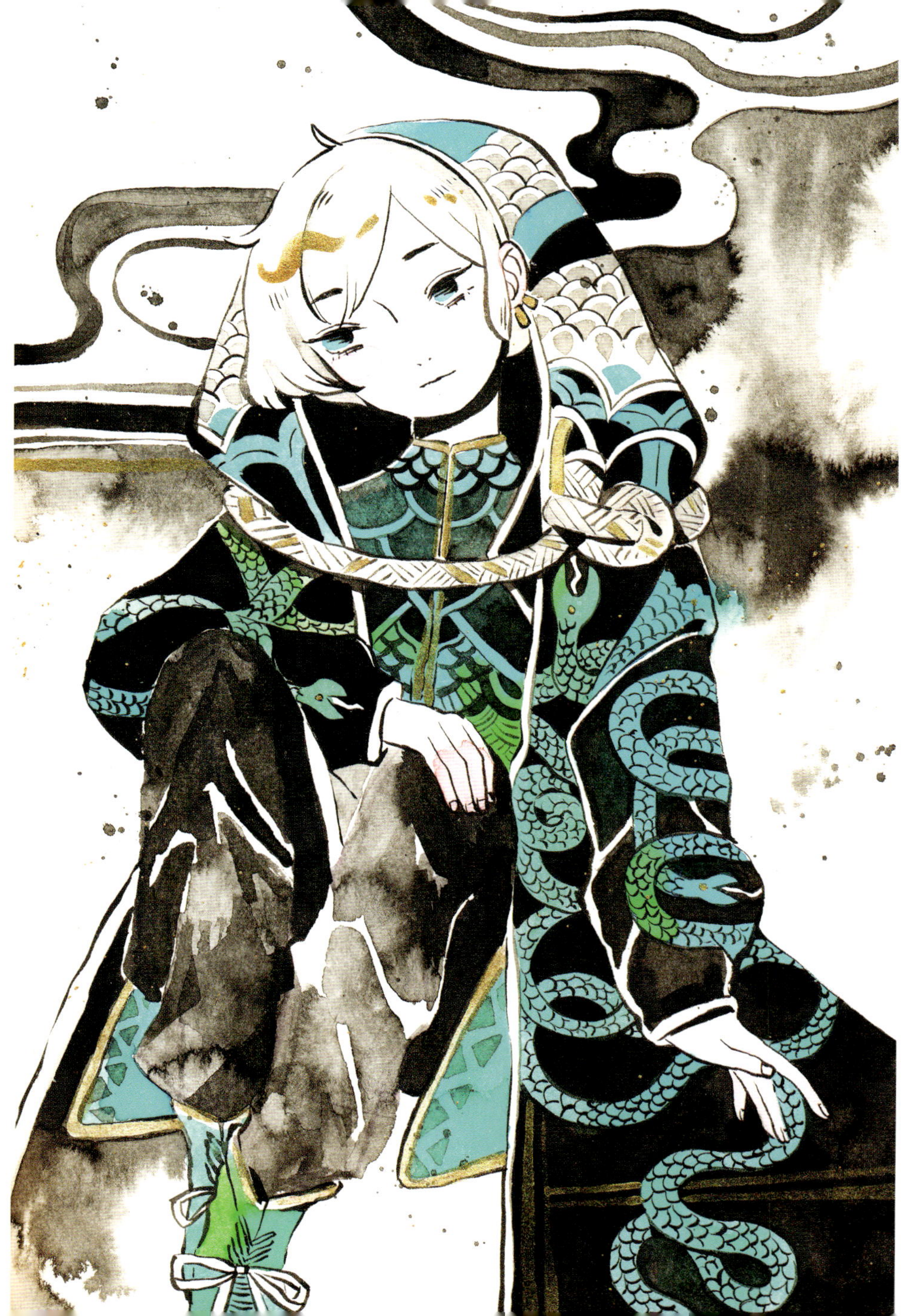

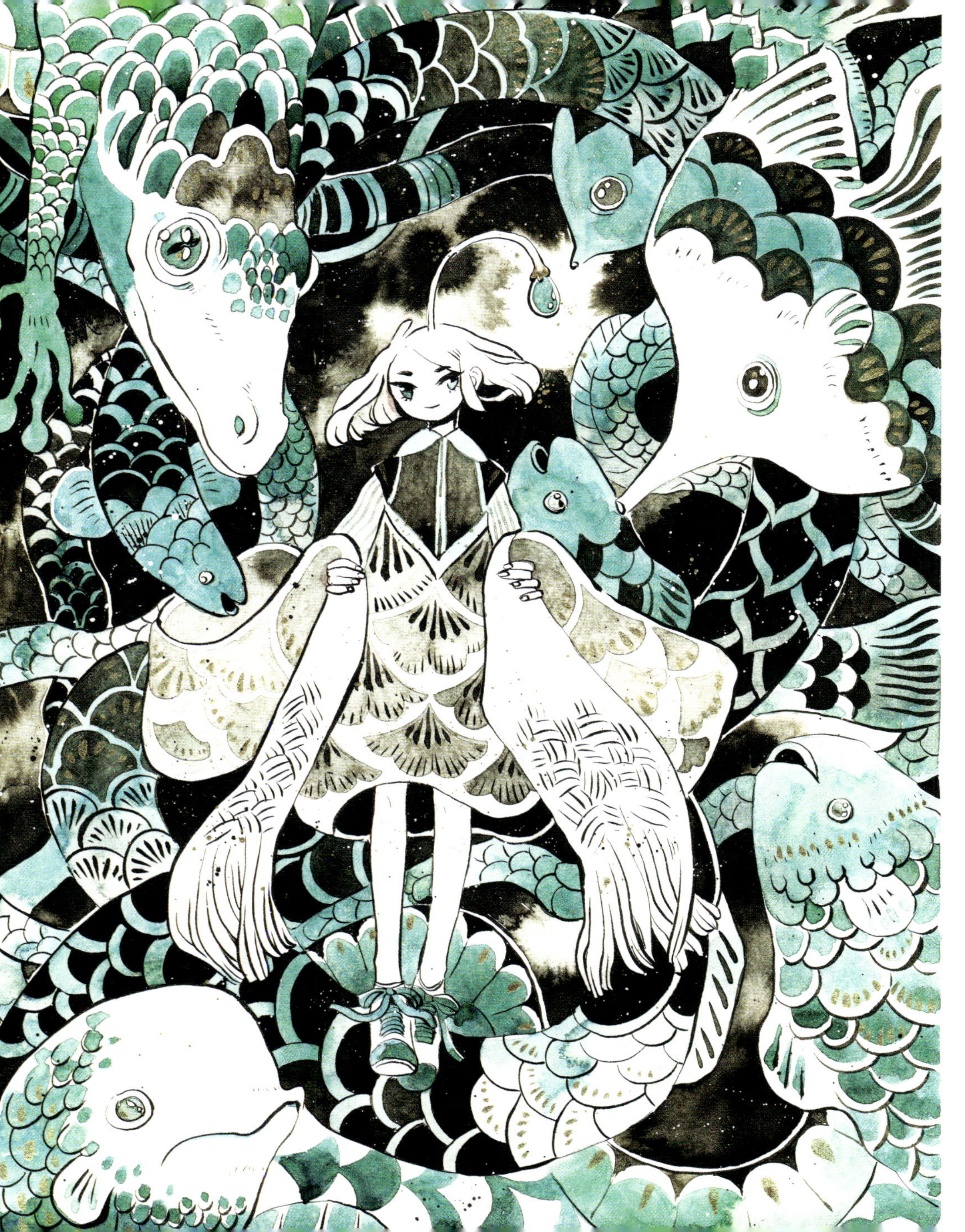

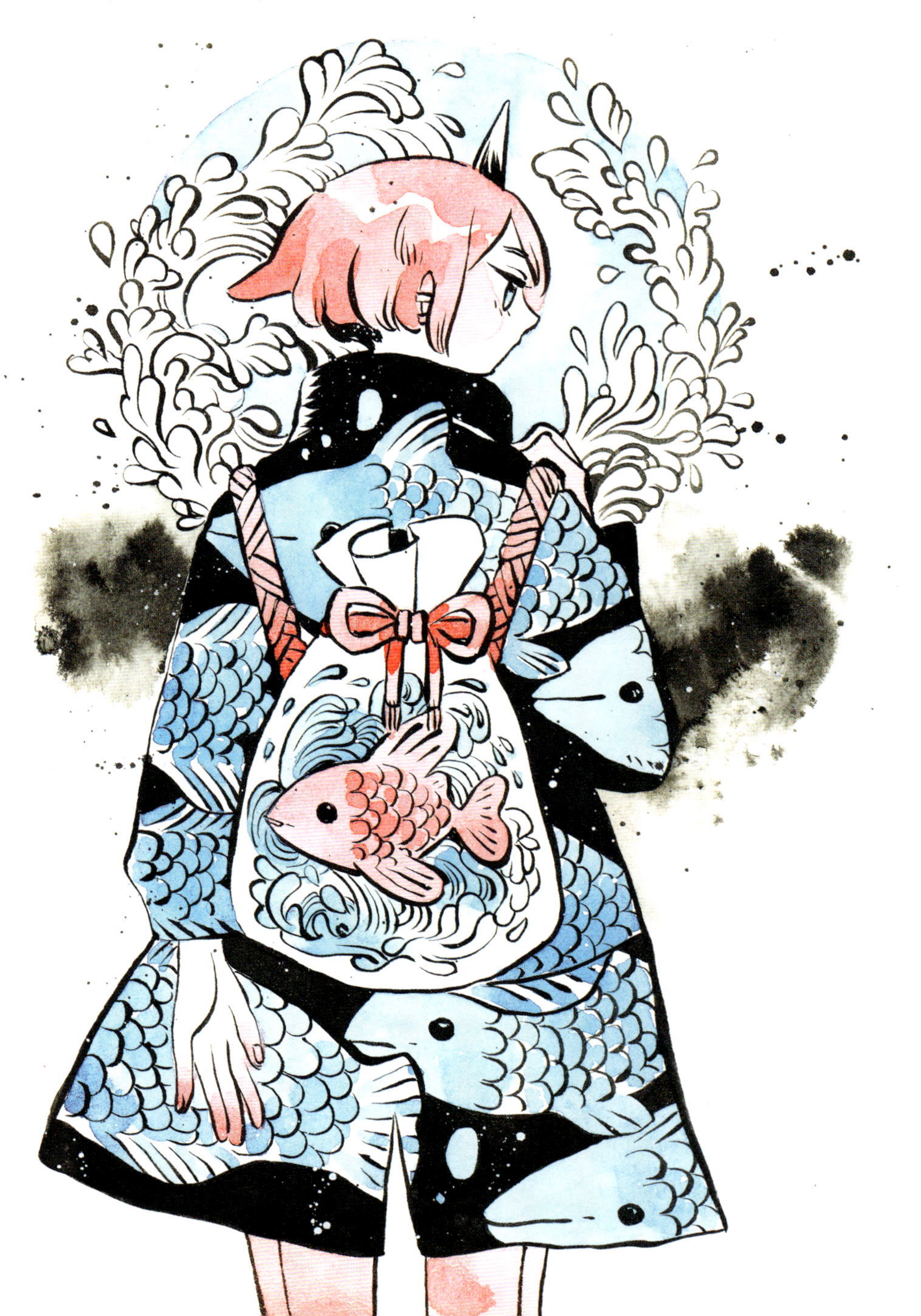

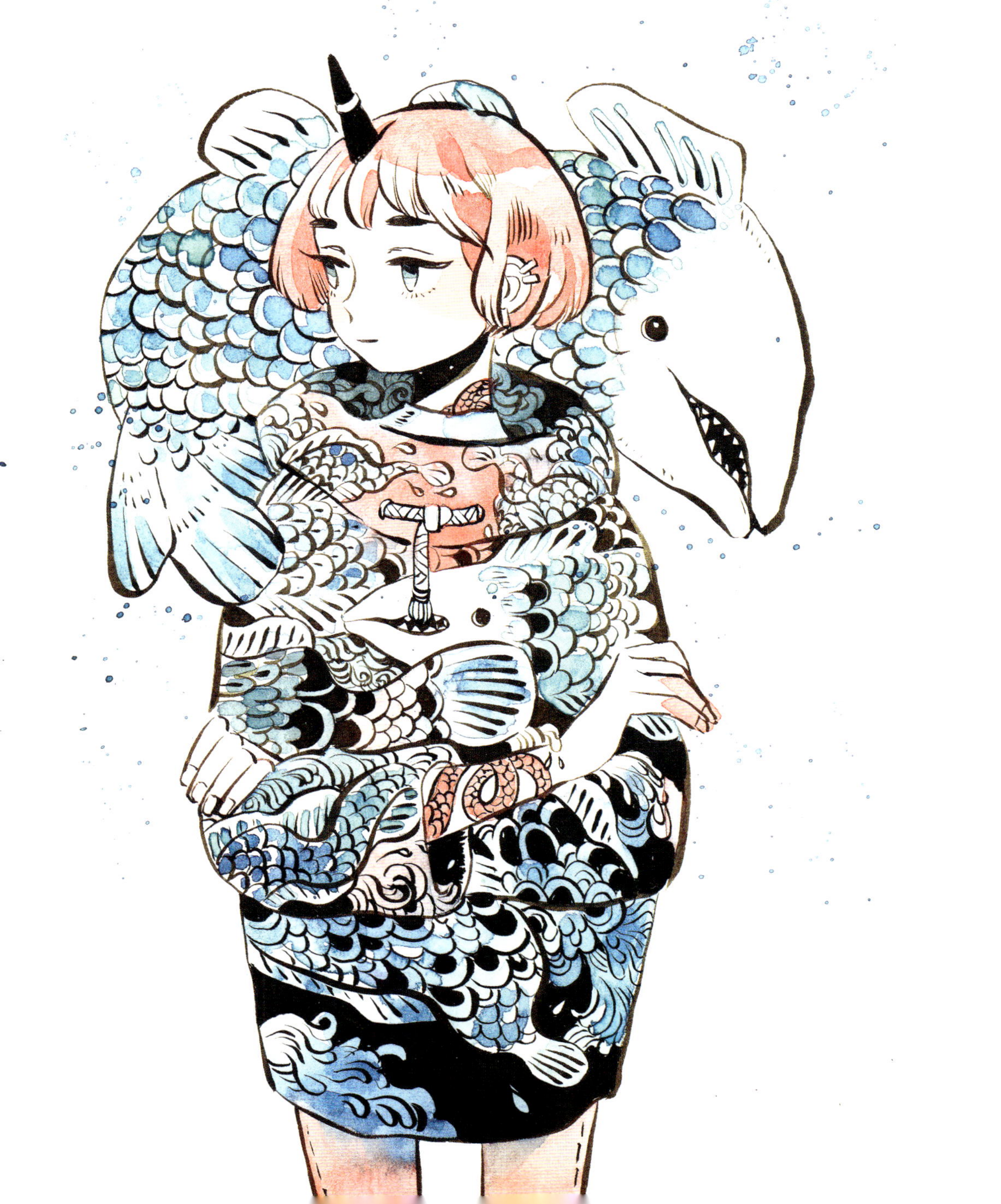

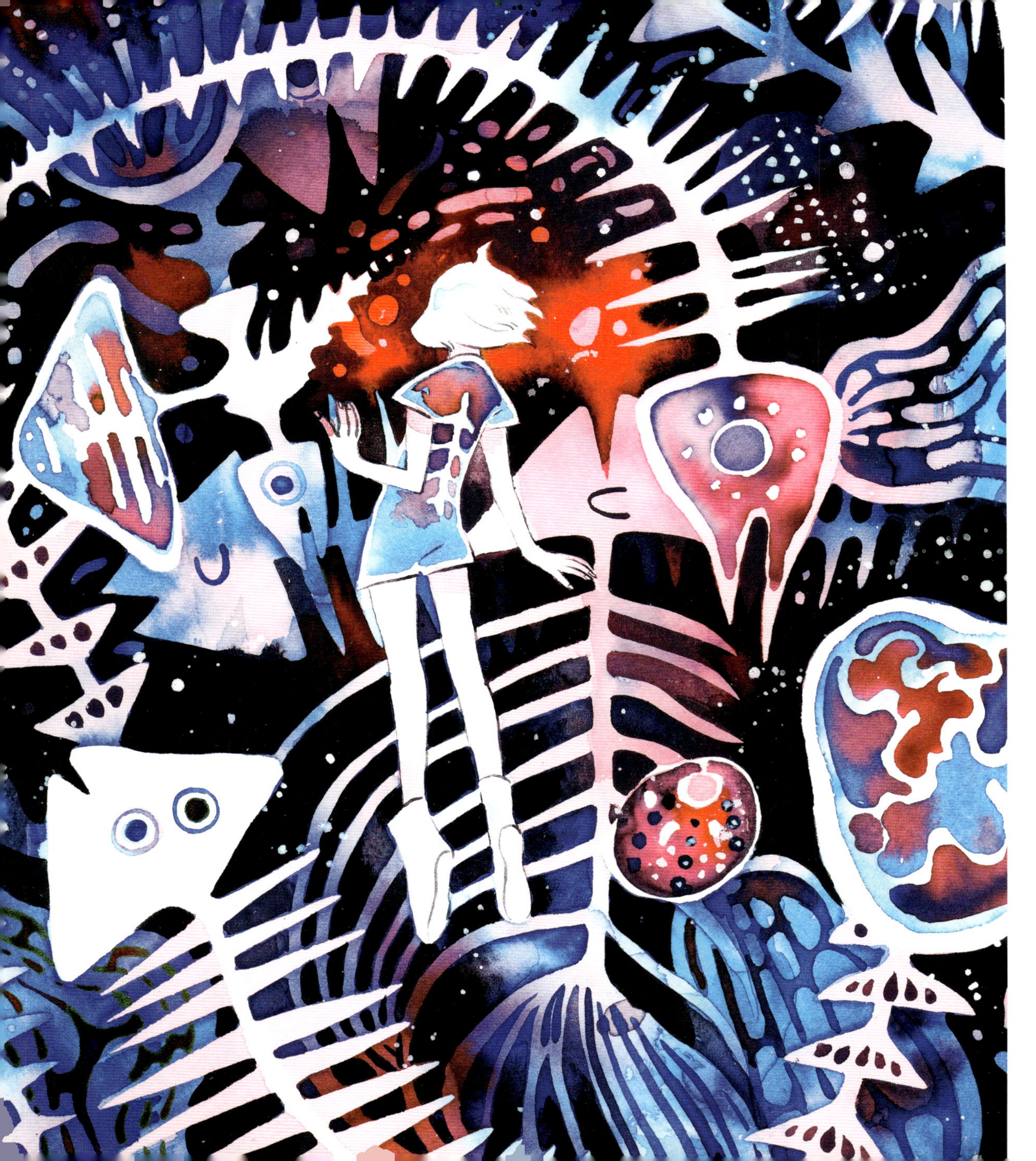

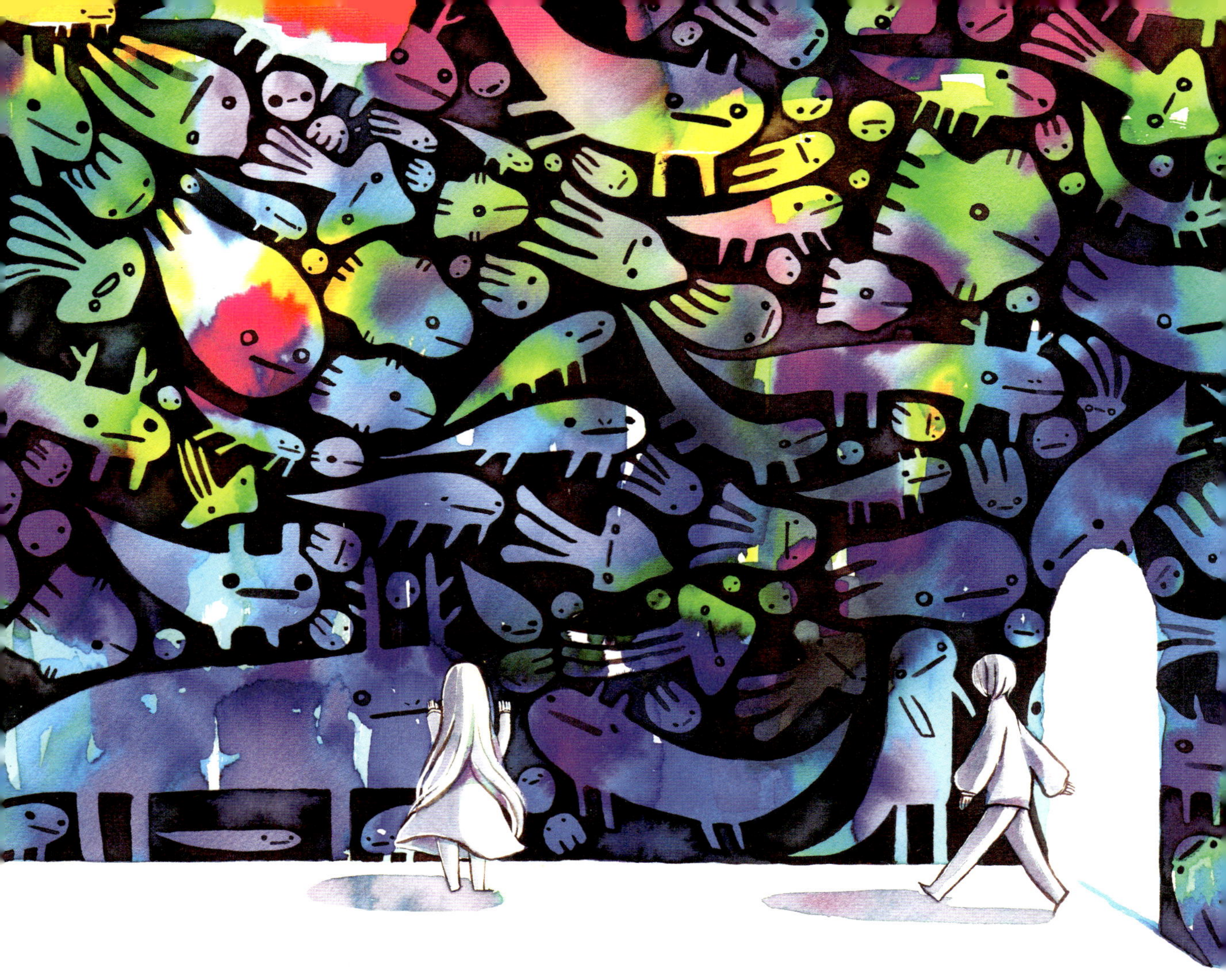

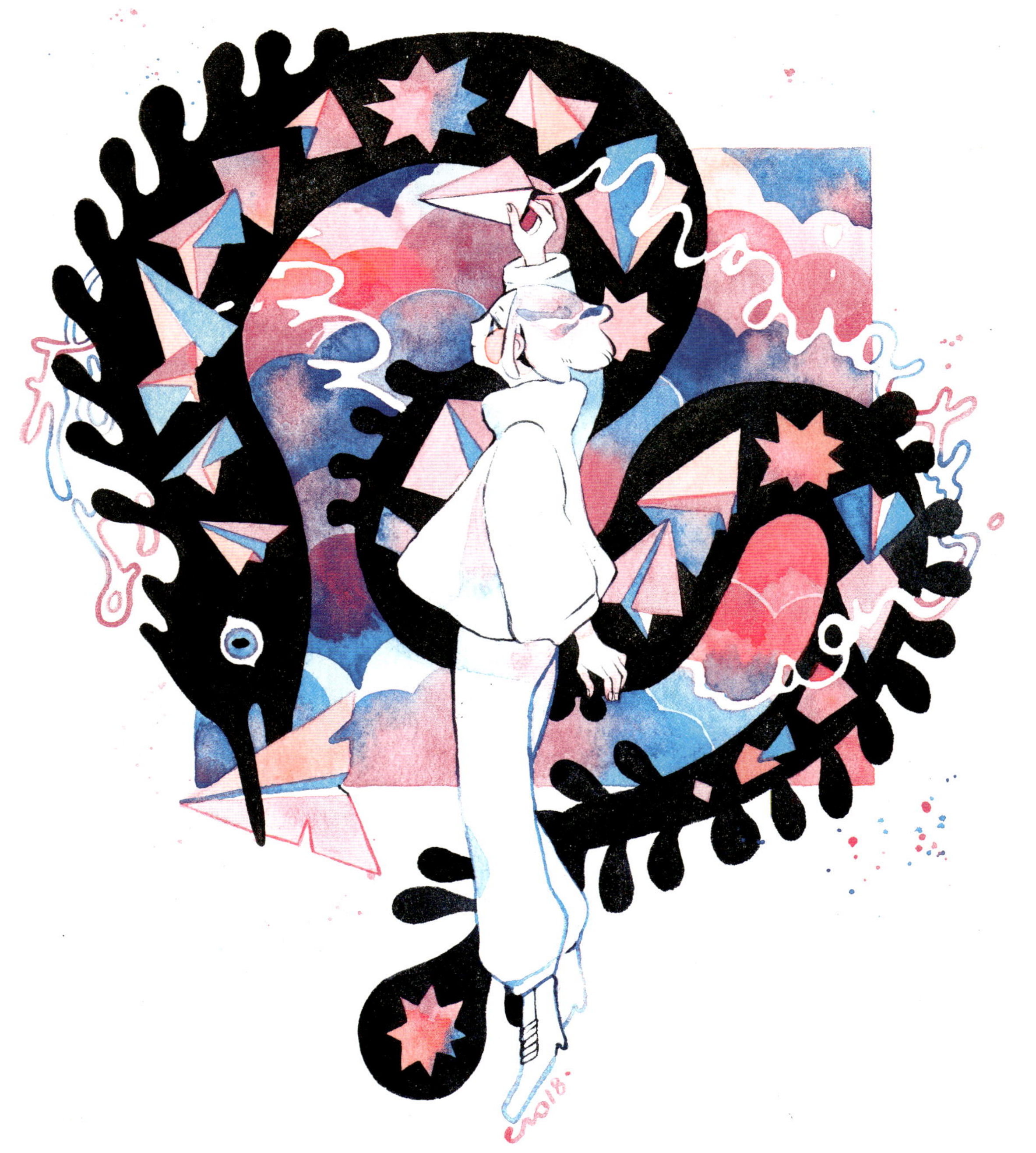

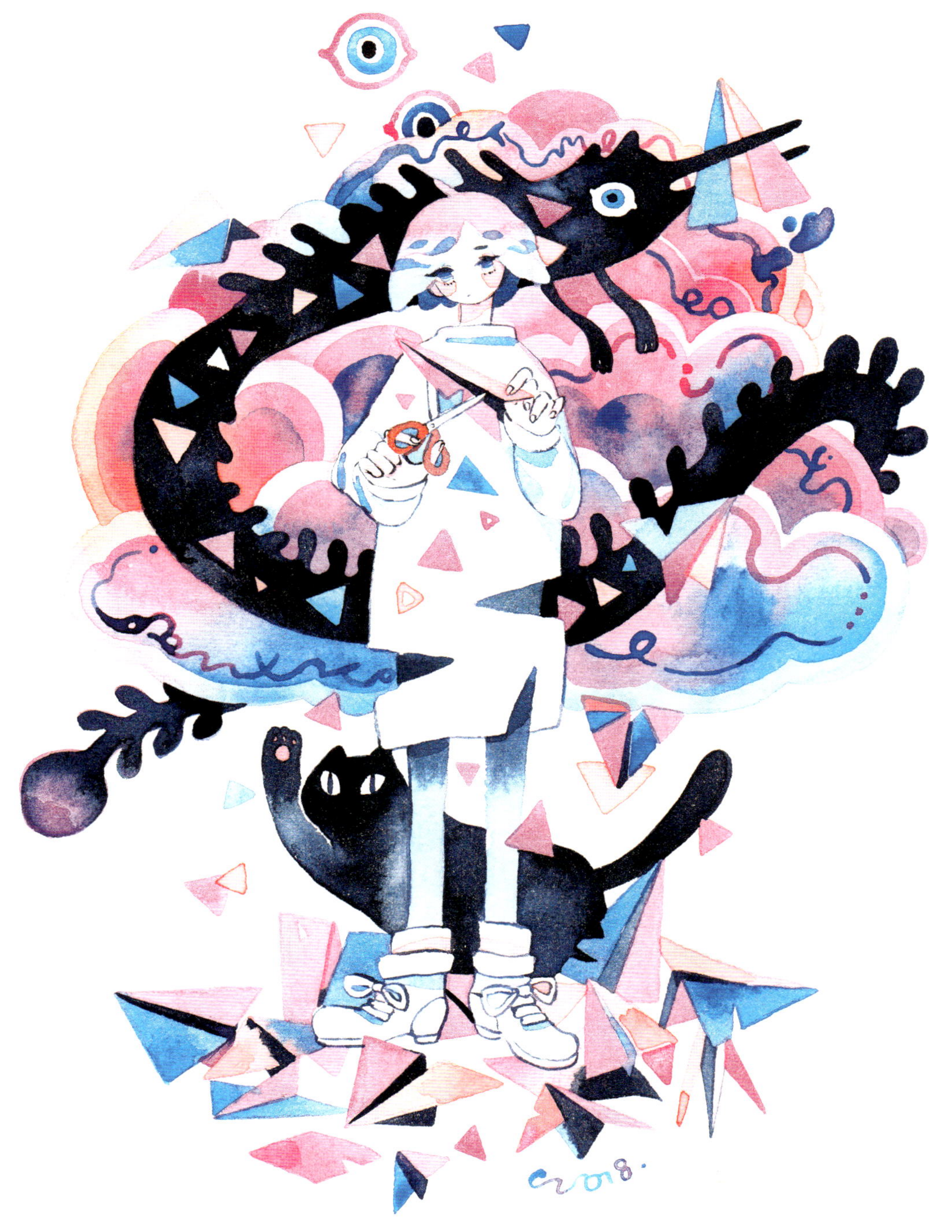

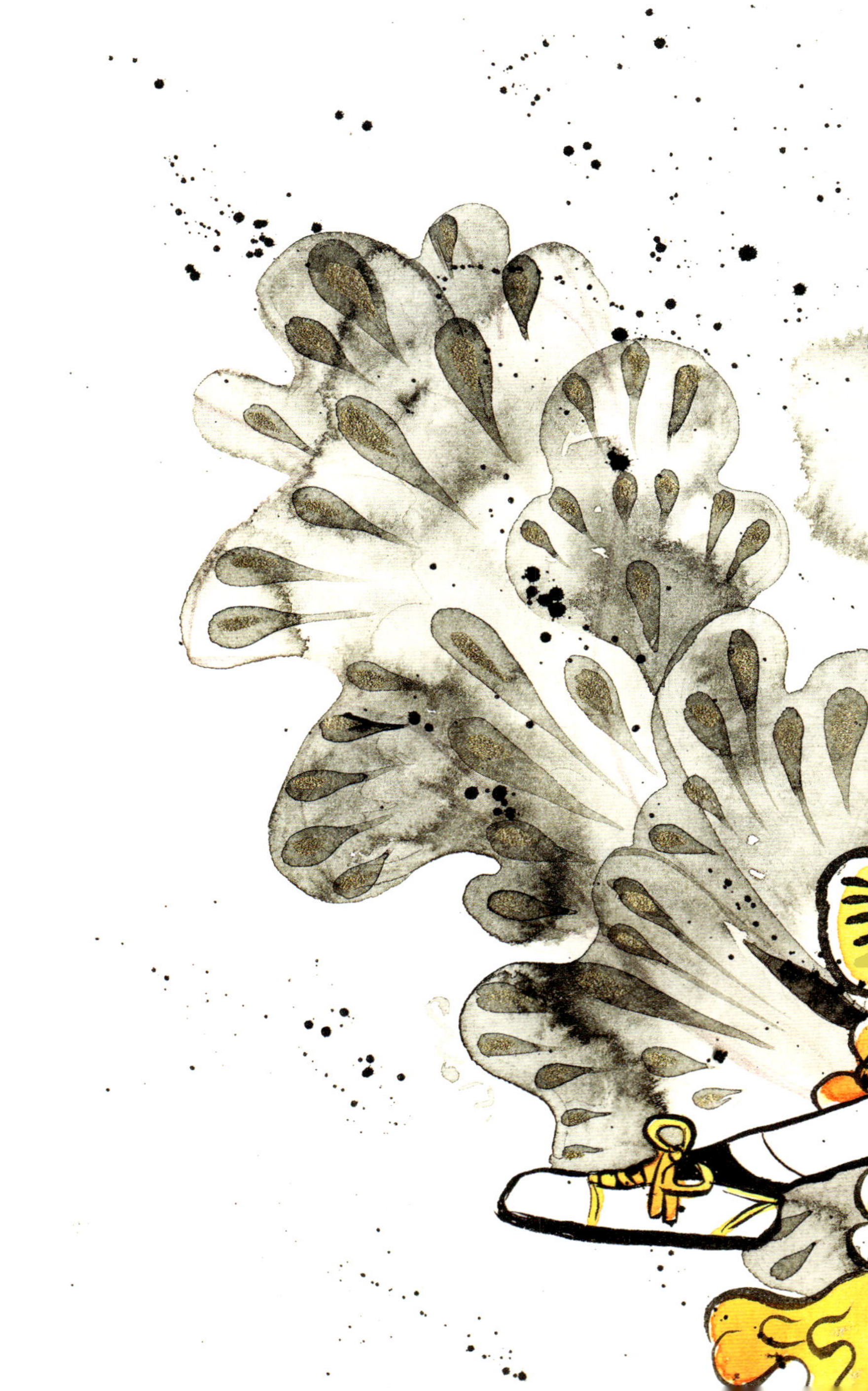

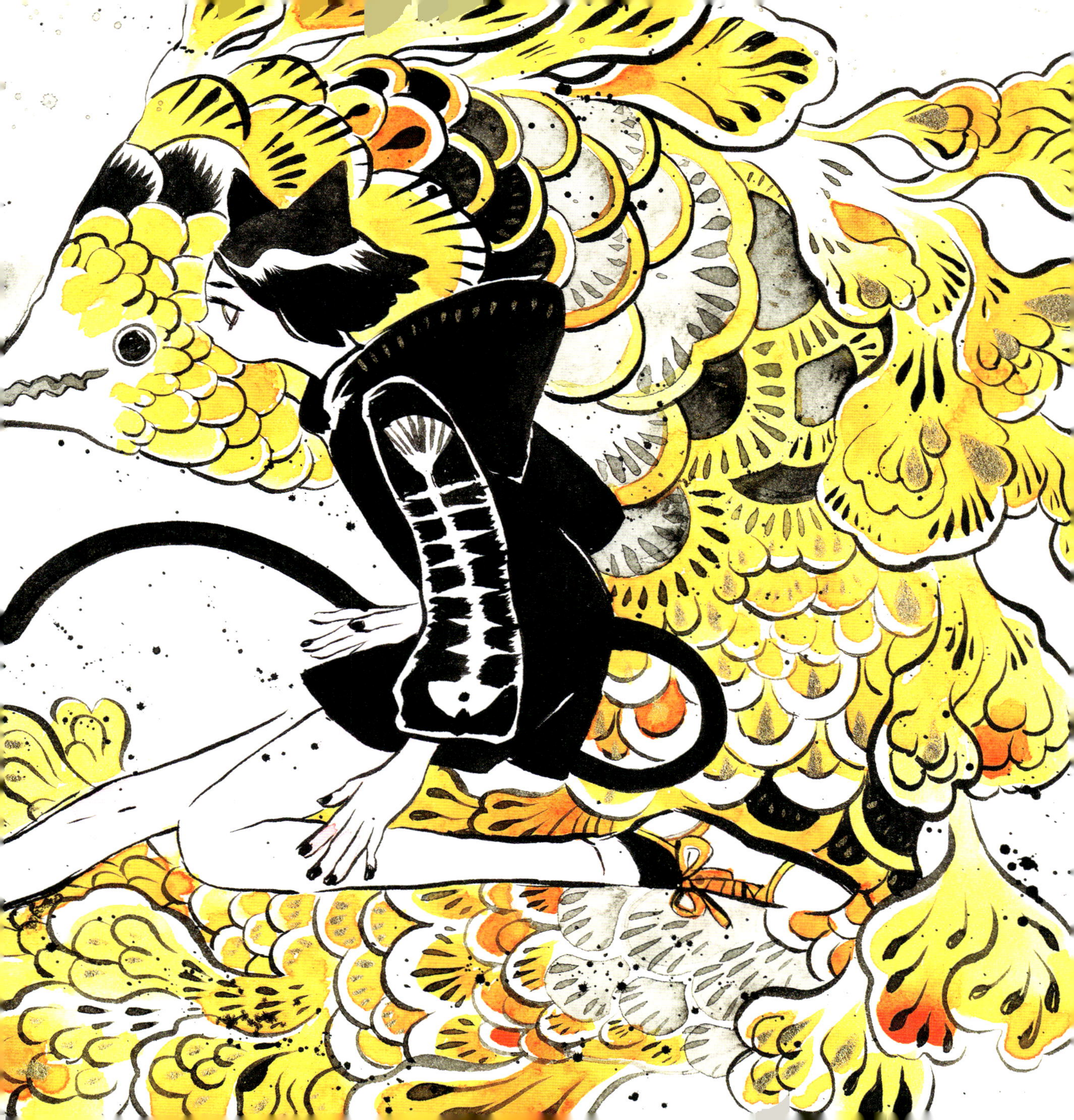

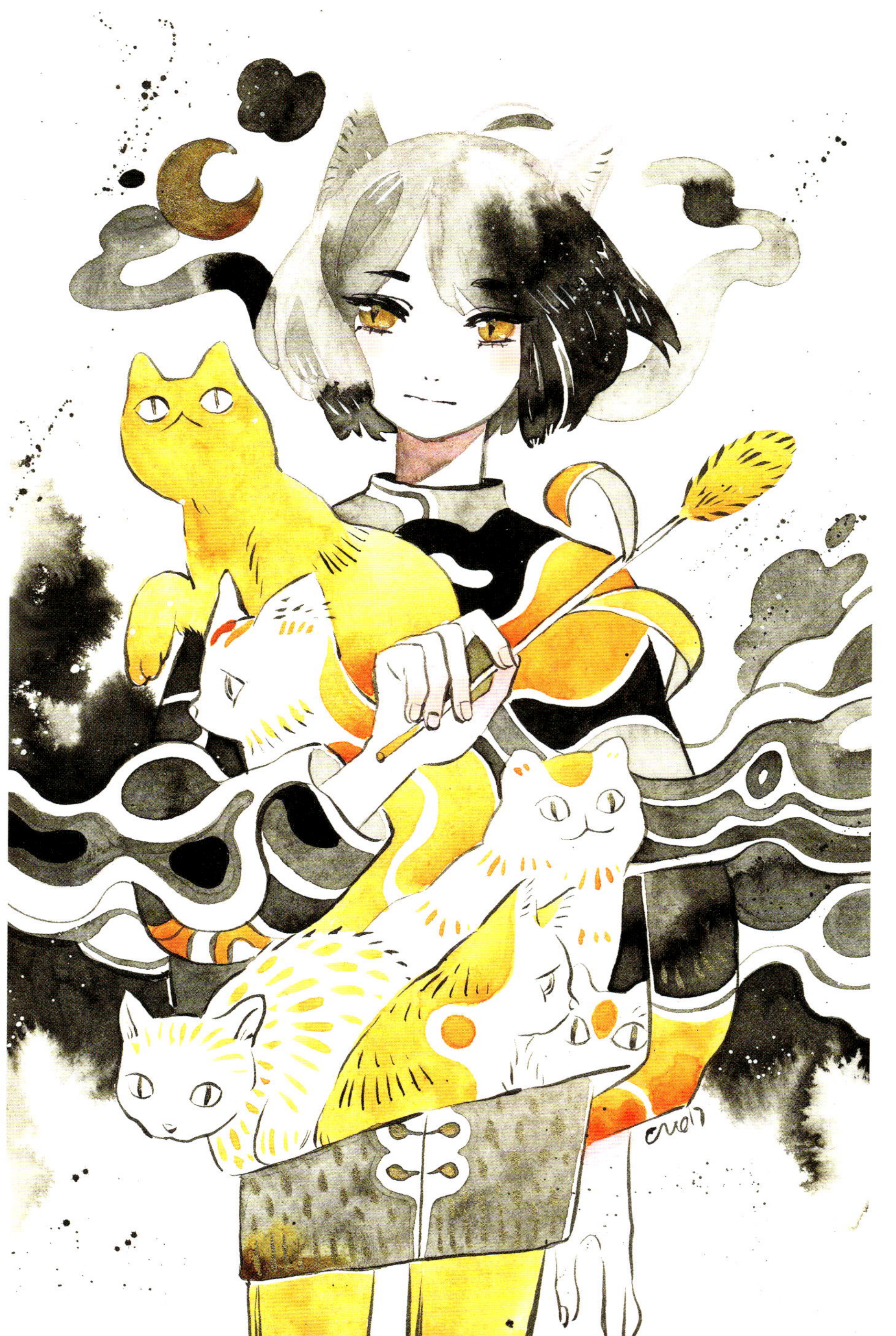

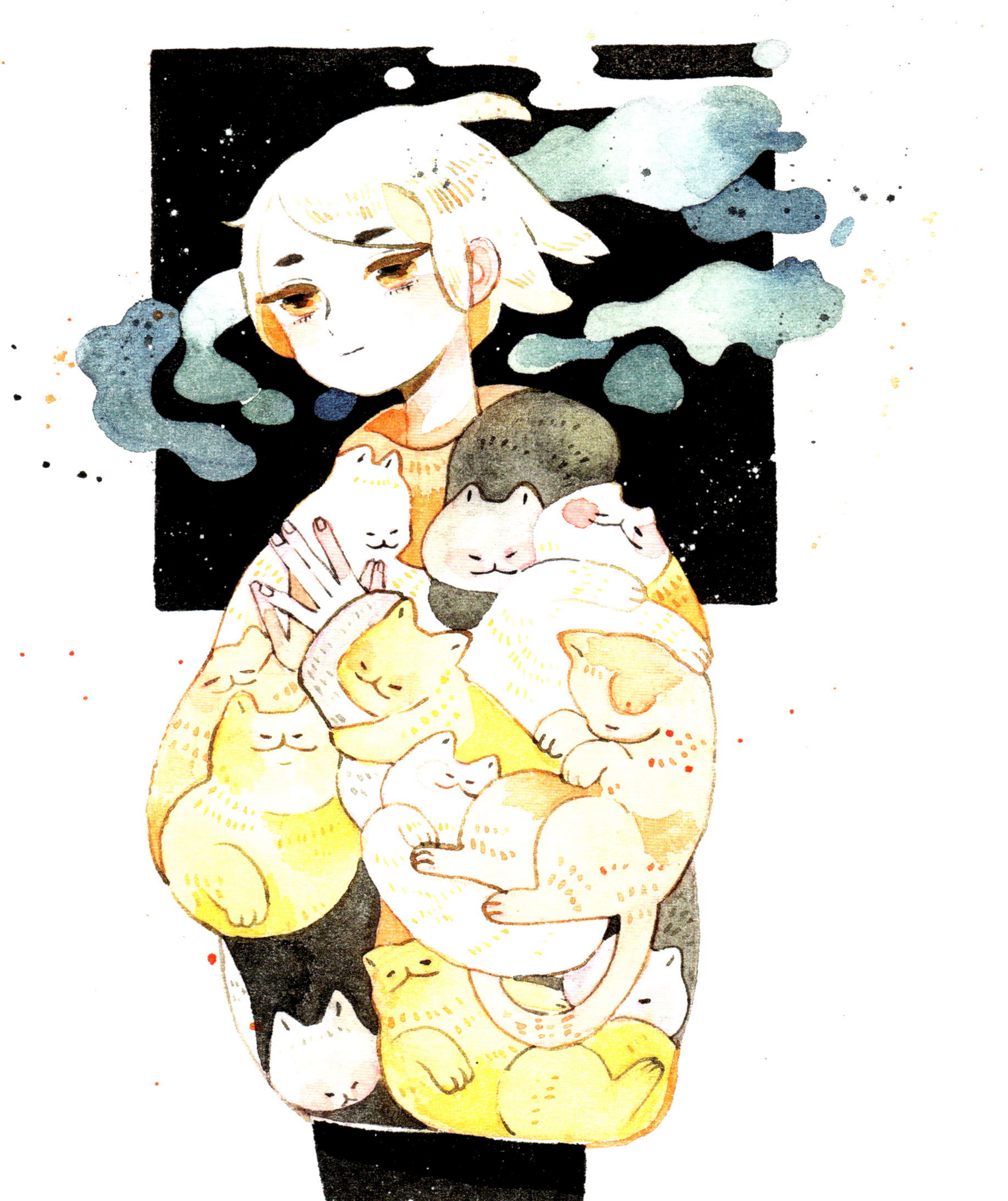

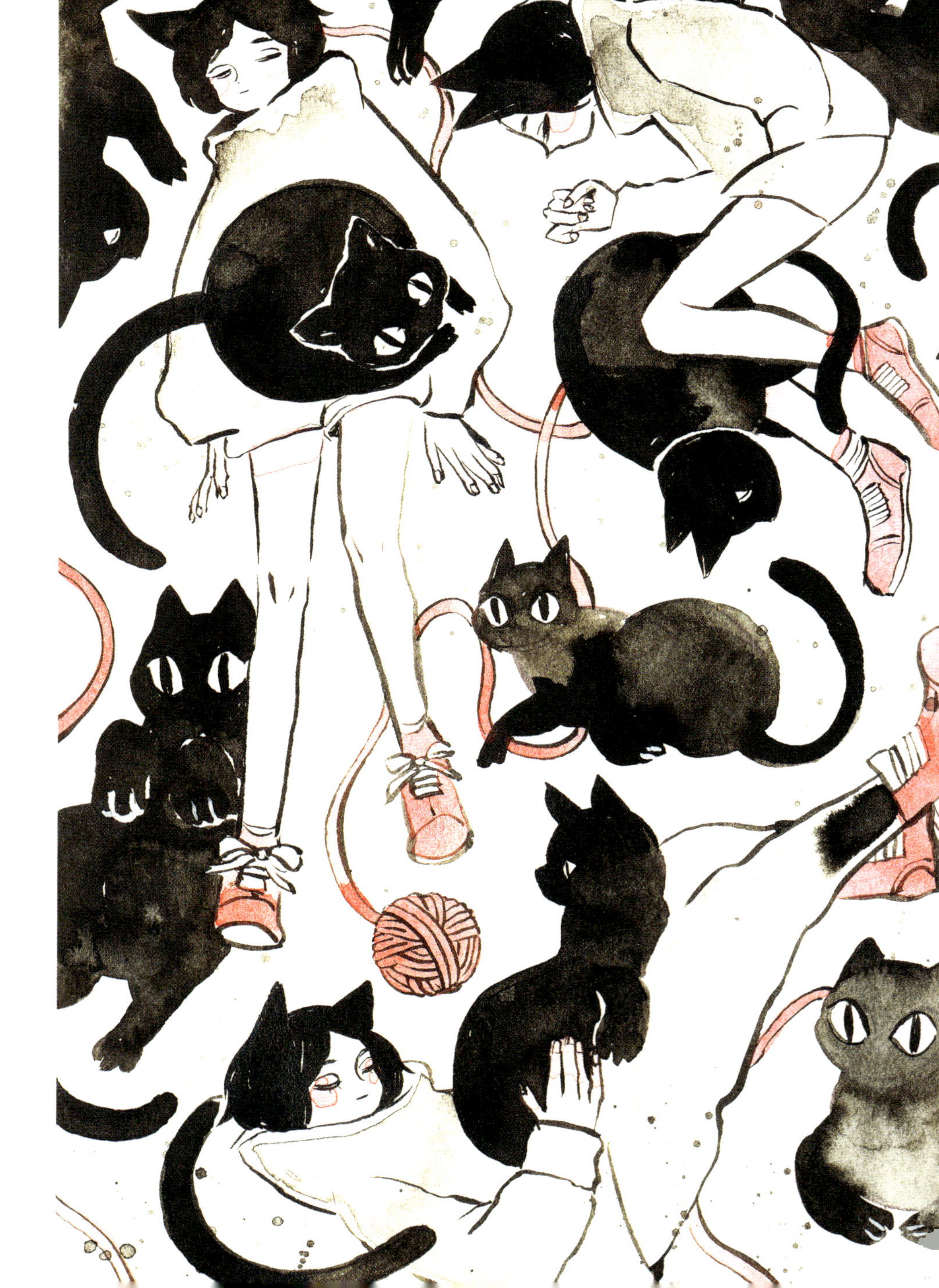

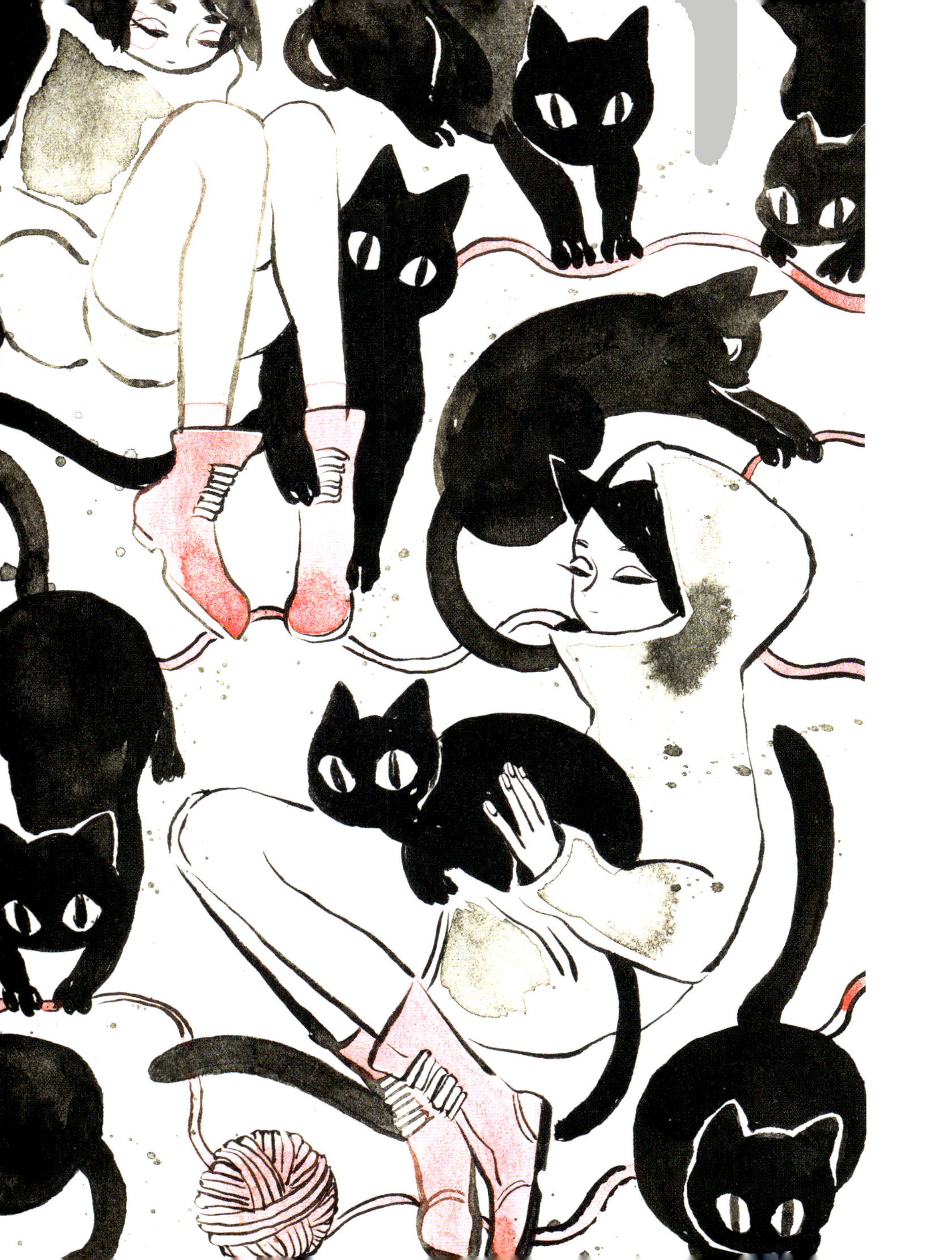

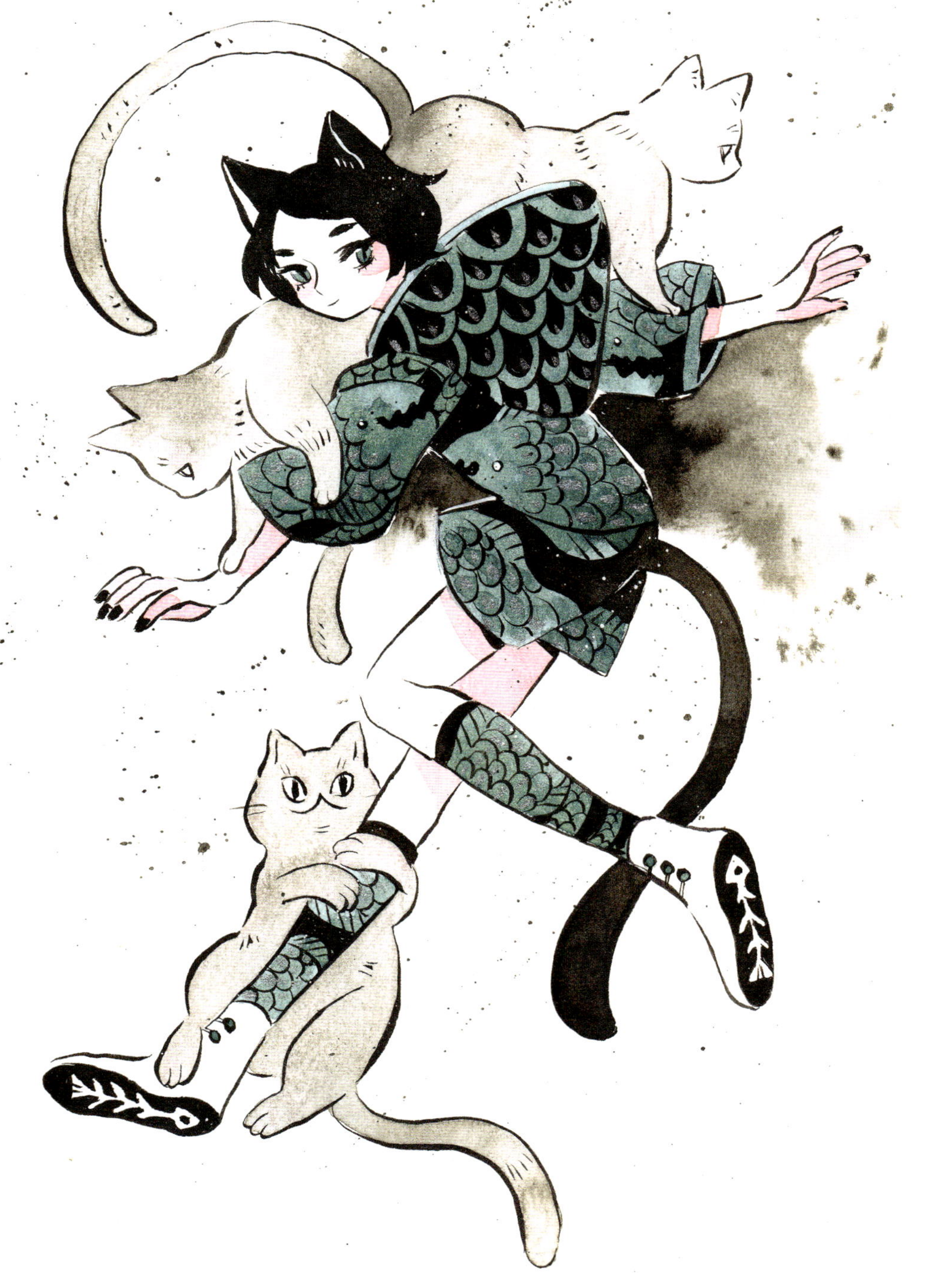

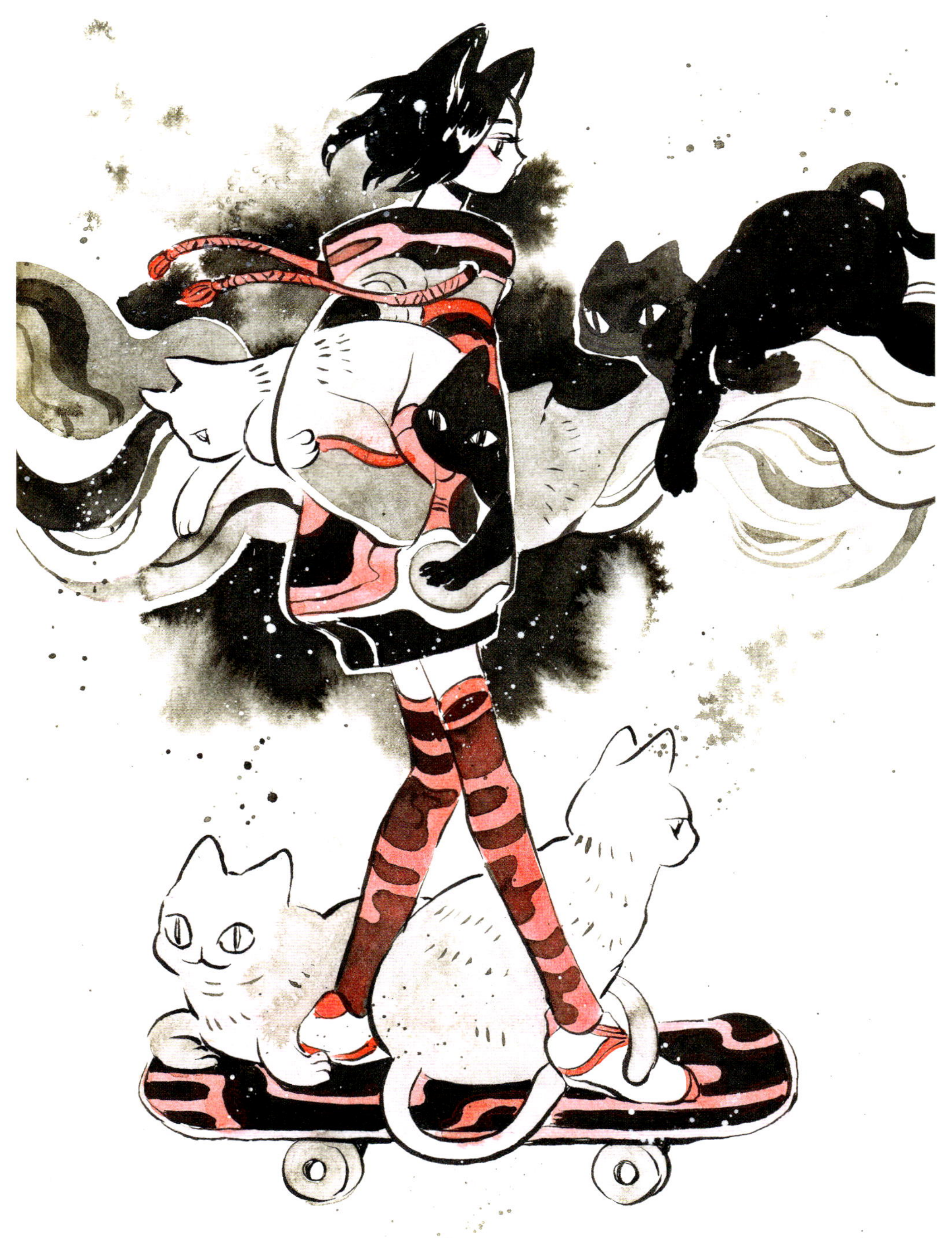

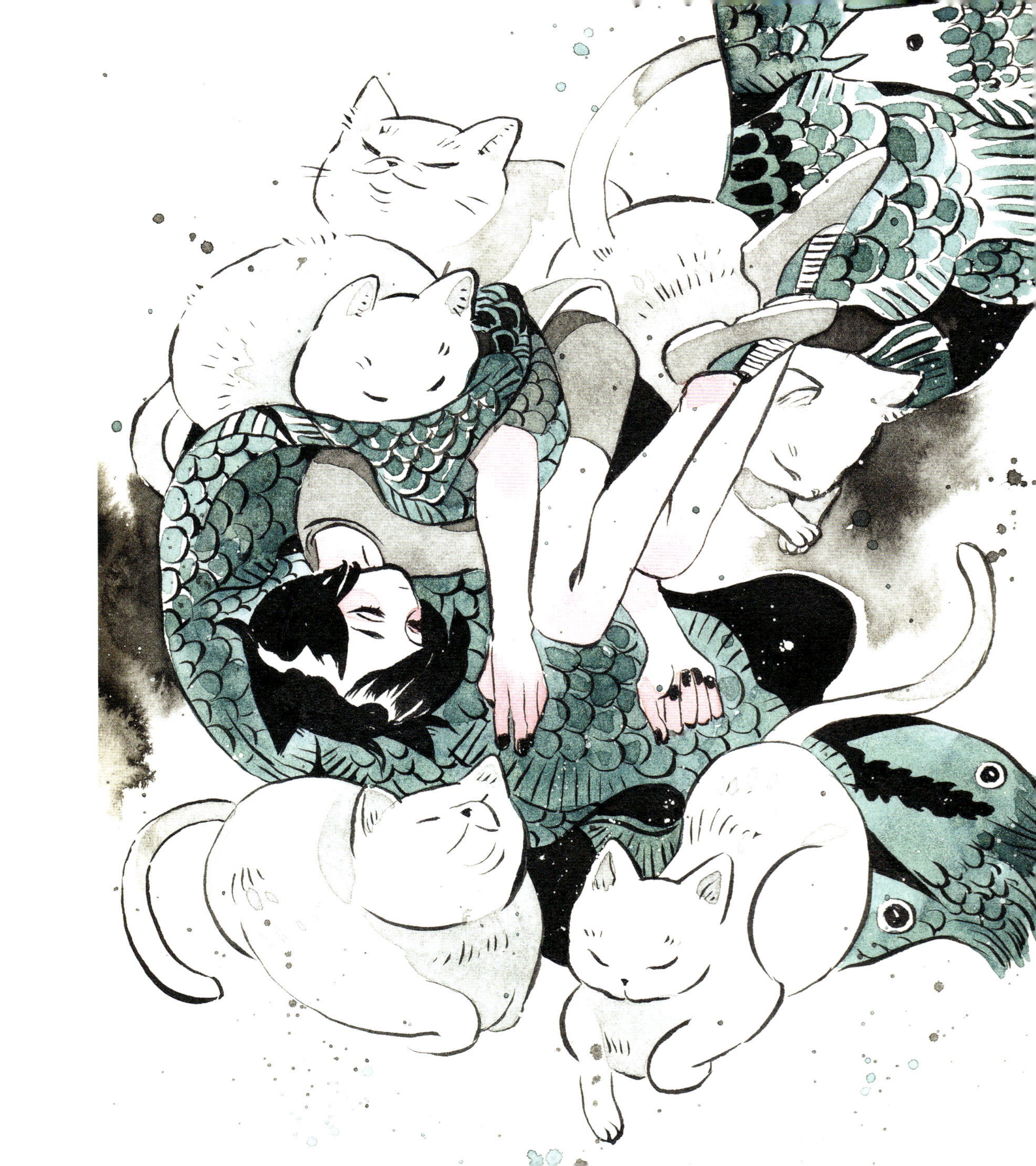

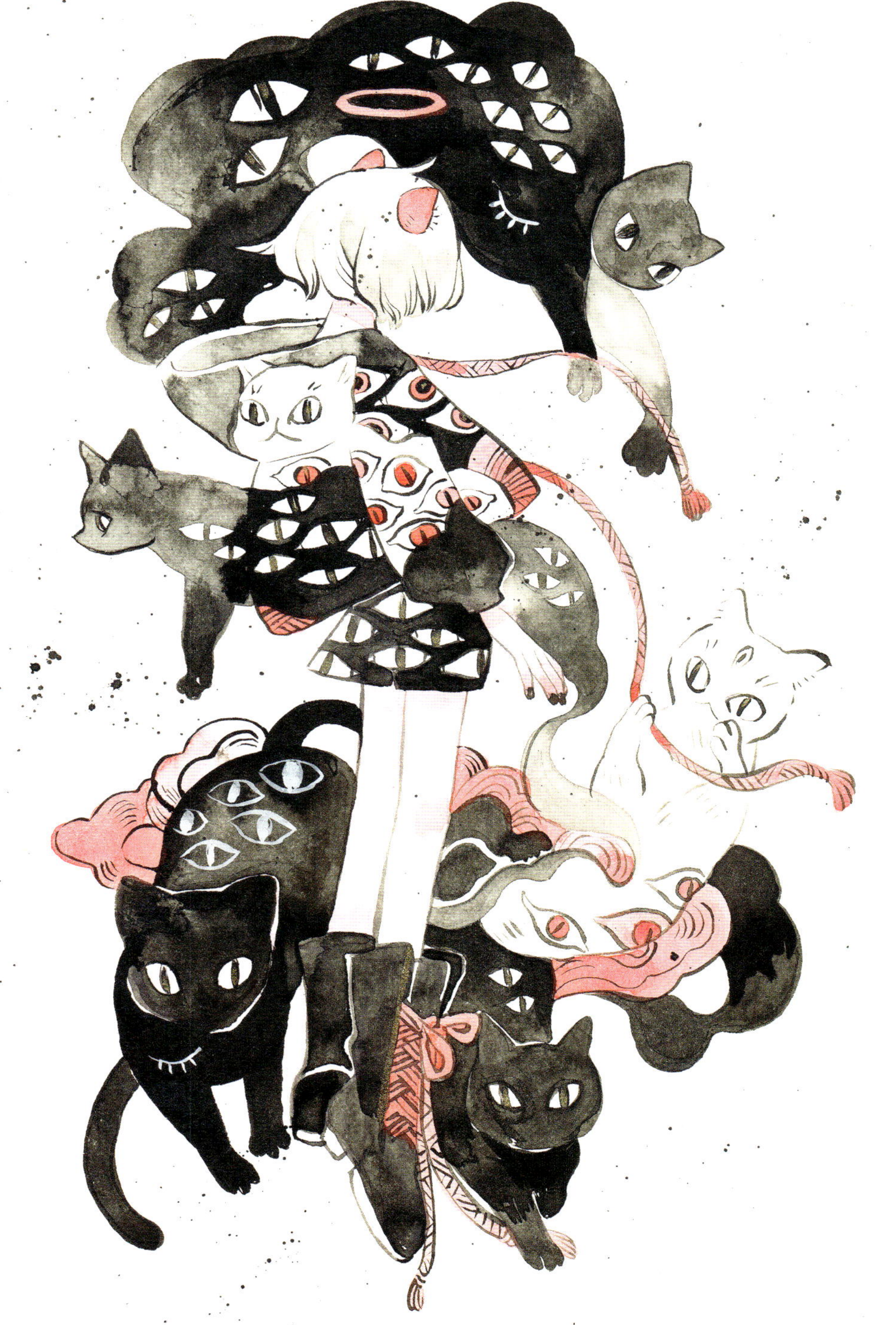

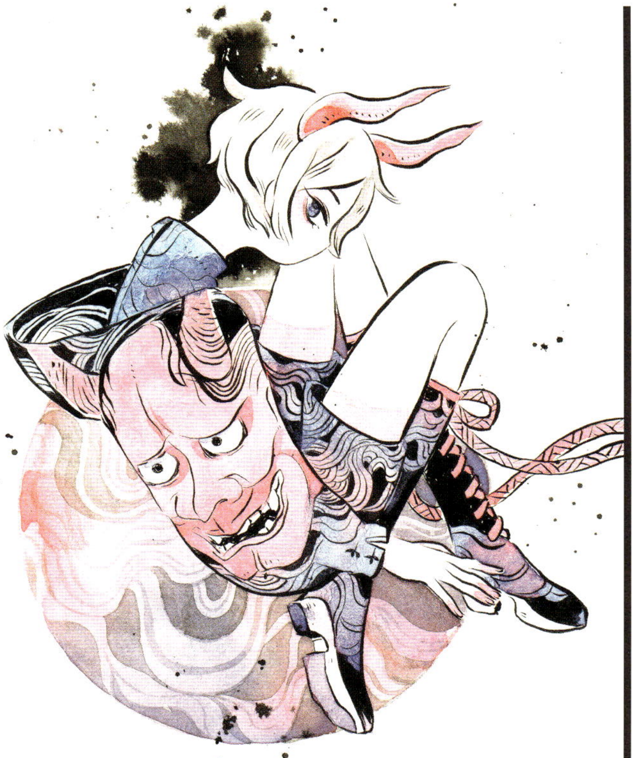

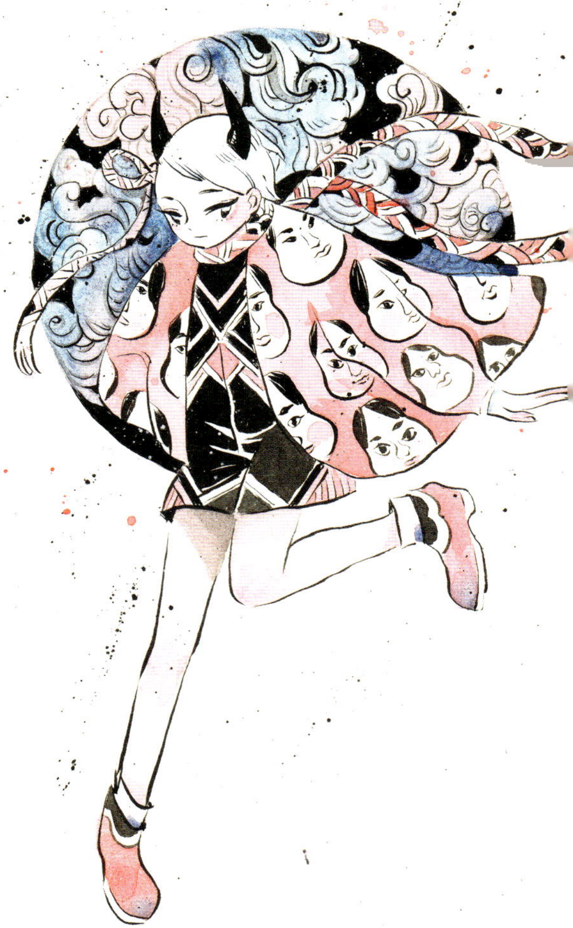

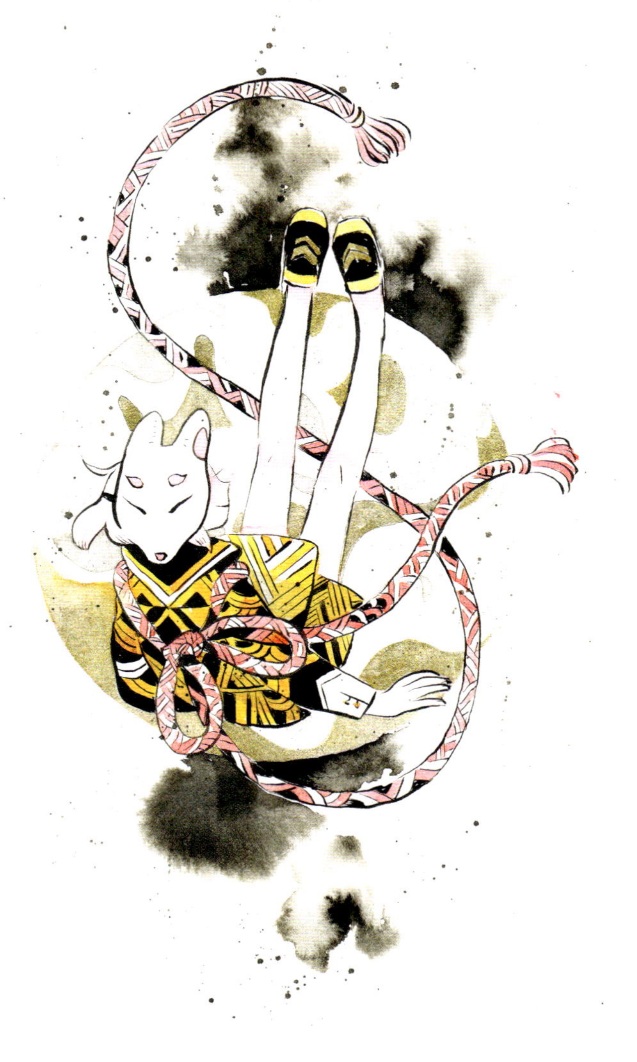

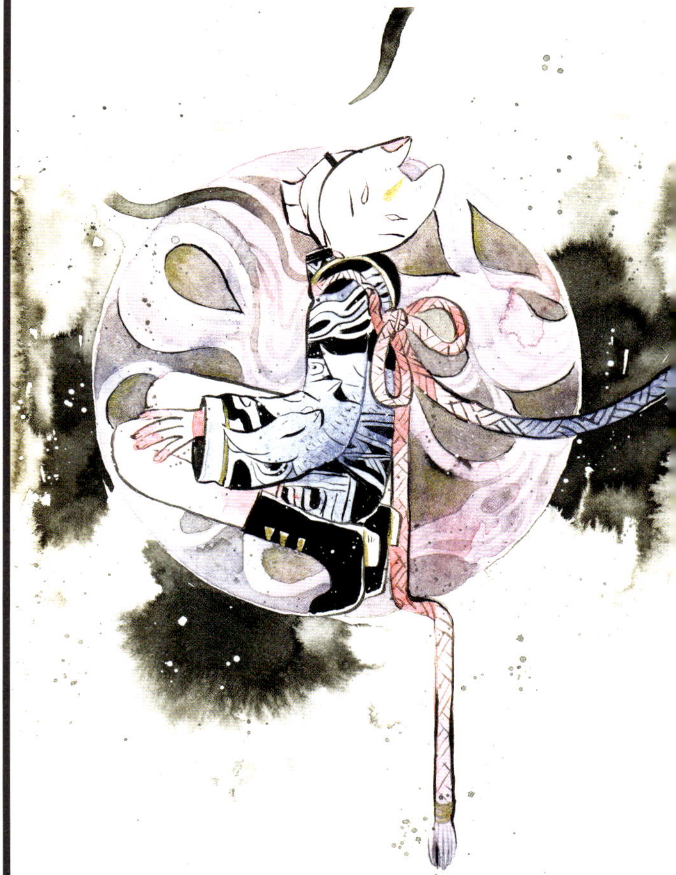

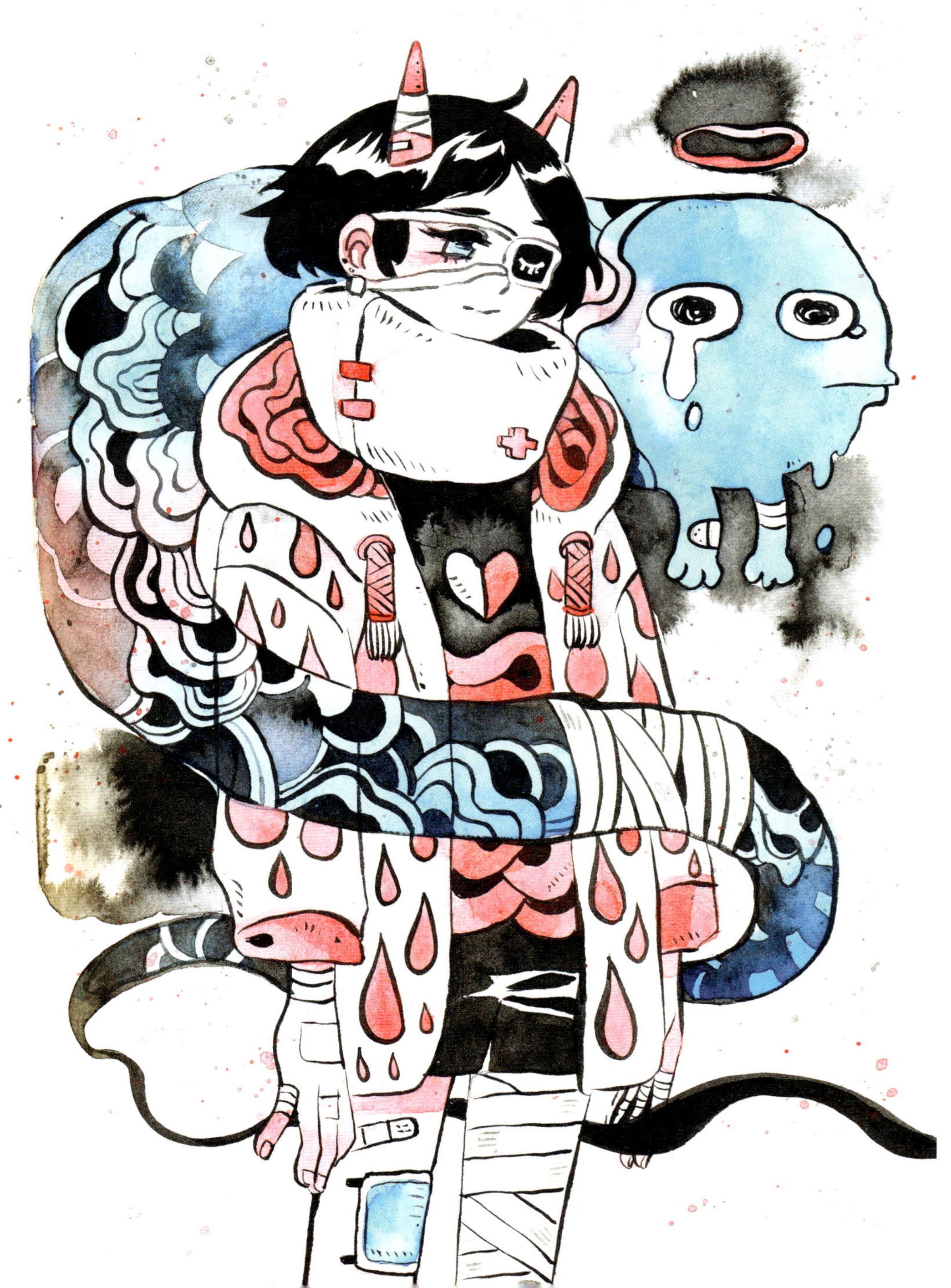

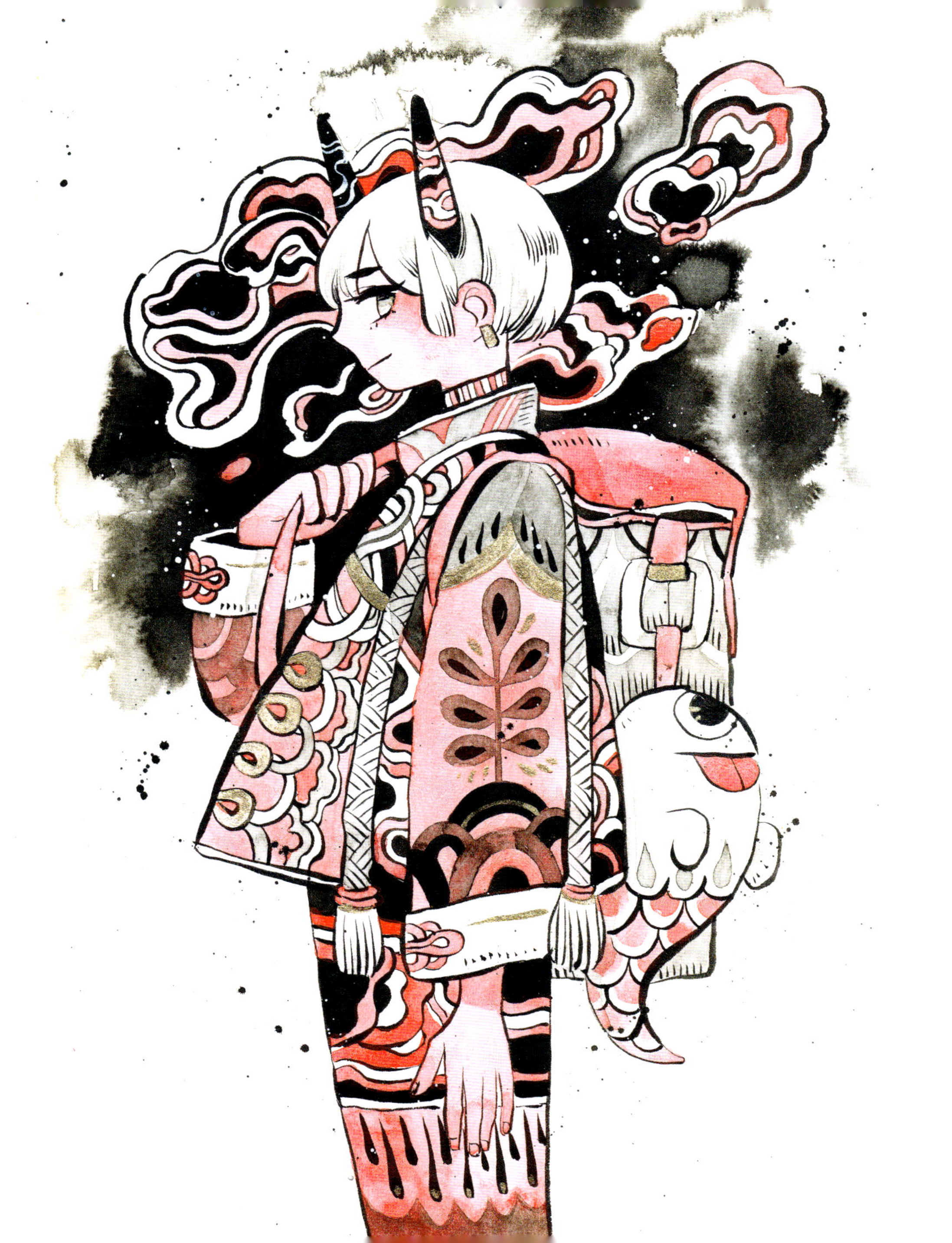

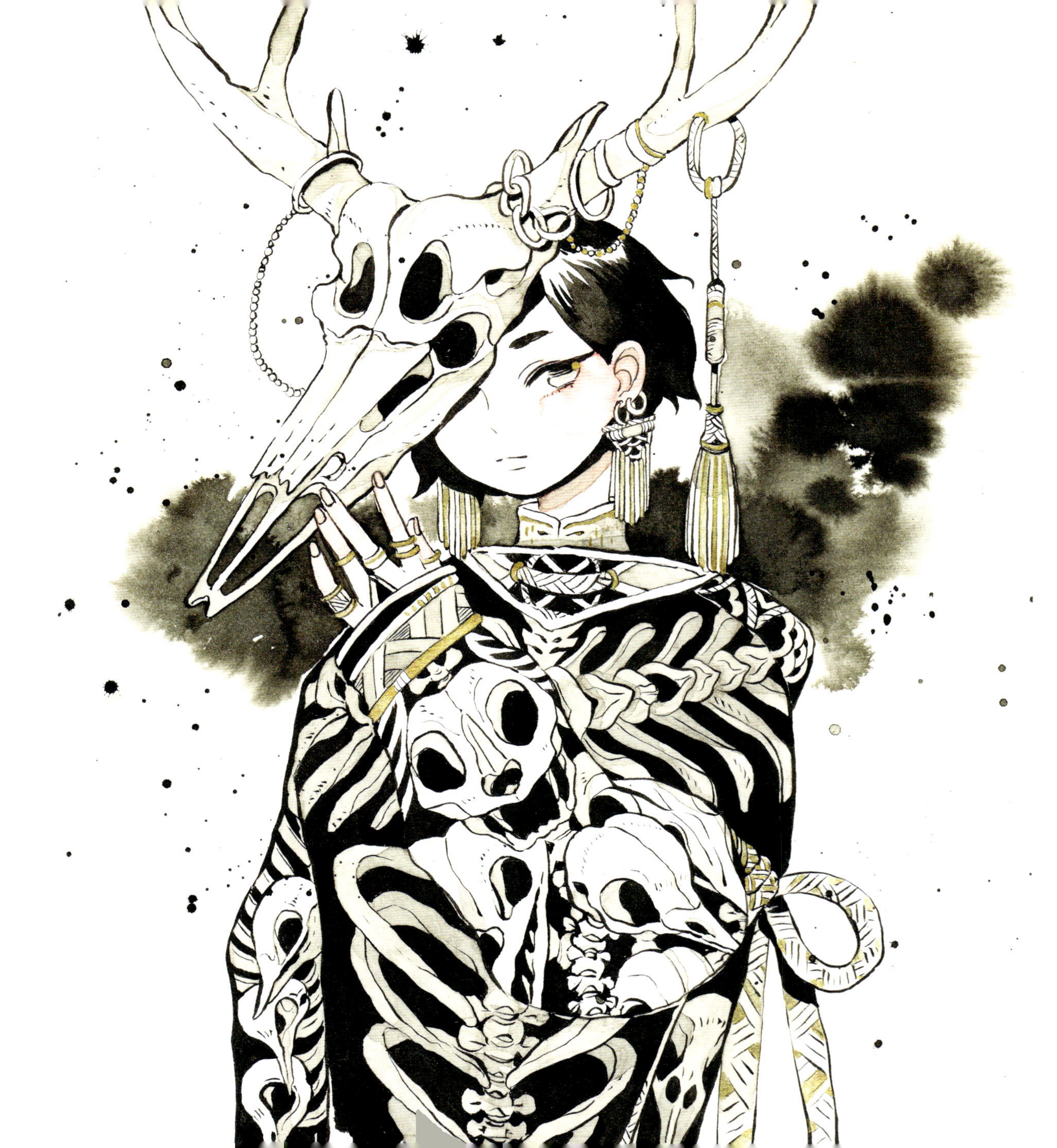

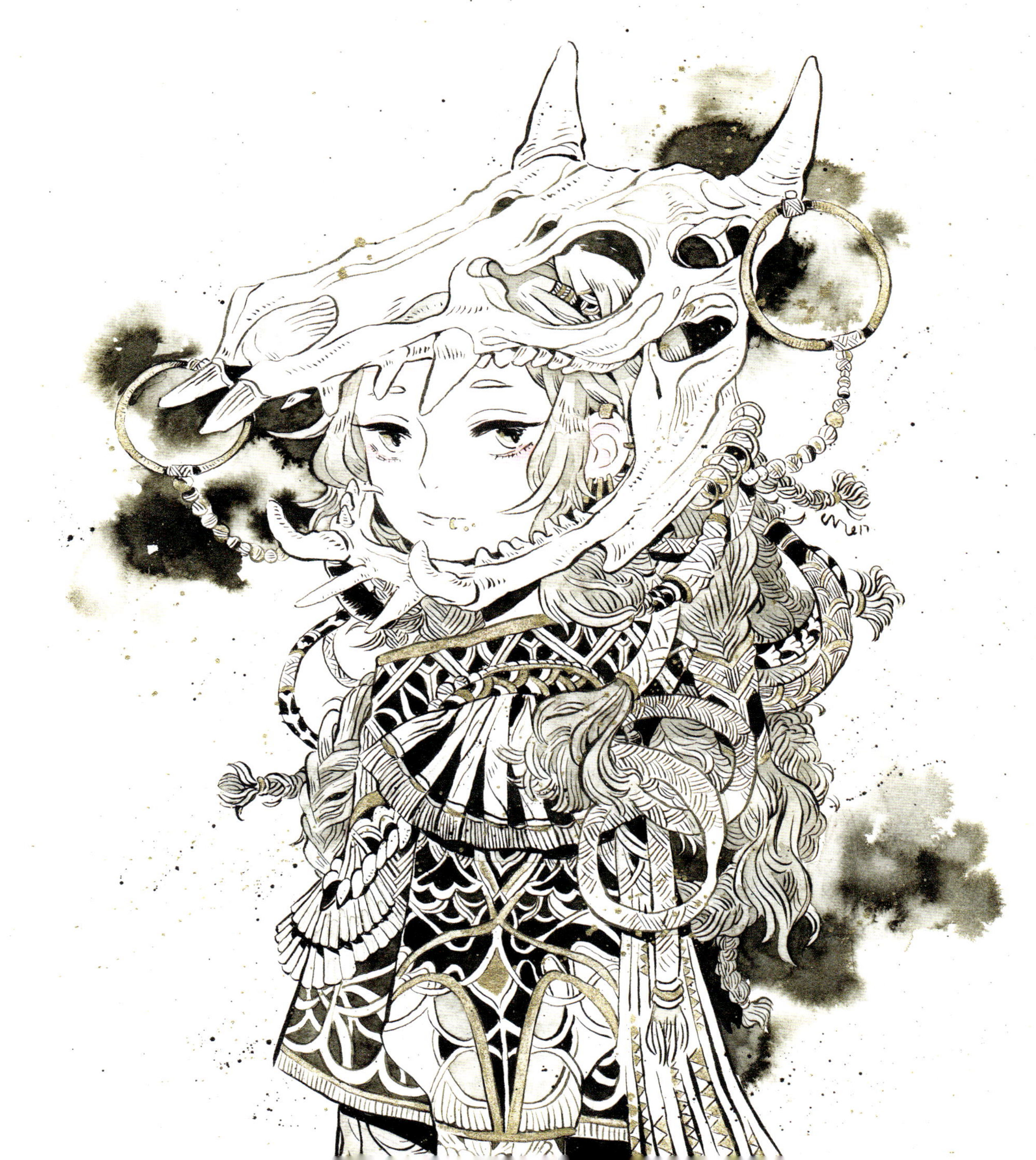

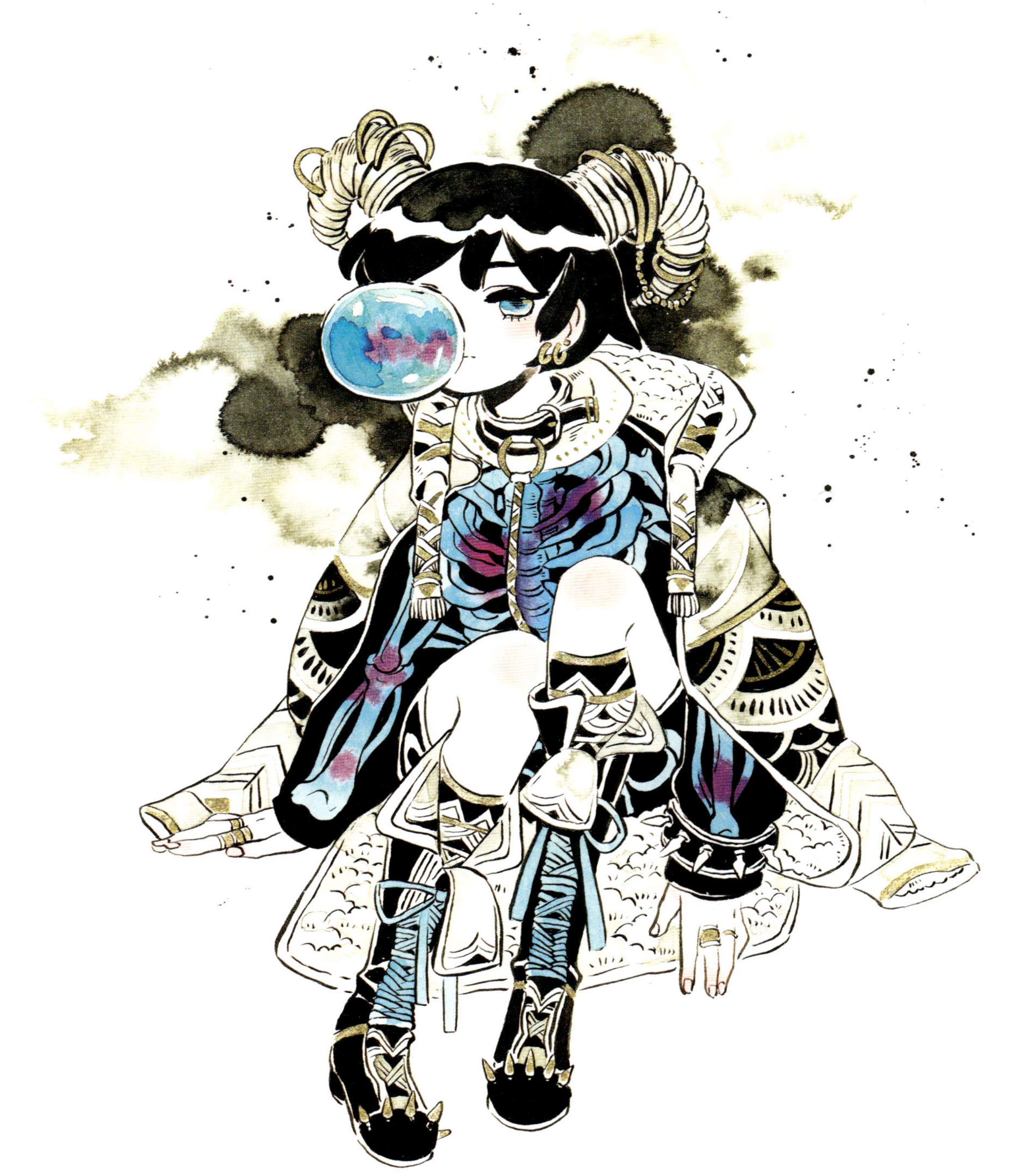

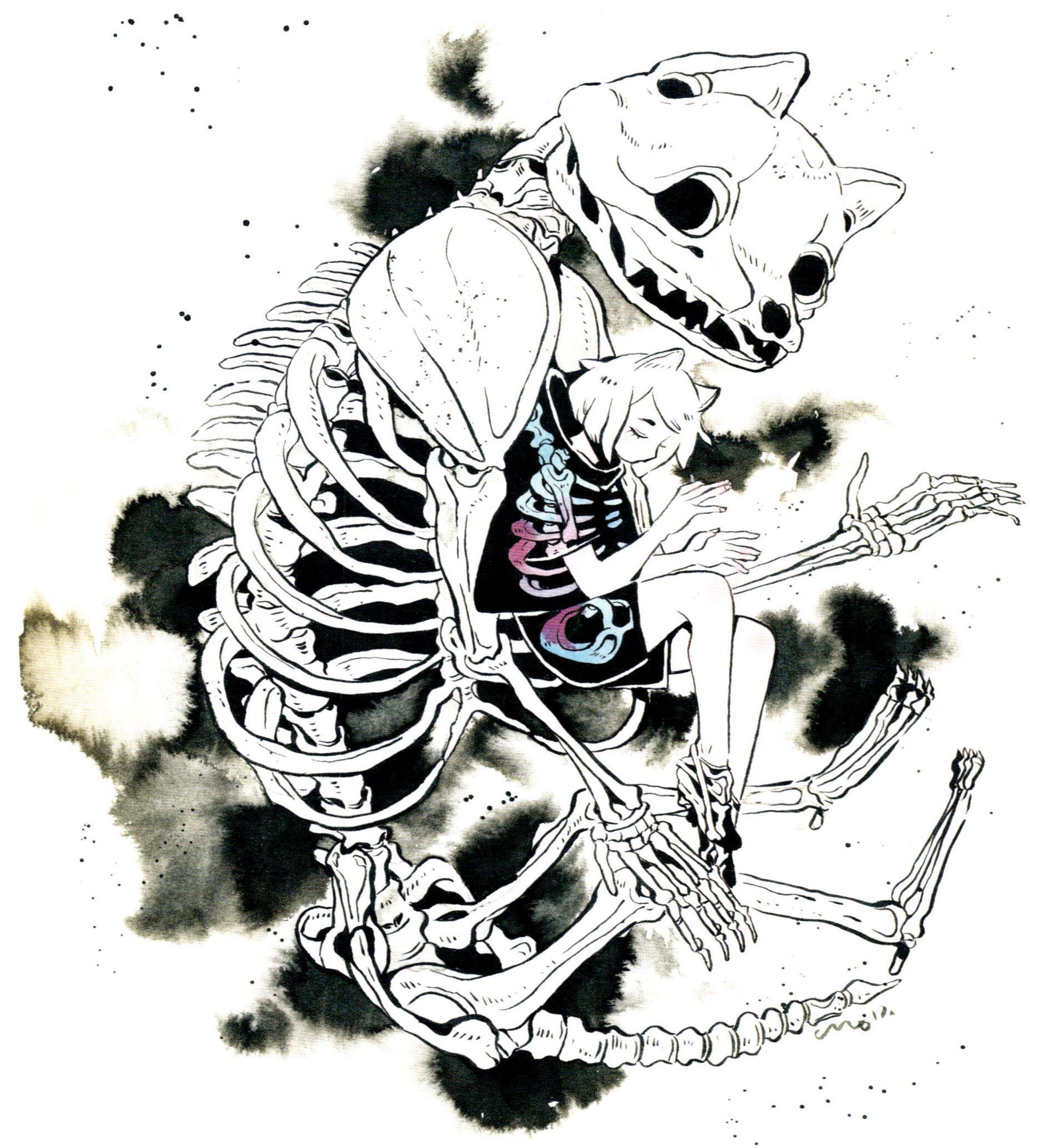

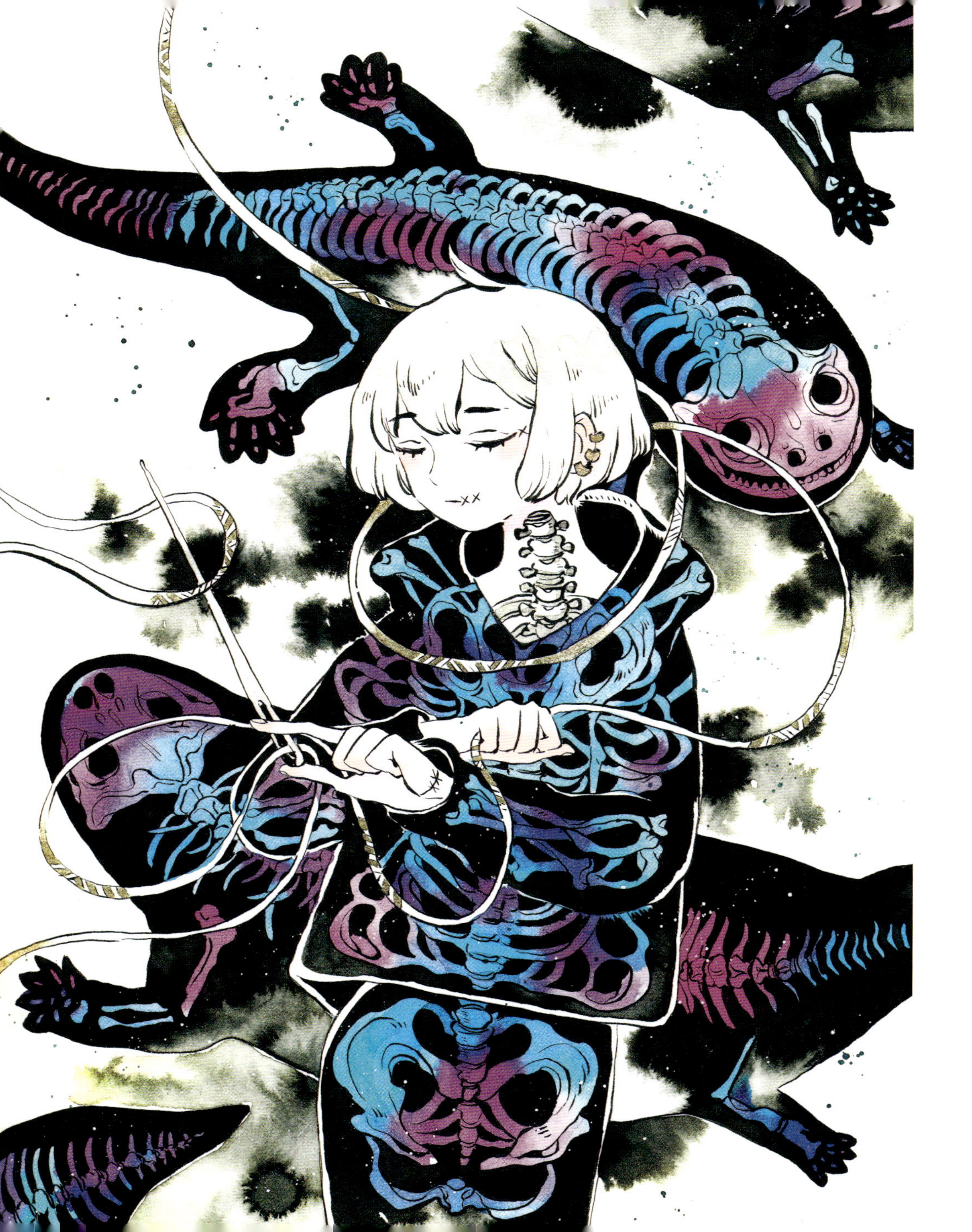

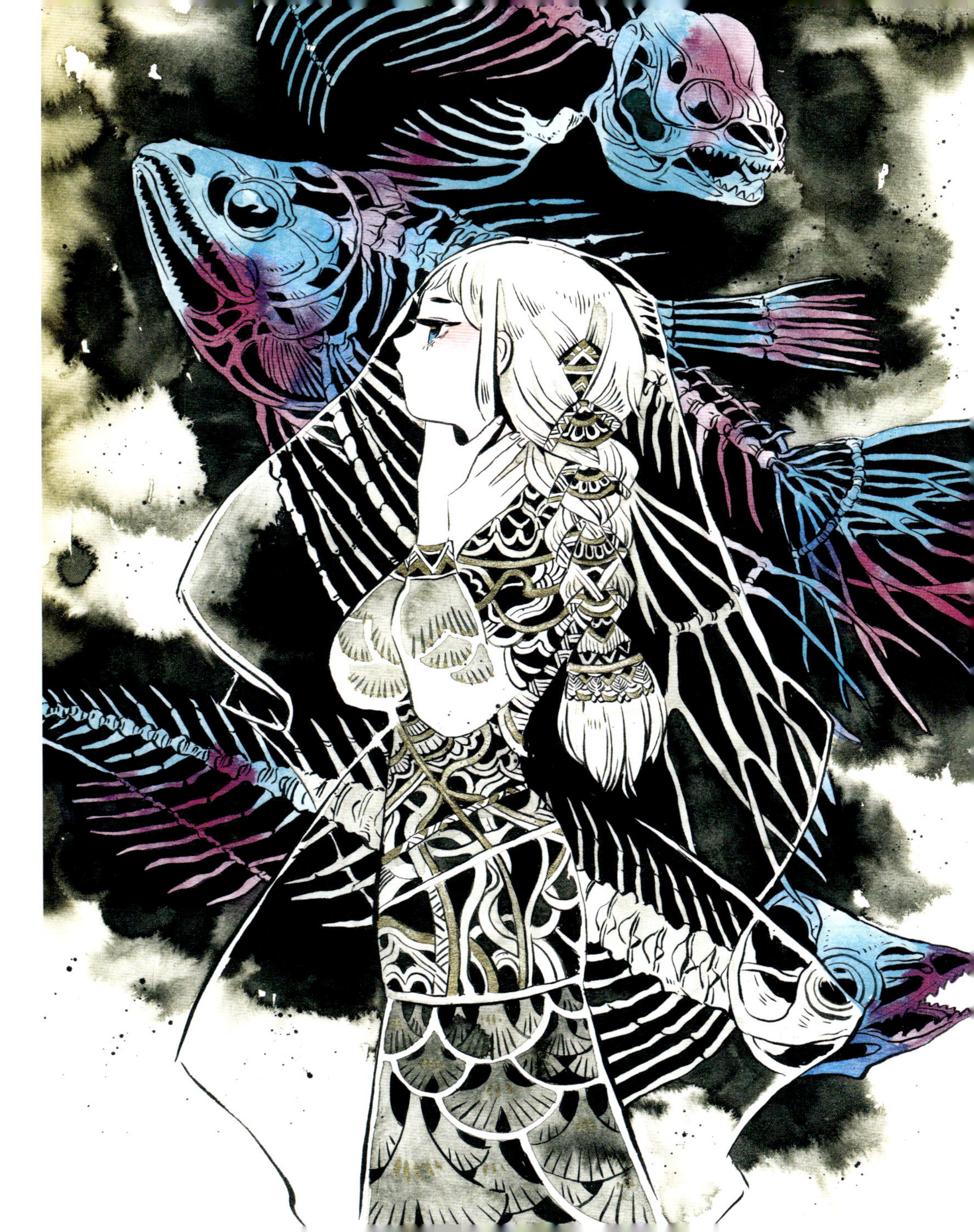

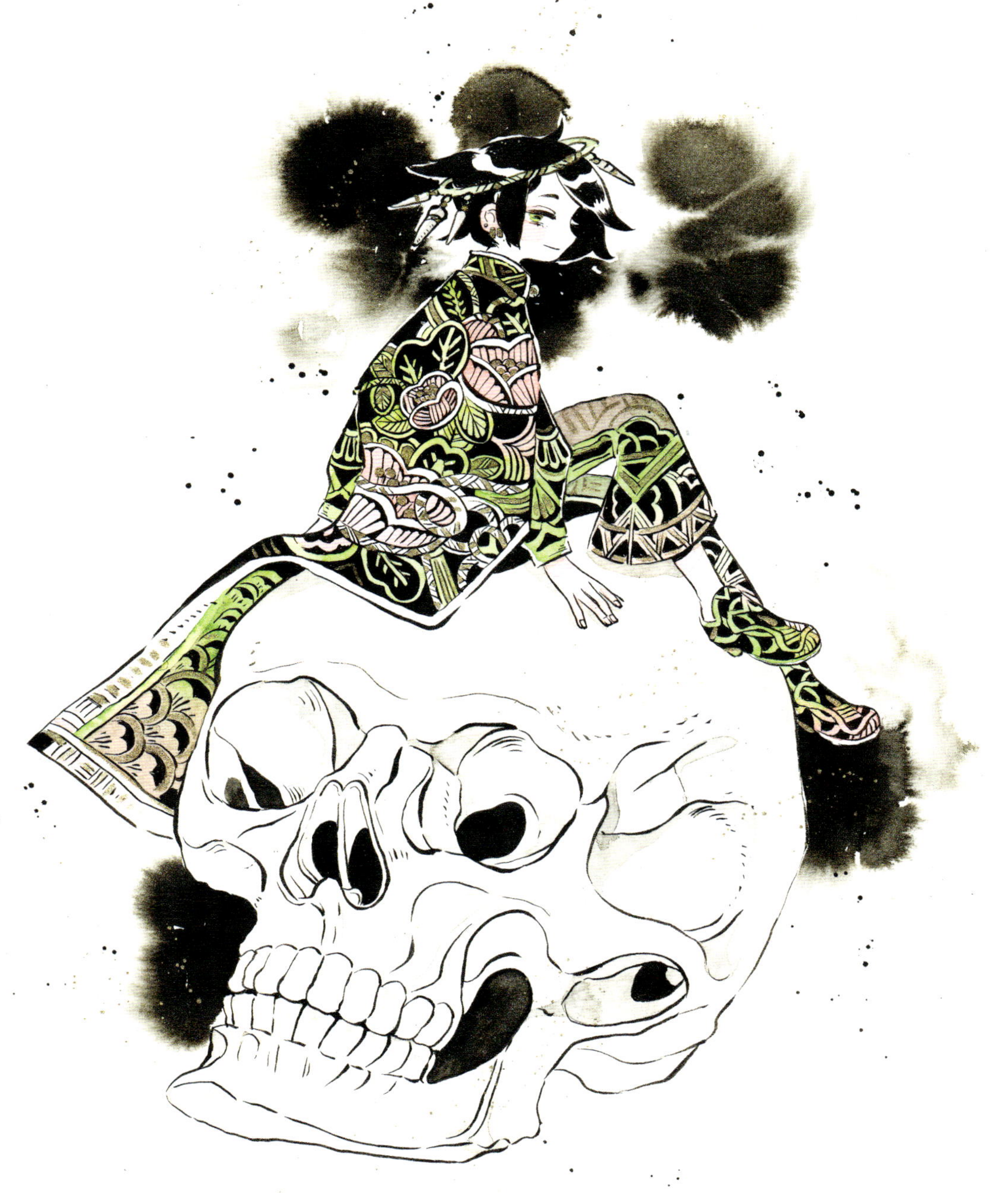

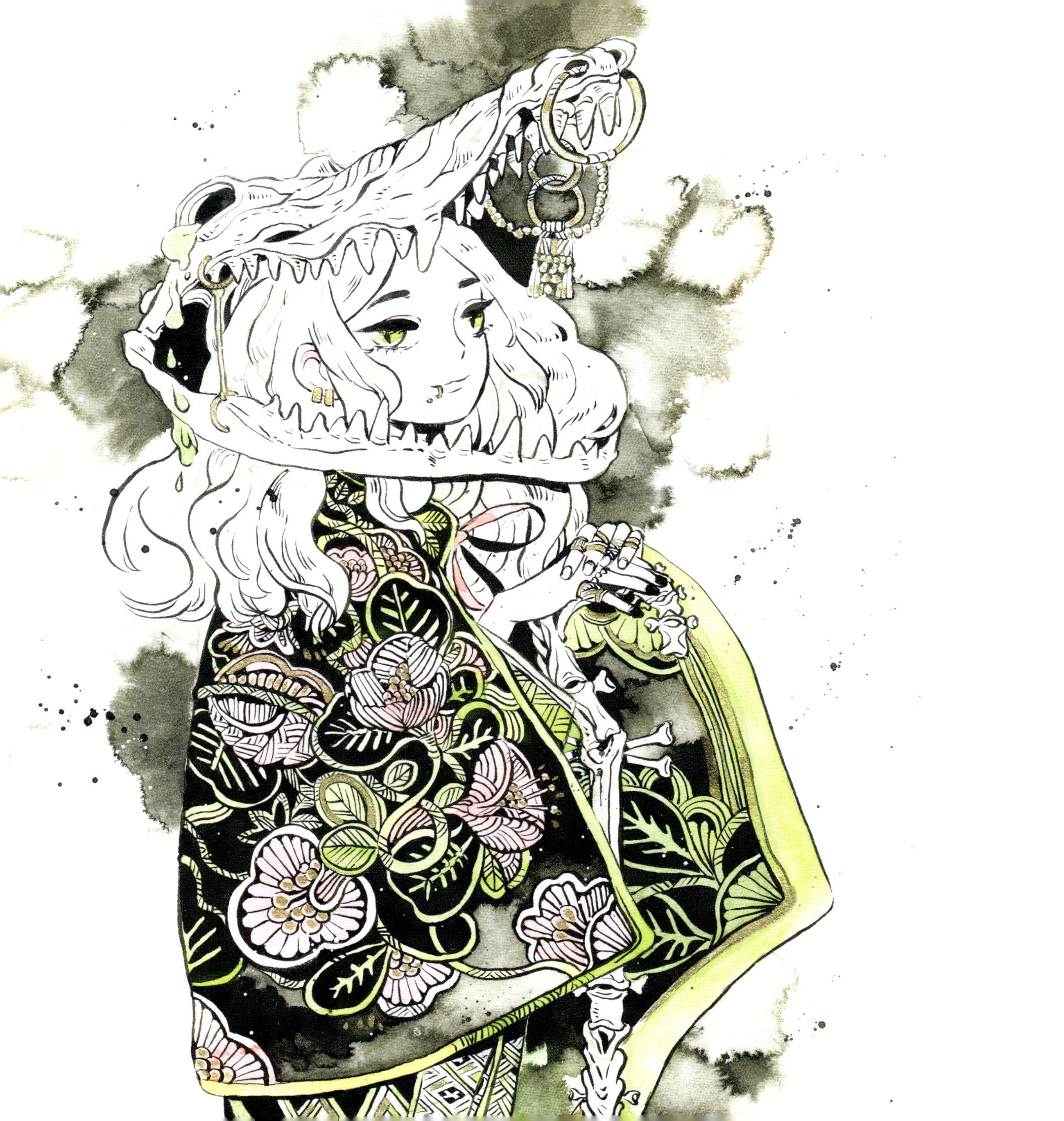

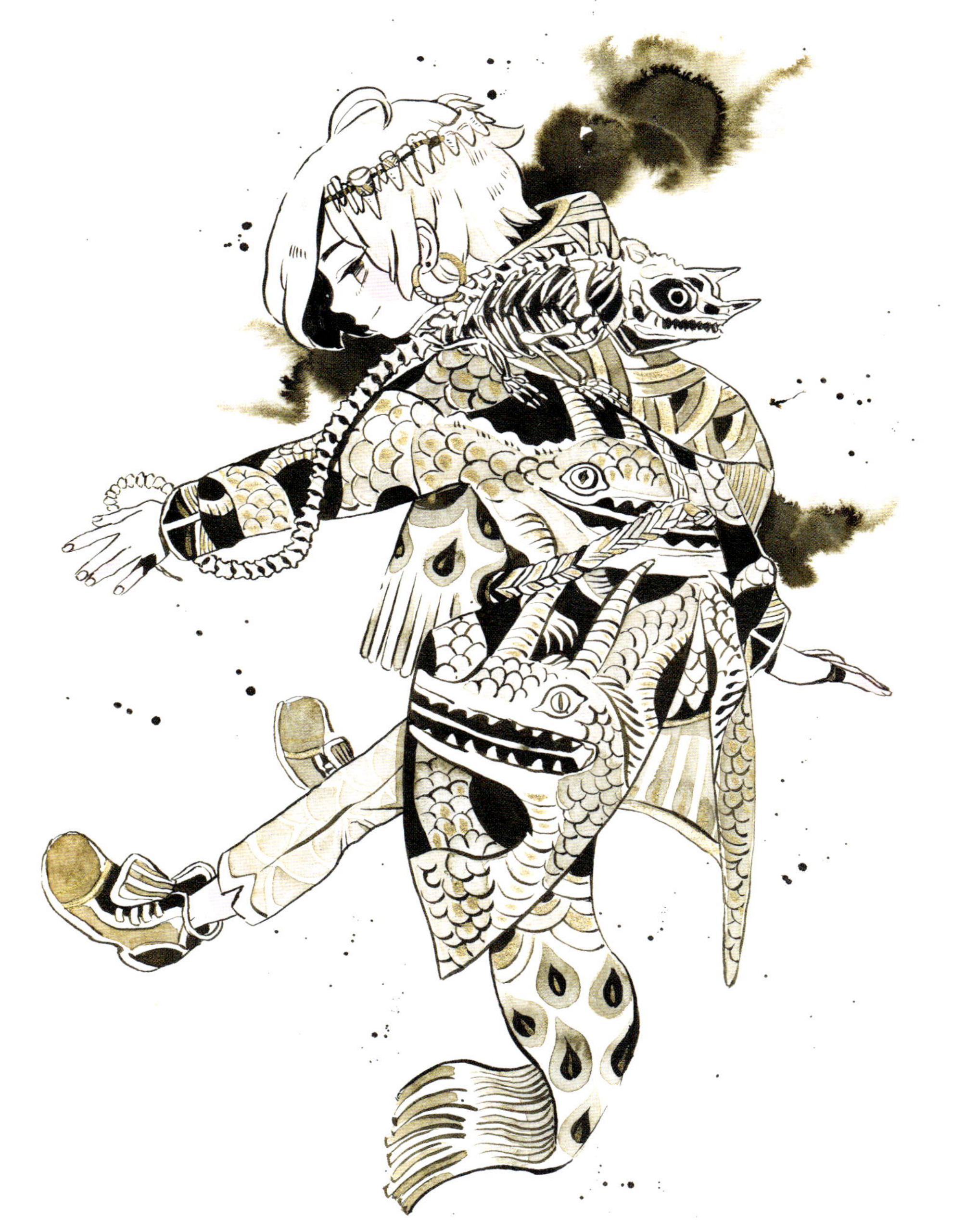

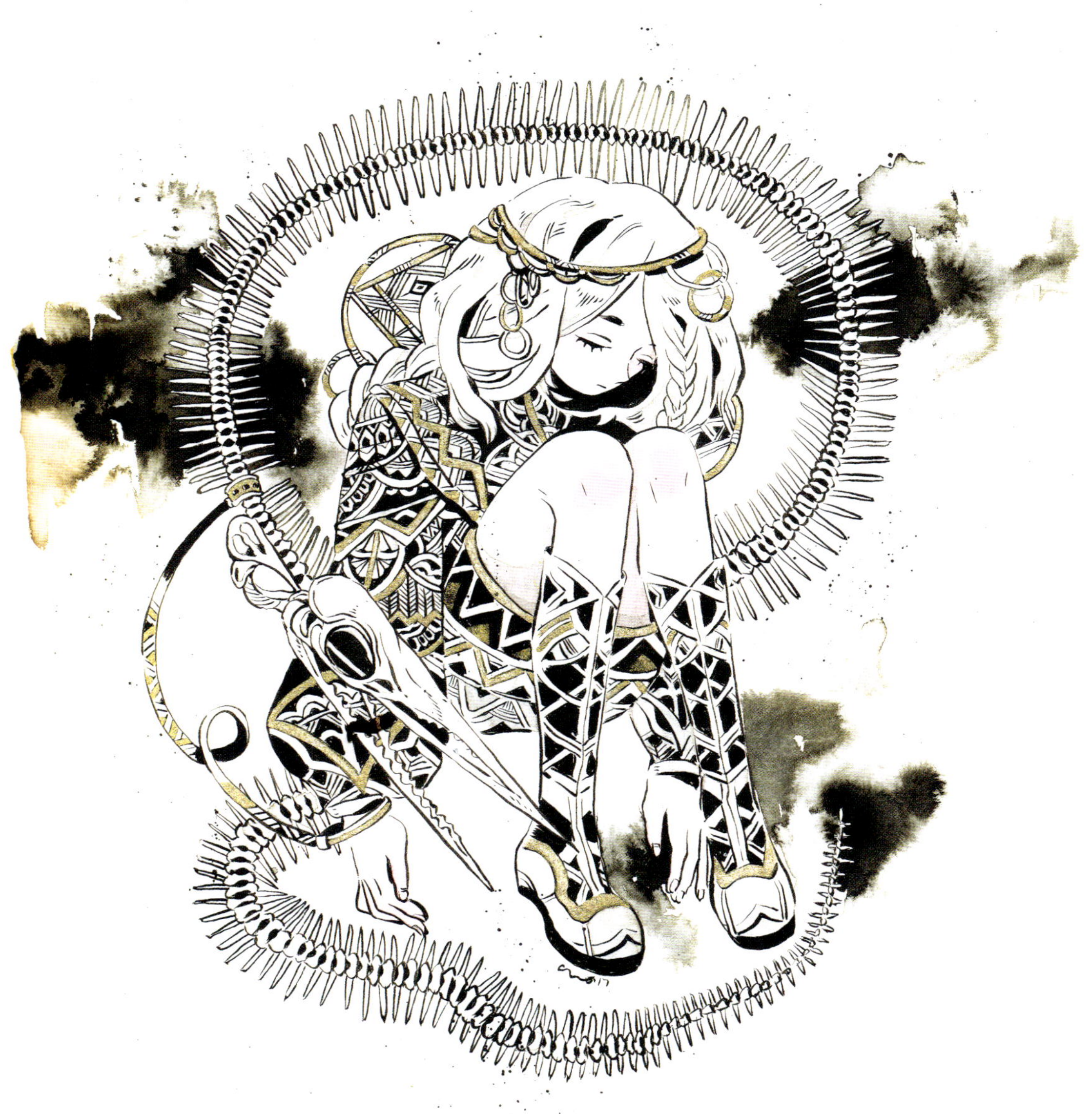

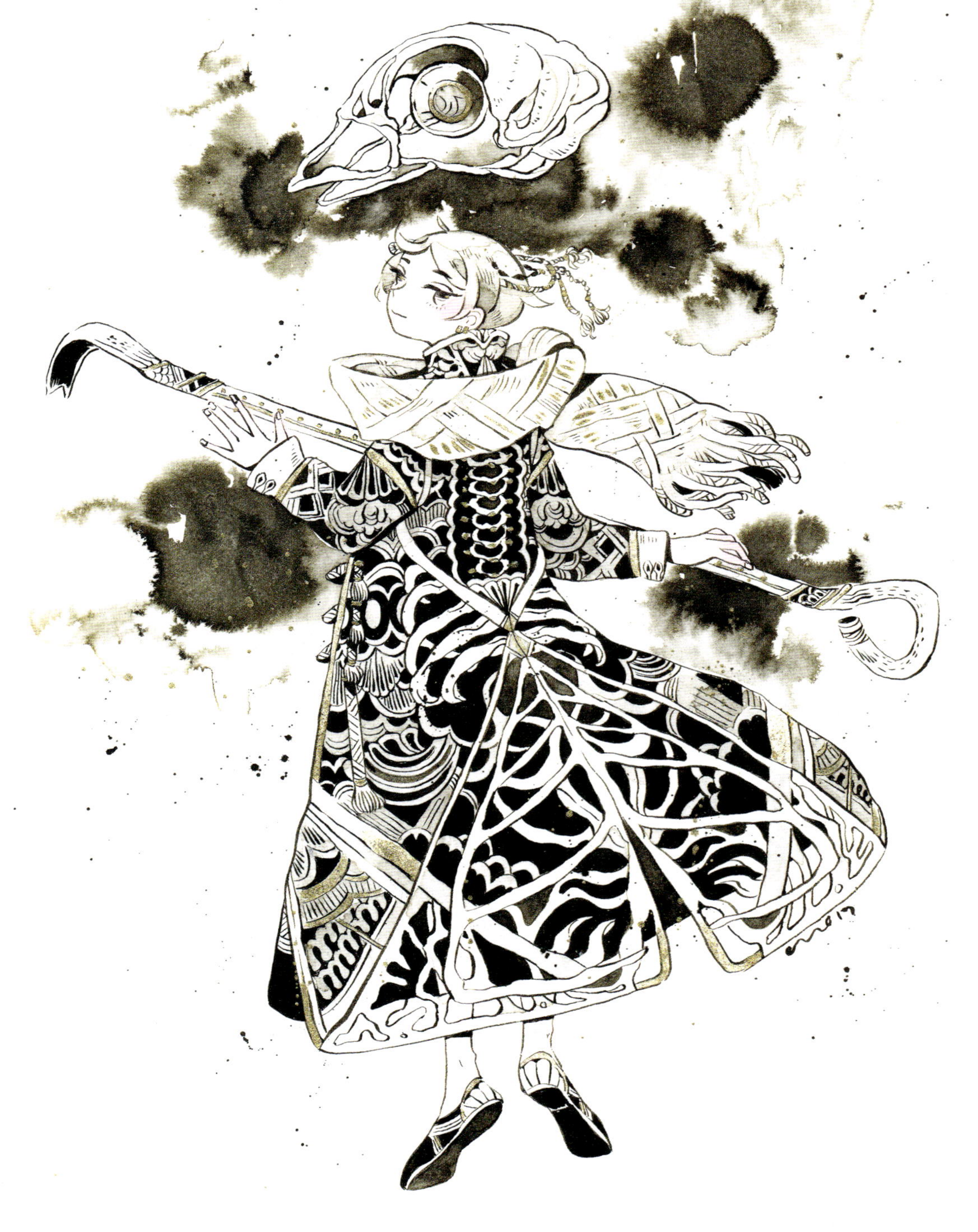

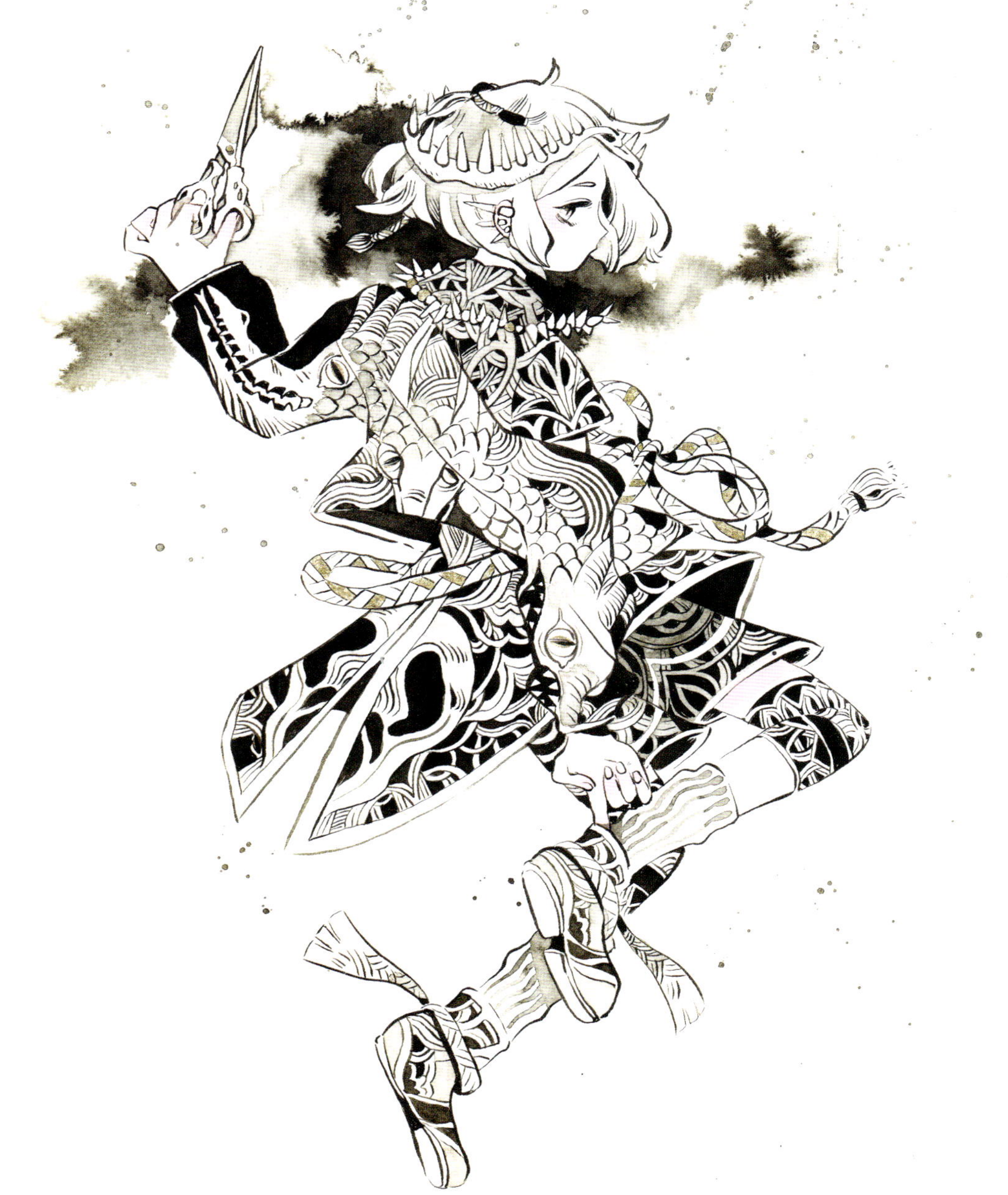

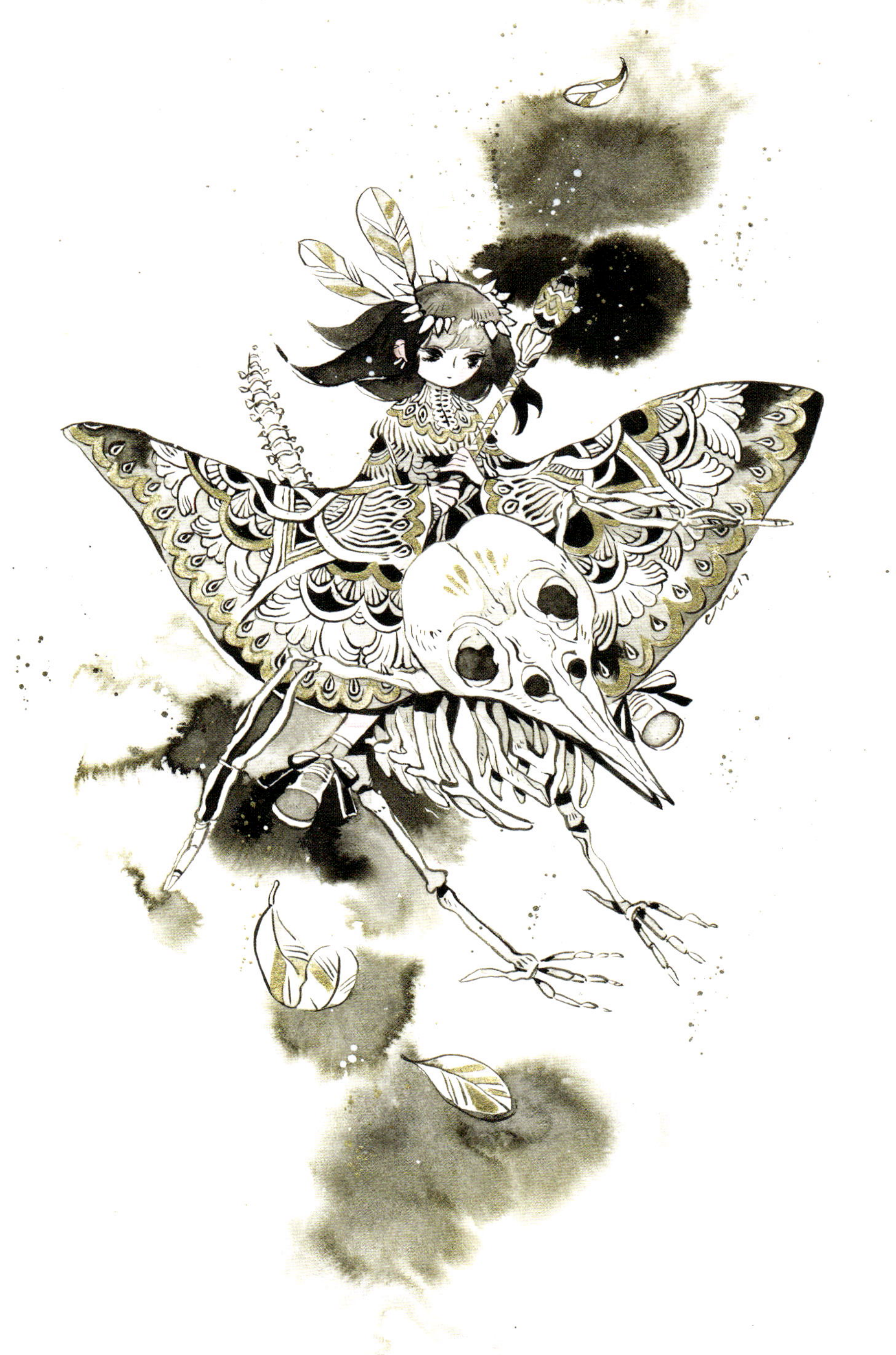

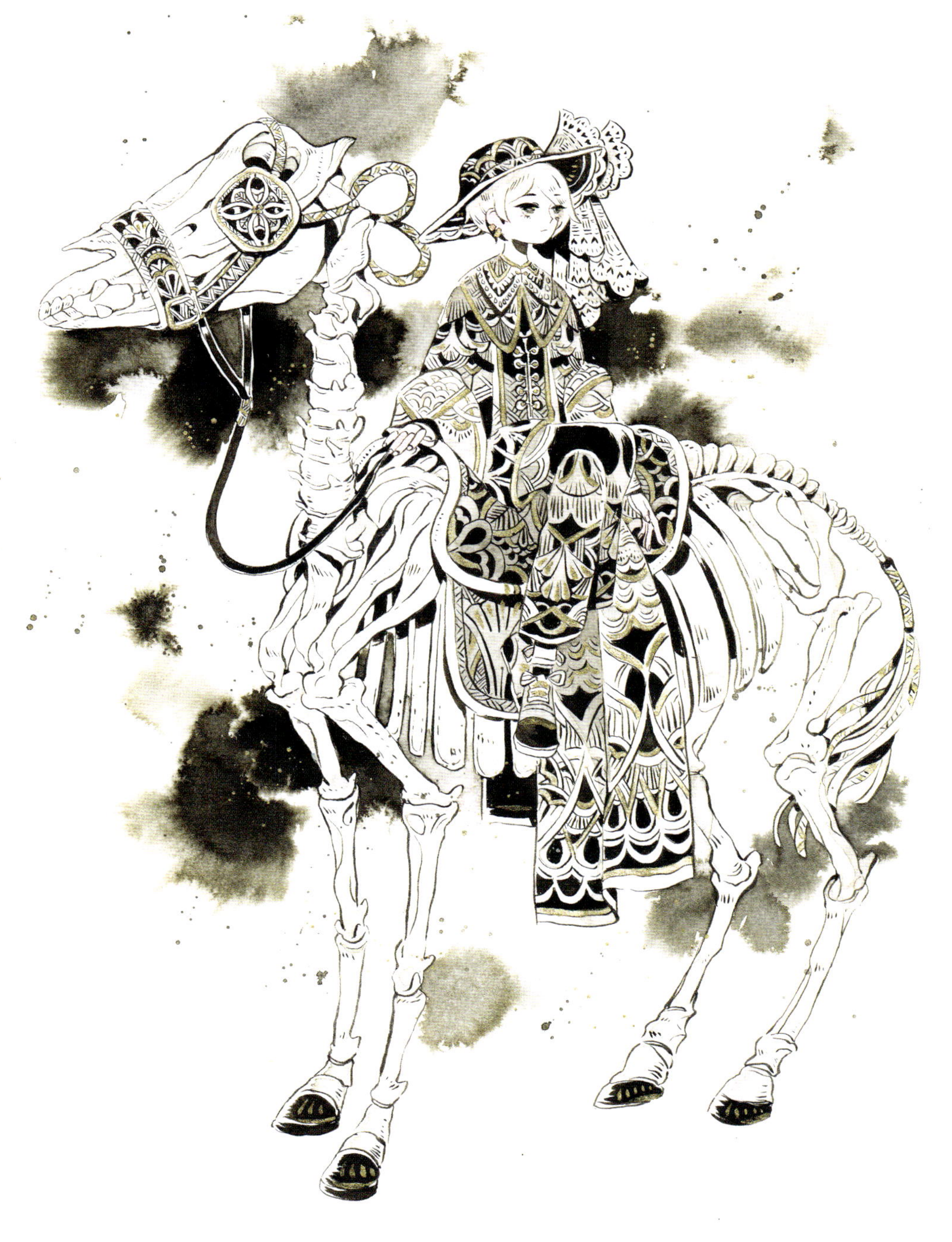

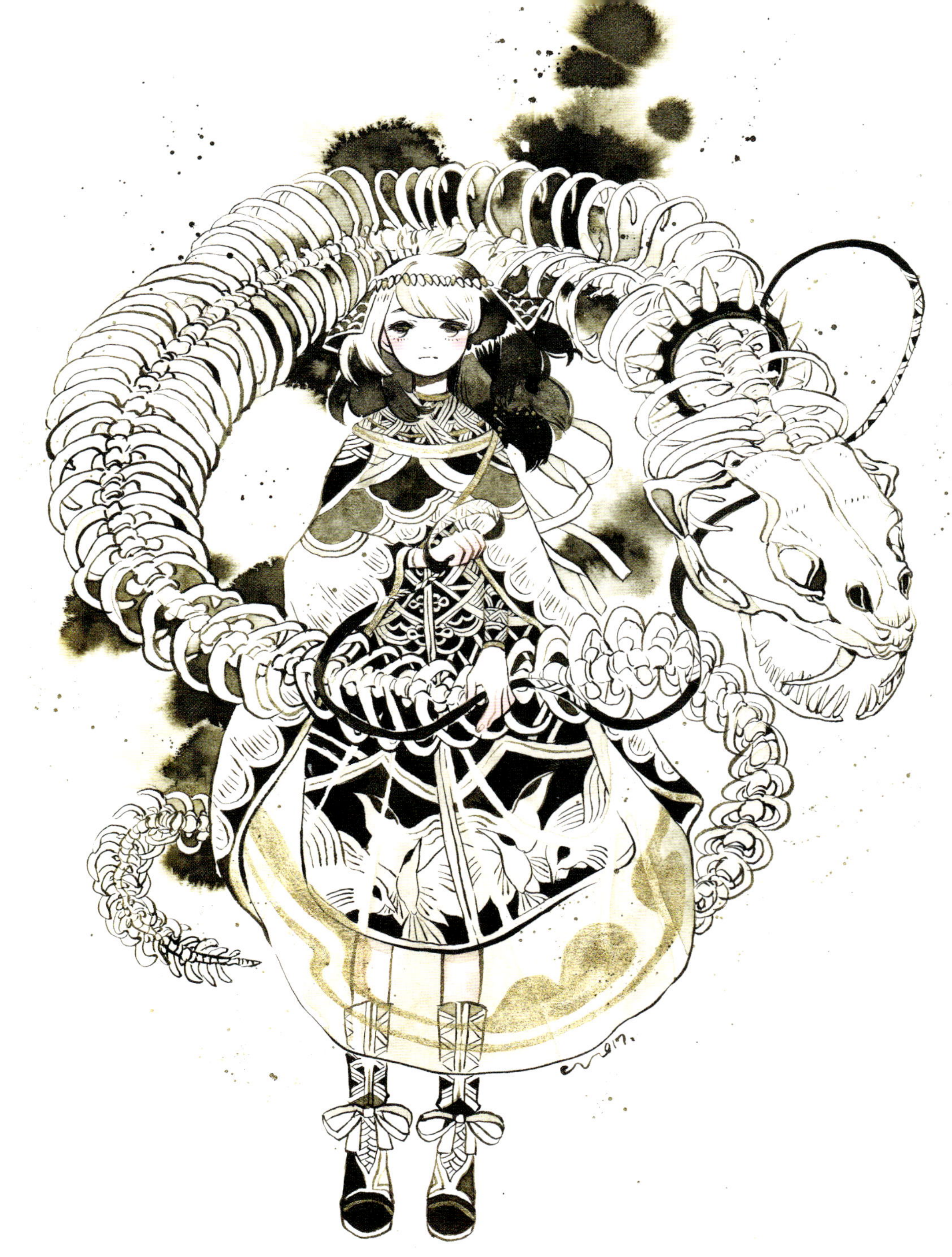

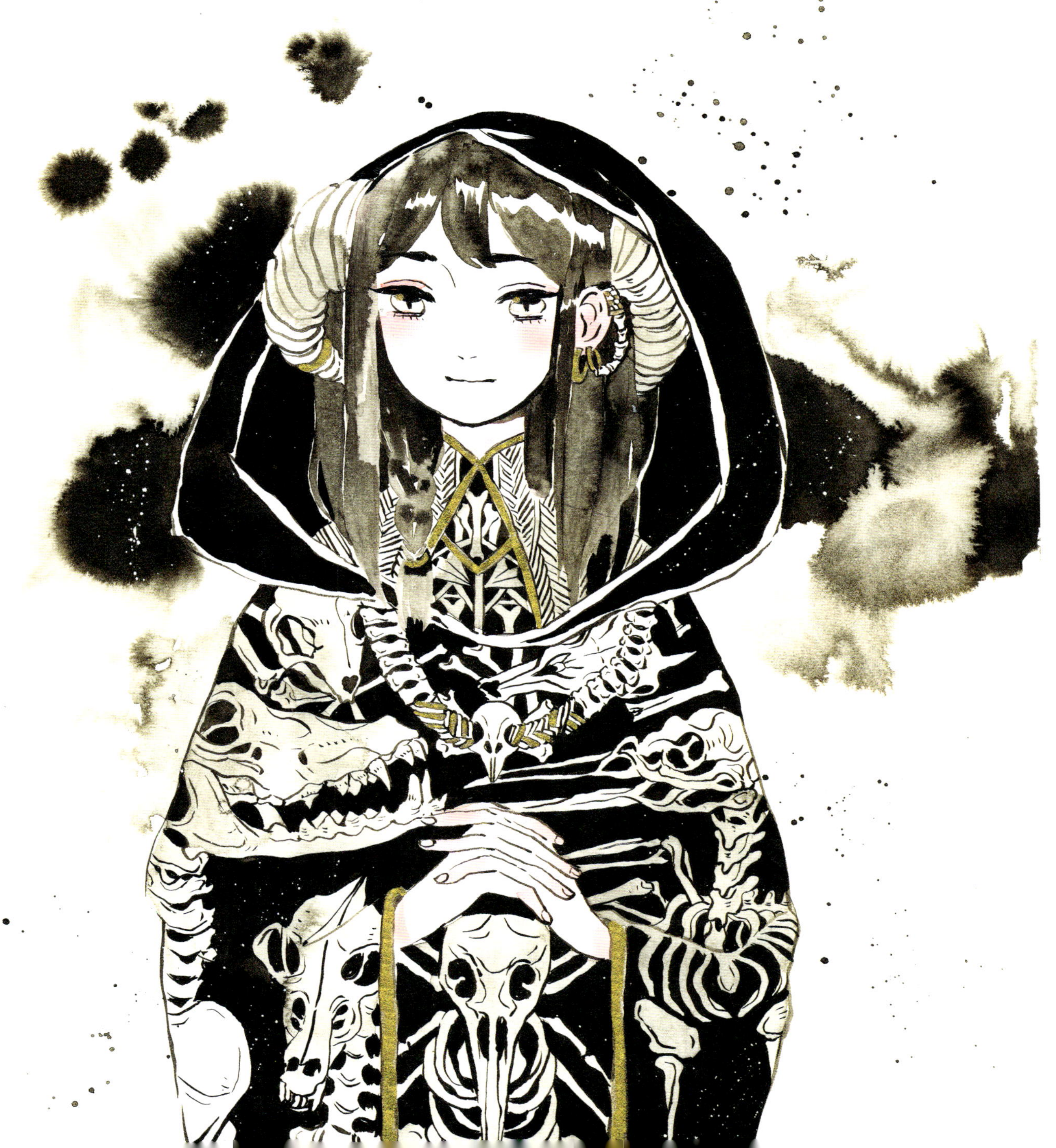

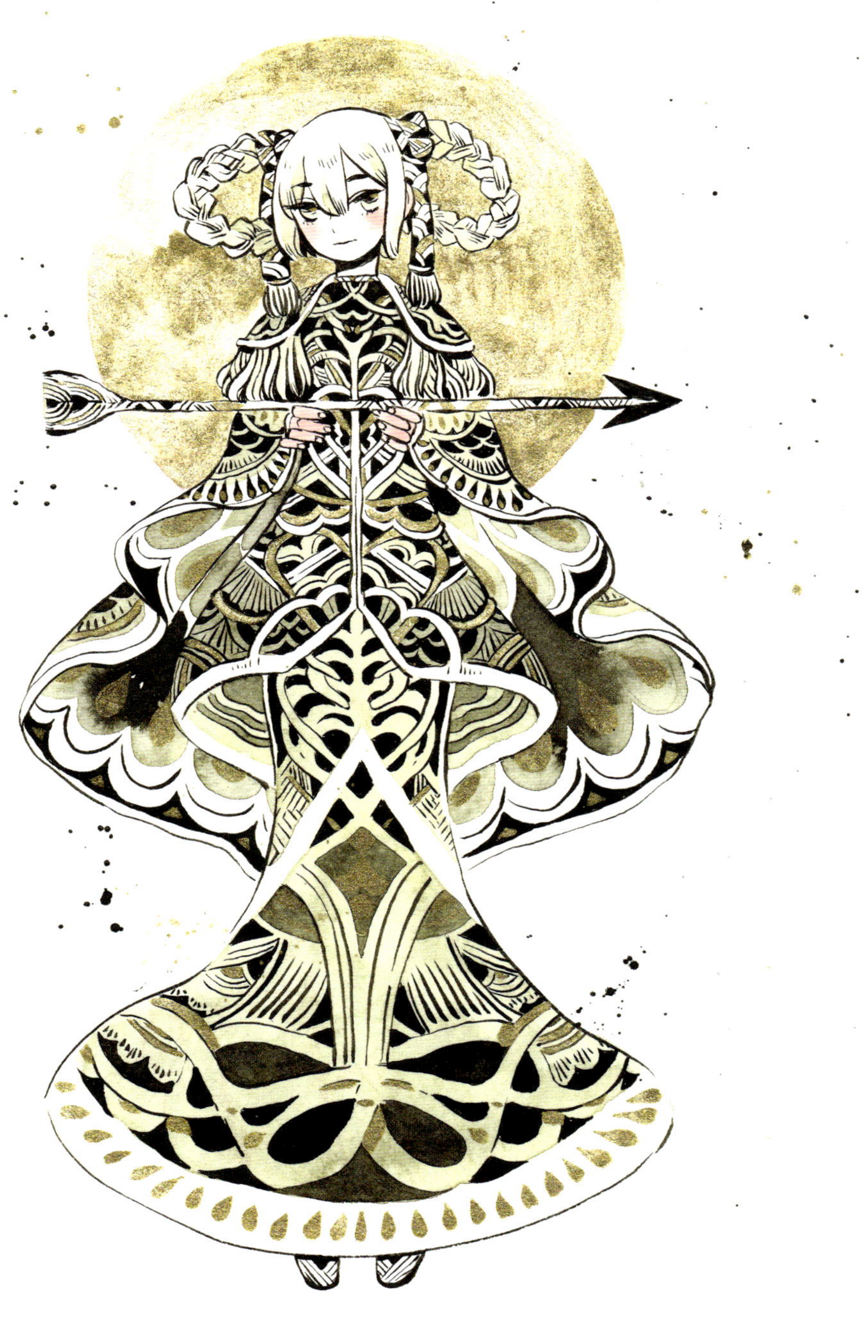

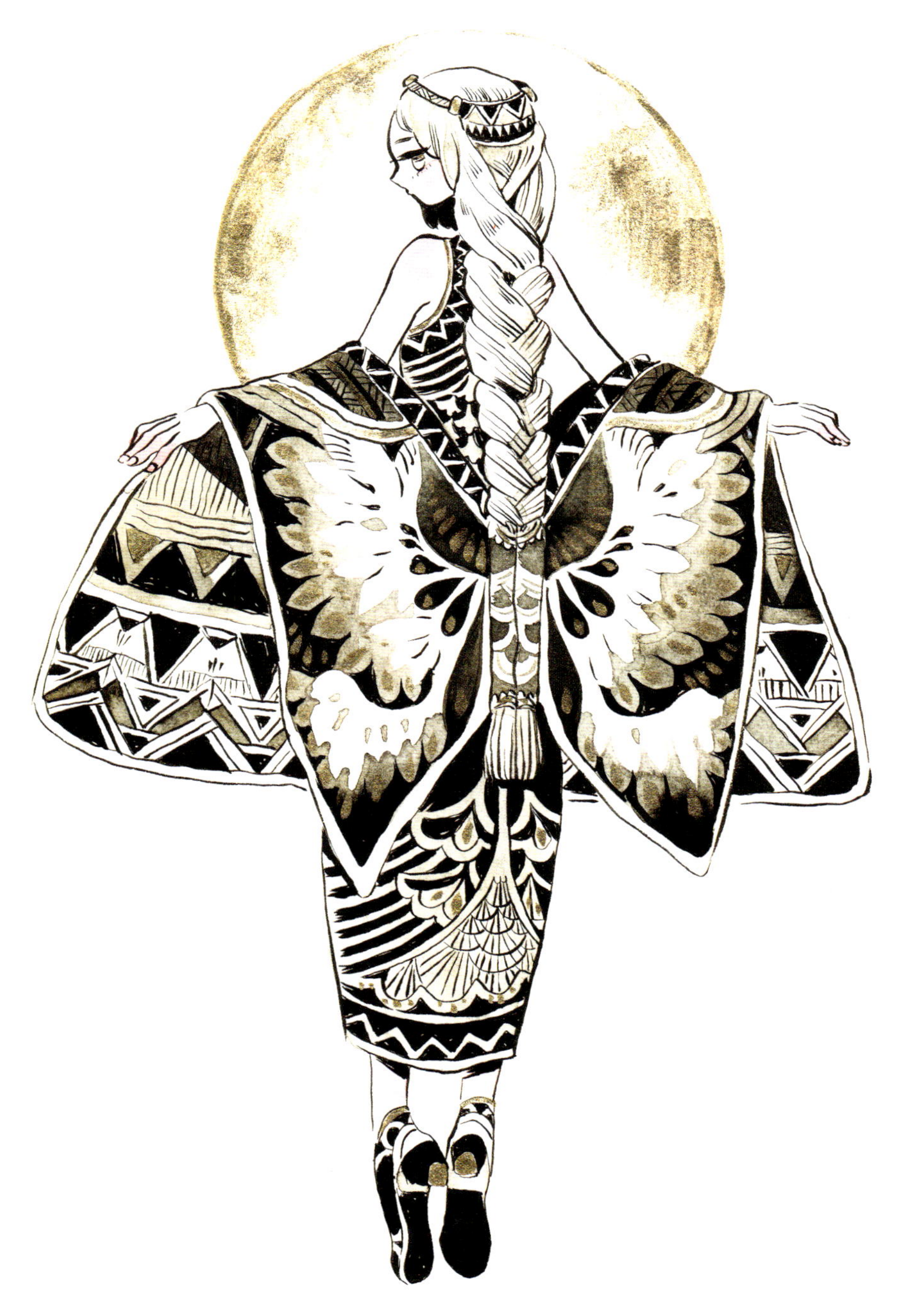

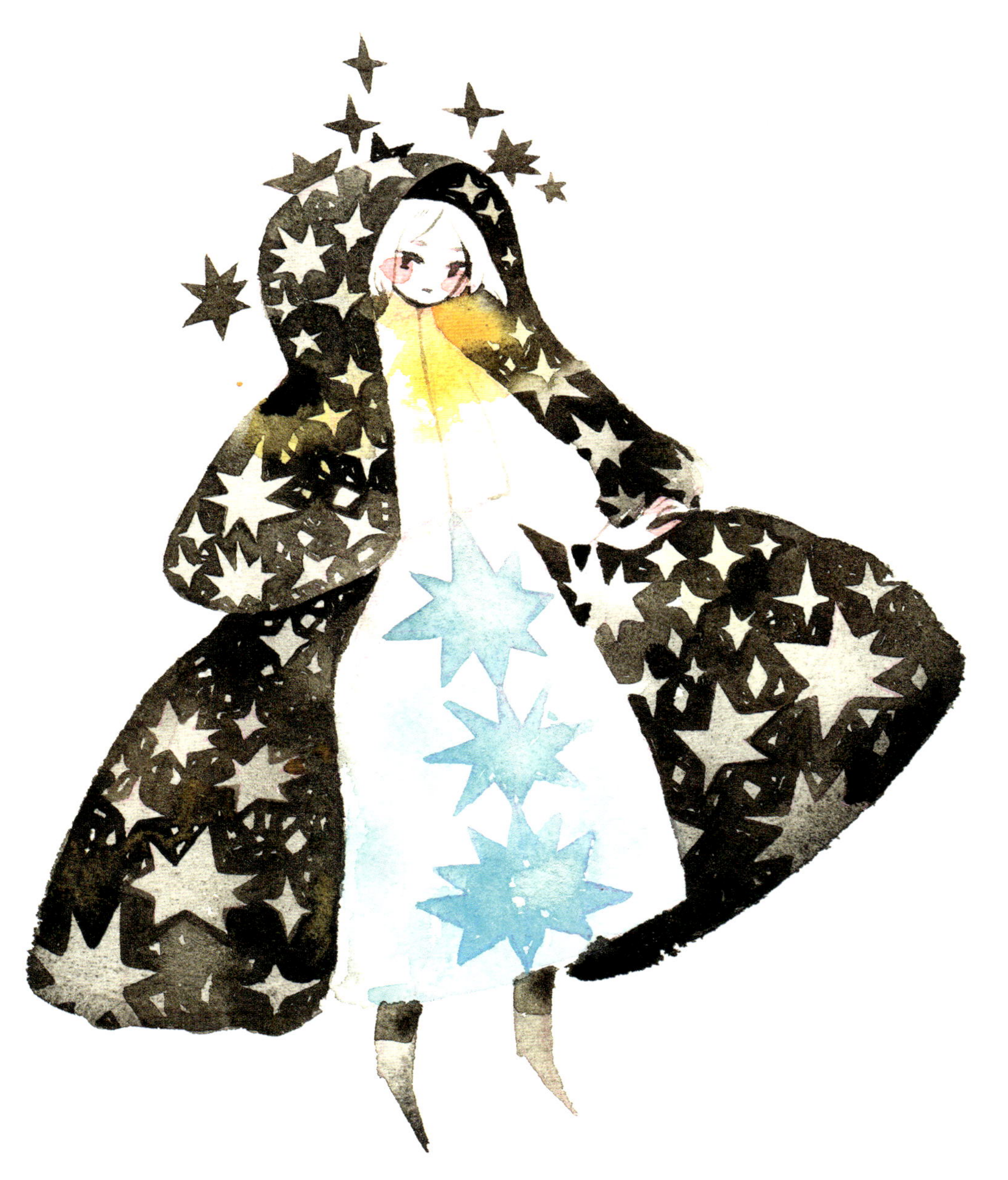

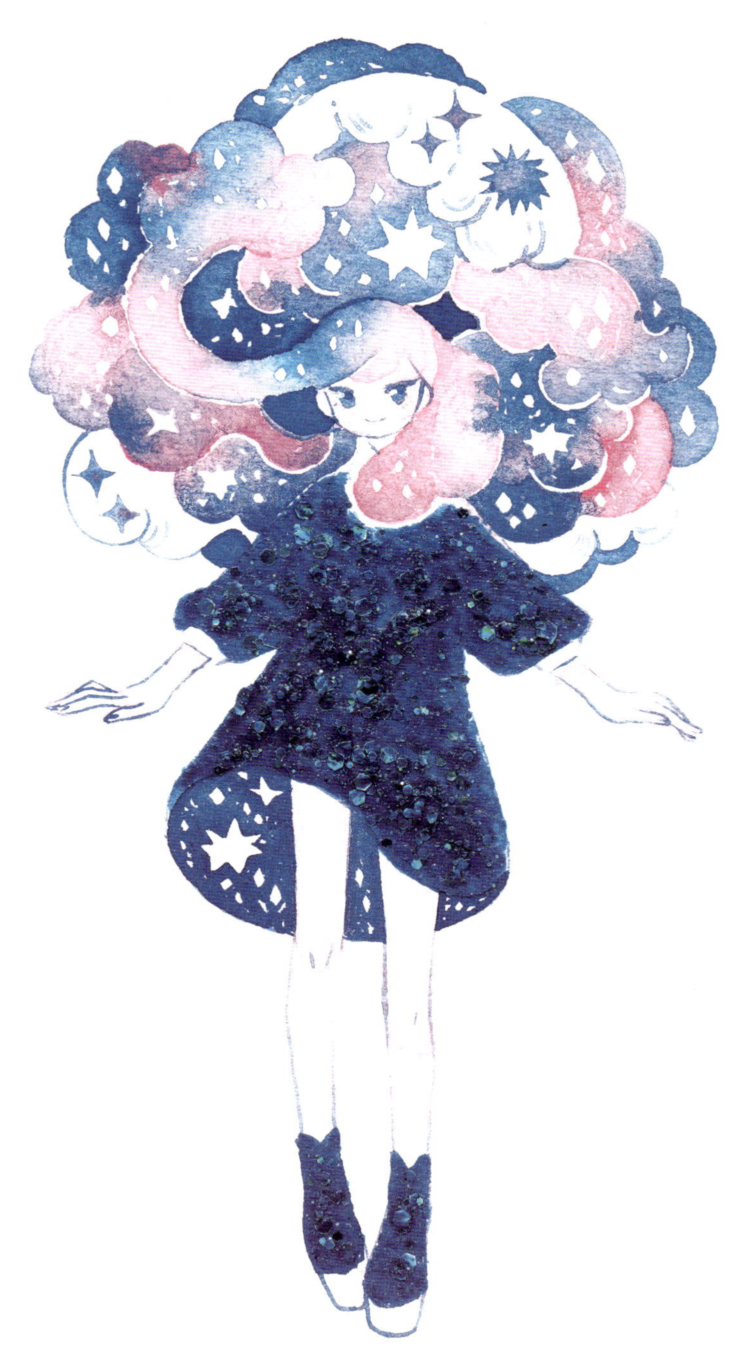

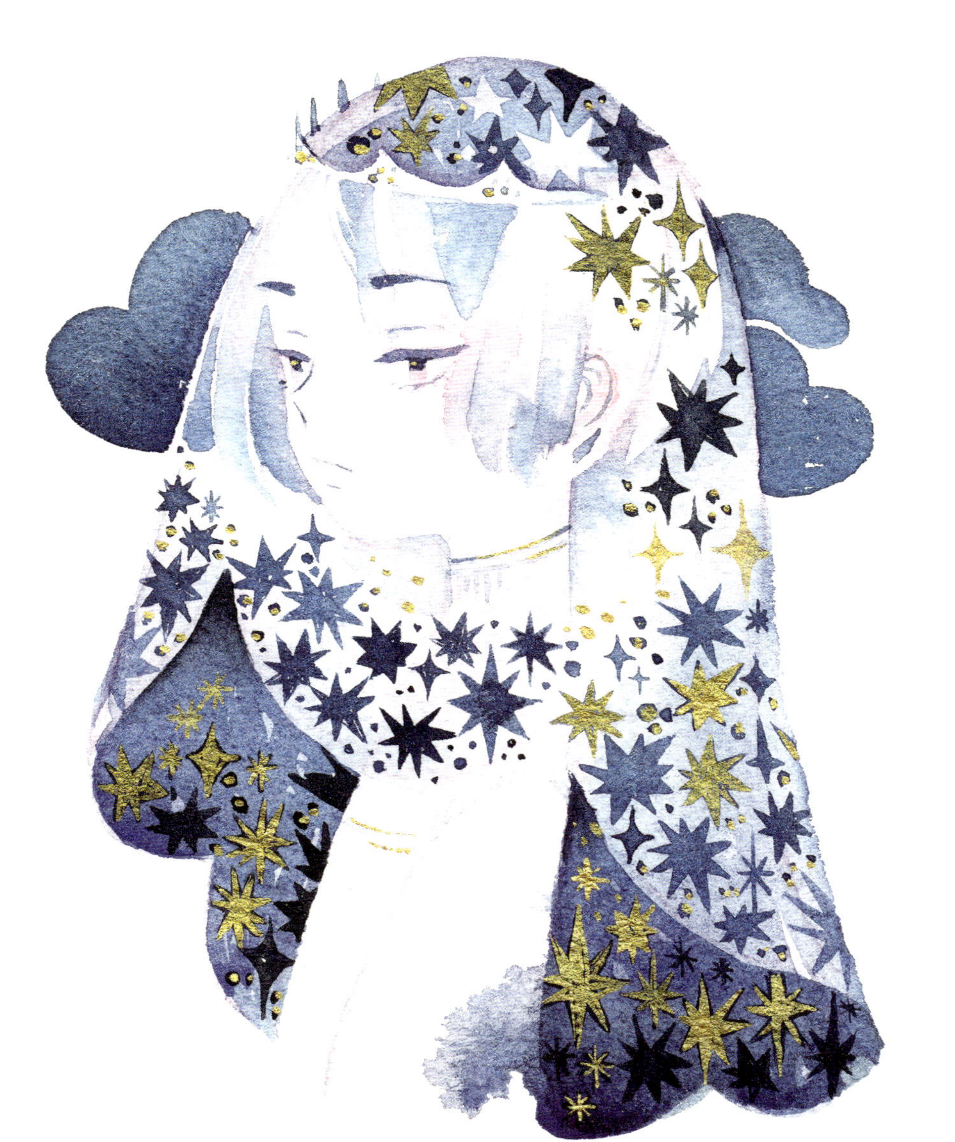

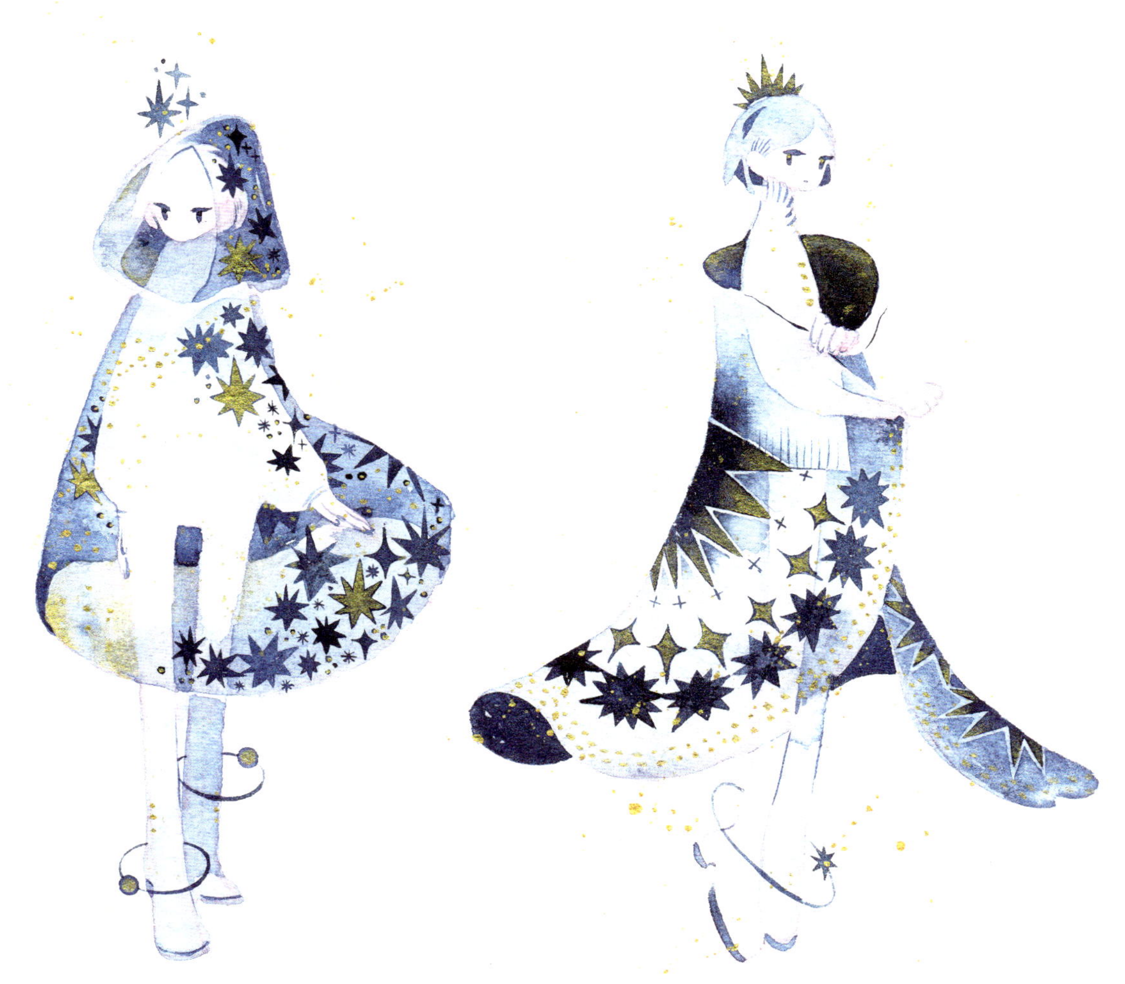

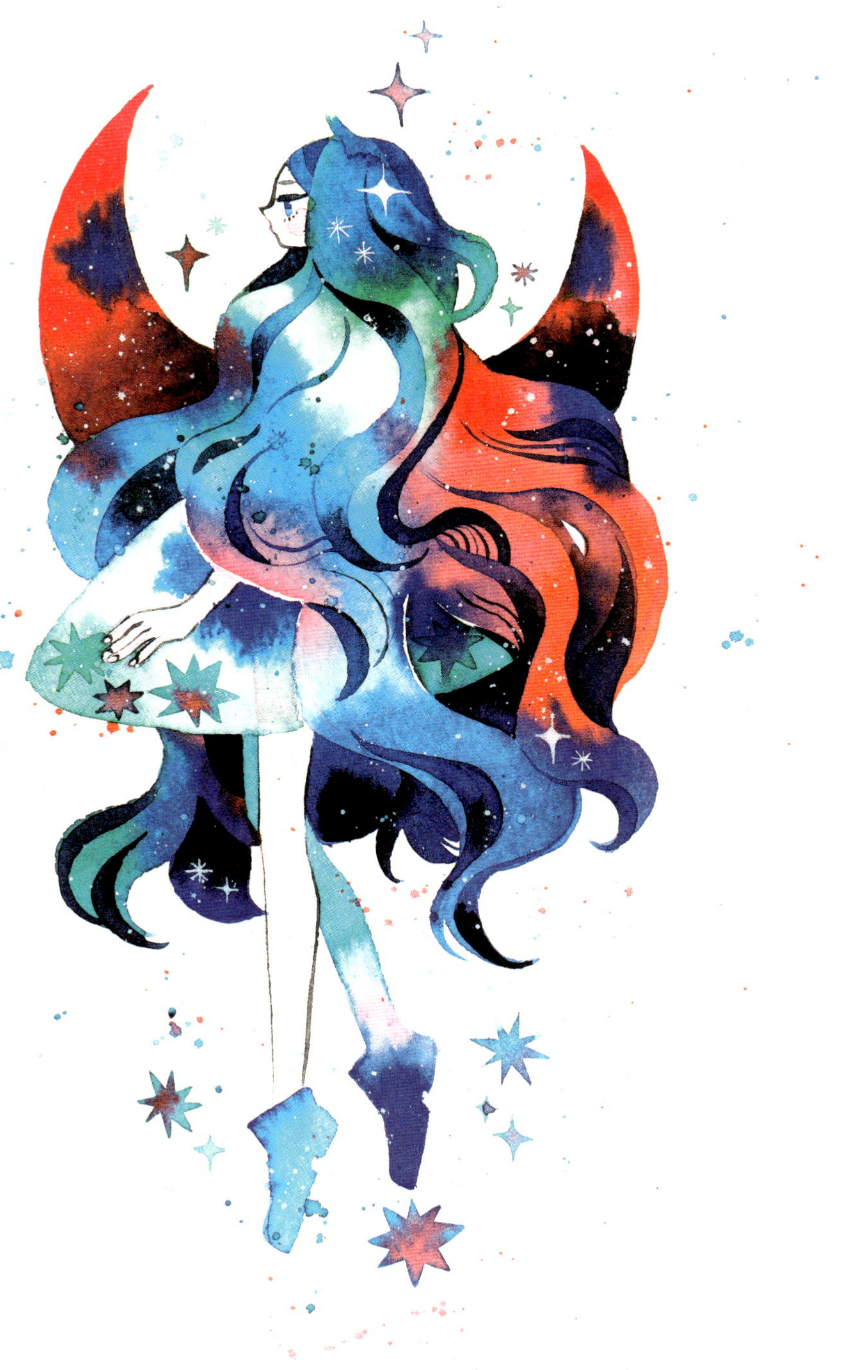

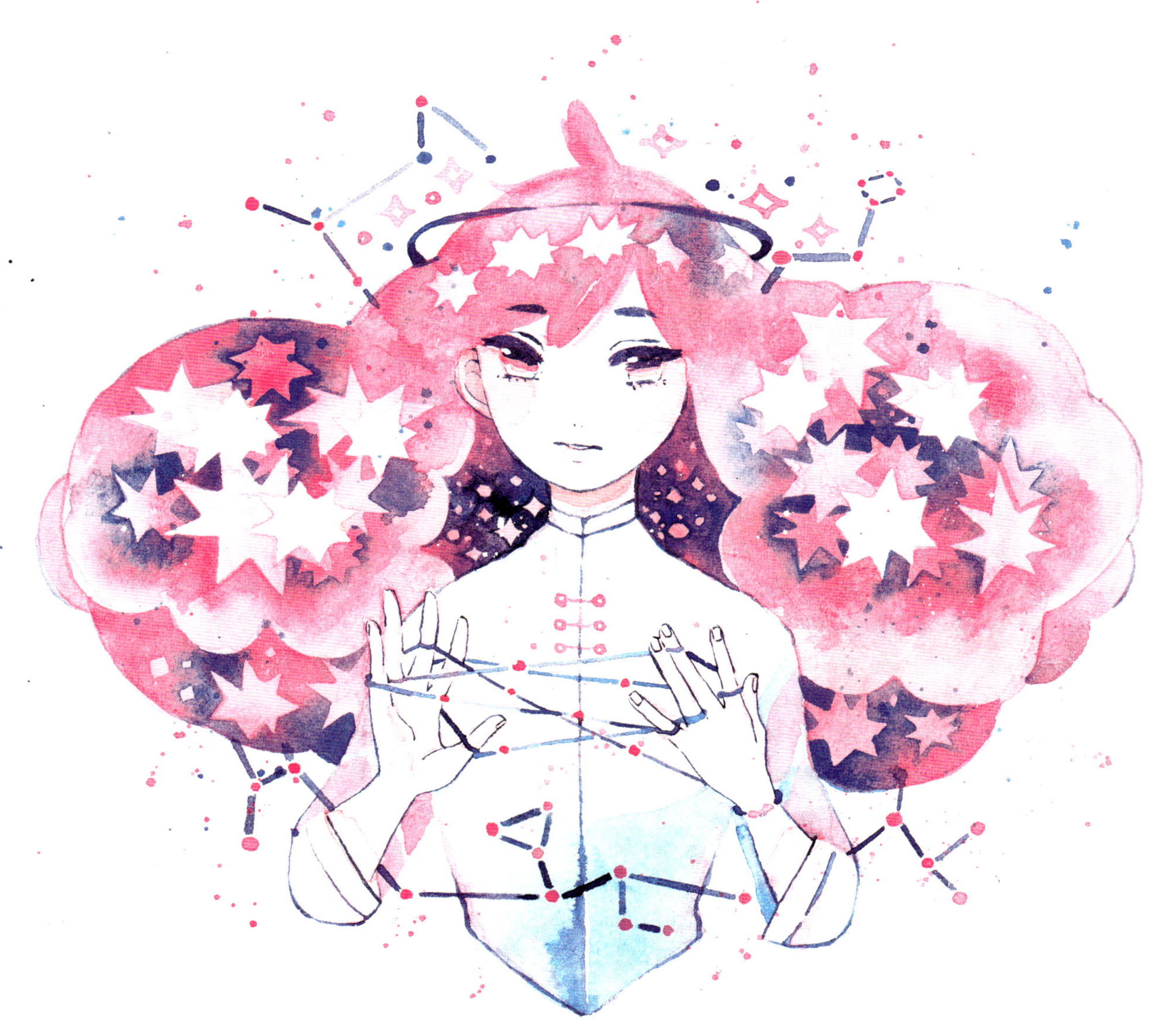

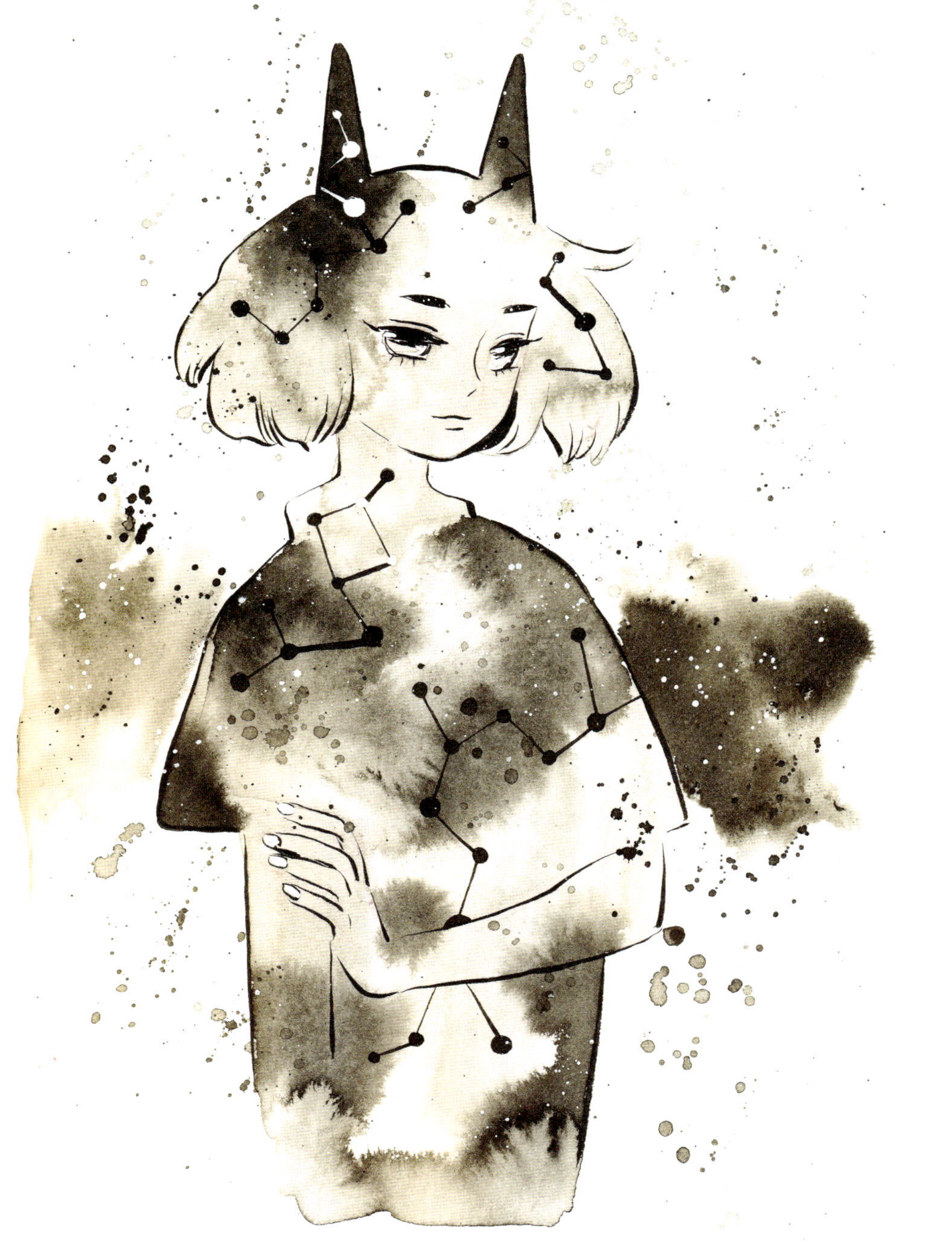

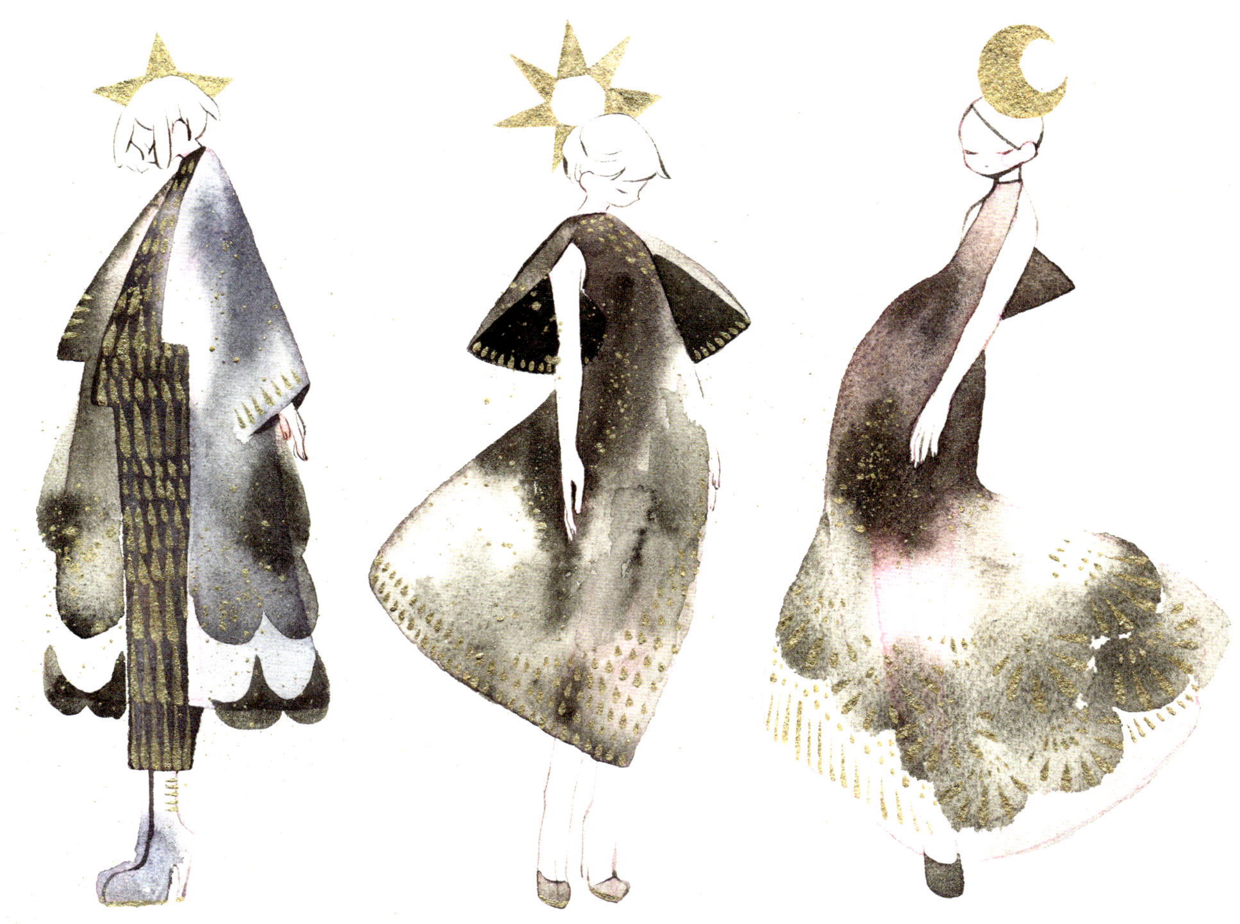

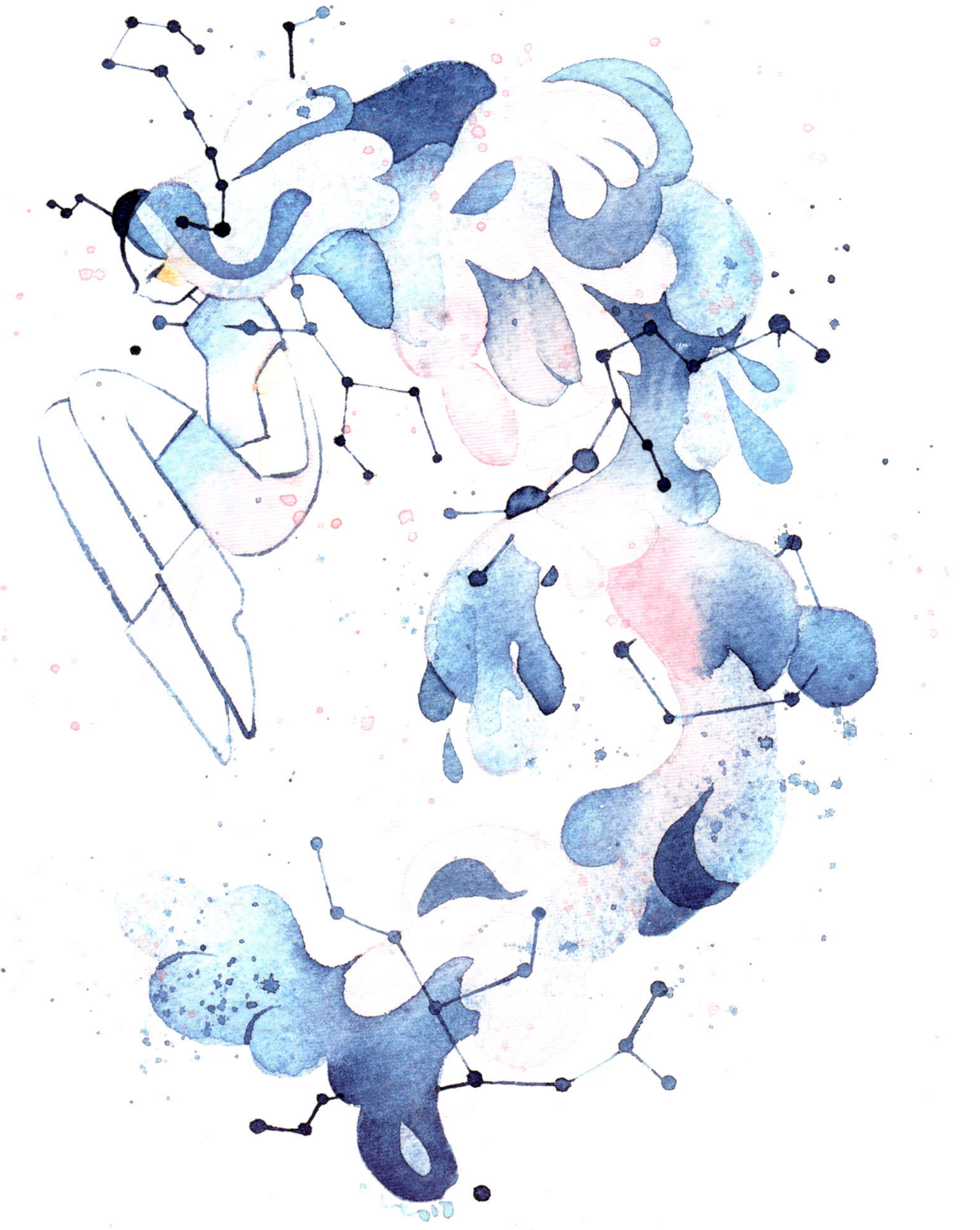

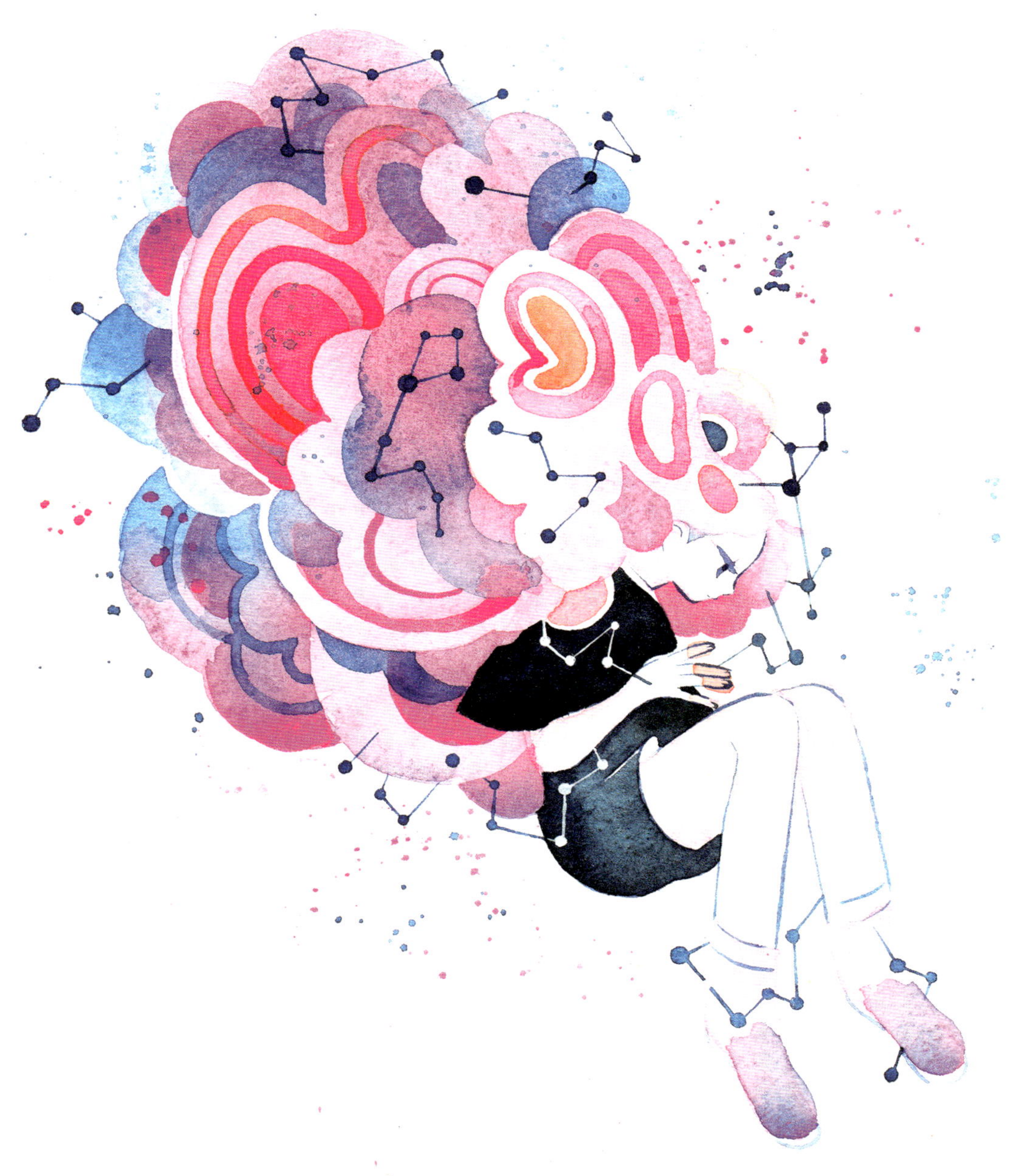

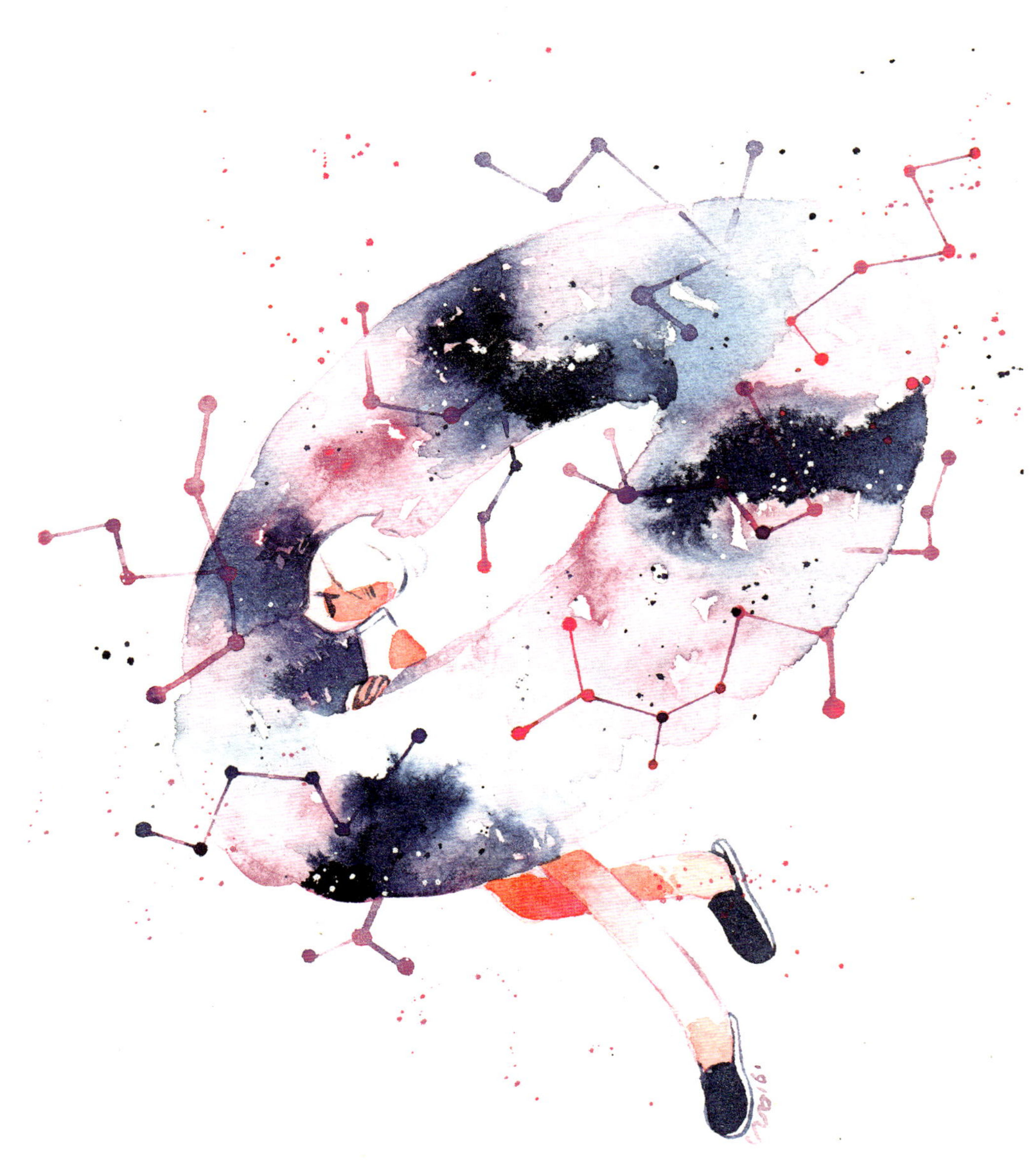

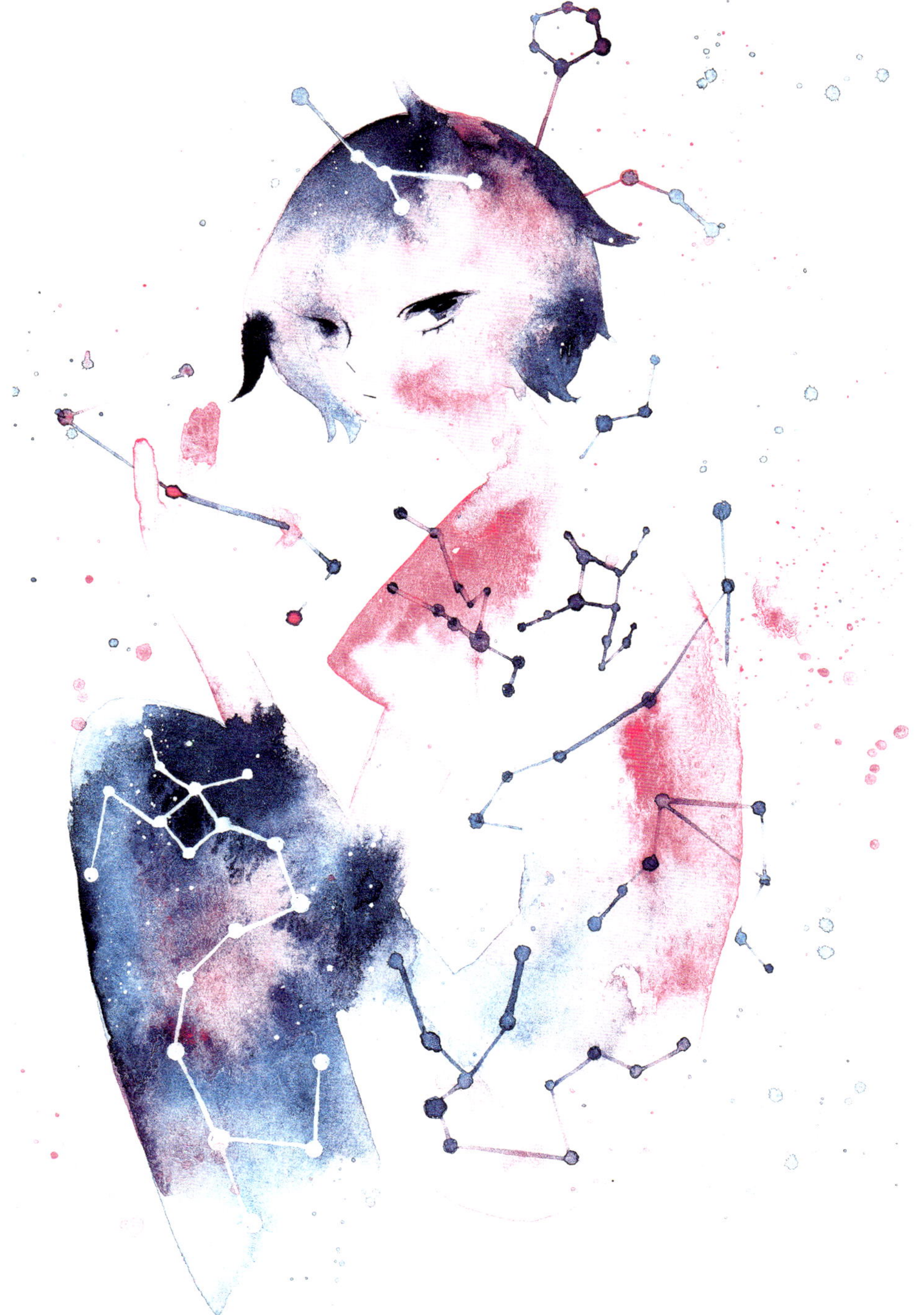

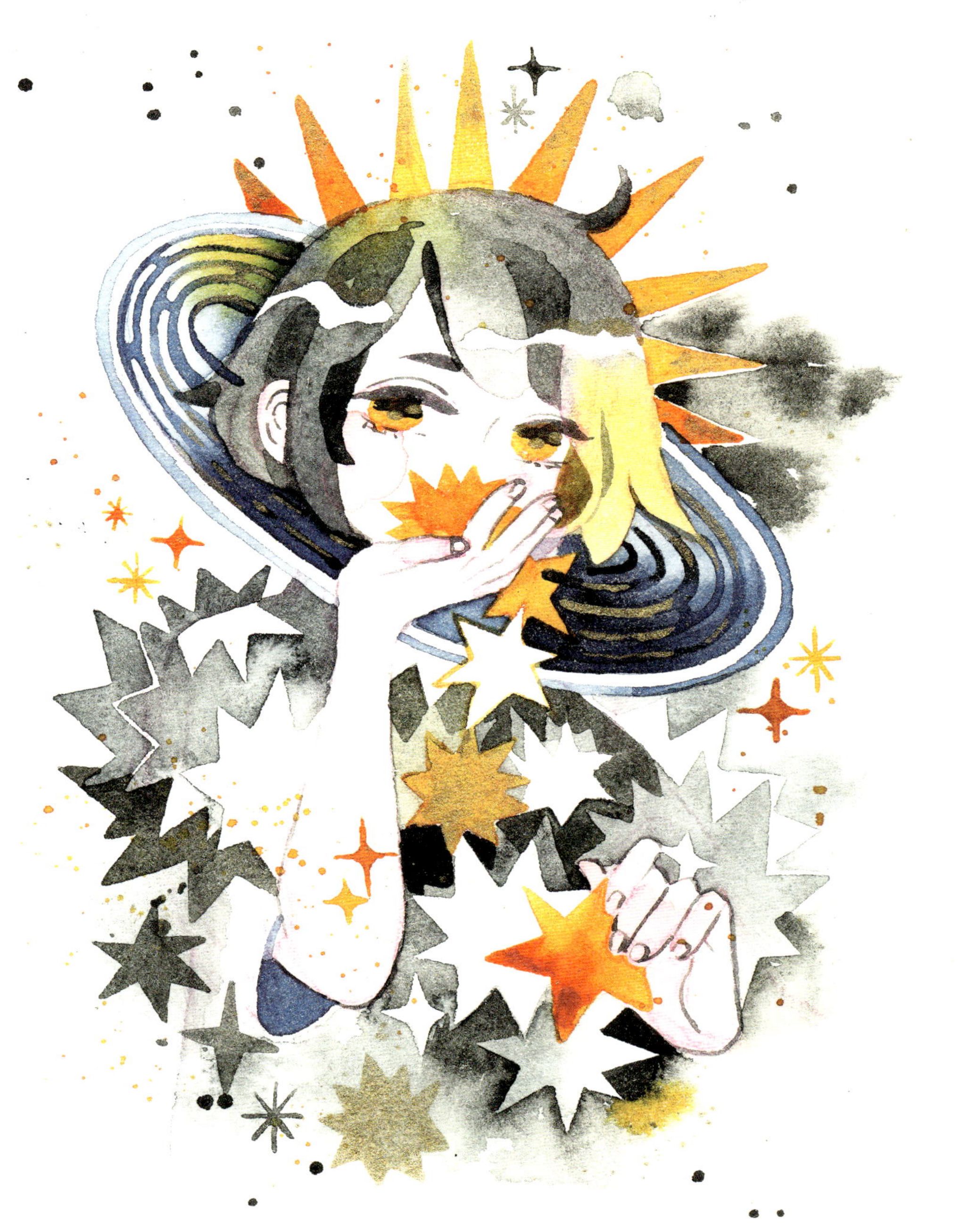

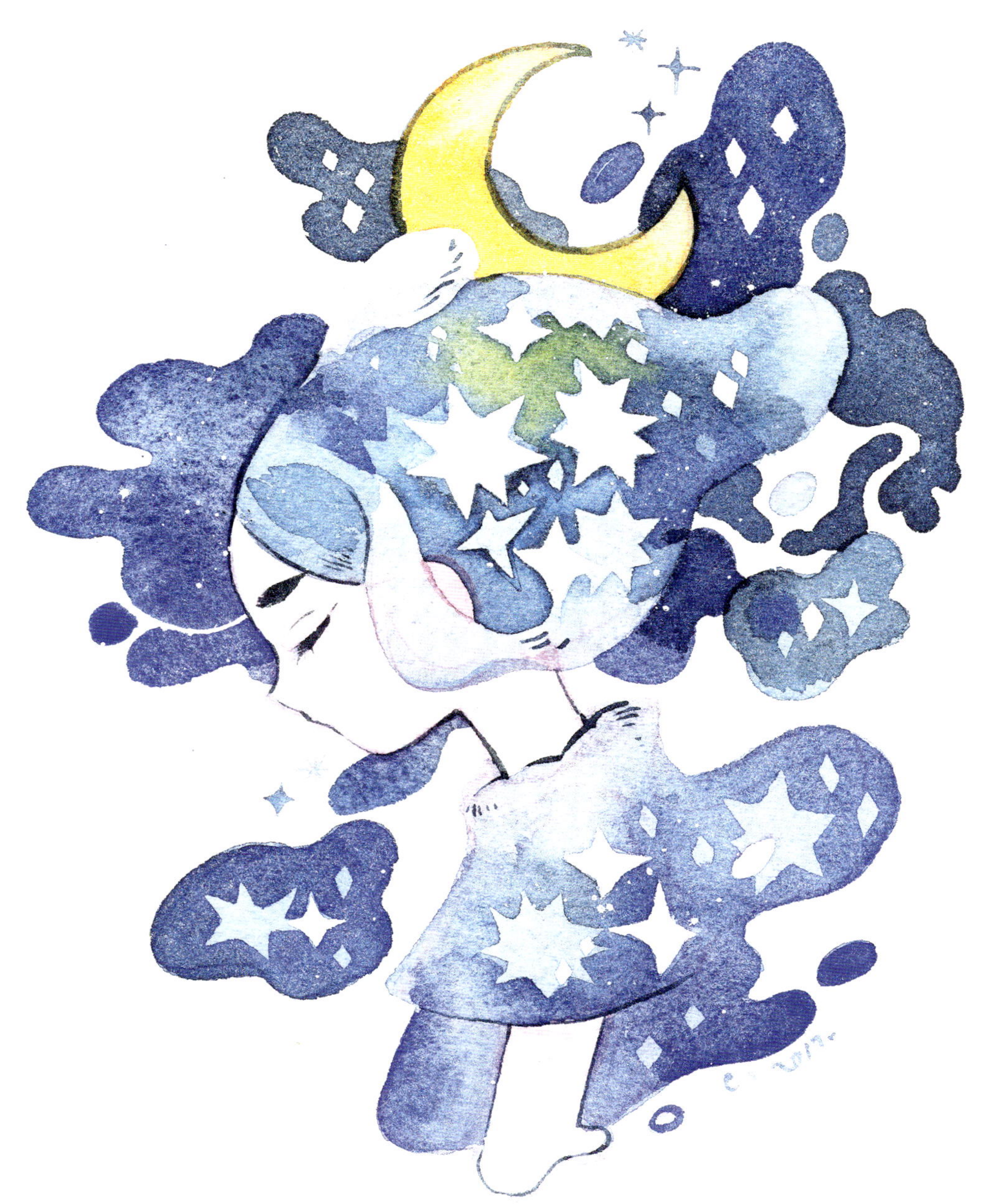

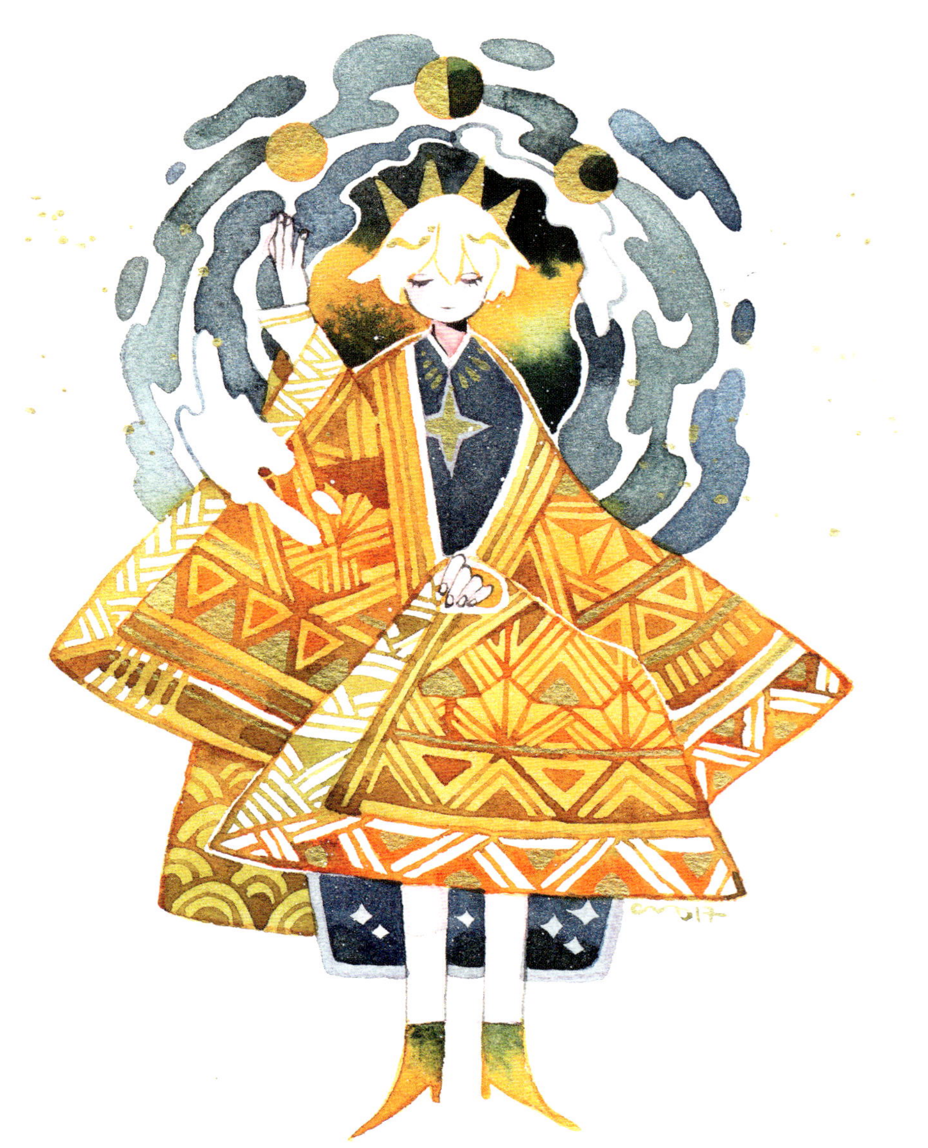

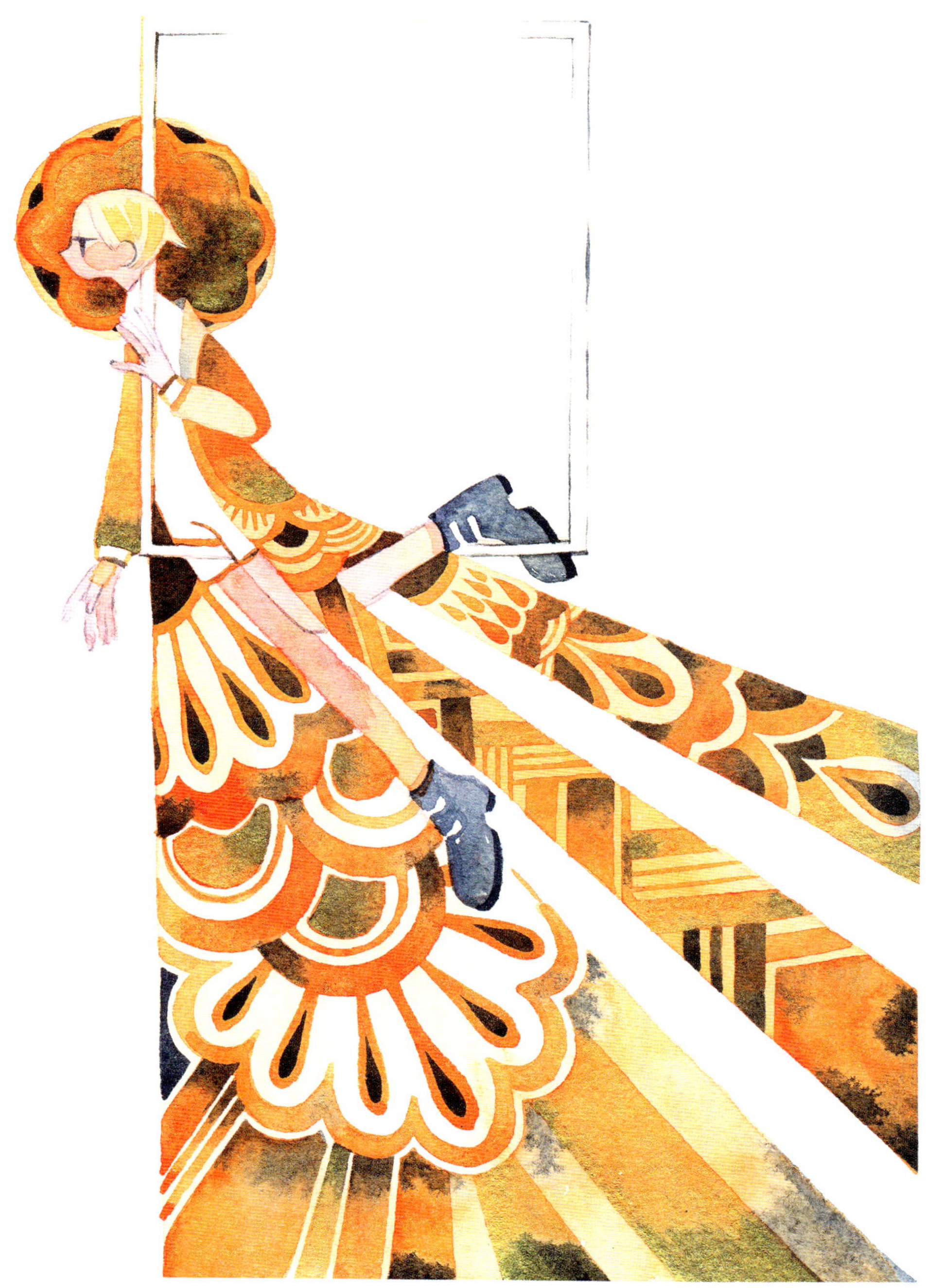

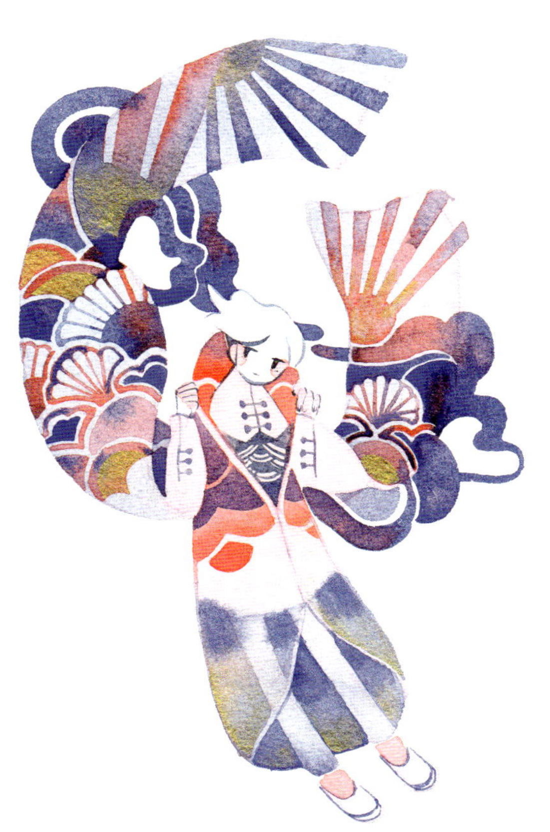
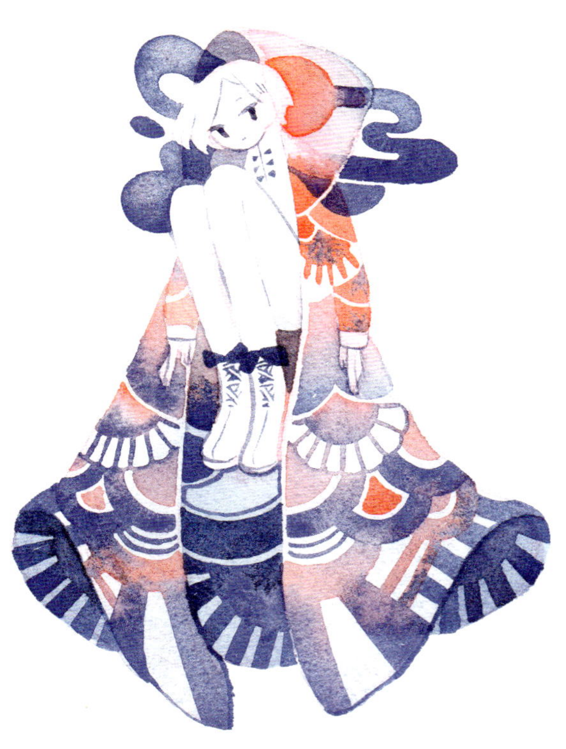

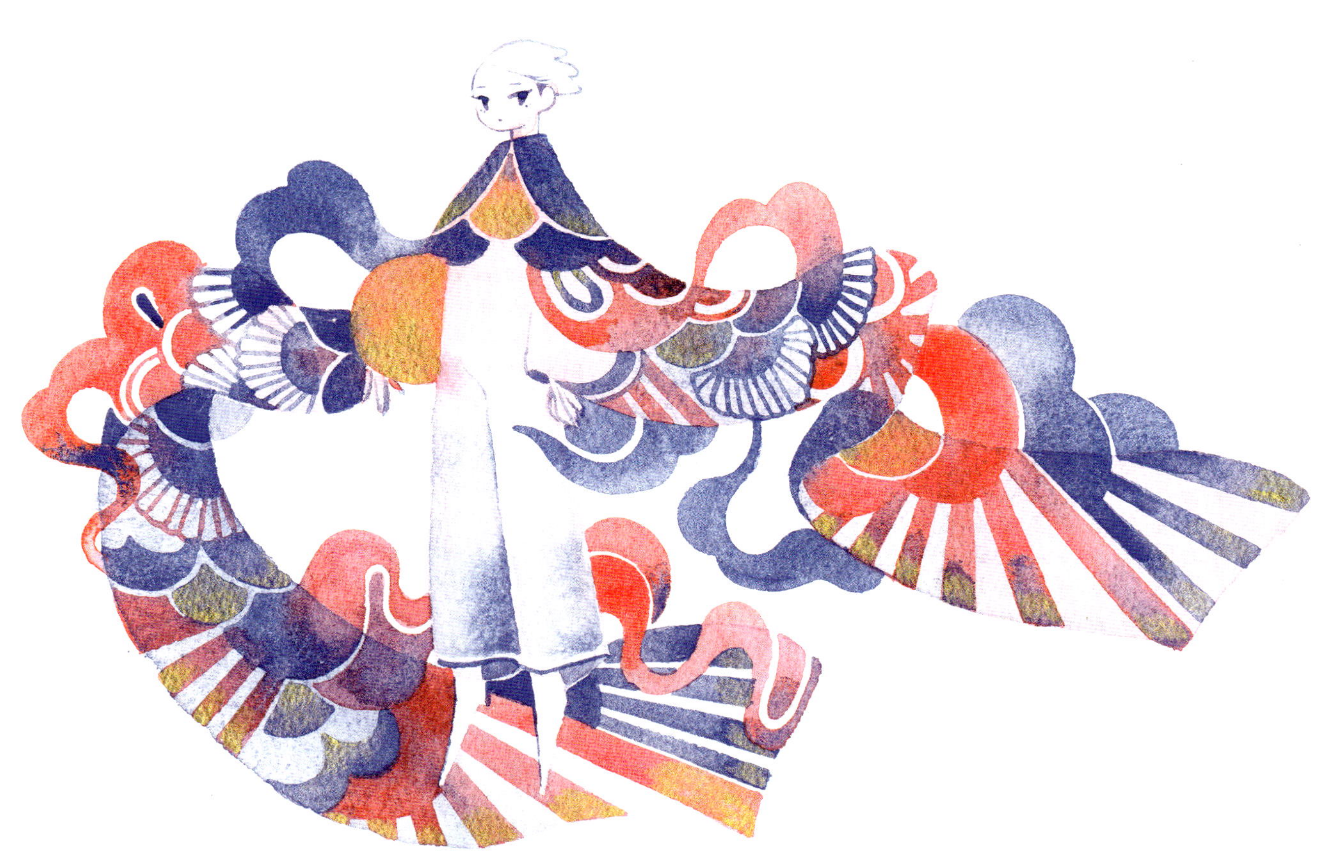

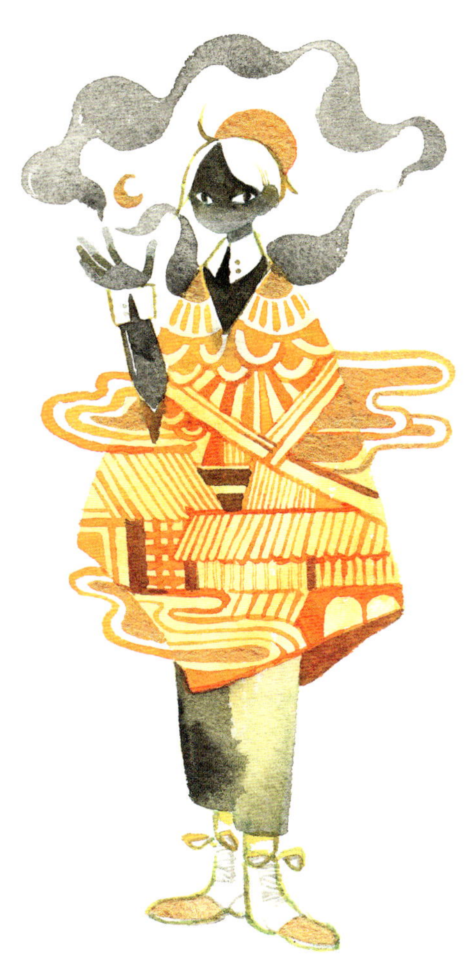
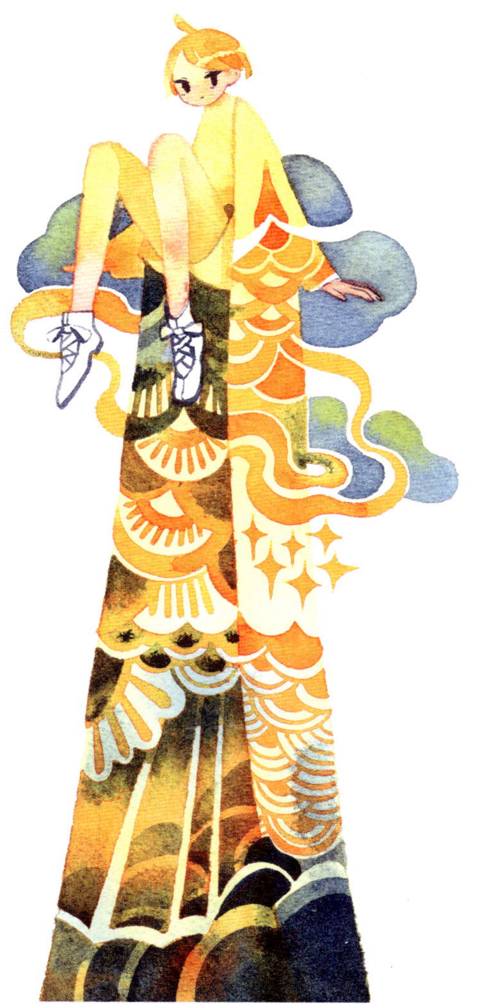

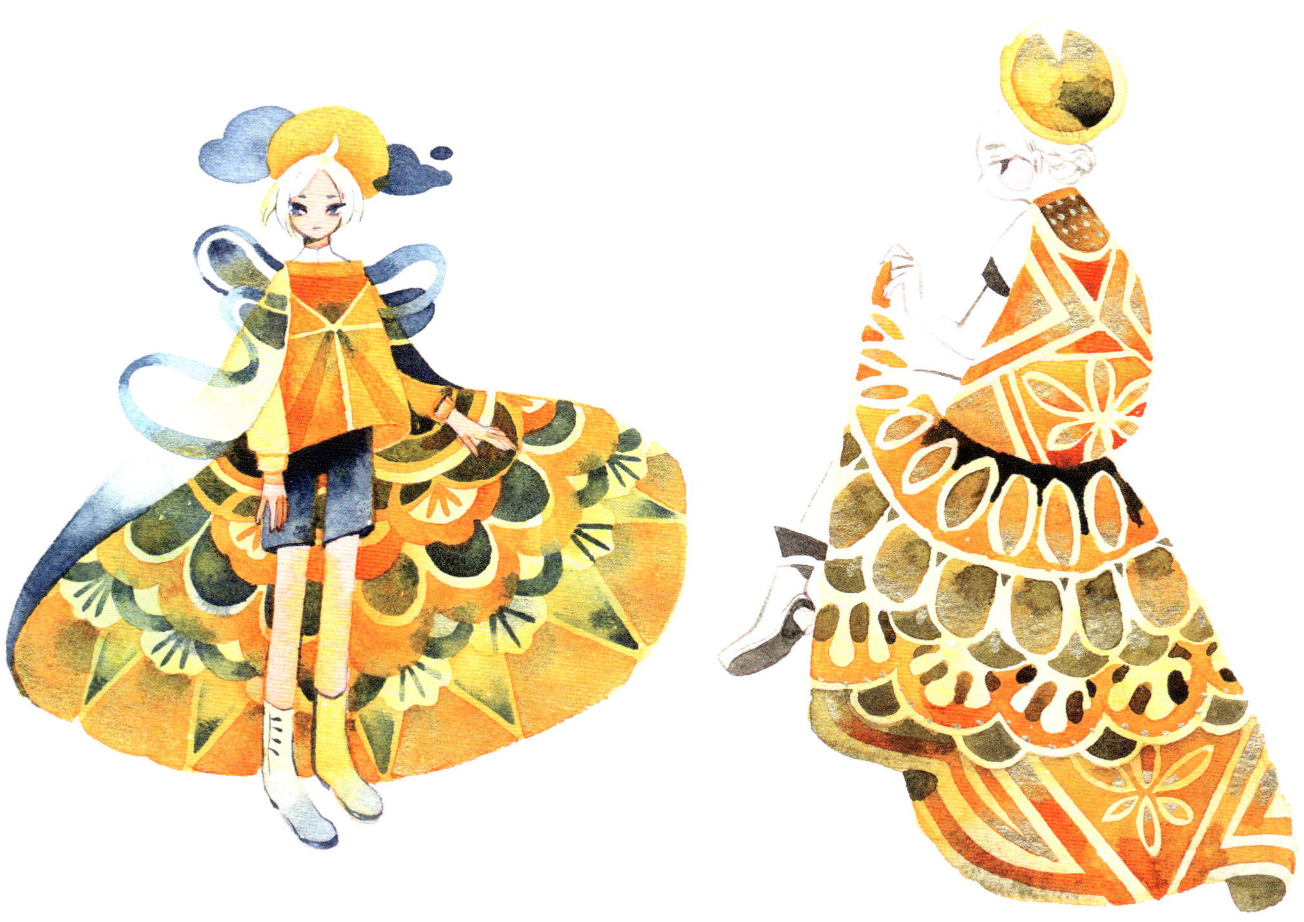

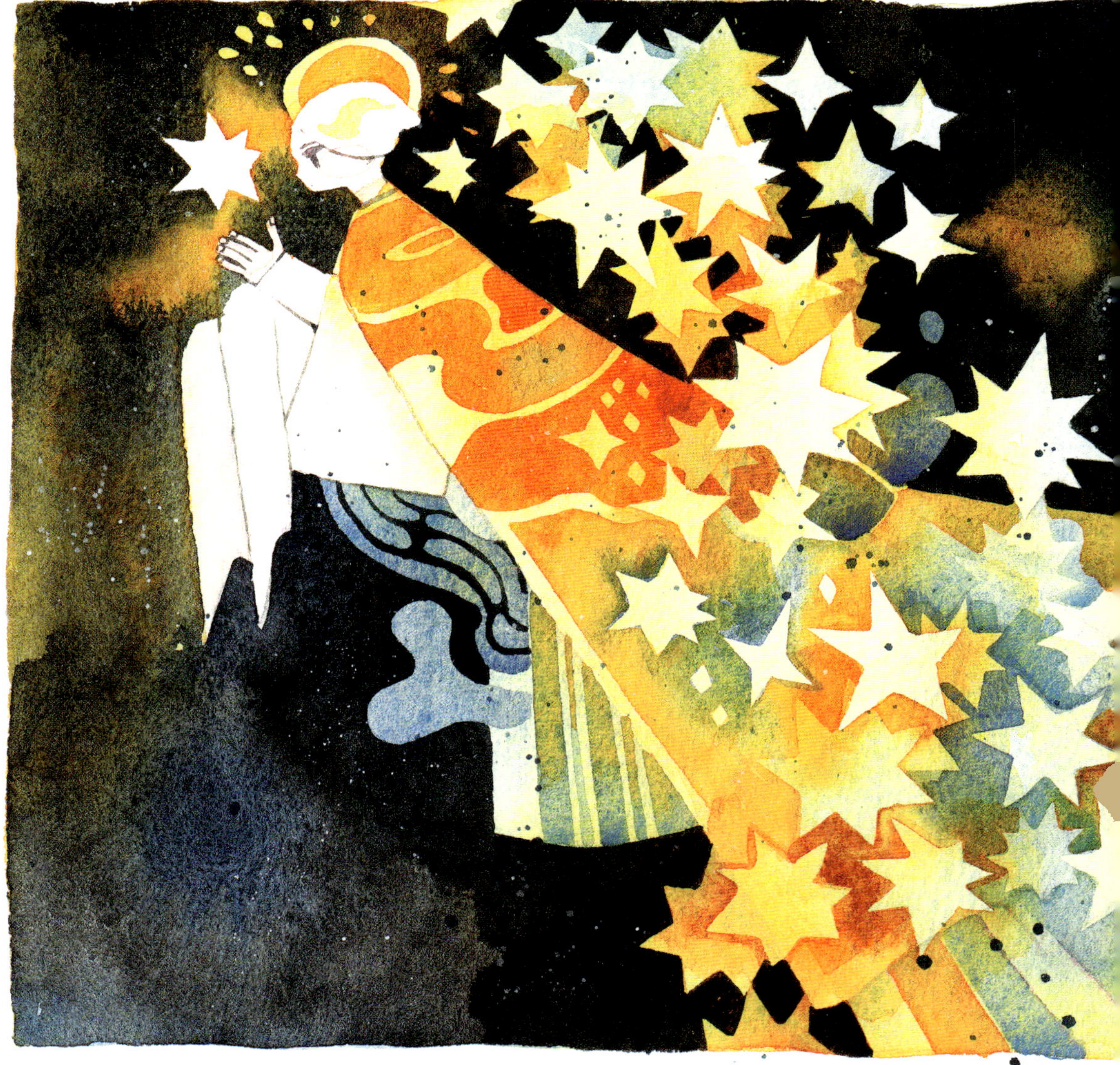

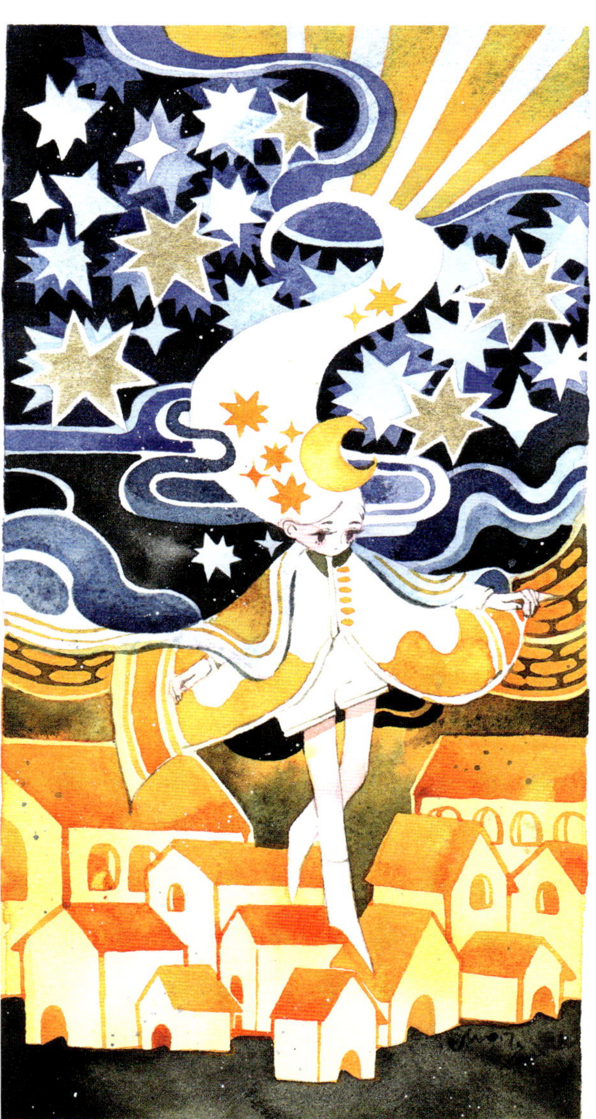

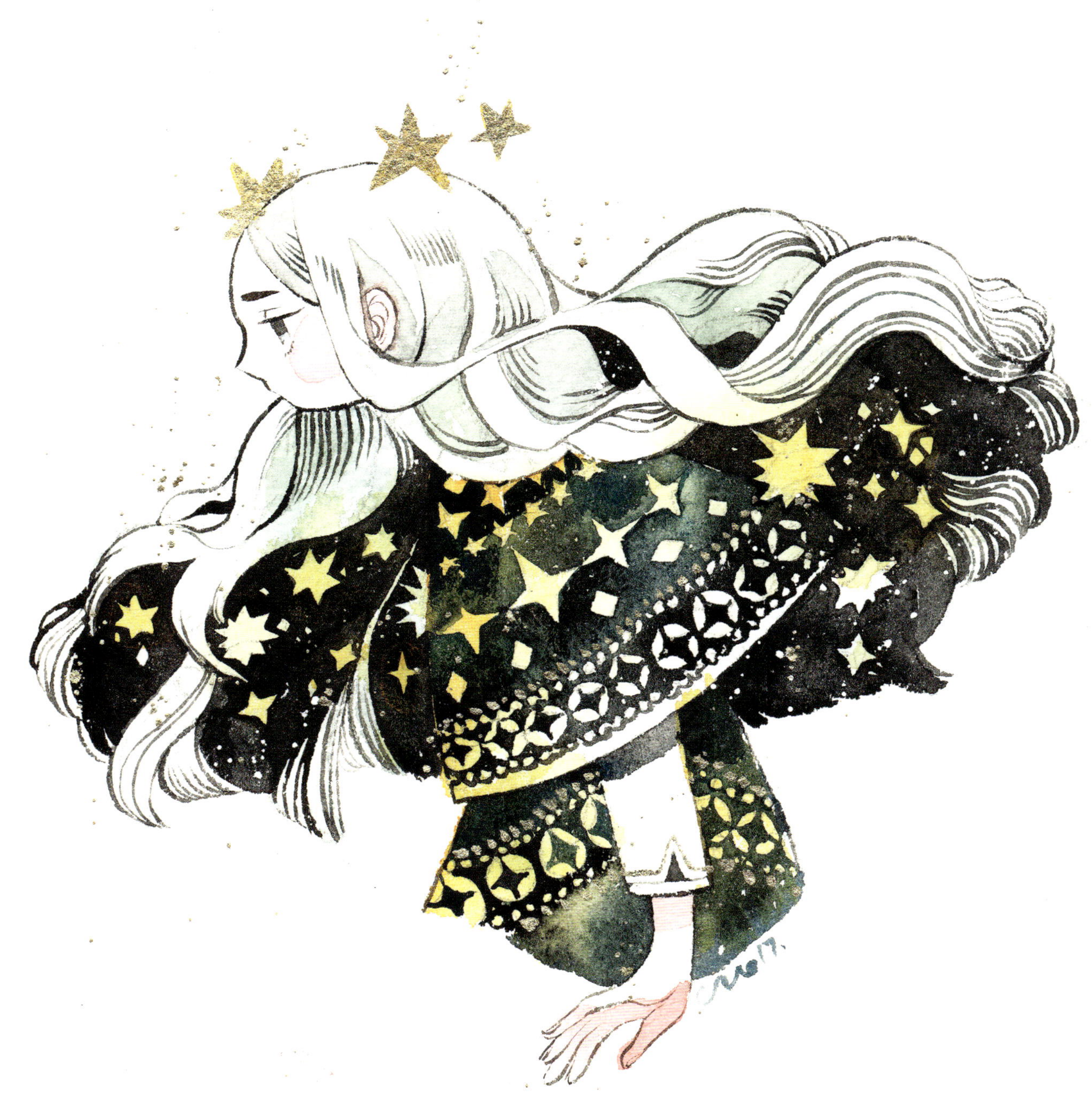

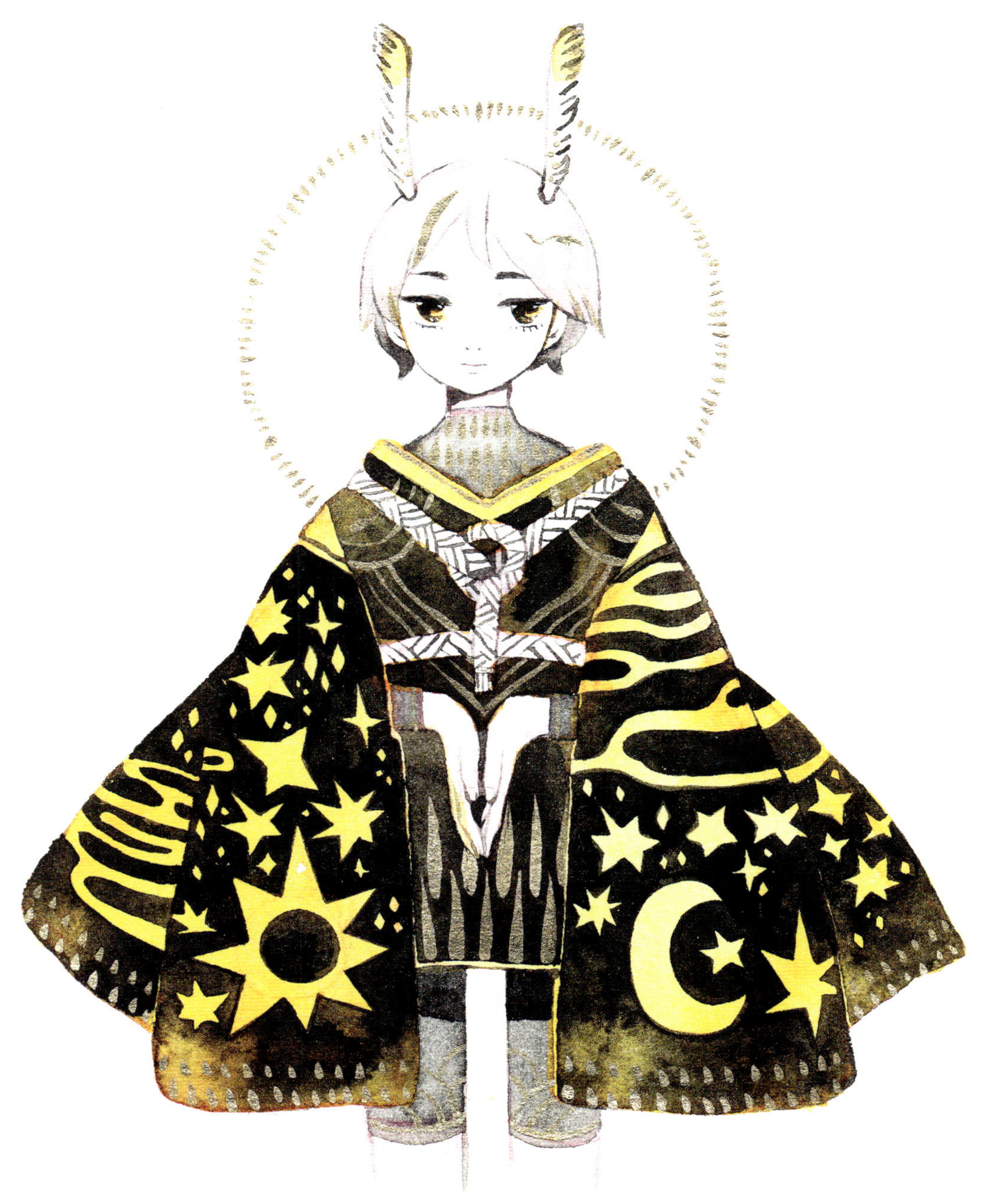

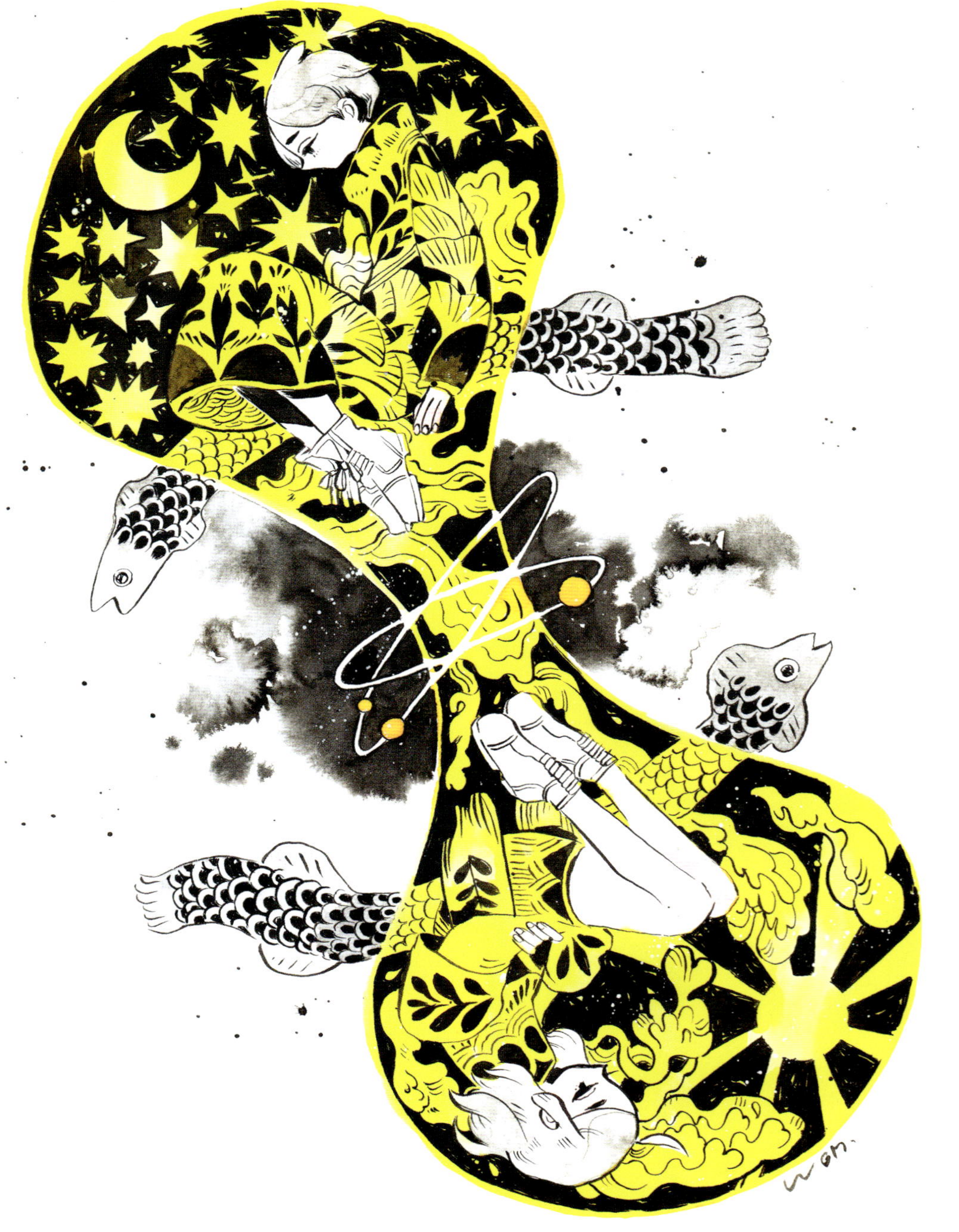

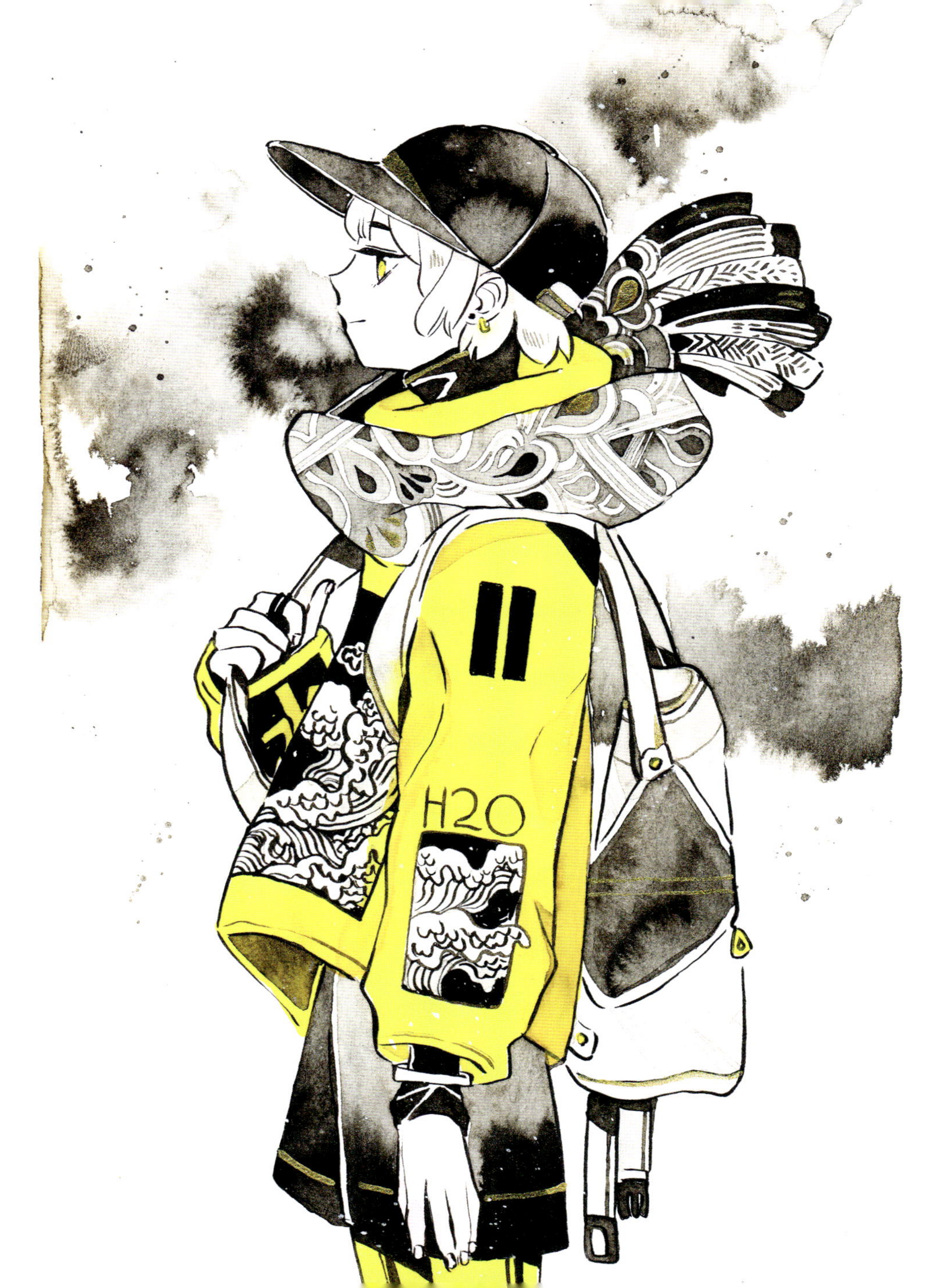
H2O

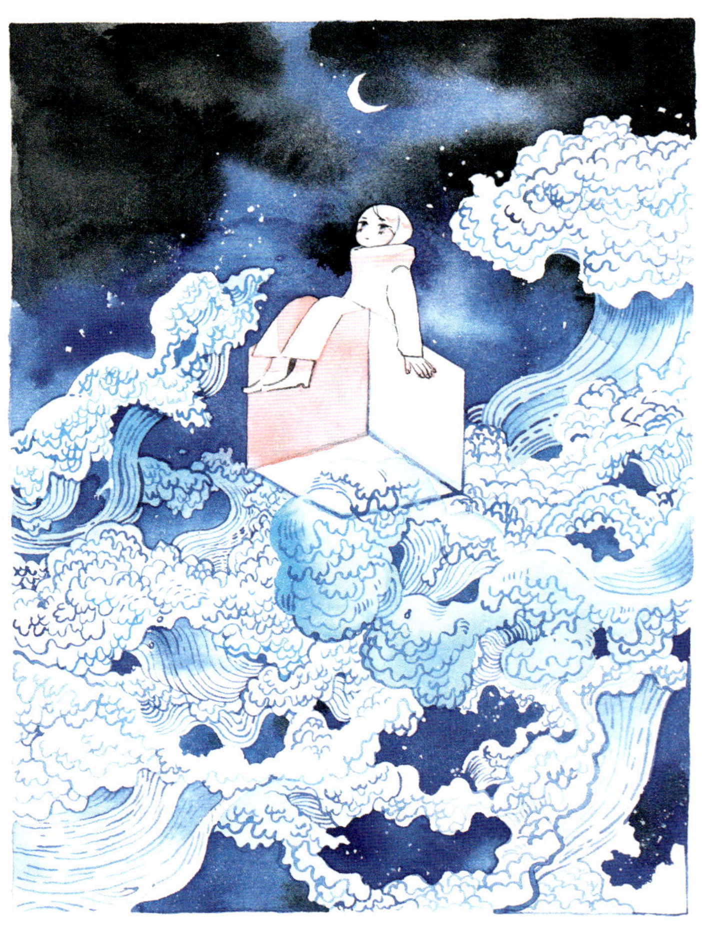

A heartfelt thank you for joining me in this journey.

旅路をともにできたみなさまに、心からの感謝を

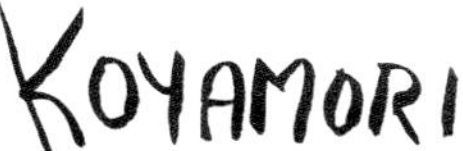

g r o w

Koyamori 画集

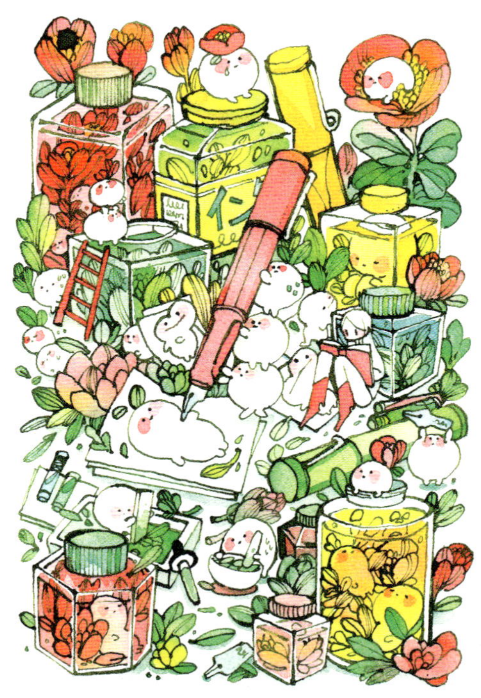

2018年10月22日　初版第1刷発行
2022年 1 月14日　　　第2刷発行

著者　Koyamori
デザイン　濱祐斗デザイン事務所
翻訳　宮内雅史
編集　道平 恵, 宮内雅史

発行人　三芳寛要
発行元　株式会社 パイ インターナショナル
〒170-0005　東京都豊島区南大塚 2-32-4
TEL 03-3944-3981　FAX 03-5395-4830
sales@pie.co.jp

印刷・製本　シナノ印刷株式会社